MODERN CURRICULUM PRESS
MATHEMATICS

Teacher's Edition

Level A

Y0-BDG-698

Royce Hargrove

Richard Monnard

Acknowledgments

Content Writers **Babs Bell Hajdusiewicz**
Phyllis Rosner
Laurel Sherman

Contributors **Linda Gojak**
William Hunt
Christine Bhargava
Jean Laird
Roger Smalley
Erdine Bajbus
Rita Kuhar
Vicki Palisin
Jeanne White
Kathleen M. Becks
Jean Antonelli
Sandra J. Heldman
Susan McKenney
Nancy Toth
Nancy Ross

Project Director **Dorothy A. Kirk**
Editors **Martha Geyen**
Phyllis Sibbing

Editorial Staff **Sharon M. Marosi**
Ann Marie Murray
Patricia Kozak
Ruth Ziccardi

Design **The Remen-Willis**
Design Group

Cover Art........© 1993 Adam Peiperl

ISBN 0–8136–3116–5 (Teacher's Edition)   0–8136–3109–2 (Pupil's Edition)

5 6 7 8 9 10   98 97

Modern Curriculum Press

Mathematics

Modern Curriculum Press

Mathematics

Modern Curriculum Press

Mathematics

Modern Curriculum Press

Mathematics

Modern Curriculum Press

Mathematics

Modern Curriculum Press

Mathematics

Modern Curriculum Press

Mathematics

Teacher's Guide

Modern Curriculum Press

Mathematics

INTRODUCING
MODERN CURRICULUM PRESS MATHEMATICS

A COMPLETE, ECONOMICAL MATH SERIES TEACHING PROBLEM-SOLVING STRATEGIES, CRITICAL-THINKING SKILLS, ESTIMATION, MENTAL-MATH SKILLS, AND ALL BASIC MATH CONCEPTS AND SKILLS!

Modern Curriculum Press Mathematics is an alternative basal program for students in grades K-6. This unique developmental series is perfect for providing the flexibility teachers need for ability grouping. Its design encourages thinking skills, active participation, and mastery of skills within the context of problem-solving situations, abundant practice to master those skills, developed models students actively work with to solve problems, and reinforcement of problem-solving and strategies. Other features like these provide students with solid math instruction.

- Each lesson begins with a developed model that teaches algorithms and concepts in a problem-solving situation.

- Students are required to interact with the model by gathering data needed to solve the problem.

- A developmental sequence introduces and extends skills taught in the basal curriculum—including statistics, logic, and probability.

- An abundant practice of math skills ensures true mastery of mathematics.

- Estimation and mental math skills are stressed in all computational and problem-solving activities.

- Calculator activities introduce students to basic calculator skills and terms.

- Comprehensive **Teacher's Editions** provide abundant additional help for teachers in features like **Correcting Common Errors, Enrichment,** and **Extra Credit,** and the complete **Table of Common Errors.**

Modern Curriculum Press Mathematics is a comprehensive math program that will help students develop a solid mathematics background. This special sampler will show you how:

- **Developed Models** begin each lesson, demonstrate the algorithm and concept in a problem-solving situation, and get students actively involved with the model.

- **Getting Started** provides samples of the concept or skill that is taught and allows the teacher to observe students' understanding.

- **Practice, Apply,** and **Copy and Do** activities develop independent skills where students practice the algorithm and apply what they have learned in the lesson or from a previous lesson. **Excursion** activities extend the math skill and are fun to do.

- **Problem Solving** pages introduce students to the techniques of problem solving using a four-step model. **Apply** activities on these pages allow students to use problem-solving strategies they have learned in everyday situations. The second half of the page focuses on higher-order thinking skills.

- **Chapter Test** pages provide both students and teachers with a checkpoint that tests all the skills taught in the chapter. There are alternative Chapter Tests based on the same objectives at the end of each student book.

- **Cumulative Review** pages maintain skills that have been taught not only in the previous chapter, but all skills taught up to this point. A standardized test format is used beginning at the middle of the second grade text.

- **Calculator** pages teach students the various functions and the basic skills needed to use calculators intelligently.

- **Teacher Edition** pages feature reduced student pages with answers, objectives, suggestions for **Teaching the Lesson, Materials, Correcting Common Errors, Enrichment,** and more.

A Developed Model Gets Students To Think, Actively Participate, And Understand Math Skills!

The major difference between *Modern Curriculum Press Mathematics* and other math programs is the developed model in which students actively work. Every lesson of *Modern Curriculum Press Mathematics* features concept development based on this developed model. Students are required to interact with this model discriminating what data is needed to solve the problem. This process teaches and reinforces their thinking skills and gets them actively involved providing the motivation to read and understand. The four-step teaching strategy of SEE, PLAN, DO, CHECK successfully increases students' understanding and provides a firm foundation for total math master of skills.

■ One major objective is the focus of every two-page lesson.

■ An algorithm or a model word problem keeps students interested and involved and provides a purpose for learning.

Dividing by 4

Therese is using baskets of flowers to decorate the tables.

r of flowers that
asket.

o make up.

the baskets.

rs, we divide

wers into each basket.

nplete the number sentences.

2.
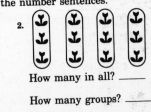

How many in all? _____

How many groups? _____

How many in each group? _____

$12 \div 4 =$ _____

ces.

4 = _____   5. $8 \div 4 =$ _____   6. $32 \div 4 =$ _____

Reviewing Addition Facts

Aaron left home early one morning to walk to the library, before he went to school. How many blocks did he walk on his way to school?

Home •

• Library

• School

We want to know the number of blocks Aaron walked all together.

We know that he walked _____ blocks from his house to the library.

He walked another _____ blocks from the library to school.

To find the total number of blocks, we add

_____ and _____.

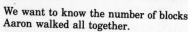

0 1 2 3 4 5 6 7 8 9 10 11 12 13 14 15 16 17 18

$7 + 6 =$ _____

↗ ↗ ↑
addends sum

$\begin{array}{r} 7 \\ + 6 \end{array}$ ← addends

← sum

$7 + 6 = 13$ is called a **number sentence**.

Aaron walked _____ blocks from his home to school.

Getting Started

Complete the number sentences.

1. $4 + 2 =$ _____   2. $7 + 9 =$ _____   3. $8 + 3 =$ _____

4. $2 + 9 =$ _____   5. $5 + 6 =$ _____   6. $8 + 8 =$ _____

Add.

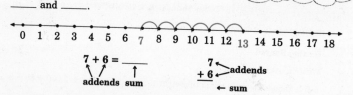

7. $\begin{array}{r} 8 \\ + 7 \end{array}$ 8. $\begin{array}{r} 4 \\ + 1 \end{array}$ 9. $\begin{array}{r} 9 \\ + 9 \end{array}$ 10. $\begin{array}{r} 5 \\ + 5 \end{array}$ 11. $\begin{array}{r} 3 \\ + 6 \end{array}$ 12. $\begin{array}{r} 9 \\ + 4 \end{array}$

3

Students interact with the artwork to gather data needed to solve problems. This interaction helps develop higher-order thinking skills.

Each objective is introduced in a problem-solving setting developing problem-solving thinking skills.

The four-step teaching method of SEE, PLAN, DO, CHECK guides students easily through the development of each skill.

■ Students SEE the "input" sentences and the artwork and use them to help solve the problems. This allows them to be actively involved in their work.

■ Students PLAN how they are going to solve problems using their reasoning skills to determine what operations are needed.

■ Students use the model to help DO the problem. Each developed model shows students how to do the algorithm.

■ To CHECK understanding of the math skill, a concluding sentence reinforces the problem-solving process.

■ Important math vocabulary is bold-faced throughout the text and defined in context and in the glossary.

■ A check (√) points out important concepts to which students should give special attention.

Subtracting Fractions with Unlike

Duncan is feeding the chickens on his uncle's farm. When he started, there were $4\frac{1}{2}$ buckets of chicken feed. How much feed has he used?

We want to know how much chicken feed Duncan has used.

We know that he started with ____ buckets

of feed, and he has ____ buckets left.

To find the amount used, we subtract the amount left from the original amount.

We subtract ____ from ____.

To subtract fractions with unlike denominators follow these steps:

Rename the fractions as equivalent fractions with the least common denominator

$$4\frac{1}{2} = 4\frac{2}{4}$$
$$-1\frac{1}{4} = 1\frac{1}{4}$$

Subtract the fractions.

$$4\frac{1}{2} = 4\frac{2}{4}$$
$$-1\frac{1}{4} = 1\frac{1}{4}$$
$$\frac{1}{4}$$

Duncan has used ____ buckets of feed.

Getting Started

Subtract.

1. $15\frac{5}{8}$
   $-7\frac{1}{3}$

2. $87\frac{2}{3}$
   $-39\frac{1}{6}$

3.

Copy and subtract.

5. $\frac{7}{8} - \frac{1}{4} =$ ____

6. $\frac{5}{6} - \frac{1}{2} =$ ____

7. $\frac{9}{10} - \frac{6}{15} =$ ____

Place Value through Thousands

The government space agency plans to sell used moon buggies to the highest bidders. What did Charley pay for the one he bought?

We want to understand the cost of Charley's moon buggy.

Charley paid exactly ____.
To understand how much money this is, we will look at the place value of each digit in the price.

✔ The numbers 0, 1, 2, 3, 4, 5, 6, 7, 8 and 9 are called **digits**. The position of the digit decides its place value.

thousands	hundreds	tens	ones
___	___	___	___

In 7,425, the digit 4 represents hundreds, and the

digit 7 represents ____.
Numbers can be written in **standard** or **expanded form**.

Standard Form	Expanded Form
7,425	7,000 + 400 + 20 + 5

We say Charley paid **seven thousand, four hundred**

twenty-five dollars. We write ____.

Getting Started

Write in standard form.

1. five thousand, six hundred fifty-eight ____

2. 3,000 + 50 + 8 ____

Write in words.

3. 6,497

4. 823

5. 9,045

Write the place value of the red digits.

6. 3,948

7. 9,603

8. 7,529

9. $5,370

7

TEACHER-GUIDED PRACTICE ACTIVITIES CHECK STUDENTS' UNDERSTANDING OF MATH CONCEPTS!

Getting Started activities provide the opportunity for students to try to do what they've just learned and for teachers a chance to check understanding. These activities also allow the teacher to evaluate students' progress in a particular objective before continuing on in the lesson. A complete **Table of Common Errors** can be found in the **Teacher's Editions.** This list helps the teacher diagnose and correct those errors identified by research to be the most common. Lesson plans offer specific suggestions for dealing with each individual error, so the teacher can concentrate on those are where students need help. Showing t teacher ways to keep errors from hap pening by alerting to common mistakes, will make teaching math go more smoothly.

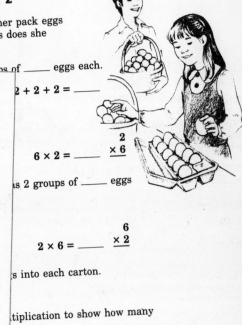

Multiplying, the Factor 2

Sun Li is helping her mother pack eggs in cartons. How many eggs does she pack into each carton?

_____ 6 groups of _____ eggs each.

$2 + 2 + 2 =$ _____

$6 \times 2 =$ _____ $\begin{array}{r} 2 \\ \times 6 \\ \hline \end{array}$

_____ 2 groups of _____ eggs

$2 \times 6 =$ _____ $\begin{array}{r} 6 \\ \times 2 \\ \hline \end{array}$

_____ s into each carton.

_____ tiplication to show how many

2. $2 + 2 + 2 + 2 + 2 =$ _____

$5 \times 2 =$ _____

$2 \times 5 =$ _____

4. $2 \times 6 =$ _____   5. $\begin{array}{r} 4 \\ \times 2 \\ \hline \end{array}$ 6. $\begin{array}{r} 2 \\ \times 2 \\ \hline \end{array}$

(one hundred nineteen) **119**

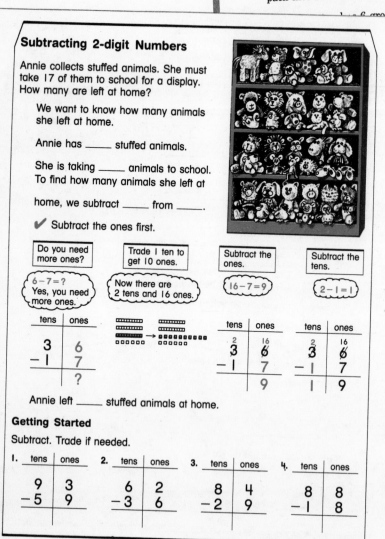

Subtracting 2-digit Numbers

Annie collects stuffed animals. She must take 17 of them to school for a display. How many are left at home?

We want to know how many animals she left at home.

Annie has _____ stuffed animals.

She is taking _____ animals to school. To find how many animals she left at home, we subtract _____ from _____.

✔ Subtract the ones first.

Do you need more ones?	Trade 1 ten to get 10 ones.	Subtract the ones.	Subtract the tens.
$6 - 7 = ?$ Yes, you need more ones.	Now there are 2 tens and 16 ones.	$16 - 7 = 9$	$2 - 1 = 1$

tens	ones
3	6
−1	7
	?

tens	ones
²3̶	¹⁶6̶
−1	7
	9

tens	ones
²3̶	¹⁶6̶
−1	7
1	9

Annie left _____ stuffed animals at home.

Getting Started

Subtract. Trade if needed.

1. tens	ones
9	3
−5	9

2. tens	ones
6	2
−3	6

3. tens	ones
8	4
−2	9

4. tens	ones
8	8
−1	8

Subtracting 2-digit numbers, with trading

(one hundred forty-nine) **149**

- Samples that the students work allow the teacher to check students' understanding of the skill.

- Students gain both confidence and competence in working these problems.

- If the objective is not fully grasped by the student, the **Table of Common Errors** will help the teacher deal with each individual type of error.

- Students gain a deeper understanding of the basic algorithm introduced in the developed model.

- New skills are reinforced through the sample problems students work right on the spot.

- Teachers observe any typical student errors before continuing additional work in the lesson.

- Teacher-guided practice activities will encourage classroom discussion.

- **Getting Started** activities help the teacher to single out predictable errors quickly.

- All samples found in the **Getting Started** activities prepare students to work the exercises found in the next part of the lesson.

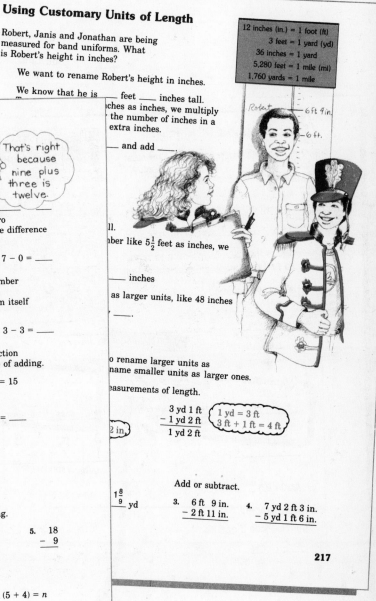

Using Customary Units of Length

Robert, Janis and Jonathan are being measured for band uniforms. What is Robert's height in inches?

We want to rename Robert's height in inches.

We know that he is ___ feet ___ inches tall.

| 12 inches (in.) = 1 foot (ft) |
| 3 feet = 1 yard (yd) |
| 36 inches = 1 yard |
| 5,280 feet = 1 mile (mi) |
| 1,760 yards = 1 mile |

ches as inches, we multiply the number of inches in a extra inches.

___ and add ___.

ll.

ber like $5\frac{1}{2}$ feet as inches, we

___ inches

as larger units, like 48 inches

o rename larger units as name smaller units as larger ones.

easurements of length.

3 yd 1 ft		1 yd = 3 ft
− 1 yd 2 ft		3 ft + 1 ft = 4 ft
1 yd 2 ft		

2 in.

$1\frac{8}{9}$ yd

Add or subtract.

3. 6 ft 9 in.
    − 2 ft 11 in.

4. 7 yd 2 ft 3 in.
    − 5 yd 1 ft 6 in.

217

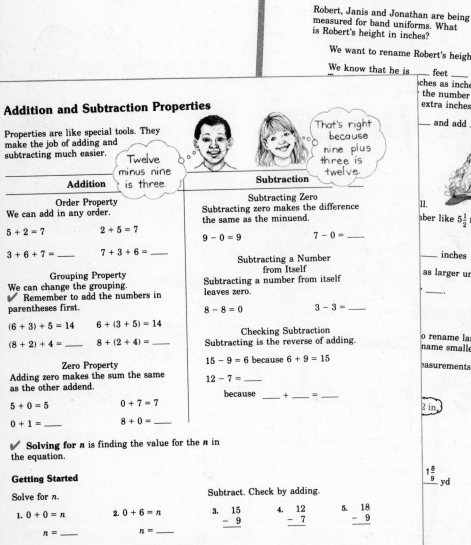

Addition and Subtraction Properties

Properties are like special tools. They make the job of adding and subtracting much easier.

Twelve minus nine is three.

That's right because nine plus three is twelve.

Addition

Order Property
We can add in any order.

5 + 2 = 7   2 + 5 = 7

3 + 6 + 7 = ___   7 + 3 + 6 = ___

Grouping Property
We can change the grouping.
✔ Remember to add the numbers in parentheses first.

(6 + 3) + 5 = 14   6 + (3 + 5) = 14

(8 + 2) + 4 = ___   8 + (2 + 4) = ___

Zero Property
Adding zero makes the sum the same as the other addend.

5 + 0 = 5   0 + 7 = 7

0 + 1 = ___   8 + 0 = ___

Subtraction

Subtracting Zero
Subtracting zero makes the difference the same as the minuend.

9 − 0 = 9   7 − 0 = ___

Subtracting a Number from Itself
Subtracting a number from itself leaves zero.

8 − 8 = 0   3 − 3 = ___

Checking Subtraction
Subtracting is the reverse of adding.

15 − 9 = 6 because 6 + 9 = 15

12 − 7 = ___

because ___ + ___ = ___

✔ **Solving for *n*** is finding the value for the *n* in the equation.

Getting Started

Solve for *n*.

1. 0 + 0 = *n*

   n = ___

2. 0 + 6 = *n*

   n = ___

Subtract. Check by adding.

3. 15
    − 9

4. 12
    − 7

5. 18
    − 9

Add. Check by grouping the addends another way.

6. 5
    3
    + 4

7. 2
    6
    + 3

8. 6
    3
    + 4

9. (5 + 2) + 6 = *n*

   n = ___

10. 3 + (5 + 4) = *n*

    n = ___

3

INDEPENDENT PRACTICE ACTIVITIES PROVIDE PLENTY OF DRILL, PRACTICE, AND EXTENSION IN A VARIETY OF FORMATS!

The purpose of building skills is to ensure that students can use and apply those skills. That goal can only be reached when skills are clearly and systematically taught and then practiced. With *Modern Curriculum Press Mathematics*, the teacher can be assured that students will have abundant opportunities to practice their newly-learned math skills. The variety of practice activities allows the teacher to meet the needs of every student. Working independently helps students strengthen new skills, become more confident, and increase their understanding. Practice helps students learn. Some students need more practice than others to help them catch on. *Modern Curriculum Press Mathematics* offers a variety of practice situations so that students stay on target with what they are learning.

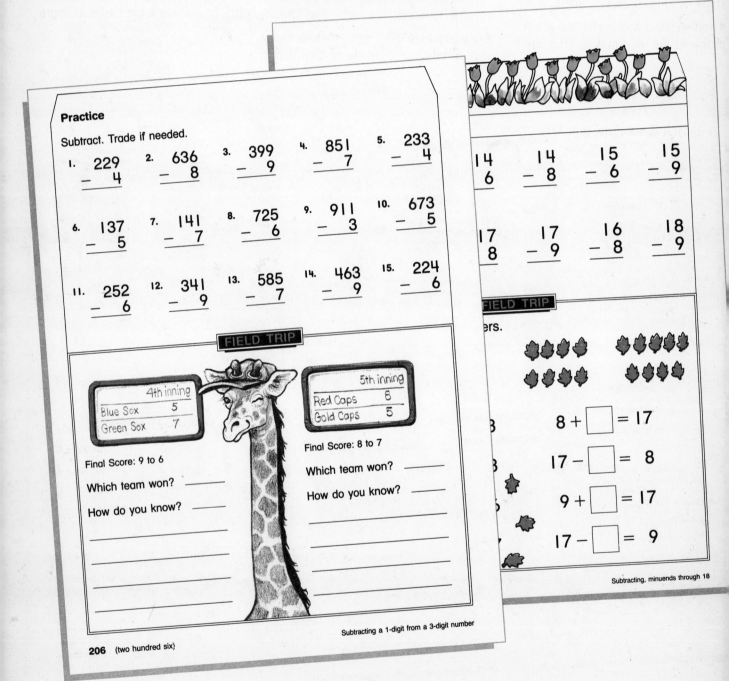

Practice

Subtract. Trade if needed.

1. 229 − 4
2. 636 − 8
3. 399 − 9
4. 851 − 7
5. 233 − 4

6. 137 − 5
7. 141 − 7
8. 725 − 6
9. 911 − 3
10. 673 − 5

11. 252 − 6
12. 341 − 9
13. 585 − 7
14. 463 − 9
15. 224 − 6

FIELD TRIP

4th inning
Blue Sox	5
Green Sox	7

Final Score: 9 to 6

Which team won? _____

How do you know? _____
_____
_____
_____

5th inning
Red Caps	6
Gold Caps	5

Final Score: 8 to 7

Which team won? _____

How do you know? _____
_____
_____
_____

206 (two hundred six)

Subtracting a 1-digit from a 3-digit number

14 − 6   14 − 8   15 − 6   15 − 9

17 − 8   17 − 9   16 − 8   18 − 9

FIELD TRIP

...ers.

$8 + \square = 17$

$17 - \square = 8$

$9 + \square = 17$

$17 - \square = 9$

Subtracting, minuends through 18

The teacher can begin the process of individual mastery by assigning **Practice** exercises that students can work independently.

- *Modern Curriculum Press Mathematics* integrates problem solving into the practice activities with **Apply** problems. Some of these problems relate to the algorithm. However, some require previously-learned skills encouraging students to think and maintain skills.

- Both vertical and horizontal forms of problems are used making students more comfortable with forms found in standardized test formats.

- An emphasis on practical skills encourages learning by applying math to everyday situations.

- Independent practice provides more opportunities for application and higher-order thinking skills.

- The variety of practice activities keeps students motivated and interested in learning.

- **Copy and Do** exercises check students' ability to assemble an algorithm from an equation and gives them practice in transferring information.

- **Excursion** activities extend the basic skill work and are fun to do. The teacher can challenge the more capable students with these mind-stretching activities.

- Giving students ample opportunities to practice and strengthen new skills builds solid skill development and helps the teacher more easily measure the results.

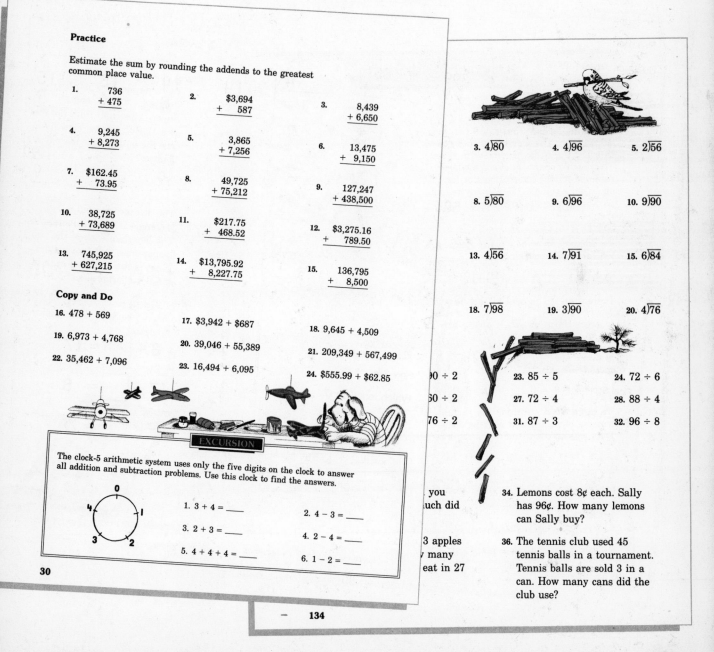

Practice

Estimate the sum by rounding the addends to the greatest common place value.

1. 736
   + 475

2. $3,694
   +   587

3. 8,439
   + 6,650

4. 9,245
   + 8,273

5. 3,865
   + 7,256

6. 13,475
   + 9,150

7. $162.45
   +   73.95

8. 49,725
   + 75,212

9. 127,247
   + 438,500

10. 38,725
   + 73,689

11. $217.75
   + 468.52

12. $3,275.16
   +   789.50

13. 745,925
   + 627,215

14. $13,795.92
   +   8,227.75

15. 136,795
   +   8,500

Copy and Do

16. 478 + 569
17. $3,942 + $687
18. 9,645 + 4,509
19. 6,973 + 4,768
20. 39,046 + 55,389
21. 209,349 + 567,499
22. 35,462 + 7,096
23. 16,494 + 6,095
24. $555.99 + $62.85

EXCURSION

The clock-5 arithmetic system uses only the five digits on the clock to answer all addition and subtraction problems. Use this clock to find the answers.

1. 3 + 4 = ____
2. 4 − 3 = ____
3. 2 + 3 = ____
4. 2 − 4 = ____
5. 4 + 4 + 4 = ____
6. 1 − 2 = ____

30

3. 4)80   4. 4)96   5. 2)56

8. 5)80   9. 6)96   10. 9)90

13. 4)56   14. 7)91   15. 6)84

18. 7)98   19. 3)90   20. 4)76

23. 85 ÷ 5   24. 72 ÷ 6
27. 72 ÷ 4   28. 88 ÷ 4
31. 87 ÷ 3   32. 96 ÷ 8

34. Lemons cost 8¢ each. Sally has 96¢. How many lemons can Sally buy?

36. The tennis club used 45 tennis balls in a tournament. Tennis balls are sold 3 in a can. How many cans did the club use?

134

T-9

MATH COMES ALIVE WHEN STUDENTS LEARN TO INTEGRATE COMPUTATION, PROBLEM-SOLVING STRATEGIES, AND REASONING TO MAKE DECISIONS FOR THEMSELVES!

Problem-solving pages present lessons that increase understanding with a four-step teaching strategy: SEE, PLAN, DO, CHECK. *Modern Curriculum Press Mathematics* offers step-by-step instruction in how to understand word problems as well as varied practice in actually using the skills learned. Each lesson focuses on a different problem-solving strategy. These strategies develop students' higher-order thinking skills and help them successfully solve problems. Step-by-step, students will understand the question, find the information needed, plan a solution, and then check it for accuracy. This develops students' critical-thinking skills and ability to apply what they've learned to solve problems that go beyond basic operations.

■ Word problems utilize high-interest information and focus on everyday situations.

PROBLEM SOLVING

Drawing a Picture

A parking lot has 9 rows of 8 parking spaces each. The fourth and fifth spaces in every third row have trees in them. The outside spaces in every row are reserved for the handicapped or for emergency vehicles. How many regular parking spaces are there in the lot?

★ SEE

We want to know how many spaces are left for regular parking.

There are _____ rows of parking spaces.

There are _____ spaces in each row.

In every third row, _____ spaces are lost to trees.

In every row _____ spaces are used for special vehicles.

★ PLAN

We can draw a picture of the parking lot, crossing out the closed parking spaces. Then we can count the regular spaces left.

★ DO

We count _____ spaces left for regular parking.

★ CHECK

We can check by adding the spaces open in each row.

4 + 6 + 6 + 4 + 6 + 6 + 4 + 6 + 6 = _____

each problem.

2. A Super-Duper ball bounces twice its height when it is dropped. Carl dropped a Super-Duper ball from the roof of a 12-foot garage. How high will the ball bounce after 5 bounces?

4. The distance around a rectangle is 10 centimeters. The length of each of the two longer sides is 3 centimeters. What is the length of each of the two shorter sides?

6. What 7 coins together make 50 cents?

173

- Step by step, students learn to understand the question, find the information they need, plan a method of solution, find an answer, and check it for accuracy.

- Every step of the process is organized so that students truly understand how to arrive at the solution.

- The problem-solving banner alerts students that they are involved in a problem-solving lesson. These focused lessons remind students how to approach problems and how to use skills and specific strategies already learned.

- Learning to integrate computation, problem-solving strategies, and reasoning makes math come alive for students.

- Problems incorporate previously taught computational skills—focusing students' minds on the problem-solving process itself.

- Problem-solving applications appear in every problem-solving lesson. This frequent practice reduces apprehension and builds confidence.

- Practice in applying the strategies gives students a chance to use skills in routine and non-routine problems.

- In every chapter, problem-solving strategies and critical-thinking skills are developed, applied, and reinforced.

- Students choose appropriate strategies to solve problems and are challenged to formulate their own problems and to change the conditions in existing problems.

PROBLEM SOLVING

Collecting Data, Determining Missing Data

Which of the following is the tallest structure: Sears Tower in Chicago, CN Tower in Toronto, World Trade Center in New York or the John Hancock Center in Chicago?

★ SEE

We want to find out which is the tallest structure. We do not have enough information to solve this problem.

★ PLAN

We need to find the height of each structure. We can

find this information by looking in _____. Once we have this information we can compare the heights to find the tallest structure.

★ DO

Use a reference book such as an encyclopedia or an almanac to find the height of each structure.

Sears Tower _____

CN Tower _____

World Trade Center _____

John Hancock Center _____

The _____ is the tallest of the four structures.

★ CHECK

We can check by verifying this data in another reference book, and by listing the heights of the four structures in order from largest to smallest.

2. Roll a pair of dice 30 times and record the number of times each sum appears. Perform the experiment a second time. What sum appears most often? What sum appears least often?

4. Toss a coin 50 times and record the number of heads and tails. Which side of the coin appears most often?

6. Record the dates of the coins available in your classroom. How many years difference exist between the newest and oldest coin?

8. An arithmetic game is created by adding the values of certain U.S. currency. Since a portrait of George Washington appears on a $1 bill and a portrait of Abraham Lincoln appears on the $5 bill, we say that George Washington + Abraham Lincoln = $6. Find the value of Thomas Jefferson + Alexander Hamilton + Woodrow Wilson.

CHAPTER TEST PAGES PROVIDE A VEHICLE FOR STUDENT EVALUATION AND FEEDBACK!

Every chapter in *Modern Curriculum Press Mathematics* concludes with a **Chapter Test.** These tests provide the opportunity for students to demonstrate their mastery of recently acquired skills. **Chapter Test** pages enable the teacher to measure all the basic skills students have practiced in the lesson and evaluate their understanding. The focus of these pages is the assessing of mastery of algorithms. An adequate number of sample problems are provided to accomplish this. This important checkpoint helps the teacher to better meet individual student-computational needs.

▪ **Chapter Test** pages are carefully correlated to what has been taught throughout the entire series.

▪ **Chapter Test** pages assess students' mastery of all the skills taught in the lesson.

▪ All directions are written in an easy-to-follow format.

▪ Both vertical and horizontal forms of problems are used making students more comfortable with exercises found in standardized tests.

▪ In the back of each student book, there is an alternate **Chapter Test** for each chapter based on the same objectives covered in the first test.

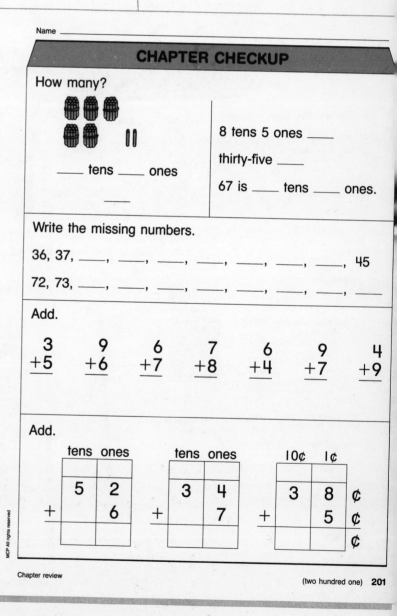

11
CHAPTER TEST

Divide.

1. $15 \div 3 =$ ___   2. $4\overline{)12}$ 3. $2\overline{)10}$

5. $5\overline{)40}$ 6. $21 \div 3 =$ ___   7. 14

9. $4\overline{)16}$ 10. $45 \div 9 =$ ___   11. $6 \div$

13. $3\overline{)24}$ 14. $28 \div 4 =$ ___   15. $5\overline{)1}$

17. $9 \div 3 =$ ___   18. $25 \div 5 =$ ___   19. 4

21. $2\overline{)16}$ 22. $20 \div 4 =$ ___   23. 24

Write the missing numbers. Check your an
with multiplication or division.

25. $15 \div 5 =$ ___   26. $9 \times 4 =$ ___   27. 6

29. $4\overline{)28}$ 30. ___ $\times 8 = 40$ 31.

33. ___ $\times 9 = 18$ 34. $4 \times 4 =$ ___   35.

37. $12 \div 3 =$ ___   38. $2\overline{)8}$ 39.

41. $4\overline{)8}$ 42. $12 \div 2 =$ ___   43.

Name ___

CHAPTER CHECKUP

How many?

___ tens ___ ones

___

8 tens 5 ones ___

thirty-five ___

67 is ___ tens ___ ones.

Write the missing numbers.

36, 37, ___, ___, ___, ___, ___, ___, ___, 45

72, 73, ___, ___, ___, ___, ___, ___, ___

Add.

| 3 | 9 | 6 | 7 | 6 | 9 | 4 |
|+5 |+6 |+7 |+8 |+4 |+7 |+9 |

Add.

tens	ones
5	2
+	6

tens	ones
3	4
+	7

10¢	1¢
3	8	¢
+	5	¢
		¢

Chapter review

(two hundred one) **201**

T-12

SYSTEMATIC MAINTENANCE IS PROVIDED AT EVERY LEVEL WITH CUMULATIVE REVIEW PAGES!

Every chapter contains a **Cumulative Review** page that provides an ongoing refresher course in basic skills. These pages maintain the skills that have been taught in the chapter plus the skills learned in previous chapters.

Cumulative Review pages actually reach back into the text for a total maintenance of skills. **Cumulative Review** pages are progressive instruction because they build on the foundation laid earlier for a thorough and sequential program of review. A standardized test format is used beginning at the middle of the second grade. Students

will benefit by gaining experience in dealing with this special test format.

■ A variety of problems done in standardized test format give students a better chance to score well on these tests.

■ Directions are minimal and easy to understand.

■ Design elements on every test are the same found on standardized tests.

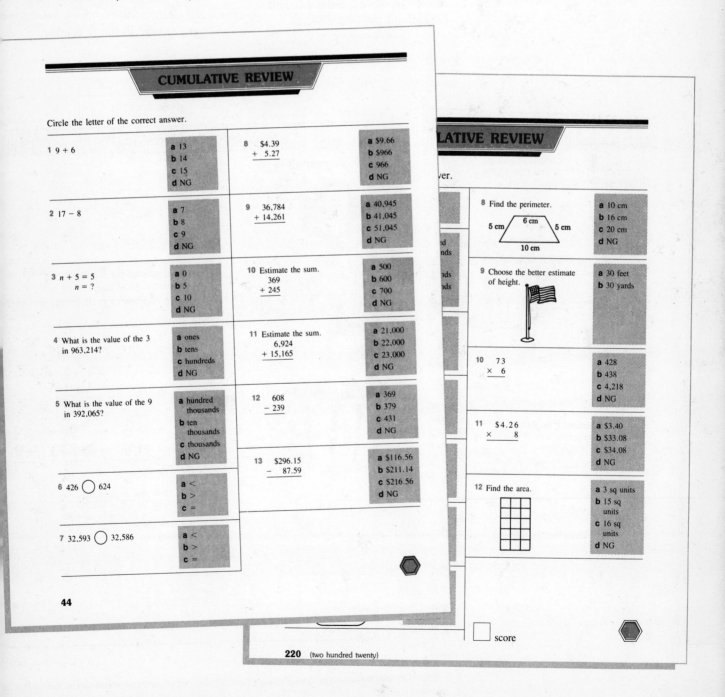

CUMULATIVE REVIEW

Circle the letter of the correct answer.

1 9 + 6
a 13
b 14
c 15
d NG

2 17 − 8
a 7
b 8
c 9
d NG

3 $n + 5 = 5$
$n = ?$
a 0
b 5
c 10
d NG

4 What is the value of the 3 in 963,214?
a ones
b tens
c hundreds
d NG

5 What is the value of the 9 in 392,065?
a hundred thousands
b ten thousands
c thousands
d NG

6 426 ◯ 624
a <
b >
c =

7 32,593 ◯ 32,586
a <
b >
c =

8 $4.39
+ 5.27
a $9.66
b $966
c 966
d NG

9 36,784
+ 14,261
a 40,945
b 41,045
c 51,045
d NG

10 Estimate the sum.
369
+ 245
a 500
b 600
c 700
d NG

11 Estimate the sum.
6,924
+ 15,165
a 21,000
b 22,000
c 23,000
d NG

12 608
− 239
a 369
b 379
c 431
d NG

13 $296.15
− 87.59
a $116.56
b $211.14
c $216.56
d NG

44

CUMULATIVE REVIEW

...ver.

8 Find the perimeter.
5 cm 6 cm 5 cm
10 cm
a 10 cm
b 16 cm
c 20 cm
d NG

9 Choose the better estimate of height.
a 30 feet
b 30 yards

10 73
× 6
a 428
b 438
c 4,218
d NG

11 $4.26
× 8
a $3.40
b $33.08
c $34.08
d NG

12 Find the area.
a 3 sq units
b 15 sq units
c 16 sq units
d NG

☐ score

CALCULATOR LESSONS PROVIDE EXCITING LEARNING ACTIVITIES AND ADD INTEREST AND PRACTICALITY TO MATH!

Calculator lessons are found throughout *Modern Curriculum Press Mathematics*. The activities are used in many ways—to explore number patterns, to do calculations, to check estimations, and to investigate functions. Each **Calculator** lesson is designed to help students learn to use and operate calculators while they reinforce and improve their mathematical skills.

■ **Calculator** lessons teach students to use simple calculators while reinforcing chapter content.

■ **Calculator** lessons introduce student to basic calculator skills and terms.

■ Practical calculator activities promo student involvement as they take an active part in what they are learning.

■ Students learn, practice, and apply critical-thinking skills as they use calculators.

Practice

Complete these calculator codes.

1. $85 \div 5 =$ ☐

2. $57 \div 3 =$ ☐

4. $96 \div 6 =$ ☐

6. $90 \div 9 =$ ☐

8. $63 \div 7 \times 8 =$ ☐

10. $75 \div 5 \times 6 =$ ☐

12. $216 - 158 \div 2 =$ ☐

14. Nathan can jog 5 miles in 65 minutes. How long will it take Nathan to jog 8 miles?

16. Bananas are on sale at 6 for 96¢. How much do 8 bananas cost?

EXCURSION

2. The sum of 2 numbers is 60. Their difference is 12. What are the numbers?

4. Five times one number is three more than six times another number. The difference between the numbers is 1. What are the numbers?

Calculators, the Division Key

Natalie is packing lunches for a picnic. She needs to buy 5 apples. How much will Natalie pay for the 5 apples?

Apples 3 for 51¢

We want to know the price for 5 apples.

We know that _____ apples cost _____.

To find the cost of 5 apples, we first find the cost of 1 by dividing _____ by _____. Then, we multiply the cost of 1 apple by _____.

This can be done on the calculator in one code.

$\cdot\, 51 \div 3 \times 5 =$ ☐

Natalie will pay _____ for 5 apples.

Complete these calculator codes.

1. $42 \div 7 =$ ☐

2. $76 \div 2 =$ ☐

3. $96 \div 4 =$ ☐

4. $52 \div 4 =$ ☐

5. $36 \div 9 \times 7 =$ ☐

6. $84 \div 4 \times 3 =$ ☐

7. $72 \div 6 \times 9 =$ ☐

8. $75 \div 5 \times 9 =$ ☐

139

PLAN CLASSROOM-READY MATH LESSONS IN MINUTES WITH COMPREHENSIVE TEACHER'S EDITIONS!

The **Teacher's Editions** of *Modern Curriculum Press Mathematics* are designed and organized with the teacher in mind. The full range of options provides more help than ever before and guarantees efficient use of the teacher's planning time and the most effective results for efforts exerted.

Each **Teacher's Edition** provides an abundance of additional **Enrichment, Correcting Common Errors** and application activities. Plus they contain a complete **Error Pattern Analysis.** The teacher will also find reduced student pages with answers, objectives, suggestions for teaching lessons, materials, **Mental Math** exercises, and more.

■ There's no need for the teacher to struggle with two separate books because student pages are reduced in the **Teacher's Edition.**

■ Clear headings and notes make it easy for the teacher to find what is needed before teaching the lesson.

■ The teacher will be more effective with lesson plans that are always complete in two pages and include everything needed.

■ Student **Objectives** set a clear course for the lesson goal.

Time to the Half-hour
pages 163-164

Objective

To practice telling time to the hour and half-hour

Materials

*Demonstration clock
*Two pencils of different lengths

Mental Math

Which is less?
1. 2 dimes or 5 nickels (2 dimes)
2. 14 pennies or 2 nickels (2 nickels)
3. 5 nickels or 4 dimes (5 nickels)
4. 1 quarter or 2 dimes (2 dimes)
5. 6 nickels or 1 quarter (1 quarter)

Skill Review

Show times to the hour and half hour on the demonstration clock. Have students write the time on the board. Now have a student set the clock to show an hour or half-hour. Have the student ask another student to write the time on the board. Have a student write a time for the hour or half-hour and invite another student to place the hands on the clock to show the times.

Name _____

Match the clocks

Telling time to the hour and half-hour

Teaching page 163

On the demonstration clock, start at 12:00 and slowly move the minute hand around the clock. Ask students to tell what the hour hand does as the minute hand moves around the clock face. (moves slowly toward the next number) Tell students the minute hand moves around the clock face 60 minutes while the hour hand moves from one number to the next. Tell students there are 60 minutes in 1 hour.

Ask students to tell where the hour hand is on the first clock. (between 5 and 6) Ask where the minute hand is. (on 6) Ask the time. (5:30) Tell students to find 5:30 in the center column and trace the line from the clock to 5:30. Tell students to draw a line from each clock to its time.

Multiplying, the Factor 5
pages 125-126

Objective

To multiply by the factor 5

Materials

Mental Math

Ask students to multiply 4 by:
1. the number of ears one person has. ($4 \times 2 = 8$)
2. the number of feet two students have. ($4 \times 4 = 16$)
3. the number of noses in a crowd of 7. ($4 \times 7 = 28$)
4. the number of their toes. ($4 \times 10 = 40$)

Skill Review

Have students make up a multiplication chart. Tell them to write 2, 3, 4 along the top, 2 through 10 along the side. Tell them to fill in the chart by multiplying each top number by each side number.

Multiplying, the Factor 5

Each key on a calculator has a special job to do. How many keys are there on the calculator keyboard?

We need to find the total number of keys on the calculator.

We can see there are ___5___ rows of keys.

Each row has ___5___ keys.

We can add. $5 + 5 + 5 + 5 + 5 = $ ___25___

We can also multiply.

$5 \times 5 = $ ___25___ $\begin{array}{r} 5 \\ \times 5 \\ \hline 25 \end{array}$

There are ___25___ keys on the calculator keyboard.

Getting Started

Use both addition and multiplication to show how many are in the picture.

1.

$5 + 5 + 5 + 5 = $ ___20___
$4 \times 5 = $ ___20___
$5 \times 4 = $ ___20___

Multiply.

2. $\begin{array}{r} 3 \\ \times 5 \\ \hline 15 \end{array}$ 3. $\begin{array}{r} 8 \\ \times 5 \\ \hline 40 \end{array}$ 4. $5 \times 6 = $ ___30___   5. $9 \times 5 = $ ___45___

(one hundred twenty-five) **125**

Teaching the Lesson

Introducing the Problem Have students look at the calculator illustrated while you read the problem. Identify the question and explain that there are several ways they could answer it. Have students read the information sentences, filling in the information required. (5 rows, 5 keys) Read each sentence and tell students to do the indicated operation in their text while one student writes it on the board. Read the solution sentence aloud and have a student give the answer while the others complete that sentence in their texts. (30)

Developing the Skill Have students start at 5 and count aloud by five's through 50. Ask a volunteer to continue through 100. Explain that this may seem easy because they are used to counting out nickels. Because five is also half of ten, and when counting by fives, every other number will be a multiple of ten. Now write these addition problems on the board and have students work them: $5 + 5 = $, $5 + 5 + 5 = $, $5 + 5 + 5 + 5 = $. (10, 15, 20) Next to each of these problems write the multiplication problem that corresponds. (5×2, 5×3, 5×4) Have volunteers put the rest of the addition and multiplication problems for the factor five on the board, 5×5 through 5×10.

- A list of **Materials** helps the teacher reduce class preparation time.

- The **Mental Math** exercise gives the teacher an opportunity to brush-up on skills at the beginning of each day's lesson.

- **Skill Review** bridges new skills with previously-taught skills for total reinforcement.

- The **Teaching the Lesson** section is meant to give practical suggestions for introducing the problem and developing the skill. Specific suggestions for an effective presentation of the model are made in **Introducing the Problem.**

- In **Developing the Skill,** the teacher i given suggestions for presenting and developing the algorithm, skill, and/or concept. Where practical, recommendations are made for the use of manipulatives.

Zeros in Minuend

pages 69-70

Objective

To subtract 4- or 5-digit numbers when minuends have zeros

Materials

*thousands, hundreds, tens, ones jars
*place value materials

Mental Math

Tell students to answer true or false:

1. 776 has 77 tens. (T)
2. 10 hundreds < 1,000. (F)
3. 46 is an odd number. (F)
4. 926 can be rounded to 920. (F)
5. 72 hours = 3 days. (T)
6. $42 \div 6 > 7 \times 1$. (F)
7. 1/3 of 18 = 1/2 of 12. (T)
8. perimeter = L × W. (F)

Skill Review

Write 4 numbers of 3- to 5-digits each on the board. Have students arrange the numbers in order, from the least to the greatest, and then read the numbers as they would appear if written from the greatest to the least. Repeat for more sets of 4 or 5 numbers.

Subtracting, More Minuends with Zeros

The Susan B. Anthony School held its annual fall Read-a-Thon. How many more pages did the fifth grade read than the second-place class?

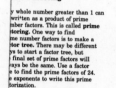

Class Reading Records

Fourth Grade — 3,795 pages
Fifth Grade — 5,003 pages
Sixth Grade — 4,056 pages

We want to know how many more pages the fifth grade read than the second-place class.

We know the fifth grade read ___5,003___ pages.

The second-place class is the ___sixth___ grade.

It read ___4,056___ pages.
To find the difference between the number of pages, we subtract ___4,056___ from ___5,003___.

✔ Remember to trade from one place value at a time.

$$\begin{array}{r} 9\ 9 \\ 4\ \not{10}\ \not{10}\ 13 \\ 5{,}003 \\ -4{,}056 \\ \hline 947 \end{array}$$

The fifth grade read ___947___ more pages than the sixth grade.

Getting Started

Subtract.

1. $\begin{array}{r} 3{,}005 \\ -1{,}348 \\ \hline 1{,}657 \end{array}$
2. $\begin{array}{r} \$40.09 \\ -\ \ 9.75 \\ \hline \$30.34 \end{array}$
3. $\begin{array}{r} 3{,}300 \\ -1{,}856 \\ \hline 1{,}444 \end{array}$

4. $\begin{array}{r} \$50.00 \\ -\ 27.26 \\ \hline \$22.74 \end{array}$
5. $\begin{array}{r} 8{,}512 \\ -7{,}968 \\ \hline 544 \end{array}$
6. $\begin{array}{r} \$90.17 \\ -\ 20.87 \\ \hline \$69.30 \end{array}$

Copy and subtract.

7. 26,007 − 18,759
   7,248
8. 70,026 − 23,576
   46,450
9. $900.05 − $267.83
   $632.22

69

Teaching the Lesson

Introducing the Problem Have a student read the problem. Ask students what 2 problems are to be solved. (which class read the second-highest number of pages and how many more pages the first-place fifth graders read) Ask students how we can find out which class came in second place. (arrange numbers from the table in order from greatest to least) Ask a student to write the numbers from greatest to least on the board. (5,003, 4,056, 3,795) Have students complete the sentences and work through the model problem with them.

Developing the Skill Write **4,000−2,875** vertically on the board. Ask students if a trade is needed to subtract the ones column. (yes) Tell students that since there are no tens and no hundreds, we must trade 1 thousand for 10 hundreds. Show the 3 thousands and 10 hundreds left. Now tell students we can trade 1 hundred for 10 tens. Show the trade with 9 hundreds and 10 tens left. Tell students we can now trade 1 ten for 10 ones. Show the trade so that 9 tens and 10 ones are left. Tell students we can now subtract each column beginning with the ones column and working to the left. Show students the subtraction to a solution of **1,125.** Remind students to add the subtrahend and the difference to check the work. Repeat for more problems with zeros in the minuend.

Prime Factoring

Any whole number greater than 1 can be written as a product of prime number factors. This is called **prime factoring.** One way to find prime number factors is to make a factor tree. There may be different ways to start a factor tree, but the final set of prime factors will always be the same. Use a factor tree to find the prime factors of 24. Use exponents to write this prime factorization.

$$24$$
(factor tree)

$$2 \times 2 \times 2 \times 3$$
$$2^3 \times 3$$

$$3 \times 2 \times 2 \times 2$$
$$3 \times 2^3$$

✔ Remember, the exponent tells how many times to use the base number as a factor. $2^3 = 2 \times 2 \times 2$

Getting Started

Complete each factor tree.

1. 20
2. 36
3. 50

Write each prime factorization using exponents if possible.

4. 8 2^3
5. 35 5×7
6. 48 $2^4 \times 3$
7. 72 $2^3 \times 3^2$
8. 400 $2^4 \times 5^2$

99

Developing the Skill Point out that when a prime number is used more than once in the prime factoring, it can be expressed with an **exponent.** Remind students that 2^3 is the same as $2 \times 2 \times 2$. Stress that the 3 in 2^3 is an exponent, and that this exponent tells the number of times 2 is used as a factor. Have students complete each of the following factor trees and then write each prime factorization using exponents:

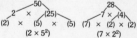

50
(2) × (25)
       (5) × (5)
(2×5^2)

28
7 × (4)
    (2) × (2)
(7×2^2)

...composite ...ctors. Tell ...e factor ...n aloud, ...he tree ...r tree on ...at a num- ...f prime ...d. Have ...f each

s the

FREQUENT ATTENTION IS GIVEN TO CORRECTING COMMON ERRORS, ENRICHMENT AND OPTIONAL EXTRA-CREDIT ACTIVITIES!

These comprehensive **Teacher's Editions** are intended to provide the teacher with a convenient, well-structured approach to teaching mathematics. From motivating introductory exercises to challenging extension activities, *Modern Curriculum Press*

Mathematics **Teacher's Editions** suggest a complete step-by-step plan to insure successful learning. The succinct lesson plans help the teacher provide solid math instruction to students.

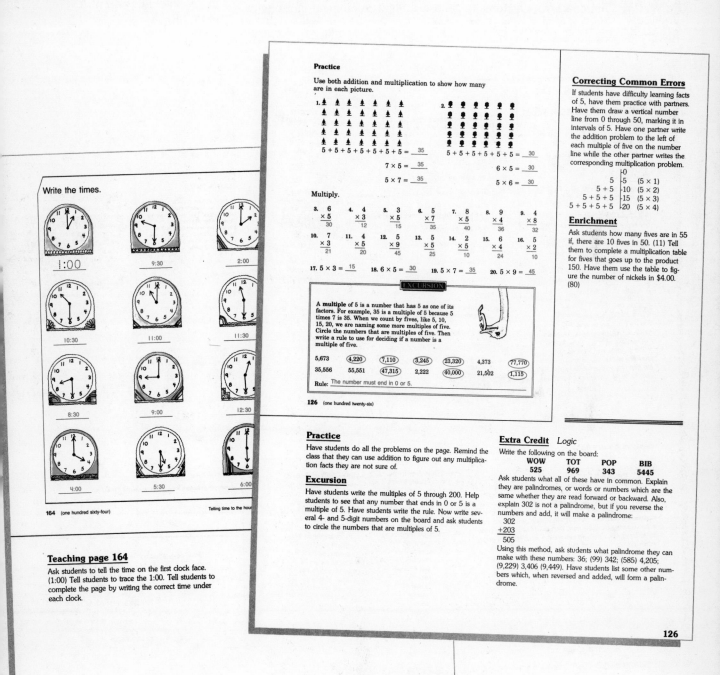

Write the times.

1:00   9:30   2:00

10:30   11:00   11:30

8:30   9:00   12:30

4:00   5:30   6:00

164 (one hundred sixty-four)   Telling time to the hour

Teaching page 164

Ask students to tell the time on the first clock face. (1:00) Tell students to trace the 1:00. Tell students to complete the page by writing the correct time under each clock.

164

Practice

Use both addition and multiplication to show how many are in each picture.

1. $5 + 5 + 5 + 5 + 5 + 5 + 5 =$ ___35___

$7 \times 5 =$ ___35___

$5 \times 7 =$ ___35___

2. $5 + 5 + 5 + 5 + 5 =$ ___30___

$6 \times 5 =$ ___30___

$5 \times 6 =$ ___30___

Multiply.

3. $\begin{array}{r} 6 \\ \times 5 \\ \hline 30 \end{array}$ 4. $\begin{array}{r} 4 \\ \times 3 \\ \hline 12 \end{array}$ 5. $\begin{array}{r} 3 \\ \times 5 \\ \hline 15 \end{array}$ 6. $\begin{array}{r} 5 \\ \times 7 \\ \hline 35 \end{array}$ 7. $\begin{array}{r} 8 \\ \times 5 \\ \hline 40 \end{array}$ 8. $\begin{array}{r} 9 \\ \times 4 \\ \hline 36 \end{array}$ 9. $\begin{array}{r} 4 \\ \times 8 \\ \hline 32 \end{array}$

10. $\begin{array}{r} 7 \\ \times 3 \\ \hline 21 \end{array}$ 11. $\begin{array}{r} 4 \\ \times 5 \\ \hline 20 \end{array}$ 12. $\begin{array}{r} 5 \\ \times 9 \\ \hline 45 \end{array}$ 13. $\begin{array}{r} 5 \\ \times 5 \\ \hline 25 \end{array}$ 14. $\begin{array}{r} 2 \\ \times 5 \\ \hline 10 \end{array}$ 15. $\begin{array}{r} 6 \\ \times 4 \\ \hline 24 \end{array}$ 16. $\begin{array}{r} 5 \\ \times 2 \\ \hline 10 \end{array}$

17. $5 \times 3 =$ ___15___   18. $6 \times 5 =$ ___30___   19. $5 \times 7 =$ ___35___   20. $5 \times 9 =$ ___45___

EXCURSION

A multiple of 5 is a number that has 5 as one of its factors. For example, 35 is a multiple of 5 because 5 times 7 is 35. When we count by fives, like 5, 10, 15, 20, we are naming some more multiples of five. Circle the numbers that are multiples of five. Then write a rule to use for deciding if a number is a multiple of five.

5,673   ④,220   ⑦,110   ③,245   ㉓,320   4,373   ㊆㊆,770

35,556   55,551   ㊸,315   2,222   ㊵,000   21,502   ①,115

Rule: The number must end in 0 or 5.

126 (one hundred twenty-six)

Practice

Have students do all the problems on the page. Remind the class that they can use addition to figure out any multiplication facts they are not sure of.

Excursion

Have students write the multiples of 5 through 200. Help students to see that any number that ends in 0 or 5 is a multiple of 5. Have students write the rule. Now write several 4- and 5-digit numbers on the board and ask students to circle the numbers that are multiples of 5.

Correcting Common Errors

If students have difficulty learning facts of 5, have them practice with partners. Have them draw a vertical number line from 0 through 50, marking it in intervals of 5. Have one partner write the addition problem to the left of each multiple of five on the number line while the other partner writes the corresponding multiplication problem.

	0	
5	5	(5×1)
$5 + 5$	10	(5×2)
$5 + 5 + 5$	15	(5×3)
$5 + 5 + 5 + 5$	20	(5×4)

Enrichment

Ask students how many fives are in 55 if, there are 10 fives in 50. (11) Tell them to complete a multiplication table for fives that goes up to the product 150. Have them use the table to figure the number of nickels in $4.00. (80)

Extra Credit   *Logic*

Write the following on the board:

WOW	TOT	POP	BIB
525	969	343	5445

Ask students what all of these have in common. Explain they are palindromes, or words or numbers which are the same whether they are read forward or backward. Also, explain 302 is not a palindrome, but if you reverse the numbers and add, it will make a palindrome:

$\begin{array}{r} 302 \\ +203 \\ \hline 505 \end{array}$

Using this method, ask students what palindrome they can make with these numbers: 36; (99) 342; (585) 4,205; (9,229) 3,406 (9,449). Have students list some other numbers which, when reversed and added, will form a palindrome.

126

- Follow up activities focus on **Correcting Common Errors, Enrichment,** and **Extra Credit** suggestions.

- In the **Correcting Common Errors** feature, a common error pattern is explored and a method of remediation is recommended. Collectively, all the **Correcting Common Errors** features in any chapter constitute a complete set of the common errors likely to be committed by the students when working in that area of mathematics.

- **Enrichment** activities are a direct extension of the skills being taught. Students can do these activities on their own while the teacher works with those students who need more help.

- **Extra Credits** are challenging independent activities to expand the mathematical experiences of the students. The **Extra Credit** section encompasses a wide variety of activities and projects and introduces and extends skills taught in the normal basal curriculum—including statistics, logic, and probability.

Practice

Subtract.

1.	3,004 − 2,356	2.	8,002 − 5,096	3.	3,891 − 1,750	4.	$20.08 − 15.99
	648		2,906		2,141		$4.09
5.	4,020 − 1,865	6.	$87.00 − 28.59	7.	3,007 − 2,090	8.	$50.06 − 37.08
	2,155		$58.41		917		$12.98
9.	19,006 − 8,275	10.	20,006 − 14,758	11.	$400.26 − 236.58	12.	$793.42 − 253.87
	10,731		5,248		$163.68		$539.55

Copy and Do

13. 4,001 − 2,756   1,245
14. $70.05 − $26.59 $43.46
15. 8,060 − 7,948   112
16. 7,007 − 2,468   4,539
17. 21,316 − 12,479   8,837
18. 14,000 − 8,396   5,604
19. $100.21 − $93.50 $6.71
20. 60,004 − 51,476   8,528
21. 52,006 − 9,037   42,969
22. $800.00 − $275.67 $524.33
23. 34,612 − 29,965   4,647
24. 50,010 − 36,754   13,256

Apply

Use the chart on page 69 to help solve these problems.

25. How many pages did the three classes read all together?   12,854 pages

26. How many more pages did the sixth grade read than the fourth grade?   261 pages

70

Correcting Common Errors

Some students may bring down the numbers that are being subtracted when there are zeros in the minuend.

INCORRECT	CORRECT
	9
	2 10 10
3,006	3,006
− 1,425	− 1,425
2,421	1,581

Have students work in pairs and use play money to model a problem such as $300 − $142, where they see that they must trade 3 hundreds for 2 hundreds, 9 tens, and 10 ones before they can subtract.

Enrichment

Tell students to find out the year in which each member of their family was born, and make a chart to show how old each will be in the year 2000.

3. 28
7 × 4
2 × 2

6. 75
3 × 25
5 × 5

... ossible.

10. 64   2⁶
11. 66   2 × 3 × 11

15. 180 $2^2 \times 3^2 \times 5$
16. 225 $3^2 \times 5^2$

7 are examples of twin
... 43, 71 and 73
... irror primes. 13 and 31 are
... 9 and 97
... its factors except itself.
... the perfect numbers less

Correcting Common Errors

Some students do not write the prime factorization of a number correctly because they cannot identify prime numbers. Have them work with partners to name all the prime numbers from 1 to 50 and write them on an index card. The students can use these cards as a guide for this work.

Enrichment

Provide this alternative method of dividing to find prime factorization of a number. Tell students they must always divide by a prime number.

$$
\begin{array}{r|l}
2 & 36 \\
2 & 18 \\
3 & 9 \\
& 3
\end{array}
\qquad 36 = 2^2 \times 3^2
$$

Have students use this method to find the prime factorization of:
120 ($2^3 \times 3 \times 5$); 250 ($5^3 \times 2$); 1,000 ($2^3 \times 5^3$); 72 ($3^2 \times 2^3$)

Practice

Remind students to begin with the ones column, work to the left and trade from one place value at a time. Have students complete the page independently.

Extra Credit   *Biography*

An American inventor, Samuel Morse, struggled for many years before his inventions, the electric telegraph and Morse code were recognized. Morse was born in Massachusetts in 1791, and studied to be an artist. On a trip home from Europe, Morse heard his shipmates discussing the idea of sending electricity over wire. Intrigued, Morse spent the rest of the voyage formulating his ideas about how this could be accomplished. Morse taught at a university in New York City, and used his earnings to continue development of his telegraph. After five years, Morse demonstrated his invention, but found very little support. After years of requests for support, Congress finally granted Morse $30,000 to test his invention. He dramatically strung a telegraph wire from Washington, D.C. to Baltimore, Maryland, and relayed the message, "What hath God wrought" using Morse code. Morse's persistence finally won him wealth and fame. A statue honoring him was unveiled in New York City one year before his death in 1872.

... prob-
... tly.

... enes as
... ect num-
... o com-

Extra Credit   *Applications*

Have a student write the primary United States time zones across the board. Discuss how this pattern continues around the world. Divide students into groups and provide them with globes or flat maps. Have students choose various cities in the United States and elsewhere in the world, and determine what the time would be in those cities when it is 6:00 AM in their home city. Have students make another list of cities without times indicated to exchange with classmates to figure time comparisons.

100

Grades K-3

Bake and Taste. Tucson, AZ: MindPlay, 1990. (Apple, IBM)

Educators looking for a slightly different program might be interested in *Bake and Taste.* Students are guided through the process of making a dessert of their choosing. In the course of the baking fun, students work on the skills of measuring, counting, and figuring fractions. The desserts can really be baked and eaten. Teacher or parent involvement is necessary for nonreaders.

Elastic Lines: The Electronic Geoboard. Education Development Center. Pleasantville, NY: Sunburst Communications, 1989. (Apple, IBM)

This is a simulation of rubber bands being stretched over pegboards of variable size and type. Students can practice the skills of visualizing shapes in space and estimating. Primary students will enjoy the most elementary of the concepts in this program that is recommended for Grades 2 through 8.

Exploring Measurement, Time, and Money, Level II. Dayton, NJ: IBM, 1990. (IBM)

This program combines a tutorial with drill and practice focusing on linear measurement, time measurement, and money. Students practice such skills as comparing measurements and making change.

Hop to It! Pleasantville, NY: Sunburst Communications, 1990. (Apple)

This program focuses on using problem solving skills to better understand addition, subtraction, and the number line. Students must choose the operation that will help animals capture objects along a number line. The number line can begin anywhere between −10 and 10.

KidsMath. Scotts Valley, CA: Great Wave Software, 1989. (Macintosh)

KidsMath offers eight games to help students learn basic math skills such as addition, subtraction, multiplication, division, and fractions. Students will be delighted with the attractive graphics and animations.

Math Rabbit. Fremont, CA: The Learning Company, 1989. (Apple, IBM, Macintosh)

A colorful program which introduces basic number concepts such as counting, addition, subtraction, and number relationships. Recommended for preschool to Grade 1.

Math Shop Jr. Jefferson City, MO: Scholastic, 1989. (Apple, IBM, Mac)

As they pretend to run stores in a mall, students work on real-life situations in which they use addition, subtraction, multiplication, division, odd and even numbers, estimation, and coins.

New Math Blaster Plus. Torrance, CA: Davidson & Associates, 1990. (Apple, IBM, Mac)

With its fast-paced, arcade-like games, this program will be a favorite of all students. It includes problems in addition, subtraction, multiplication, division, fractions, decimals, and percents. Teachers can print customized tests.

Number Munchers. Minneapolis, MN: MECC, 1986. (Apple, IBM, Mac)

Students control a number-munching monster. If the monster eats the correct answer, the student moves on to the next level. The program drills concepts such as multiples 2–20, factoring of numbers 3–99, prime numbers 1–99, equality and inequality.

NumberMaze. Scotts Valley, CA: Great Wave Software, 1988. (Mac)

To travel through the mazes, students must answer questions involving basic math concepts. Some word problems are included.

Picture Chompers. Minneapolis, MN: MECC, 1990. (Apple)

Students practice classification skills in this fast-paced game. User guides a pair of teeth around a grid and the teeth eat objects of specified color, pattern, size, or shape.

Stickybear Math. Norfolk, CT: Optimum Resource, Inc., 1984. (Apple, IBM)

Students solve simple addition and subtraction problems to get the colorful Stickybear out of sticky situations.

Super Solvers: Treasure Mountain! Fremont, CA: The Learning Company, 1990. (IBM)

This program builds problem-solving skills as students try to foil the prankster Morty Maxwell who has stolen the enchanted crown. Math, reading, thinking, and science skills are required.

Winker's World of Patterns. Scotts Valley, CA: Wings for Learning, 1990. (Apple, IBM)

Students practice recognizing and remembering patterns involving colors, numbers, and words.

Scope and Sequence

	K	1	2	3	4	5	6
READINESS							
Attributes	■						
Shapes	■	■					
Colors	■	■	■				
NUMERATION							
On-to-one correspondence	■						
Understanding numbers	■	■	■				
Writing numbers	■	■					
Counting objects	■	■	■				
Sequencing numbers	■	■	■	■	■		
Numbers before and after	■	■	■	■	■		
Ordering numbers			■	■	■	■	■
Comparing numbers	■	■	■	■	■	■	■
Grouping numbers	■	■	■	■	■		
Ordinal numbers	■	■	■	■			
Number words		■	■	■	■	■	■
Expanded numbers		■	■	■	■	■	■
Place value		■	■	■	■	■	■
Skip-counting		■	■	■	■	■	
Roman numerals			■	■	■		
Rounding numbers				■	■	■	■
Squares and square roots				■			

Scope and Sequence	K	1	2	3	4	5	6
Primes and composites				■	■	■	■
Multiples					■	■	■
Least common multiples						■	■
Greatest common factors						■	■
Exponents							■
ADDITION							
Addition facts	■	■	■	■	■	■	■
Fact families		■	■	■	■	■	
Missing addends	■	■	■	■	■		
Adding money	■	■	■	■	■	■	■
Column addition		■	■	■	■	■	■
Two-digit addends		■	■	■	■	■	
Multidigit addends			■	■	■	■	■
Addition with trading		■	■	■	■	■	■
Basic properties of addition				■	■	■	■
Estimating sums				■	■	■	■
Addition of fractions				■	■	■	■
Addition of mixed numbers				■	■	■	■
Addition of decimals				■	■	■	■
Rule of order				■	■	■	■
Addition of customary measures						■	■

Scope and Sequence

	K	1	2	3	4	5	6
Addition of integers							■
SUBTRACTION							
Subtraction facts	■	■	■	■	■	■	■
Fact families		■	■	■	■	■	
Missing subtrahends		■	■				
Subtracting money	■	■	■	■	■	■	■
Two-digit numbers		■	■	■	■	■	
Multidigit numbers			■	■	■	■	■
Subtraction with trading		■	■	■	■	■	■
Zeros in the minuend				■	■	■	■
Basic properties of subtraction				■	■	■	■
Estimating differences				■	■	■	■
Subtraction of fractions				■	■	■	■
Subtraction of mixed numbers						■	■
Subtraction of decimals				■	■	■	■
Rule of order				■	■	■	■
Subtraction of customary measures						■	■
Subtraction of integers							■
MULTIPLICATION							
Multiplication facts			■	■	■	■	■
Fact families			■	■	■		

Scope and Sequence

	K	1	2	3	4	5	6
Missing factors					■		
Multiplying money			■	■	■	■	■
Multiplication by powers of ten				■	■	■	■
Multidigit factors				■	■	■	■
Multiplication with trading				■	■	■	■
Basic properties of multiplication			■	■	■	■	■
Estimating products				■	■	■	■
Rule of order				■	■	■	■
Multiples					■	■	■
Least common multiples						■	■
Multiplication of fractions						■	■
Factorization						■	■
Multiplication of mixed numbers							■
Multiplication of decimals					■	■	■
Exponents							■
Multiplication of integers							■
DIVISION							
Division facts				■	■	■	■
Fact families				■	■		
Divisibility rules				■		■	■
Two-digit quotients				■	■	■	■

Scope and Sequence

	K	1	2	3	4	5	6
Remainders				■	■	■	■
Multidigit quotients					■	■	■
Zeros in quotients					■	■	■
Division by multiples of ten					■	■	■
Two-digit divisors					■	■	■
Properties of division					■	■	
Averages				■	■	■	■
Greatest common factors						■	■
Division of fractions						■	■
Division of mixed numbers						■	■
Division of decimals						■	■
Division by powers of ten						■	■
MONEY							
Counting pennies	■	■	■	■	■		
Counting nickels	■	■	■	■	■		
Counting dimes	■	■	■	■	■		
Counting quarters		■	■	■	■		
Counting half-dollars				■	■	■	
Counting dollar bills		■		■	■	■	
Writing dollar and cents signs		■	■	■	■	■	■
Matching money with prices	■	■	■				

Scope and Sequence

	K	1	2	3	4	5	6
Determining amount of change	■	■	■				
Determining sufficient amount		■	■				
Determining which coins to use		■	■				
Addition	■	■	■	■	■	■	■
Subtraction	■	■	■	■	■	■	■
Multiplication			■	■	■	■	■
Division					■	■	■
Rounding amounts of money				■	■	■	■
Finding fractions of amounts					■	■	■
Buying from a menu or ad			■	■	■	■	■

FRACTIONS

	K	1	2	3	4	5	6
Understanding equal parts	■	■	■	■			
One half	■	■	■	■			
One fourth	■	■	■	■			
One third	■	■	■	■			
Identifying fractional parts of figures			■	■	■	■	■
Identifying fractional parts of sets			■	■	■	■	■
Finding unit fractions of numbers				■	■	■	
Equivalent fractions				■	■	■	■
Comparing fractions				■	■	■	■
Simplifying fractions					■	■	■

Scope and Sequence

	K	1	2	3	4	5	6
Renaming mixed numbers					■	■	■
Addition of fractions				■	■	■	■
Subtraction of fractions				■	■	■	■
Addition of mixed numbers					■	■	■
Subtraction of mixed numbers						■	■
Multiplication of fractions						■	■
Factorization						■	■
Multiplication of mixed numbers						■	■
Division of fractions						■	■
Division of mixed numbers						■	■
Renaming fractions as decimals							■
Renaming fractions as percents							■
DECIMALS							
Place value				■	■	■	■
Reading decimals				■	■	■	■
Writing decimals				■	■	■	■
Converting fractions to decimals				■	■	■	■
Writing parts of sets as decimals				■	■	■	
Comparing decimals				■	■	■	■
Ordering decimals							■
Addition of decimals				■	■	■	■

Scope and Sequence

	K	1	2	3	4	5	6
Subtraction of decimals				■	■	■	■
Rounding decimals				■		■	■
Multiplication of decimals					■	■	■
Division of decimals						■	■
Renaming decimals as percents							■
GEOMETRY							
Polygons	■	■	■	■	■	■	■
Sides and corners of polygons			■	■	■		
Lines and line segments					■	■	■
Rays and angles					■	■	■
Measuring angles						■	■
Symmetry			■			■	■
Congruency				■	■	■	■
Similar figures					■	■	■
Circles						■	■
MEASUREMENT							
Non-standard units of measure	■	■					
Customary units of measure		■	■	■	■	■	■
Metric units of measure	■	■	■	■	■	■	■
Renaming customary measures					■	■	■
Renaming metric measures					■	■	■

Scope and Sequence

	K	1	2	3	4	5	6
Selecting appropriate units			■	■	■	■	
Estimating measures		■	■	■	■	■	
Perimeter by counting	■	■	■				
Perimeter by formula			■	■	■	■	■
Area of polygons by counting			■	■			
Area of polygons by formula					■	■	■
Volume by counting				■			
Volume by formula					■	■	■
Addition of measures						■	■
Subtraction of measures						■	■
Circumference of circles							■
Area of circles							■
Surface area of space figures							■
Estimating temperatures				■			
Reading temperature scales			■	■			
TIME							
Ordering events	■						
Relative time	■						
Matching values	■	■	■	■	■		
Calendars	■	■	■	■			
Days of the week	■	■	■	■			

Scope and Sequence

	K	1	2	3	4	5	6
Months of the year	■	■	■	■			
Telling time to the hour	■	■	■	■			
Telling time to the half-hour		■	■	■			
Telling time to the five-minutes			■	■	■		
Telling time to the minute			■	■	■		
Understanding AM and PM					■		
Time zones					■		
GRAPHING							
Tables		■	■	■	■	■	■
Bar graphs	■	■	■	■	■	■	■
Picture graphs			■	■	■		■
Line graphs					■	■	■
Circle graphs						■	■
Tree diagrams						■	
Histograms							■
Ordered pairs				■	■	■	■
PROBABILITY							
Understanding probability					■	■	■
Listing outcomes					■	■	■
Means and medians						■	
Circle graphs						■	■

Scope and Sequence

	K	1	2	3	4	5	6
Tree diagrams						■	■
Histograms							■
RATIOS AND PERCENTS							
Understanding ratios					■	■	■
Equal ratios						■	■
Proportions							■
Scale drawings						■	■
Ratios as percents						■	■
Percents as fractions						■	■
Fractions as percents						■	■
Finding the percents of numbers						■	■
INTEGERS							
Understanding integers							■
Addition of integers							■
Subtraction of integers							■
Multiplication of integers							■
Graphing integers on coordinate planes							■
PROBLEM SOLVING							
Creating an algorithm from a word problem		■	■	■	■	■	■
Selecting the correct operation		■	■	■	■	■	■
Using data			■	■	■	■	■

Scope and Sequence

	K	1	2	3	4	5	6
Reading a chart			■	■	■	■	■
Using a four-step plan				■	■	■	■
Drawing a picture				■	■	■	■
Acting it out				■	■	■	■
Making a list				■	■	■	■
Making a tally				■	■	■	
Making a table				■	■	■	■
Making a graph				■	■	■	
Guessing and checking					■	■	■
Looking for a pattern					■	■	■
Making a model					■		
Restating the problem					■	■	■
Selecting notation					■	■	■
Writing an open sentence					■	■	■
Using a formula					■	■	■
Identifying a subgoal						■	■
Working backwards						■	■
Determining missing data						■	■
Collecting data						■	■
Solving a simpler but related problem						■	■
Making a flow chart							■

Scope and Sequence

	K	1	2	3	4	5	6
CALCULATORS							
Calculator codes				■	■	■	■
Equal key				■	■	■	■
Operation keys				■	■	■	■
Square root key				■			
Clear key				■	■	■	■
Clear entry key				■	■	■	■
Money				■	■	■	■
Unit prices				■	■	■	
Fractions				■	■		
Percents					■		
Banking				■	■	■	
Inventories					■		
Averages					■		
Rates						■	■
Formulas						■	■
Cross multiplication							■
Functions							■
Binary numbers							■
Repeating decimals							■
Statistics							■

This **Table of Common Errors** is designed to help the teacher understand the thinking patterns and potential errors that students commonly commit in the course of learning the content in *Modern Curriculum Press Mathematics*. Familiarity with this list can help the teacher forestall errant thinking and save much time used in reteaching.

In the **Correcting Common Errors** feature in each lesson in *Modern Curriculum Press Mathematics*, abundant suggestions are made to remediate situations where students might have misconceptions of other difficulties with a skill. These suggestions make frequent use of manipulatives and cooperative learning.

Numeration

1. The student transposes digits when writing the number of objects in a picture.

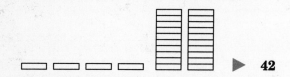 ▶ **42**

2. When counting objects in an array, the student counts some objects twice or fails to count each object in the array.

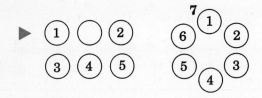

3. The student mistakes one number for another because it has been carelessly written.

4. When writing numerals for a number that is expressed in words, the student fails to write zeros as placeholders where they are needed.

   Write five hundred four in numerals.

   ▶ **54**

5. The student confuses the names of place values.

6. The student fails to write the money sign and/or decimal point in an answer involving money.

   $$\begin{array}{r} \$3.52 \\ +\quad 2 \\ \hline \end{array}$$
   ▶ **804**

7. The student does not relate money to what has been learned about place value.

   For example, the student does not relate dimes to tens place.

8. When ordering whole numbers, the student incorrectly compares single digits regardless of place value.

   For example, the student thinks that *203 is less than 45 because 2 is less than 4 and 3 is less than 5.*

9. The student rounds down when the last significant digit is 5.

   ▶ $75 \approx$ **70**

10. The student rounds progressively from digit to digit until the designated place value is reached.

    Round $3.45 to dollars.

    ▶ $3.45 ≈ **$3.50** ≈ **$4**

11. When counting past twenty, the student incorrectly repeats the number pattern between ten and twenty.

    ▶   . . . eighteen, nineteen, twenty, **twenty-eleven, twenty-twelve** . . .

12. The student changes the common interval when skip-counting.

    ▶   2, 4, 6, 8, **11, 14, 17**

13. The student starts off skip-counting but reverts to a counting series after a few numbers.

    ▶   3, 6, 9, **10, 11, 12,** . . .

14. The student fails to count money from the largest bills and coins to the smallest.

15. The student thinks since five pennies equal a nickel, that other coin relationships are also based on a five to one ratio.

    ▶   **5** quarters = 1 dollar

16. The student counts all coins as one cent regardless of their value.

17. The student confuses the greater than and less than signs.

    ▶   56 < 29
        34 > 55

Addition and Subtraction

1. The student is unsure of the basic facts of addition and/or subtraction.

2. The student copies the problem incorrectly.

    Find the sum of 6, 5, and 9.

    ▶
    ```
      6
      4
    +9
    ```
    19

3. The student makes simple addition errors when adding numbers with two or more digits.

    ```
     25
    +63
    ```
    ▶   87

4. The student thinks that a number plus zero is zero.

    ▶   **6 + 0 = 0**

5. The student adds during a subtraction computation, or vice versa.

    ```
     56      75
    +23     −28
    ```
    ▶   **33**   **103**

6. The student computes horizontal equations from left to right regardless of the operation.

    ▶   3 + 2 × 5 = 25

7. The student adds or subtracts before multiplying or dividing in a horizontal equation.

▶ $3 \times 4 + 6 \times 2 = 60$

8. When doing a computation involving several numbers, the student omits a number.

Find the sum of 23, 36, 54, and 75.

$$
\begin{array}{r}
23 \\
36 \\
+75 \\
\hline
\mathbf{134}
\end{array}
$$

9. The student forgets the partial sum when adding a column of addends.

$$
\begin{array}{r}
\mathbf{3} \\
\mathbf{9} \\
+4 \\
\hline
\mathbf{4}
\end{array}
$$

10. The student omits the regrouped value.

$$
\begin{array}{r}
75 \\
+46 \\
\hline
\mathbf{111}
\end{array}
$$

11. The student fails to rename and places more than one digit in a column in an addition problem.

$$
\begin{array}{r}
\mathbf{36} \\
+78 \\
\hline
\mathbf{1,014}
\end{array}
$$

12. In an addition problem, the student writes the tens digit as part of the sum and regroups the ones.

$$
\begin{array}{r}
\mathbf{4} \\
36 \\
+78 \\
\hline
\mathbf{141}
\end{array}
$$

13. The student renames when it is not necessary.

$$
\begin{array}{r}
\mathbf{1} \\
32 \\
+45 \\
\hline
\mathbf{87}
\end{array}
$$

14. In an addition problem with a zero in the first addend, the student aligns the digits of the second addend with the nonzero digits in the first.

Add 307 and 12.

$$
\begin{array}{r}
307 \\
+1\ 2 \\
\hline
\mathbf{409}
\end{array}
$$

15. The student does not align the numbers properly when adding or subtracting whole numbers.

$$
\begin{array}{r}
62 \\
+39 \\
\hline
\mathbf{659}
\end{array}
$$

16. The student rounds the answer rather than the components of the problem.

Estimate the sum of 35 and 49.

$$
\begin{array}{r}
35 \\
+49 \\
\hline
\mathbf{84} \approx \mathbf{80}
\end{array}
$$

17. The student incorrectly adds from left to right.

$$
\begin{array}{r}
1 \\
37 \\
+82 \\
\hline
\mathbf{110}
\end{array}
$$

18. The student confuses addition and subtraction by one with either addition and subtraction of zero or with multiplication by one.

▶ $5 + 1 = \mathbf{5}$
$5 - 1 = \mathbf{5}$

19. The student makes simple subtraction errors when subtracting numbers with two or more digits.

$$
\begin{array}{r}
116 \\
\cancel{2}\cancel{6} \\
-19 \\
\hline
\mathbf{6}
\end{array}
$$

20. The student thinks that a number minus zero is zero.

    ▶ $6 - 0 = 0$

21. The student thinks that zero minus another number is zero.

    ▶ $0 - 6 = 0$

22. When creating fact families, the student incorrectly applies commutativity to subtraction.

    $$8 - 5 = 3$$
    $$8 - 3 = 5$$
    ▶ $5 - 8 = 3$
    ▶ $3 - 8 = 5$

23. The student brings down the digit in the subtrahend when the corresponding minuend digit is a zero.

    $$\begin{array}{r} 50 \\ +36 \\ \hline \end{array}$$
    ▶ 26

24. In a multidigit subtraction problem, the student correctly renames the zero in the tens place but does not decrease the digit to the left of the zero.

    ▶ $$\begin{array}{r} {\scriptstyle 9\,13} \\ 4\,\cancel{0}\,\cancel{3} \\ -2\,5\,6 \\ \hline 2\,4\,7 \end{array}$$

25. In a multidigit subtraction problem, the student ignores the zero and regroups from the digit to the left of the zero.

    ▶ $$\begin{array}{r} {\scriptstyle 3\ \ 13} \\ \cancel{4}\,0\,\cancel{3} \\ -2\,5\,6 \\ \hline 5\,7 \end{array}$$

26. In a multidigit subtraction problem, the student correctly regroups from the digit to the left of the zero and renames the zero as ten, but fails to reduce the ten by one when the second regrouping is done.

    ▶ $$\begin{array}{r} {\scriptstyle 1\,10\,14} \\ \cancel{2}\,\cancel{0}\,\cancel{4} \\ -1\,5\,5 \\ \hline 5\,9 \end{array}$$

27. The student does not regroup, but finds the difference between the smaller digit and the larger one regardless of their position and function.

    $$\begin{array}{r} 35 \\ -29 \\ \hline \end{array}$$
    ▶ 14

28. The student does not decrease the digit to the left after regrouping.

    ▶ $$\begin{array}{r} {\scriptstyle 15} \\ 3\,\cancel{5} \\ -2\,9 \\ \hline 1\,6 \end{array}$$

29. Instead of regrouping in a subtraction problem, the student incorrectly thinks that if you take a larger digit from a smaller one, there will be nothing left.

    $$\begin{array}{r} 35 \\ -29 \\ \hline \end{array}$$
    ▶ 10

30. In regrouping, the student thinks that the renamed value is found by subtracting the two digits of the same place value.

    ▶ $$\begin{array}{r} {\scriptstyle 5\,13} \\ 4\,\cancel{9}\,\cancel{3} \\ -\ \ 4\,5 \\ \hline 4\,1\,8 \end{array}$$

Multiplication

1. The student does not understand the connection between repeated addition and multiplication.

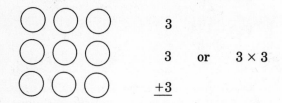

3
3   or   3 × 3
+3

2. The student is unsure of the basic multiplication facts.

3. The student mistakes a multiplication sign for an addition sign, or vice versa.

   ▶ 6 × 3 = **9**
      6 + 3 = **18**

4. The student thinks that one times any number is one.

   ▶ 35 × **1** = **1**

5. The student confuses multiplication by zero with multiplication by one thinking that any number times zero is that number.

   ▶ 36 × **0** = **36**

6. The student makes simple multiplication mistakes in multidigit multiplication problems.

   $3.46
   ×2
   ▶ $6.72

7. The student is unsure of how many zeros should be in the product when multiplying by a multiple of ten.

   20
   ×3
   ▶ **600**

8. The student multiplies the digits from left to right.

   36
   ×3
   ▶ **918**

9. The student fails to regroup and writes both digits in the product.

   45
   ×**3**
   ▶ **1,215**

10. The student writes the tens digit as part of the product and regroups the ones.

    2
    36
    ×2
    ▶ **81**

11. The student does not regroup or fails to add the regrouped value.

    36
    ×**2**
    ▶ **62**

12. When multiplying numbers, the student adds the regrouped digit before multiplying.

    1
    36
    ×2
    ▶ **82**

Division

1. The student fails to understand the connection between division and multiplication.

   For example, the student does not see the relationship between the fact $3 \times 2 = 6$ and $6 \div 2 = 3$.

2. The student is unsure of the basic division facts.

3. In a division problem, if either term is one, the student thinks the answer must be one.

   ▶ $6 \div 1 = 1$
   $1 \div 6 = 1$

4. The student confuses division by one with division by the same number.

   ▶ $6 \div 6 = 6$
   $6 \div 1 = 1$

5. The student does not realize that division by zero has no meaning.

   ▶ $6 \div 0 = 6$
   $0 \div 0 = 0$

6. The student places the initial quotient digit over the wrong place value in the dividend.

   ▶
   $$\begin{array}{r} 77 \text{ R1} \\ 2\overline{)15} \\ 14 \\ \hline 15 \\ 14 \\ \hline 1 \end{array}$$

7. The student ignores initial digits in the dividend that are less than the divisor.

   ▶
   $$\begin{array}{r} 2 \text{ R1} \\ 2\overline{)15} \\ 4 \\ \hline 1 \end{array}$$

8. The first estimated partial quotient is too low so the student subtracts and divides again and places the extra digit in the quotient.

   ▶
   $$\begin{array}{r} 1\,14 \\ 3\overline{)72} \\ 3 \\ \hline 4 \\ 3 \\ \hline 12 \\ 12 \\ \hline \end{array}$$

9. The student fails to subtract the last time or fails to record the remainder as part of the quotient.

   ▶
   $$\begin{array}{r} 11 \\ 3\overline{)35} \\ 3 \\ \hline 5 \\ 3 \\ \hline \end{array}$$

10. The student records the remainder as the last digit of the quotient.

    ▶
    $$\begin{array}{r} 112 \\ 3\overline{)35} \\ 3 \\ \hline 5 \\ 3 \\ \hline 2 \end{array}$$

11. The student records a remainder that is larger than the divisor.

    ▶
    $$\begin{array}{r} 11 \text{ R5} \\ 3\overline{)38} \\ 3 \\ \hline 8 \\ 3 \\ \hline 5 \end{array}$$

12. When checking a division problem, the student fails to add the remainder after multiplying the quotient by the divisor.

```
    15 R1
  3)46            15
    3            ×3
    16     ▶    45
    15
    1
```

13. The student incorrectly subtracts in a division problem.

```
       16
     3)38
       3
  ▶   18
      18
```

14. The student fails to subtract before bringing down the next digit in a division problem.

```
       11 R1
     3)54
       3
  ▶    4
       3
       1
```

15. The student incorrectly multiplies in a division problem.

```
       14 R2
     3)54
  ▶    4
      14
      12
      2
```

Measurement

1. The student is confused about how to read fractional measures on a ruler.

   Measure the tape to the nearest quarter-inch.

   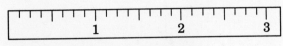

   ▶ **2 inches**

2. The student does not properly align the object to be measured with the point that represents zero on the ruler.

   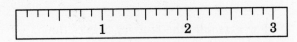

3. The student reads the small hand of a standard clock as minutes and the large hand as hours.

   ▶ **1:15**

4. When the hour hand is between two numbers, the student reads the time for the next hour.

   ▶ **7:50**

5. The student counts the minutes after the hour by starting at the hour hand.

   ▶ **4:20**

6. The student becomes confused about identifying days beyond those in the first week on a calendar.

7. The student uses an incorrect frame of reference when relating temperatures with real-life activities.

8. The student is unfamiliar with the object for which he or she must make an estimate.

Geometry

1. The student does not understand the concept of a two-dimensional figure.

2. The student does not understand the concept of surface area.

3. The student confuses the names of basic polygons.

4. The student thinks any figure is a square if it has 4 equal sides.

 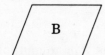

For example, the student thinks that figure A and **B** are both squares.

5. The student does not understand that the relative position of a figure has no effect on the figure's shape.

For example, the student thinks that figure **B** is **not** a square.

6. The student identifies a line as a line of symmetry, even though it does not create two congruent parts.

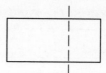

7. The student thinks that right angles must always have the same orientation.

For example, the student thinks that **only** angle A is a right angle.

8. The student omits one or more of the dimensions of a polygon when computing its perimeter.

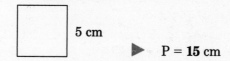

9. The student confuses the names of basic solid figures.

Fractions

1. The student counts the wrong number of parts of a picture when naming equivalent fractions.

   Write a fraction to represent the shaded parts.

    ▶ $\dfrac{3}{4}$

2. The student transposes the numerator and the denominator of a fraction.

3. To find equivalent fractions, the student uses addition or subtraction instead of multiplication or division.

   ▶ $\dfrac{2}{3} + \dfrac{3}{3} = \dfrac{5}{3}$

4. When comparing fractions, the student compares only the numerators.

   ▶ $\dfrac{2}{3} < \dfrac{3}{5}$

5. When comparing fractions with the same numerator, the student compares only the denominators.

   ▶ $\dfrac{1}{4} > \dfrac{1}{3}$

6. When adding fractions, the students add both the numerators and the denominators.

   ▶ $\dfrac{1}{3} + \dfrac{1}{3} = \dfrac{2}{6}$

7. The student fails to multiply by the numerator when finding a fractional part of a number.

   ▶ $\dfrac{2}{5}$ of 15 = 3

Decimals

1. The student confuses the terms used for place values in decimal numbers with those in whole numbers.

   Find the place value of the underlined digit in 4.6̲3.

   ▶ **tens**

2. When writing decimal numbers, the student misplaces the nonzero digit.

   Write three and four hundredths in numerals.

   ▶ **3.4**

3. The student omits the decimal point in a decimal number.

   Write fourteen hundredths in numerals.

   ▶ **14**

4. When ordering decimal numbers, the student's answer is based on the number of digits rather than their value.

   For example, the student thinks that 0.23 **is larger than** 0.4 because 23 is larger than 4.

5. When rounding decimal numbers, the student replaces values beyond the designated place value with zeros.

   Round 0.65 to tenths.

   ▶ **0.60**

6. When adding or subtracting decimal numbers, the student operates on the whole number parts and the decimal parts of the numbers separately.

   $$\begin{array}{r} 4.6 \\ +3.9 \\ \hline \end{array}$$
   ▶ **7.15**

7. The student places the decimal point in the wrong place in a decimal answer.

   $$\begin{array}{r} 4.6 \\ +3.9 \\ \hline \end{array}$$
   ▶ **.715**

Graphing

1. The student fails to divide by the number of addends when computing the average of a group of numbers.

   Find the average of 16, 25, 80, 44, and 90.

   ```
        16
        25
        80
        44
       +90
   ▶   255
   ```

2. The student always divides by 2 or some other constant number when calculating an average.

   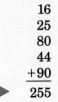

   ```
    16          127 R1
    25    ▶   2)255
    80
    44
   +90
    255
   ```

3. The student reverses the numbers in an ordered pair.

   For example, the student thinks that (3,2) **is the same as** (2,3).

4. The student reads the next larger interval on the scale when reading a bar graph.

   ▶ **6**

5. The student does not refer to a scale when interpreting a picture graph.

   How many books does Tony have?

   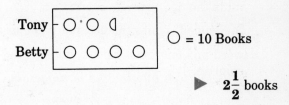

   ○ = 10 Books

   ▶ $2\frac{1}{2}$ books

Problem Solving

1. The student's answer is based only on the size of the objects.

   For example, the student thinks a nickel is worth more than a dime.

2. The student uses the wrong operation or operations to solve a problem.

3. The student does not read the problem but chooses the operation based on the relative size of the numbers in the problem.

4. The student does not read the problem carefully, but selects key words to determine the operation or operations.

5. The student thinks that all numbers in a word problem must be used to get the solution.

6. The student does not use all the relevant information given in a problem.

7. When comparing cost, the student does not find the unit cost of each product.

8. The student thinks that a lower cost always means the better buy.

9. The student does not answer the question posed in the problem.

10. The student is confused because the problem contains unfamiliar words or situations.

    For example, the student does not know that there are 52 cards in a standard deck of cards.

11. The student does not find all the possible solutions because he or she does not create a systematic list.

12. The student does not collect enough data to establish a pattern.

13. The student misreads a chart or table used in a problem.

14. The student's diagram does not faithfully depict the situation in the problem.

15. The student does not check if the data that is being tested makes sense in the problem.

16. The student is confused about what to do with a remainder in a real situation involving division.

17. The student does not check to see that the answer is reasonable.

Calculators

1. The student enters the incorrect codes into the calculator.

2. The student does not enter the codes into the calculator in the correct order.

3. The student does not relate the equal sign on a calculator with the repeated addition function.

4. When entering a subtraction into a calculator, the student enters the subtrahend before the minuend.

5. When entering a division into a calculator, the student enters the divisor before the dividend.

6. The student fails to enter a decimal point at the appropriate place in a calculator code.

MODERN CURRICULUM PRESS Level A
MATHEMATICS

Richard Monnard Royce Hargrove

Project Editor.............................. Dorothy A. Kirk
Editor....................................... Martha Geyen
Design and Production............ Remen-Willis Design Group
Illustration.... Roberta Holmes-Landers, Doug Roy, Valerie Felts
Cover Art............................ © 1993 Adam Peiperl

This book is the property of:

Book No. ________ Enter information in spaces below as instructed.

State ______________________

Province ______________________

County ______________________

Parish ______________________

School district ______________________

Other ______________________

Issued to	Year Used	CONDITION ISSUED	CONDITION RETURNED

PUPILS to whom this textbook is issued must not write on any page or mark any part of it in any way, consumable textbooks excepted.

1. Teachers should see that the pupil's name is clearly writen in ink in the spaces above in every book issued.
2. The following items should be used in recording the condition of this book: New; Good; Fair; Poor; Bad.

MODERN CURRICULUM PRESS
13900 Prospect Road, Cleveland, Ohio 44136
A Paramount Communications Company

Table of Contents

1 and 2

pages 1-2

Objectives

To recognize concepts of 1 and 2
To write 1 and 2

Materials

2 counters
Felt or sandpaper 1 and 2

Mental Math

Which is larger?
1. a horse or ant (horse)
2. a mouse or you (you)
3. a dog or whale (whale)
4. a cat or bee (cat)
5. a horse or house (house)

Skill Review

Hold up a pencil and ask a student to hand you another one. Have students count them with you. Repeat with an eraser, book, chalk, etc.

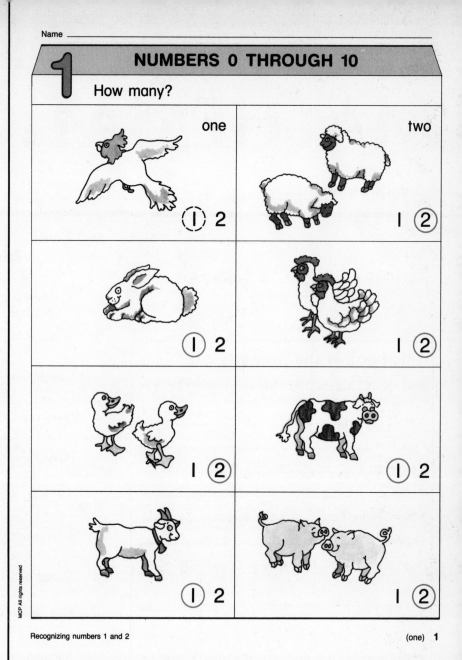

Teaching page 1

Hold up one object and ask how many. (1) Have students tell how many as you show other single objects. Write a **1** and **one** on the board. Repeat for the number 2. Tell students that 2 is one more than 1. Hold up one or two objects and ask students to point to the correct number and number word.

Have students look at the first picture and tell how many birds. (1) Tell students to trace the circle around the 1. Repeat for the picture of sheep. Have students complete the page independently.

1

Write the numbers.

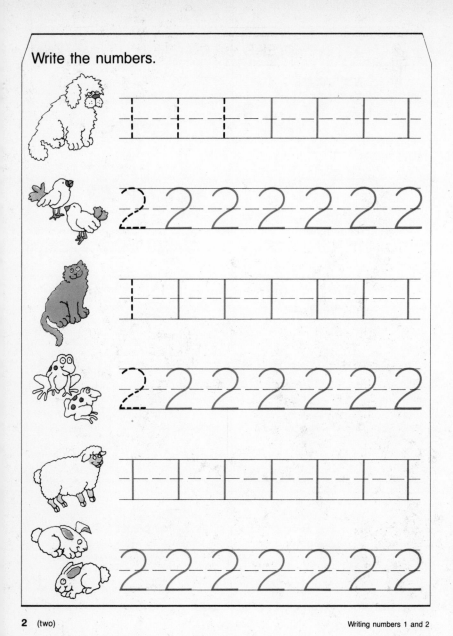

Writing numbers 1 and 2

Watch for students who have difficulty writing 1 and 2. Write a large 1 and 2 on the chalkboard. Hold up either one or two objects, have students say either "one" or "two" to tell how many, and then have them trace the numeral 1 or 2 in the air using those written on the chalkboard as a guide. Encourage them to also model each number using their index finger or two fingers, which ever the case may be.

Enrichment

1. Identify groups of 1 and 2 objects in the room.
2. Draw groups of 1 and 2 objects and write the number.
3. Work in pairs to build a person with felt or magnetic body pieces. Have partner position 1 trunk, 2 arms, 1 head, 2 legs, etc. as you name parts.

Teaching page 2

Have students write a **1** and a **2** in the air to the tune of *Mulberry Bush*:

1   We start at the top and go straight down,
    Start at the top and go straight down,
    We start at the top and go straight down,
    To write the number 1.

2   We curve around, then straight across,
    We curve around, then straight across,
    We curve around, then straight across,
    To write the number 2.

Ask students how many puppies are in the first picture. (1) Have students trace the 1's and make more 1's to the end of the row. Repeat for the row of 2's. Tell students to count the animals and write the numbers to complete each row.

Extra Credit   *Applications*

Hold up a ball and ask students to tell everything they can about it. (it is round, it is a sphere, it rolls, it is red, etc.) Ask if there is any relationship between the fact that it is round and the fact that it rolls. (Yes, it rolls because it is round.) Explain that you want the class to find pictures of things that roll. They can use old magazines in class, or you can make this an assignment to be done at home. Encourage them to use their imaginations. Point out that there are many things that are not made to be rolled, but that will roll nonetheless, such as a soup can. When each student has assembled the pictures, have them paste the pictures onto construction paper and label the collage "Things That Roll." Put all the collections on a bulletin board so students can see what others have found.

3 and 4

pages 3-4

Objectives

To recognize concepts of 3 and 4
To write 3 and 4

Materials

4 counters
Sheet of paper
Felt or sandpaper 3 and 4

Mental Math

How many do you have?
1. hands (2)
2. cheeks (2)
3. head (1)
4. lips (2)
5. neck (1)
6. eyebrows (2)
7. tongue (1)

Skill Review

Write on the chalkboard:

1   **2**

one   **two**

Tell students that one is the word for
the number 1 and two is the word
for the number 2. Now write the
words **one** and **two** on the board
again and have students write the
correct number under each word.

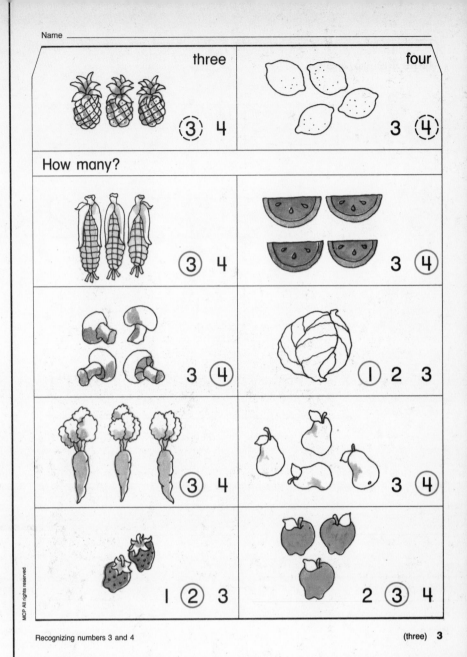

Recognizing numbers 3 and 4

(three) **3**

Teaching page 2

Hold up 2 pencils. Pick up another. Tell students that 2
and 1 more is 3. Have students count the pencils.
Write a **3** and **three** on the board. Hold up 3 pencils
and pick up another. Tell students that 3 and 1 more is
4. Have students count the pencils. Write a **4** and **four**
on the board. Pick up from 1 to 4 pencils and have
students count them with you. Ask students how many
pineapples are in the first picture. (3) Have students
trace the circle around the 3. Repeat procedure for the
4 lemons. Ask students to complete the page
independently.

3

Write the numbers.

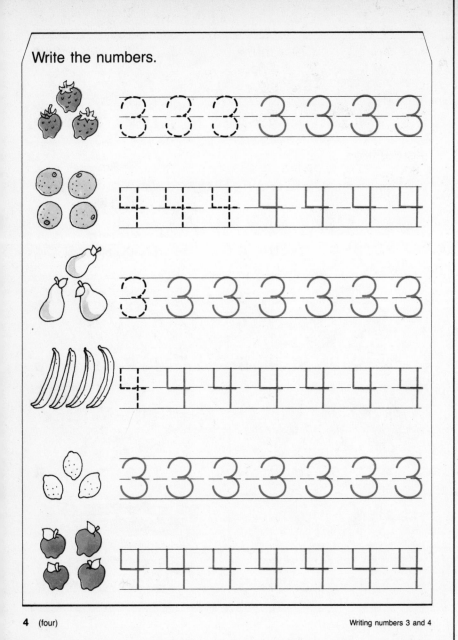

Writing numbers 3 and 4

Correcting Common Errors

Some students may need additional practice with the concepts of three and four. Show 3 counters. Have students count 1, 2, 3 to tell how many there are. Then, have them raise 3 fingers to show how many and ask volunteers to come forward and match one-to-one the counters and fingers to prove that both sets have 3 items. Repeat in a similar manner with 4 counters.

Enrichment

1. Find groups of 3 and 4 objects in the room.
2. Learn *Baa Baa Black Sheep.*
   Baa Baa Black Sheep
   Have you any wool?
   Yes sir, yes sir, Three bags full.
   One for my master, And one for my dame,
   And one for the little boy
   Who lives in the lane.
3. Draw 3 balls and color them 3 different colors. Draw 4 sticks in 4 colors.

Teaching page 4

Have students write a **3** and a **4** in the air to the tune of *Mulberry Bush:*

3   We go around and around again,
     We go around and around again,
     We go around and around again,
     To write the number 3.

4   Straight down, across, and then straight down,
     Straight down, across, and then straight down,
     Straight down, across, and then straight down,
     To write the number 4.

Have students count the strawberries and trace the 3's. Tell students to make more 3's to the end of the row. Repeat for the row of 4's. Tell students to count the pears, bananas, lemons and apples and write the numbers.

Extra Credit   *Applications*

Read the story, "The Three Bears" to the class. Ask students to draw the bears. At the same time illustrate the bears on the board and label them: big, bigger, biggest. Ask students to label their bears in the same way. On another page have students draw the three bowls, the three chairs, and the three beds. You may want students to use one color for the baby bear's things, another for the mother bear's, and a third for the father bear's. Have them label these things too: big, bigger, biggest.

4

1 through 5

pages 5-6

Objectives

To recognize concepts of 1 through 5
To write 1, 2, 3, 4, 5

Materials

5 counters
Number cards 1 through 5
Number-name cards one through five
Sheet of paper

Mental Math

Which is smaller?
1. a book or you (book)
2. a zebra or cat (cat)
3. a grape or peach (grape)
4. a sofa or chair (chair)
5. a flower or tree (flower)
6. a lake or puddle (puddle)

Skill Review

Write on the board:

1	one
2	two
3	three
4	four

Have students lay out their number and number-name cards to match those on the board.

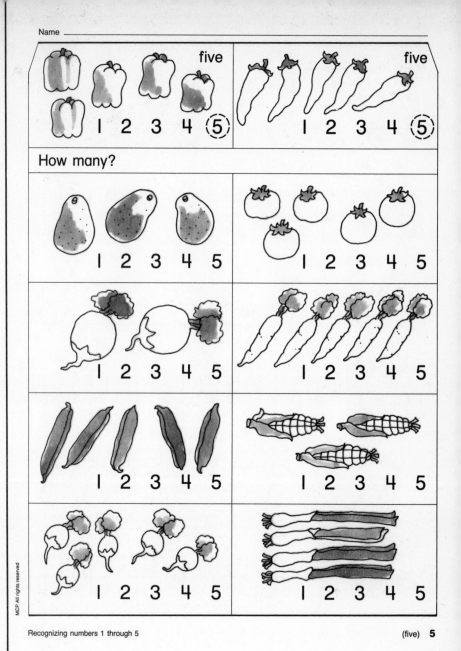

Recognizing numbers 1 through 5   (five) **5**

Teaching page 5

Have students put 4 counters on their paper. Tell them to put one more counter on the paper. Ask how many counters are 4 and 1 more. (5) Write a **5** and **five** on the board.

Have students tell how many peppers are in the first picture. (5) Ask students to trace the circle around the 5. Repeat for the next problem. Tell students to count the vegetables in each box and circle that number to complete the page.

Write the numbers.

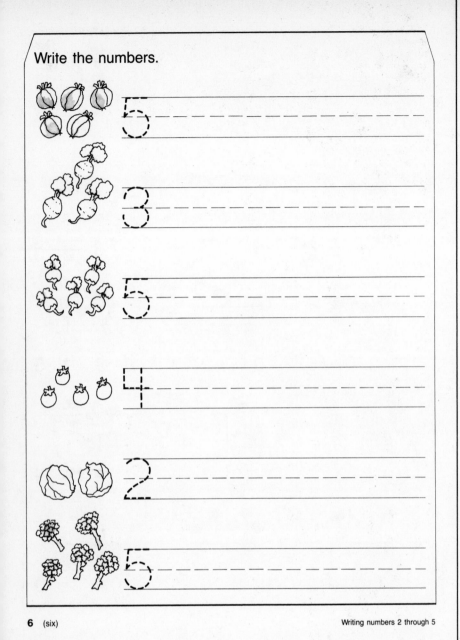

Writing numbers 2 through 5

Correcting Common Errors

To help students connect the concept of number to the number name, have them work with partners using counters and a piece of yarn. Have them use the yarn to make a circle on their desk, table, or work area. Then, as you hold up a card with one of the numbers from 1 through 5 on it, have them place that many counters inside the circle. Have partners check one another to make sure that the answers are correct.

Enrichment

1. Mix number cards and put in order. Repeat with number-name cards.
2. Work in pairs with two decks each. Match number cards to number cards and number-name cards to number-name cards.
3. Write five 5's, four 4's, three 3's, two 2's, one 1.

Teaching page 6

Write a **5** on the board. Have students write a **5** in the air.

Have students count the onions at the top of the page. Tell students to trace the 5 and make more 5's across the page. Have students count the beets in the next problem, trace the 3 and make more 3's. Tell students to complete the page in this way.

Extra Credit *Applications*

In class, slice apples on the horizontal to make slices that expose the interior star pattern of the seeds. Distribute one slice to each student. Have students identify the shape they see, and count the points (5). Provide star-shaped cookie cutters or star-shaped patterns for students to trace. Have students draw an apple seed on each point of the star. Label the points with the numerals one through five. Then let students eat and enjoy their apple slices.

0 through 5

pages 7-8

Objectives

To recognize 0 through 5 objects
To write 0, 1, 2, 3, 4, 5

Materials

*5 pencils
*6 paper cups
*15 tongue depressors or sticks

Mental Math

Name the number that tells about
your:
1. nose (1)
2. ears (2)
3. tongue (1)
4. eyes (2)
5. feet (2)
6. hands (2)

Skill Review

Write the number names on the
board as illustrated:

one two three four five
Hold up 4 pencils and ask how
many. Have a student write a **4**
under the word **four.** Repeat for 3,
5, 2 and 1.

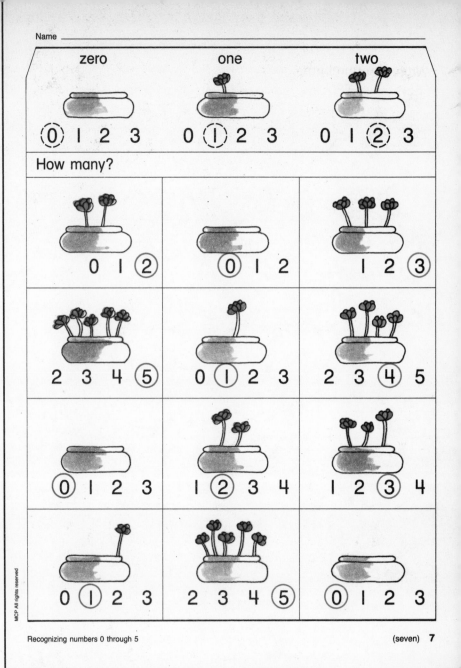

Recognizing numbers 0 through 5

(seven) **7**

Teaching page 7

Pick up 3 pencils and ask how many. Repeat with 1
and 2 pencils. Hold up an empty hand and ask how
many pencils. (none) Tell students that when we have
none, we write a **0.** Write a **0** and **zero** on the board.
Put 6 cups on the chalkboard tray. Write a **0** above
the first cup, a **1** above the second, etc., to a **5** above
the last cup. Ask a student to put 3 sticks into cup 3.
Continue to have students fill the cups with the correct
number of sticks. Ask how many sticks should go into
cup 0. (none) Have students look at the vases of
flowers. Ask how many flowers are in the first vase. (0)
Have students trace the circle around the **0.** Repeat for
the next two problems. Tell students to count the
flowers in each vase and circle the correct number.

*Indicates teacher demonstration materials.

7

Write the numbers.

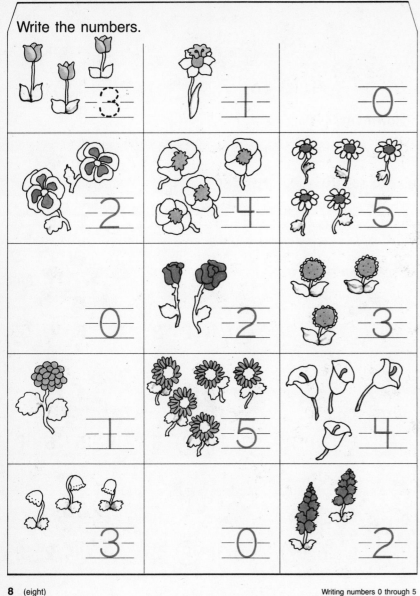

Writing numbers 0 through 5

Correcting Common Errors

Some students may need additional work with the concept of zero. Hold up 5 pencils. Have students count with you from 1 to 5. Put aside the fifth pencil and count again, this time from 1 to 4. Continue to put aside one pencil each time and count the remaining pencils. When you put aside the last pencil, hold up your empty hand and ask, "How many pencils?" (none) Discuss how "none" means "not even one." Then say, "There are no pencils.", and "We have zero pencils." Write 0 on the chalkboard.

Enrichment

1. Working with a partner, find objects in the room in groups of 2, 3, 4 and 5.
2. Make "Number Books". Write one number from 0 through 5 on each page. Draw or cut and paste 2 objects on the 2 page, 3 objects on the 3 page, etc.

Teaching page 8

Erase the numbers above the 6 cups and arrange the cups in mixed order. Have students count the sticks in each cup and write that number on the chalkboard above it. Now write the numbers on the cups and erase the board. Have students place the cups in order from 0 through 5. Have students count the flowers in the first box. (3) Tell students to trace the **3**. Ask how many flowers are in the next box. (1) Have students write a **1** in the space. Tell students to count the flowers in each box and write that number in the space.

Extra Credit *Sets*

Read the story, "The Three Bears" aloud. Prepare paper cutouts of the bears, their bowls, chairs and beds, with strips of felt on the backs. Students can dramatize the story, matching props to each bear. Have them match the cutouts, one-to-one, on a flannel board with small pieces of yard.

Select a small group of "bears" to play musical chairs. Have the class count the children representing bears and tell how many chairs are needed to have an equivalent set. Remove one chair. Which set has more members, the "bears" or the chairs? Play the game with several groups of students.

6 and 7

pages 9-10

Objectives

To recognize concepts of 6 and 7
To write 6 and 7

Materials

7 counters
Number cards 0 through 7
Number-name cards zero through seven
Sheet of paper
Felt or sandpaper 6 and 7

Mental Math

Name the number that:
1. means none (0)
2. is 1 more than 4 (5)
3. is 1 more than 0 (1)
4. rhymes with shoe (2)
5. rhymes with tree (3)

Skill Review

Sing: This old man, he played **none**; he played knickknack **on my son**. With a knickknack paddy whack, give the dog **no** bones. This old man came rolling home. Repeat the song. Pause at number words for students to show counters as "bones". (1/thumb/1 bone; 2/shoe/2 bones; 3/knee; 4/door; 5/hive) Sing again and have students show their number cards.

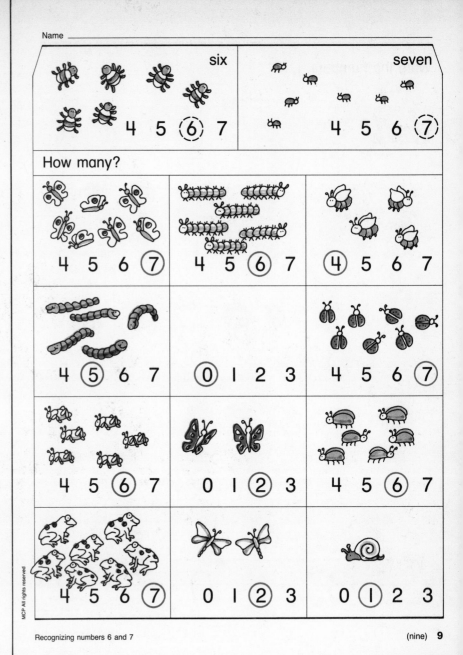

Recognizing numbers 6 and 7

(nine) **9**

Teaching page 9

Tell students to lay counters on their papers to show these sentences: **My dog had 5 bones but he looked so hungry that I gave him 1 more bone. Now he has 6 bones.** Write **6** and **six** on the board. Have a student draw 6 sticks on the board. Repeat the exercise for these sentences: **My dog had 6 bones but he looked so hungry that I gave him 1 more bone. Now he has 7 bones.** Have students count the spiders in the first box. Have students trace the circle around the 6. Repeat for 7 ants. Tell students to count the creatures in each box and circle that number.

Write the numbers.

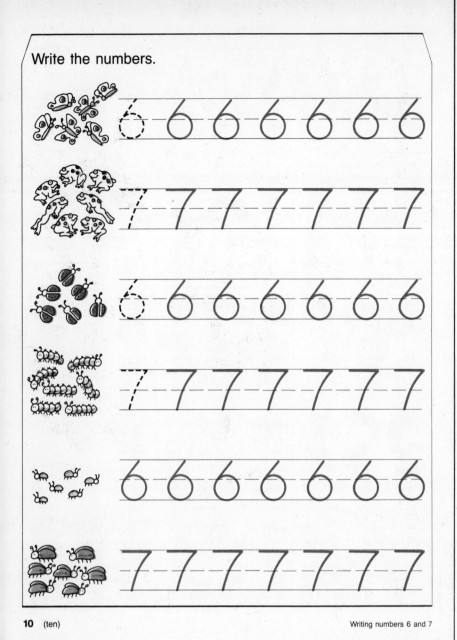

Writing numbers 6 and 7

Correcting Common Errors

Watch for students who write their numbers backwards. Practice by having them trace numbers in the air. The teacher can better detect problems of this sort by standing in the rear of the class as students trace numbers in the air.

Enrichment

1. Add pages for 6 and 7 in "Number Books".
2. Play "Concentration" with number and number-name cards. Turn all cards face down. Draw two cards. A match of the 3 and three cards earns another turn. Play until all cards have been matched.

Teaching page 10

Write a **6** several times on the chalkboard. Have students trace the numbers. Repeat for 7. Tell students to count the butterflies at the top of the page. Have students trace the 6 and make more 6's across the page. Repeat for 7 frogs. Have students complete the page.

Extra Credit   *Sets*

Fill five pairs of small paper bags so that each pair contains the same number of objects, 1 through 5. Distribute the bags to 10 students. Have students choose partners to compare the objects in their bags to see if the sets are equivalent. Have them arrange the sets in one-to-one correspondence. If the sets are unequal, they change partners until they find someone with an equivalent set. Continue the matching game with 10 more members of the class. While some students are comparing sets, the rest of the class can make worksheets by grouping from 1 to 5 stickers on one side of the paper, and 1 to 5 stickers on the other side, matching sets. Have them try to find others with equivalent sets of stickers.

8 and 9

pages 11-12

Objectives

To recognize concepts of 8 and 9
To write 5, 6, 7, 8, 9

Materials

9 counters
Felt or sandpaper 8 and 9
Sheet of paper
Number cards 1 through 7

Mental Math

How many?
1. legs on a dog (4)
2. tails on a cat (1)
3. thumbs on one hand (1)
4. thumbs on two hands (2)
5. wings on a snake (0)
6. colors on a stoplight (3)

Skill Review

Say: As I was going to St. Ives,
        I met a man with 7 wives;
        Each wife had 7 sacks,
        Each sack had 7 cats,
        Each cat had 7 kits.
        Kits, cats, sacks, and wives,
        How many were going to St.
            Ives? (1) Tell students to
listen to the poem again and show a
number card every time a number is
heard. Repeat again, substituting the
number 6 for every 7.

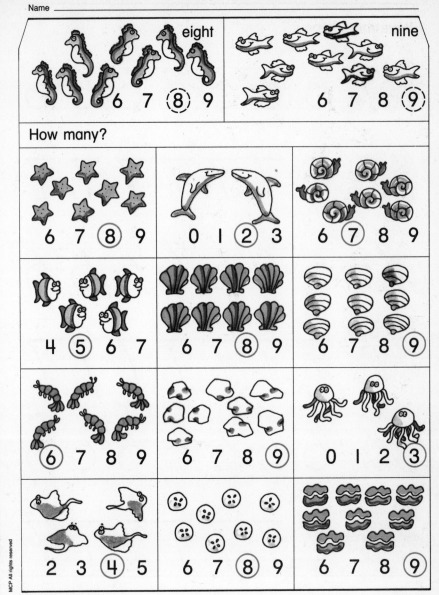

Recognizing numbers 8 and 9

(eleven) **11**

Teaching page 11

Have students count out 7 counters on their papers.
Then have students place 1 more counter with the 7.
Tell students that 7 and 1 more is 8. Write **8** and
eight on the board. Have students count with you.
Have students place 1 more counter with the 8. Tell
students that 8 and 1 more is 9. Write **9** and **nine** on
the board. Have students count with you.

Have students count the seahorses in the first box and
trace the circle around the 8. Repeat for 9 fish. Ask
students to complete the page independently.

11

Write the numbers.

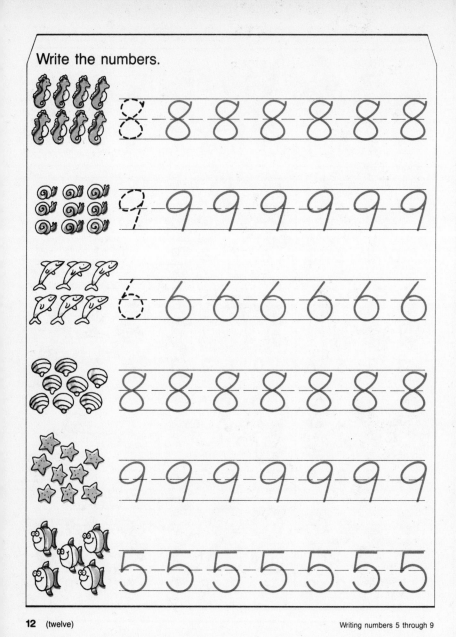

Writing numbers 5 through 9

Correcting Common Errors
Some students may lose track when they are counting a group of eight or nine objects. As they are counting, have students cross off or move to the side each object as it is counted so they will not count it again.

Enrichment
1. Add pages for 8 and 9 to "Number Books".
2. Make spinner with numbers 0 through 9. Spin and read the number pointed to.

Teaching page 12
Have students trace the felt or sandpaper 8 and 9. Tell them to look at the seahorses at the top of the page and tell how many. (8) Have students trace the 8 and complete the line with more 8's. Repeat for the snails and have students complete the page.

Extra Credit *Applications*
Ask how many of your students help set the table for meals at home. Have volunteers explain how they go about setting the table. Point out that one of the first things they do in order to set a table is to count the knives, forks and spoons; the plates and glasses; and the napkins. Illustrate a simple place setting on the board. Explain that you are going to show them the arrangement as it would appear if they were looking down on it.

Bring in plastic knives, forks, spoons, glasses, paper plates and napkins, or borrow the settings from the school cafeteria. Divide the class into groups of four, and assign each member of the group a part of the place setting. Serve a small snack as a reward when they are finished.

0 through 9

pages 13-14

Objective

To review numbers 0 through 9

Materials

9 counters
Number cards 0 through 9
Number-name cards zero through nine
Sheet of paper

Mental Math

What number is 1 more than:

1. 7 (8)
2. 0 (1)
3. 3 (4)
4. 8 (9)
5. 6 (7)
6. 1 (2)

Skill Review

Write the numbers **0** through **9** in order in a column on the board. Write the number name for each number beside it. Have students put number and number-name cards in the same order.

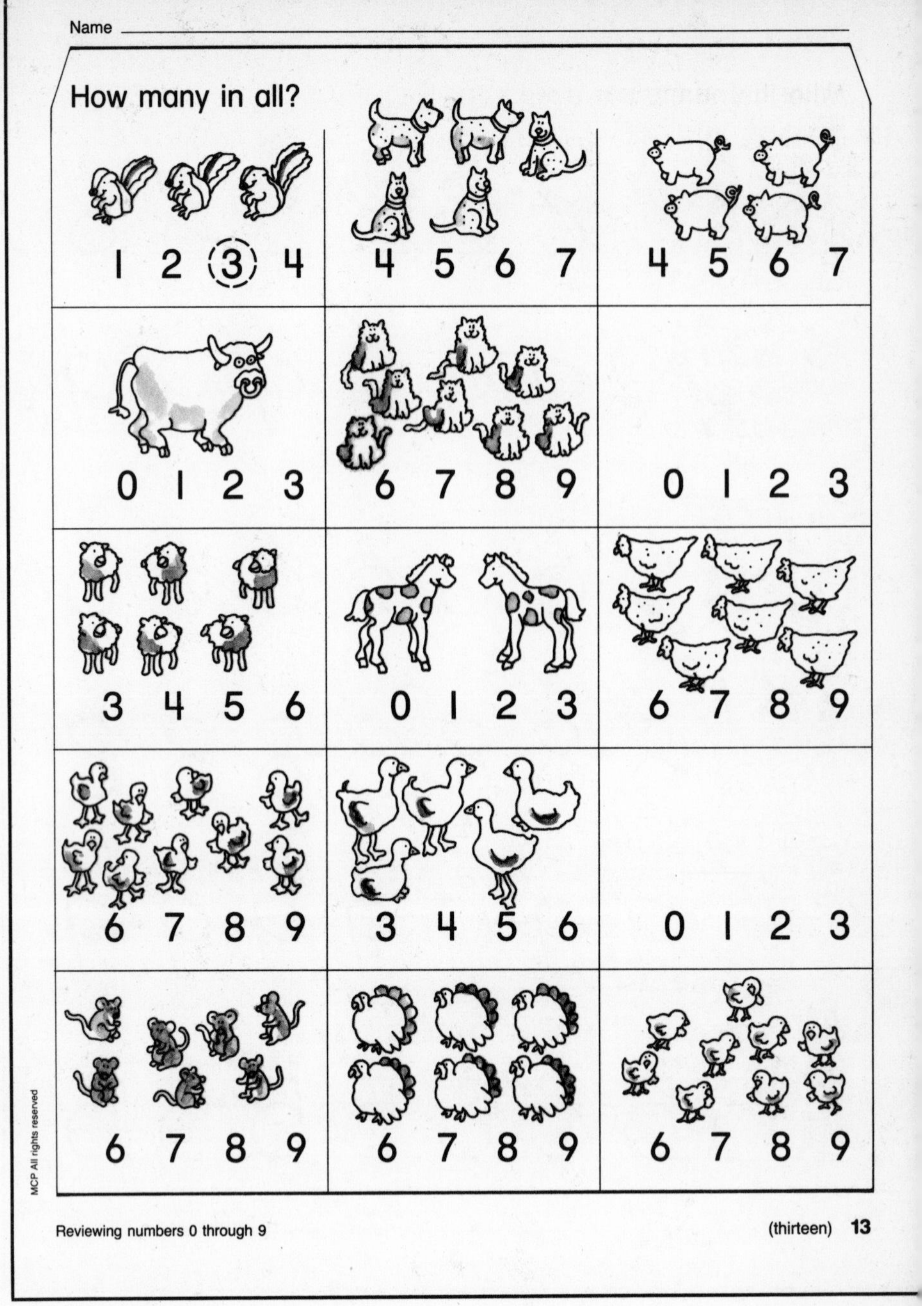

Name _____

How many in all?

1 2 ③ 4	4 5 6 7	4 5 6 7
0 1 2 3	6 7 8 9	0 1 2 3
3 4 5 6	0 1 2 3	6 7 8 9
6 7 8 9	3 4 5 6	0 1 2 3
6 7 8 9	6 7 8 9	6 7 8 9

Reviewing numbers 0 through 9

(thirteen) **13**

Teaching page 13

Draw a group of 9 objects on the board. Have students count the objects. Ask students to place that number of counters on their papers, and show that number card and number-name card. Continue counting groups randomly for 0 through 8.

Tell students to count the skunks in the first box and trace a circle around the 3. Have students count the animals in each box and circle the correct number to complete the page.

13

Write the number in each set.

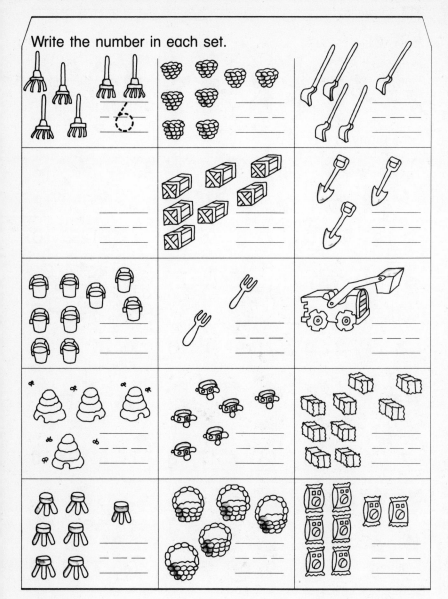

Reviewing numbers 0 through 9

Correcting Common Errors

Some students may need additional practice with 0 through 9. Have them work with partners with cards showing a number of objects on one side and the number on the other. Shuffle the cards and place them in a stack with the pictures of the objects face up. Students take turns drawing a card and writing the number that tells how many objects are on the card. If the partner agrees that it is the correct number, they turn the card over to check their answer.

Enrichment

1. Using a spinner with numbers 0 through 8, name the number that is 1 more than the number spun.
2. Draw a picture having 9 objects. Color: 3 objects red, 0 objects blue, 1 object orange, 2 objects green, 3 objects yellow.
3. Mix number cards and draw a card. Put numbers in order from that card up to 9 and from that card down to 0.

Teaching page 14

Write the numbers **0** through **9** across the board. Write the correct number name under each number. Ask students to tell the name of the number that is the least. (0) Ask for the name of the number that is the greatest. (9) Ask students if the numbers and their number names are in order from the least to the greatest. (yes) Have students place their number and number-name cards in order from the least to the greatest. Have students count the rakes in the first box and trace the number 6. Tell students to complete the page independently.

Extra Credit   *Counting*

Students can practice their counting skills with a game of "Concentration." For counting to ten, 20 playing cards are needed. Use blank index cards or uniformly-cut lightweight cardboard. Number ten of the cards from one through ten. Use the remaining ten cards to draw sets of one through ten objects. Stickers or stamped pictures could also be used. Mix the cards and set them face down. The student chooses any two cards and turns them over. If the two cards are a numeral and its matching set, the player keeps both cards. If the cards do not match, the player turns them both face down again. One student may play by turning over two cards at a time, trying to remember where potential matches may be. Two or more students may play by taking turns at choosing a pair of cards, and concentrating on the cards played by the others.

10

pages 15-16

Objectives

To recognize concept of 10
To write 0,1,2,3,4,5,6,7,8,9,10

Materials

10 counters
Number cards 0 through 10
Number-name cards zero through ten
Sheet of paper

Mental Math

What meal comes after:
1. breakfast (lunch)
2. lunch (supper)
What meal comes before:
1. lunch (breakfast)
2. supper (lunch)

Skill Review

Have students place counters on their papers to match the numbers **0** through **9** you write randomly on the board. Repeat the exercise for the number and number-name cards.

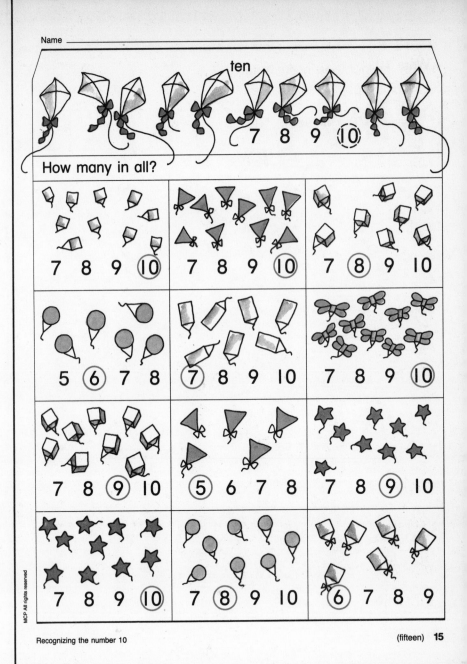

Recognizing the number 10

(fifteen) **15**

Teaching page 15

Have students place 6 counters on their papers. Tell them to put 1 more counter on their papers and tell what 6 and 1 more is. (7) Have students add another counter and tell what 7 and 1 more is. (8) Continue the process of adding 1 more counter, up to a total of 10 counters. Write **ten** on the board and tell students this is the word for 10. Write a **10** under its word and tell students a 10 is made by writing a 1 and a 0 side by side.

Have students count the kites in the example and circle the 10. Help with the next three problems to be sure students are counting the kites before circling a number. Have students complete the page independently.

15

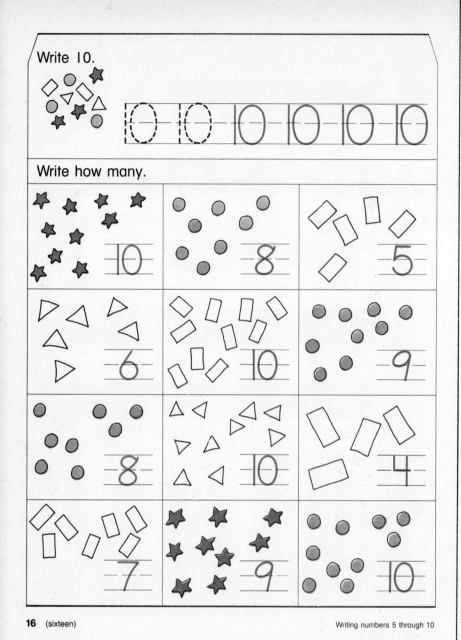

Write 10.

Write how many.

Writing numbers 5 through 10

Correcting Common Errors

Some students may have difficulty associating numbers and number names. Have them work with partners with a set of number cards and a set of number-name cards, both in mixed order. Have them take turns turning over a number card and searching through the number-name cards to find the matching number name.

Enrichment

1. Add page for 10 to "Number Books."
2. Working in pairs with two decks, match number and number-name cards.

Teaching page 16

Have students count the shapes. Tell them to trace the two 10's and complete the row. Ask students to count the shapes in the first box with you. Tell them to write a **10** beside the 10 stars. Have students count the shapes in each box and write that number in the space to complete the page.

Extra Credit *Counting*

Distribute ten small unwaxed paper plates to each student. Have students number the plates, in the center, from one through ten. Provide each student with sufficient stickers to count and place the corresponding number of stickers on each numbered plate. The stickers can be the seasonal, animal types, colored stars, small geometric shapes or labels. When they are completed, students can punch a hole in the top of each plate and tie them together in correct order with yarn.

Counting to 10

pages 17-18

Objective

To write numbers 0 through 10 in order

Materials

Number cards 0 through 10
Number-name cards zero through ten
Crayons

Mental Math

How many do you have?
1. toes (10)
2. fingers (8)
3. thumbs (2)
4. chins (1)
5. barrettes (0,1,2)
6. nostrils (2)

Skill Review

Write on the board:

3
5
10
8
7

Have students read each number as you make that number of x's beside it.

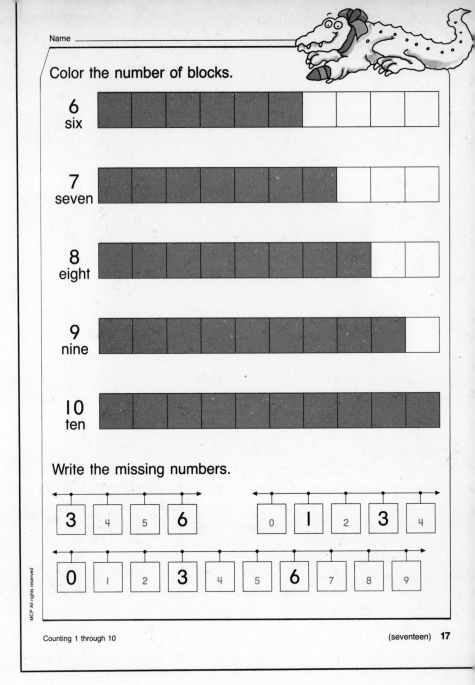

Counting 1 through 10

(seventeen) **17**

Teaching page 17

Draw a row of eleven circles on the board. Write a **0** in the first circle, a **3** in the 4th circle and a **7** in the 8th circle. Ask volunteers to fill in the missing numbers. Tell students to look at the first row of blocks. Ask students to read the number. (6) Ask if there are more than 6 boxes in that row. (yes) Tell students to color only 6 of those boxes. Help with the next row if necessary and then have students complete the last 3 rows independently. Tell students that the bottom half of this page asks them to fill in the missing numbers. Ask students to start at the 3 and count to 6. Have students fill in the missing numbers. (4,5) Tell students to fill in the missing numbers in the next two problems.

17

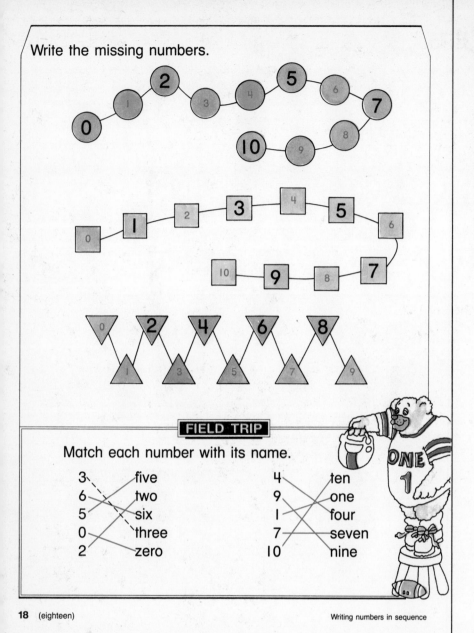

Write the missing numbers.

Correcting Common Errors
Students may need practice finding missing numbers when all are placed in order. Place the 0 through 10 number cards in order on the chalk tray. Then, while students are not looking, take away a card. Next, have them check the tray and identify the missing number. Replace the card and have the students in unison count from 0 to 10. Repeat the activity to remove other number cards.

Enrichment
1. Shuffle number cards and put in order.
2. Shuffle number-name cards and put in order.

FIELD TRIP

Match each number with its name.

3 — five
6 — two
5 — six
0 — three
2 — zero

4 — ten
9 — one
1 — four
7 — seven
10 — nine

ONE 1

18 (eighteen)

Writing numbers in sequence

Teaching page 18
Have students look at the circles joined by lines. Have them find the 0 and the 2. Ask what number comes between 0 and 2. (1) Have students write a **1** in that blank circle. Tell students to fill in the circles after the 2 and continue in order to the 10 at the end. Have students do the next two problems independently.

Field Trip
Tell students they are to match each number to its word by drawing a line from the number to its number word. Have students trace the first line and then match all the numbers independently.

Extra Credit *Counting*
Use a playground ball and a box containing cards numbered from one through ten. (You can also draw a set of shapes illustrating the given number on the back of each card.) Taking turns, have each student choose a numbered card from the box, and count the objects or read the numeral. Without telling the number to the rest of the group, the student then bounces and catches the ball the indicated number of times. Another child is chosen to identify the number, and can take a turn if their answer is correct. The class could count aloud with the bouncing to get the activity started.

Pennies through 9¢

pages 19-20

Objective

To count pennies through 9 cents

Materials

9 pennies (real or punchout)
Number cards 1 through 10
Number-name cards one through ten
Sheet of paper

Mental Math

Count to 10 from:
1. 6 (6,7,8,9,10)
2. 3
3. 9
4. 7
5. 0
6. 5

Skill Review

Teach or review:
One, Two, Buckle My Shoe
 1, 2, buckle my shoe;
 3, 4, shut the door;
 5, 6, pick up sticks;
 7, 8, lay them straight;
 9, 10, a good fat hen.
Repeat and have students hold up
their number and number-name
cards instead of saying the numbers.

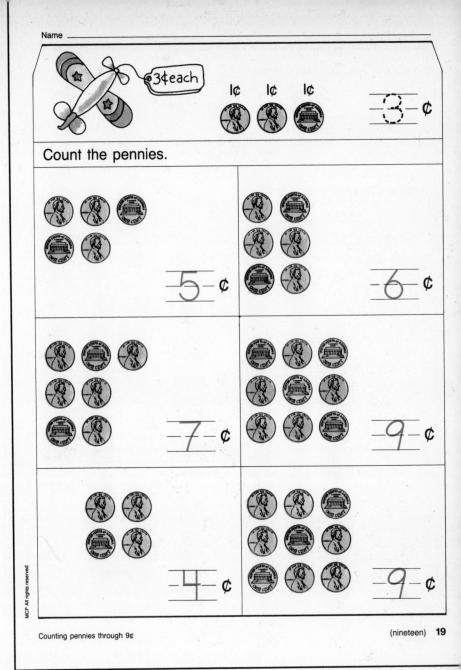

Name _____

3¢ each

1¢ 1¢ 1¢

3 ¢

Count the pennies.

5 ¢   6 ¢

7 ¢   9 ¢

4 ¢   9 ¢

Counting pennies through 9¢   (nineteen) **19**

Teaching page 19

Hold up a real penny and ask students to identify it.
Tell students a penny is a piece of money. Write **1
cent** and **1¢** on the board. Tell students we write 1
cent or 1¢ to mean 1 penny. Hold up 2 pennies and
write **2 cents** and **2¢** on the board. Have students
read these. Ask students to place 2 pennies on their
papers and say "2 cents" with you. Repeat with other
amounts through 9 cents.

Have students find the airplane and the pennies. Tell
students the airplane costs 3¢. Count the pennies with
them and ask them to trace the 3. Have students count
the pennies in the first box and write the number in
the space. (5) Tell students the **¢** sign has to be used
to mean money. Have students count the pennies in
each box and write the number in front of the ¢ sign.

19

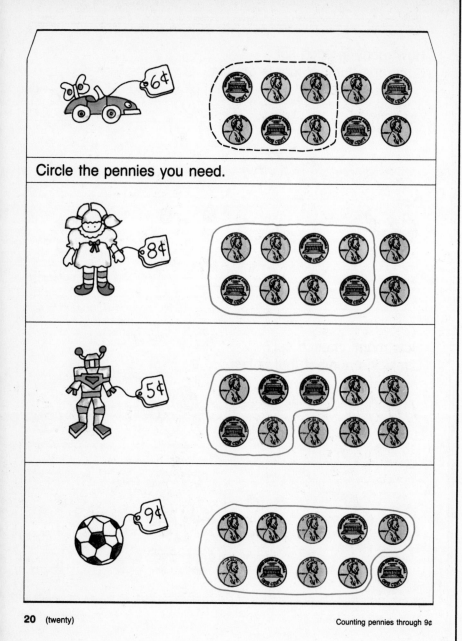

Circle the pennies you need.

Counting pennies through 9¢

Some students may have difficulty counting pennies. Have them work with partners with number cards 1 through 10 and 10 pennies. Have them take turns choosing a number card and placing the correct number of pennies on it. They then write the amount with the cents sign on a piece of paper. Both partners must agree each time the answer is correct.

Enrichment

1. Start a store in the classroom with items costing up to 9¢. Make price tags for items and then make purchases.
2. Draw an object with a price tag of 9¢ or less. Draw pennies needed to buy the object.

Teaching page 20

Have students look at the car and read its price tag. (6¢) Ask how much the car costs. (6¢) Ask students if all the pennies are needed to buy the car. (no) Tell them to trace the line around the 6 pennies to show that only 6 pennies are needed to buy the car. Help with the next problem if necessary. Have students complete the page.

Extra Credit *Counting*

Provide each student with three rectangular sheets of drawing or typing paper to make a counting book. Have them fold each sheet in half and combine the sheets to form a booklet. The folded edge can be stapled. The students title and decorate the front cover of their number books. Have them number the top of the remaining pages from one to ten. They can complete the book independently, by drawing the correct number of objects indicated by the numeral on each page. Ideas can be suggested by the class as a whole, and listed by the teacher before students begin drawing. Seasonal or unit themes can be discussed. The project can also be completed by having the students cut appropriate numbers of objects from magazines, and glue them into the booklet.

Comparing Counting

pages 21-22

Objectives

To compare two numbers to solve problems

To write numbers 0 through 10 in order

Materials

Number cards 0 through 10

Mental Math

Count backwards to 0 from:
1. 3 (3,2,1,0)
2. 5
3. 6
4. 8
5. 7

Skill Review

Dictate the amounts 0¢ through 9¢. Have student volunteers write the amounts on the board.

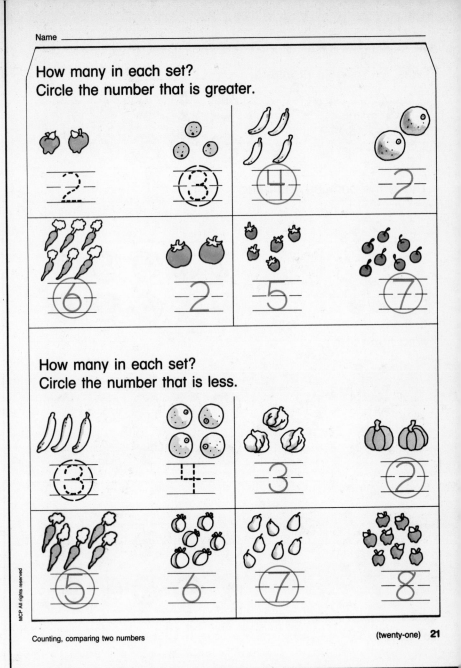

How many in each set?
Circle the number that is greater.

How many in each set?
Circle the number that is less.

Counting, comparing two numbers

(twenty-one) **21**

Teaching page 21

Place number card 5 on the chalk tray. Hold up card 6 and ask students where to place it. (after the 5) Have a student place the 6 after the 5. Repeat the procedure for card 4, then cards 7,3,8,2,9,1,10,0 in that order. Remove all the cards. Place cards 4 and 6 on the tray. Ask a student to draw the correct number of x's above each. Ask which number has more x's. (6) Tell students that we say 6 is greater than 4. Ask which number has fewer x's. (4) Tell students that 4 is less than 6. Repeat more examples as necessary.

Ask students to count the apples and oranges in the first box and trace the numbers 2 and 3. Ask which number is greater. (3) Have students trace the circle around the 3. Help with the next problem if necessary and have students complete the next 2 boxes. Then

ask students to count the bananas and grapefruit, and trace the 3 and 4. Ask which number is less. (3) Have them trace around the 3. Tell students to count the objects in the next three boxes, write each number in the space, and then circle the number that is less.

21

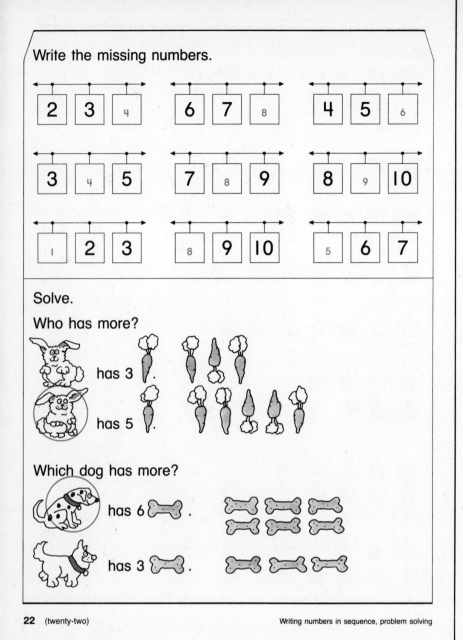

Write the missing numbers.

2	3	4		6	7	8		4	5	6

3	4	5		7	8	9		8	9	10

1	2	3		8	9	10		5	6	7

Solve.

Who has more?

has 3 🥕.

has 5 🥕.

Which dog has more?

has 6 🦴.

has 3 🦴.

22 (twenty-two)   Writing numbers in sequence, problem solving

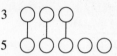

Correcting Common Errors

Some students may have difficulty deciding which number is greater. Have them use lines to match, one-to-one, the objects in one set with the objects in another. The set with some objects left over has the greater number of objects.

3 ◯◯◯
5 ◯◯◯◯◯

Enrichment

1. Practice finding and naming the total number of pages in books in your classroom.
2. Use deck of playing cards, with face cards removed, to match, place in order and compare numbers.

Teaching page 22

Write __4__ on the board. Ask a student to write the number that goes after the 4. (5) Ask a student to write the number that goes before the 4. (3) Repeat other examples as necessary. Write **5__7** on the board and ask what number goes between 5 and 7. (6) Repeat other examples as necessary. Have students look at the first 3 boxes and tell what number should go into the last box. (4) Have students complete the top half of the page independently. Read the first rebus problem. Have students count the white rabbit's carrots (3) and the grey rabbit's carrots (5). Ask which number is greater. (5) Ask who has the 5 carrots. (grey rabbit) Ask who has more carrots. (grey rabbit) Have students circle the grey rabbit. Repeat procedure for the last problem.

Extra Credit *Numeration*

Have two teams of students. Give each team an envelope containing a set of objects numbering from one through nine, and a set of number cards numbered from 0 through 9. Also give each team a card reading "greater than" and a card reading "less than." Each team chooses a set of objects from the envelope, picks a number and places the correct relationship card between the numerals. Repeat this process for all the sets and numerals. The team with the most correct answers wins.

22

Chapter Review

pages 23-24

Objective

To review 0 through 10

Materials

Number cards 1 through 10

Mental Math

Who has more?
1. Pat has 8; Pete has 3 (Pat)
2. Jan has 2; Bob has 9 (Bob)
3. Al has 6; Mary has 10 (Mary)
4. Ali has 4; Nick has 0 (Ali)
5. Joe has 6; Michelle has 7 (Michelle)
6. Ed has 1; José has 5 (José)

Skill Review

Write on the board:
(5) **6** (7)
(7) **8** (9)
(2) **3** (4)
(4) **5** (6)
(8) **9** (10)
(0) **1** (2)
Ask students to hold up the number cards that come before and after each number.

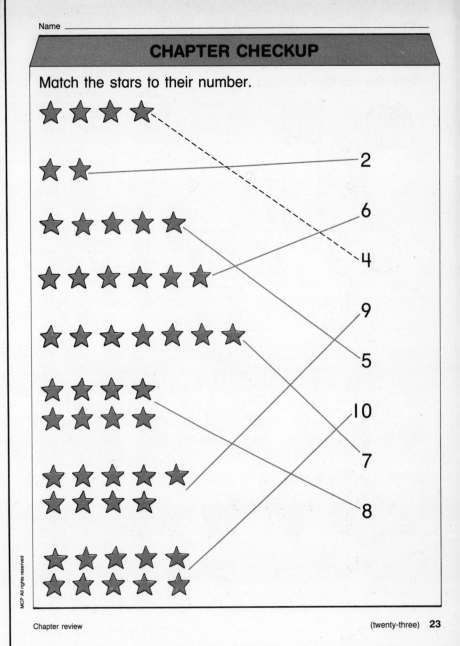

Name _____

CHAPTER CHECKUP

Match the stars to their number.

Chapter review   (twenty-three) **23**

Teaching page 23

Write on the board:
3   xxxx
5
4   x
2   xxx
0   xxxxx
1   xx

Help students match the columns by drawing a line from each number to that number of x's.

Have students count the stars in the first box and trace the line to the number 4. Have students complete the page independently.

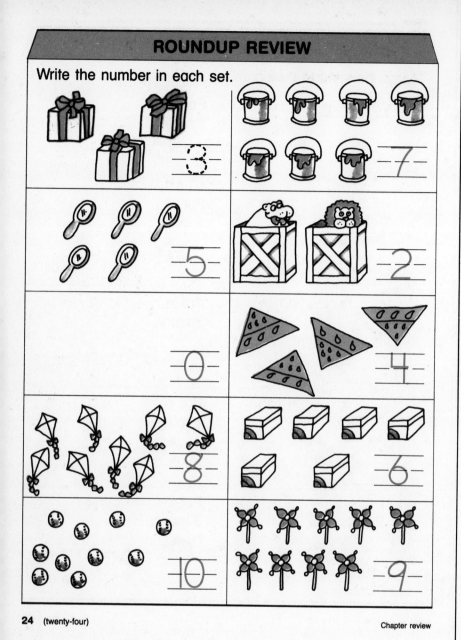

ROUNDUP REVIEW

Write the number in each set.

Chapter review

1. Practice finding numbers quickly in number books.
2. Identify items that have numbers in order. (ex. pages in books, telephones, typewriters, clocks, calendars)

Teaching page 24

Have students count the boxes in the first problem and trace the number 3. Tell students to count the objects in each box and write the number in the space.

Sums through 5

pages 25-26

Objective

To understand concept of adding for sums through 5

Materials

*Yarn or ribbon
Number cards 1 through 10
Number-name cards one through ten
5 counters
Sheet of paper

Mental Math

Name the number that comes between:

1. 4 and 6 (5)
2. 0 and 2 (1)
3. 8 and 6 (7)
4. 8 and 10 (9)
5. 1 and 3 (2)
6. 5 and 3 (4)

Skill Review

Sing *Paddywhack:*
  This old man,
  He played **none.**
  He played knickknack
  on my **son.**
  With a knickknack paddywhack.
  give the dog **no** bones.
  This old man came rolling home.
(1/thumb/1 bone; 2/shoe/2 bones; 3/knee; 4/door; 5/hive; 6/sticks; 7/heaven; 8/slate; 9/pine; 10/hen)

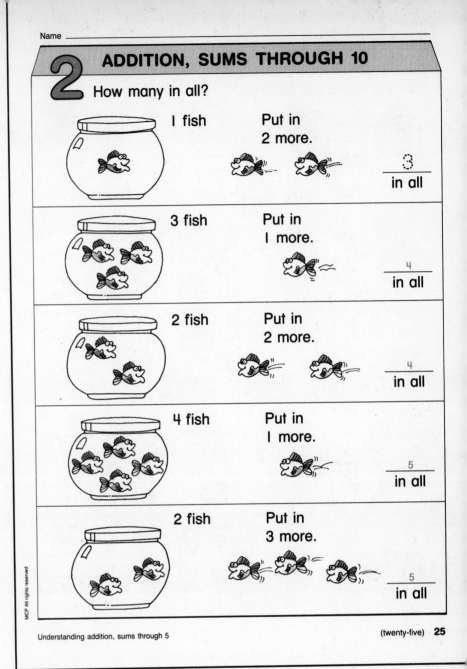

Name _____

2 ADDITION, SUMS THROUGH 10

How many in all?

1 fish	Put in 2 more.	3 in all
3 fish	Put in 1 more.	4 in all
2 fish	Put in 2 more.	4 in all
4 fish	Put in 1 more.	5 in all
2 fish	Put in 3 more.	5 in all

Understanding addition, sums through 5

(twenty-five) **25**

Teaching page 25

Make a yarn ring on the floor around 2 students. Ask students how many are in the ring.(2) Have 2 more students stand inside the ring and ask how many in all.(4) Tell the students that 2 and 2 more is 4. Repeat with other students for 1 and 1 more, and 2 and 3 more.

Have students find the first fishbowl and tell how many fish are in the bowl.(1) Ask how many are to be put in.(2) Ask how many fish in all.(3) Tell students that 1 and 2 more is 3. Have students trace the 3. Help with the next problem if necessary and have students complete the page.

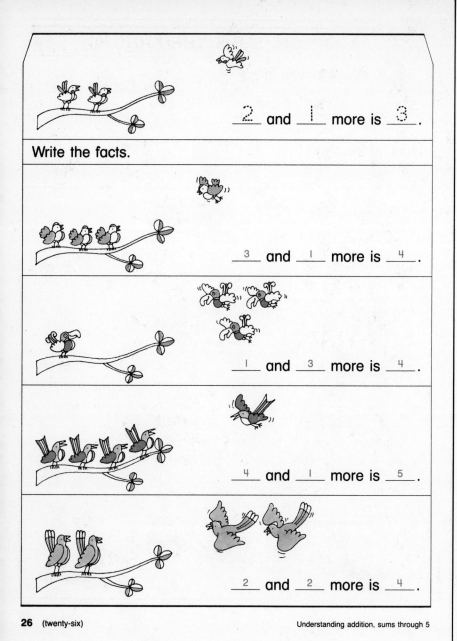

Write the facts.

_2_ and _1_ more is _3_.

_3_ and _1_ more is _4_.

_1_ and _3_ more is _4_.

_4_ and _1_ more is _5_.

_2_ and _2_ more is _4_.

Understanding addition, sums through 5

Correcting Common Errors

Some students may have difficulty telling how many in all. Have them work with partners with a bowl and counters. Direct them to place a number of counters in the bowl. When you tell them how many more to add, have them count on to find the total.

Enrichment

1. Draw a picture that shows 2 and 1 is 3.
2. Cut and paste pictures from magazines or catalogs to create a picture that shows 5 in all. Repeat for 4, 3 and 2.

Teaching page 26

Have students count the birds in the tree at the top of the page.(2) Tell them to trace the number 2 to show that there are 2 birds to start with. Ask students how many birds are flying to the tree.(1) Have students trace the 1 to show that 1 more bird is going to join the 2 birds. Have students read with you.(2 and 1 more is 3) Tell students to trace the 3 to show that there are 3 birds in all. Help students to complete the second problem. Tell students to complete the page.

Extra Credit   *Counting*

Using an empty egg carton, number the two rows of cups from one to twelve. Tape an envelope to the inside of the carton top. Cut 78 small egg shapes or squares from lightweight cardboard, and store them in the envelope.

Each student plays the game by counting and placing the correct number of markers into each numbered space. Instruct the students to collect and replace the markers in the correct storage place, when finished. As an alternative, number the spaces from one to ten, and use the remaining two spaces to store 55 beans or other small counting objects.

Sums through 5

pages 27-28

Objective

To use + and = in sums through 5

Materials

None

Mental Math

Name the number that comes:
1. before 6 (5)
2. after 2 (3)
3. before 10 (9)
4. between 3 and 5 (4)
5. after 9 (10)
6. between 8 and 6 (7)

Skill Review

Write on the board:

> **3 and 1 is 4**
> **2 and 2 is 4**
> **1 and 2 is 3**
> **4 and 1 is 5**

Have students make stories using these numbers. (ex. "I had 3 shirts and Mom bought me 1 more. Now I have 4 shirts in all.")

Name _____

2 and 1 more is ___3___.

$2 + 1 = $ ___3___

How many in all?

$1 + 1 = $ ___2___

$3 + 1 = $ ___4___

$2 + 2 = $ ___4___

$2 + 3 = $ ___5___

Addition facts, sums through 5   (twenty-seven) **27**

Teaching page 27

Write on the board: //   /   ///

> **2   and   1 more   is   3**

Write **2 + 1 = 3** on the board. Tell students this is a shorter way to write 2 and 1 more is 3. Point to each part as you read the sentence to the students, **2 plus 1 equals 3.** Tell students the equals sign tells us that 2 + 1 is the same as 3. Write **4 and 1 more is 5** on the board and ask a volunteer to write this in the shorter way. (4 + 1 = 5) Have the students read this with you. (4 plus 1 equals 5) Repeat for 2 and 3 more is 5.

Ask students how many dogs are sitting in the first picture. (2) Ask how many dogs are running to join. (1) Ask how many dogs in all. (3) Have students trace the 3. Have a student write this on the board in the shorter way. (2 + 1 = 3) Have students trace the 3 in the

sentence 2 + 1 = 3. Help with the next problem and have students complete the page.

27

How many in all?

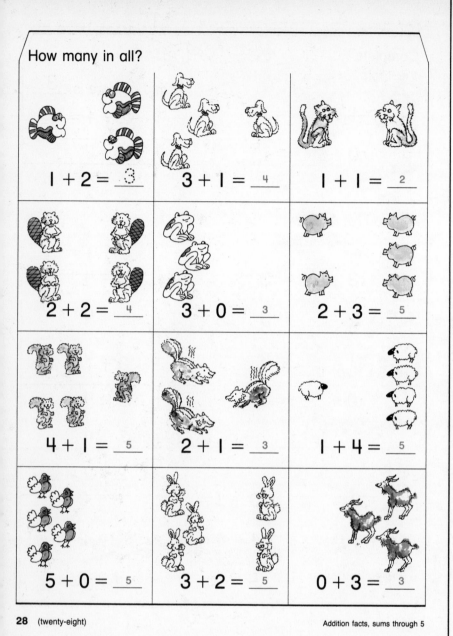

1 + 2 = 3	3 + 1 = 4	1 + 1 = 2
2 + 2 = 4	3 + 0 = 3	2 + 3 = 5
4 + 1 = 5	2 + 1 = 3	1 + 4 = 5
5 + 0 = 5	3 + 2 = 5	0 + 3 = 3

28 (twenty-eight)   Addition facts, sums through 5

Correcting Common Errors

Some students may need additional help understanding the + sign and the = sign. Have two students stand together. Ask, "How many students?" (2) Have 1 more student join the pair. Ask, "How many more?" (1) "How many in all?" (3) Write the following on the chalkboard:

$$2 \text{ and } 1 \text{ more is } 3$$
$$2 + 1 = 3$$

Repeat the activity for other facts for sums through 5.

Enrichment

1. Draw a picture that shows $3 + 1 = 4$.
2. Write a story using $4 + 1 = 5$.

Teaching page 28

Have students read the first number sentence with you. (1 plus 2 equals 3.) Ask students what the 1 tells about the fish. (1 fish is in the bowl.) Ask what the 2 tells us. (2 fish are coming to join.) Tell students the plus sign tells us to put the two numbers of fish together. Ask students what 1 and 2 more is. (3) Have students trace the 3. Help with the second problem and have students complete the page.

Extra Credit   *Numeration*

Tell students that numbers play an important role in all their daily activities. Discuss with them all the different places that they see numbers from the minute they get up in the morning, until they go to bed. Make a class list of their ideas on the board. Then tell students to look for more places to find numbers when they go home, and to make a list of these places to share with the class. The following day, allow students to write their additional ideas on the board, followed by their names. If their idea has been duplicated, they can write their name beside it, also. See who came up with the most places where numbers can be found.

Fact Families

pages 29-30

Objective

To discover fact family for sums through 5

Materials

5 counters
Sheet of paper
Yarn

Mental Math

Which is greater?
1. 8 or 9 (9)
2. 7 or 2 (7)
3. 5 or 8 (8)
4. 0 or 10 (10)
5. 6 or 3 (6)
6. 4 or 0 (4)
7. 1 or 5 (5)

Skill Review

Write on the board:

$$2 + 1 = 3$$
$$4 + 0 = 4$$
$$0 + 1 = 1$$
$$3 + 2 = 5$$
$$1 + 2 = 3$$

Have students read the sentences. (2 plus 1 equals 3, etc.)

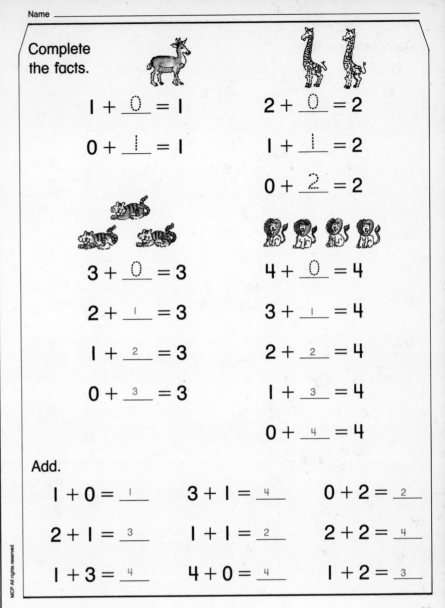

Name _____

Complete the facts.

$1 + \underline{0} = 1$ $2 + \underline{0} = 2$

$0 + \underline{1} = 1$ $1 + \underline{1} = 2$

                $0 + \underline{2} = 2$

$3 + \underline{0} = 3$ $4 + \underline{0} = 4$

$2 + \underline{1} = 3$ $3 + \underline{1} = 4$

$1 + \underline{2} = 3$ $2 + \underline{2} = 4$

$0 + \underline{3} = 3$ $1 + \underline{3} = 4$

                $0 + \underline{4} = 4$

Add.

$1 + 0 = \underline{1}$ $3 + 1 = \underline{4}$ $0 + 2 = \underline{2}$

$2 + 1 = \underline{3}$ $1 + 1 = \underline{2}$ $2 + 2 = \underline{4}$

$1 + 3 = \underline{4}$ $4 + 0 = \underline{4}$ $1 + 2 = \underline{3}$

Discovering fact families, sums through 4   (twenty-nine) **29**

Teaching page 29

Ask students to give a number sentence for **I have 3 toys and will get 1 more toy.** (3 + 1 = 4) Write **3 + 1 = 4** on the board. Have students place 3 counters on their papers and 1 counter off their papers. Ask students to give a number sentence for **I have 1 toy and am getting 3 toys.** (1 + 3 = 4) Write **1 + 3 = 4** on the board and have students show this sentence with counters on and off their papers. Continue this procedure for 0 + 4 = 4 and 4 + 0 = 4. Tell students that these are all number sentences for the sum of 4.

Have students look at the gazelle at the top of the page. Tell students they are to use 2 numbers to show the number 1. Read the sentences with the students.

(1 gazelle is joined by no gazelles; no gazelles are joined by one gazelle) Have students trace the numbers. Now have students find the 2 giraffes. Tell students they are to find all the ways to use 2 numbers to show a sum of 2. (2 + 0 = 2, 1 + 1 = 2, 0 + 2 = 2) Help students through the 3 sentences. Ask students to find the 3 tigers and tell what is to be done in this problem. (to find all the ways to use 2 numbers to show the sum of 3) Help students work this problem and then have them complete the page.

29

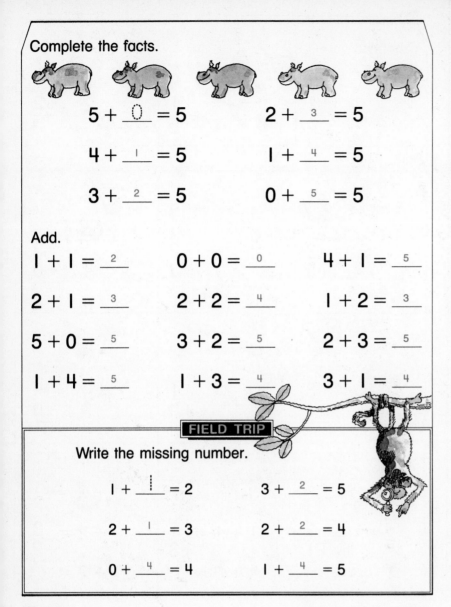

Complete the facts.

$5 + \underline{0} = 5$ $2 + \underline{3} = 5$

$4 + \underline{1} = 5$ $1 + \underline{4} = 5$

$3 + \underline{2} = 5$ $0 + \underline{5} = 5$

Add.

$1 + 1 = \underline{2}$ $0 + 0 = \underline{0}$ $4 + 1 = \underline{5}$

$2 + 1 = \underline{3}$ $2 + 2 = \underline{4}$ $1 + 2 = \underline{3}$

$5 + 0 = \underline{5}$ $3 + 2 = \underline{5}$ $2 + 3 = \underline{5}$

$1 + 4 = \underline{5}$ $1 + 3 = \underline{4}$ $3 + 1 = \underline{4}$

FIELD TRIP

Write the missing number.

$1 + \underline{1} = 2$ $3 + \underline{2} = 5$

$2 + \underline{1} = 3$ $2 + \underline{2} = 4$

$0 + \underline{4} = 4$ $1 + \underline{4} = 5$

Discovering fact families, sums through 5

Some students may have difficulty seeing that different facts can have the same sum. Have them work with partners using 5 counters. Have them use the counters to find as many different combinations to make 5 as they can. Have them write the fact each time. Then have them repeat the activity for 4 and 3.

Enrichment

1. Make fact cards for fact families of sums through 5.
2. Cut and paste pictures from catalogs or magazines to make a picture of 2 children sharing 4 toys.

Teaching page 30

Ask students to find the 5 hippos. Ask what is to be done here.(to find all the ways to show 5 using 2 numbers) Tell students this problem will show the fact family for the sum of 5. Have students trace the 5 and the 0 and complete the facts for 5. Have students look at the 3 columns of number sentences. Point out the $0 + 0$ problem by having students find that sentence first. Ask what none plus none equals.(none or zero) Tell students to do all the problems in the 3 columns.

Field Trip

Write on the board **$2 + 3 = 5$.** Ask students to read the sentence. Cover the 3 and ask students to tell what must be added to 2 to equal 5.(3) Repeat for $3 + \_\_ = 5$, $4 + \_\_ = 4$ and $0 + \_\_ = 4$. Have students

verify the 1 in the first sentence and then trace it. Tell students to write the missing number in each sentence.

Extra Credit   *Sets*

Take a tour of the school to discover how things are arranged in sets in the building. Visit the office and point out to students how the secretary groups paper clips, pens, rubber bands, mail, student cards, etc. Stop in the cafeteria to see how the staff store sets of trays, silverware, measuring equipment, straws, etc. Ask the cafeteria workers how orderly sets help them complete their jobs. Look for sets of pictures in the halls, sets of desks in classrooms, etc. Discuss why things are grouped into sets.

30

Sums of 5

pages 31-32

Objective

To add vertically for sums through 5

Materials

Dominoes

Mental Math

Who is younger?
1. Max is 10; Jill is 7 (Jill)
2. Darryl is 2; Anne is 3 (Darryl)
3. Sam is 6; Pam is 5 (Pam)
4. Ben is 7; Tim is 8 (Ben)
5. Sara is 2; John is 5 (Sara)

Skill Review

Write **2 and 2 more is 4** on the board. Ask students to make up a story for this number sentence.(ex. 2 girls were playing and 2 more came to join them) Ask a volunteer to write this sentence a shorter way.(2 + 2 = 4) Continue for the sentences 3 and 1 is 4, 5 and 0 is 5.

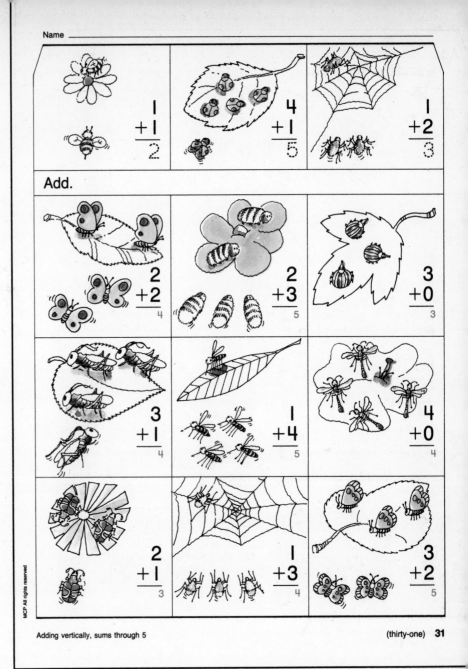

Add.

Adding vertically, sums through 5

(thirty-one) **31**

Teaching page 31

On the board draw a large domino turned horizontally and write under it as illustrated:

2 + 2 = 4

Tell students to read the number sentence with you. (2 plus 2 equals 4) Show students the real domino also turned horizontally. Now rotate the real domino in your hand and show it to the students vertically. Draw

and write the following on the board:
$$\begin{array}{r} 2 \\ +2 \\ \hline 4 \end{array}$$

Tell students to read the number sentence with you as you point to each number.(2 plus 2 equals 4) Draw another domino vertically for 3 + 1 = 4 and have students write the vertical fact. $\begin{array}{r} 3 \\ +1 \\ \hline 4 \end{array}$ Do other examples as needed.

Have students find the picture of the two bees. Ask what number sentence the bees are showing.

(1 + 1 = 2 or $\begin{array}{r} 1 \\ +1 \\ \hline 2 \end{array}$) Have students trace the 2. Talk

through the next 2 problems in the same manner and have students complete the page.

31

Add.

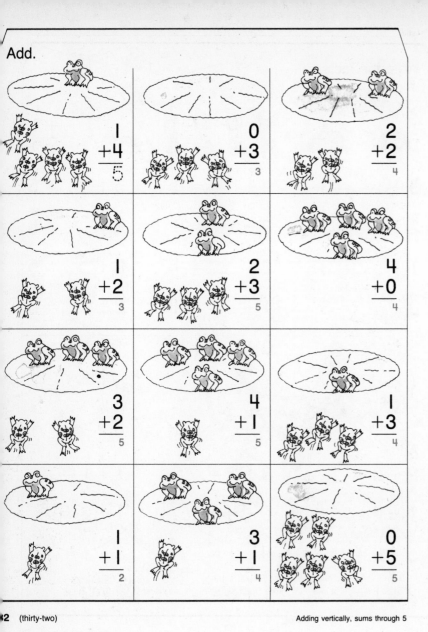

$$\begin{array}{r} 1 \\ +4 \\ \hline 5 \end{array}$$
$$\begin{array}{r} 0 \\ +3 \\ \hline 3 \end{array}$$
$$\begin{array}{r} 2 \\ +2 \\ \hline 4 \end{array}$$

$$\begin{array}{r} 1 \\ +2 \\ \hline 3 \end{array}$$
$$\begin{array}{r} 2 \\ +3 \\ \hline 5 \end{array}$$
$$\begin{array}{r} 4 \\ +0 \\ \hline 4 \end{array}$$

$$\begin{array}{r} 3 \\ +2 \\ \hline 5 \end{array}$$
$$\begin{array}{r} 4 \\ +1 \\ \hline 5 \end{array}$$
$$\begin{array}{r} 1 \\ +3 \\ \hline 4 \end{array}$$

$$\begin{array}{r} 1 \\ +1 \\ \hline 2 \end{array}$$
$$\begin{array}{r} 3 \\ +1 \\ \hline 4 \end{array}$$
$$\begin{array}{r} 0 \\ +5 \\ \hline 5 \end{array}$$

Adding vertically, sums through 5

Correcting Common Errors

Some students need extra practice adding vertically for sums through 5. Have these students work in pairs. Give each pair a worksheet with a variety of vertical problems with sums through 5. Have them draw circles or mark x's beside each addend to correspond to the number. Have them write the sum and then count the circles or x's to check the answer.

$$\begin{array}{r} 2 \ \text{x x} \\ +3 \ \text{x x x} \\ \hline 5 \ \text{x x x x x} \end{array}$$

Enrichment

1. Make vertical fact cards for fact families of sums 1 through 5.
2. Match horizontal and vertical fact cards.

Teaching page 32

Have students tell the number sentence for the frogs in the first picture. (1 plus 4 equals 5) and trace the 5. Tell students to complete the page.

Extra Credit   *Counting*

Make a counting box for each pair of students. Assemble the following materials in each box: a set of two-inch square cards numbered zero through ten, and 55 quarter-sized circles cut from construction paper. (Buttons, bottle caps or round plastic chips could be substituted.) First, have one student in a pair place the number cards in order in a column on a table. Then have the other student arrange the correct number of circles in a row next to each number card. Have students do the activity again, switching roles.

To extend the students' thinking skills, cut the circles for each number from a different color of construction paper. Some children may discover the pattern and be able to match each numeral with its corresponding colored circles. The counting in this activity can be expanded to 12, by using 78 circles.

Sums through 5

pages 33-34

Objective

To learn sums through 5

Materials

5 counters
Sheet of paper

Mental Math

Which is less?
1. 3¢ or 4¢ (3¢)
2. 7¢ or 8¢ (7¢)
3. 5¢ or 2¢ (2¢)
4. 0¢ or 3¢ (0¢)
5. 7¢ or 6¢ (6¢)
6. 8¢ or 9¢ (8¢)

Skill Review

Group the students in pairs. Using 5 counters, have the first student build a number fact for the sum of 5 and the second student write the fact. Reverse roles after each fact. Have students build all 6 facts for the sum of 5. Repeat for 3 and 4.

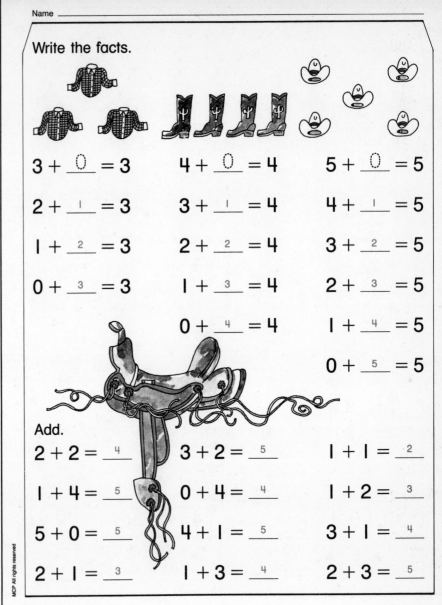

Name _____

Write the facts.

$3 + \underline{0} = 3$ $4 + \underline{0} = 4$ $5 + \underline{0} = 5$

$2 + \underline{1} = 3$ $3 + \underline{1} = 4$ $4 + \underline{1} = 5$

$1 + \underline{2} = 3$ $2 + \underline{2} = 4$ $3 + \underline{2} = 5$

$0 + \underline{3} = 3$ $1 + \underline{3} = 4$ $2 + \underline{3} = 5$

$0 + \underline{4} = 4$ $1 + \underline{4} = 5$

$0 + \underline{5} = 5$

Add.

$2 + 2 = \underline{4}$ $3 + 2 = \underline{5}$ $1 + 1 = \underline{2}$

$1 + 4 = \underline{5}$ $0 + 4 = \underline{4}$ $1 + 2 = \underline{3}$

$5 + 0 = \underline{5}$ $4 + 1 = \underline{5}$ $3 + 1 = \underline{4}$

$2 + 1 = \underline{3}$ $1 + 3 = \underline{4}$ $2 + 3 = \underline{5}$

Practice, sums through 5

(thirty-three) **33**

Teaching page 33

Ask students what 2 numbers can be added together to make zero.(0 and 0) Ask a student to write the number sentence on the board.($0 + 0 = 0$ or $\begin{matrix}0\\ +0\\ \hline 0\end{matrix}$)

Ask students to find the fact family of 2 and tell what 2 numbers can be added together to make 2.(2 and 0, 0 and 2, 1 and 1) Have students use their counters to build the number facts for the sum of 2. Tell students to complete the fact families for sums of 3, 4 and 5 and then complete the page.

33

Add.

1 +1 = 2	2 +3 = 5	4 +0 = 4	1 +4 = 5	2 +0 = 2
0 +3 = 3	2 +1 = 3	1 +0 = 1	1 +3 = 4	0 +4 = 4
4 +1 = 5	3 +2 = 5	3 +0 = 3	1 +2 = 3	0 +1 = 1
0 +2 = 2	5 +0 = 5	3 +1 = 4	2 +2 = 4	0 +5 = 5

Practice, sums through 5

Have students practice sums through 5 using flash cards with the facts without the answers on one side and the facts with the answers on the other. Have them work in pairs, taking turns quizzing each other using the cards.

Enrichment

1. Find all facts for sums through 5 that can be written 2 ways. (ex. 2 + 3 and 3 + 2)
2. Draw a picture depicting a fact. (ex. 3 + 1 = 4 can be shown by drawing 3 lollipops in one hand and 1 in the other.) Have others tell the fact shown.
3. Find facts for the family of 3 in the classroom. (ex. 2 bulletin boards and 1 more)

Teaching page 34

Have students read the first problem (1 + 1 = 2) and trace the 2. Tell students to complete the page.

Extra Credit   *Applications*

Have students write their first names and count the number of letters in them. Ask them to write the number after their name. Have them compare names with other children in the class. Whose name has the most letters? Whose name has the fewest letters? Ask them to count to see how many more letters are in a long name than a short name.

34

Fact Families
Sums 5 through 7

pages 35-36

Objectives

To discover fact families for sums of 6 and 7
To add vertically for sums 5 through 7

Materials

7 counters
Sheet of paper

Mental Math

How many?
1. wheels on a car (4)
2. roofs on a house (1)
3. people in your family (?)
4. fingernails on two hands (10)
5. letters in the word come (4)
6. hubcaps on a car (4)

Skill Review

Write the word **the** on the board. Ask students to count the letters in the word. (3) Ask students to tell a fact in the family of 3. (0 + 3, 2 + 1, 1 + 2, 3 + 0)
Continue with the following words:
I, me, take, a, ball, house, blue.

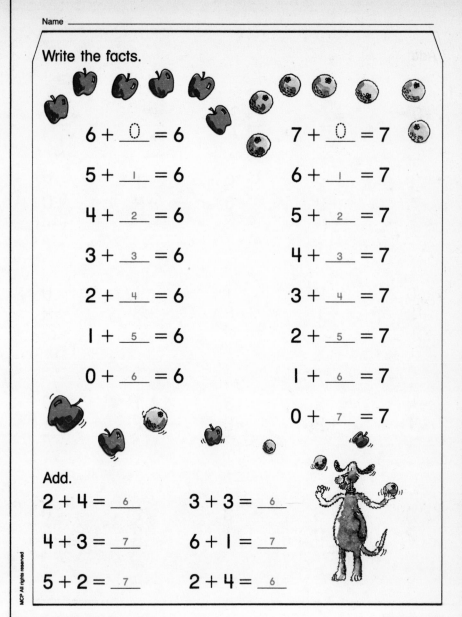

Write the facts.

$6 + \underline{0} = 6$ $7 + \underline{0} = 7$

$5 + \underline{1} = 6$ $6 + \underline{1} = 7$

$4 + \underline{2} = 6$ $5 + \underline{2} = 7$

$3 + \underline{3} = 6$ $4 + \underline{3} = 7$

$2 + \underline{4} = 6$ $3 + \underline{4} = 7$

$1 + \underline{5} = 6$ $2 + \underline{5} = 7$

$0 + \underline{6} = 6$ $1 + \underline{6} = 7$

                              $0 + \underline{7} = 7$

Add.

$2 + 4 = \underline{6}$ $3 + 3 = \underline{6}$

$4 + 3 = \underline{7}$ $6 + 1 = \underline{7}$

$5 + 2 = \underline{7}$ $2 + 4 = \underline{6}$

Discovering fact families, sums of 6 and 7   (thirty-five) **35**

Teaching page 35

Ask students to use 6 counters to build a fact in the 6 family. (6 + 0 = 6, 5 + 1 = 6, 4 + 2 = 6, 3 + 3 = 6, 2 + 4 = 6, 1 + 5 = 6, 0 + 6 = 6, in any order) Ask students how many facts are in the 6 family. (7) Have students use 1 more counter and build facts for the 7 family. Write these in vertical form on the board:

0	7	1	6	2	5	4	3
+7	+0	+6	+1	+5	+2	+3	+4
7	7	7	7	7	7	7	7

Ask students how many facts are in the 7 family. (8) Have students complete the page, using counters if they choose.

Add.

5 +0 *5*	6 +1 7	2 +3 5	0 +6 6	3 +3 6
7 +0 7	5 +1 6	4 +1 5	1 +5 6	1 +4 5
4 +2 6	5 +2 7	4 +3 7	2 +4 6	1 +6 7
3 +2 5	2 +5 7	0 +5 5	3 +4 7	0 +7 7

Adding vertically, sums 5 through 7

Correcting Common Errors

Have students who need practice with sums of 6 and 7 work with partners using counters. For each fact, they should use counters to model the problem and then count them to find the sum.

Enrichment

1. Plan a method for finding all facts in a number family.
2. Make up a story using all facts in a number family. (ex. for 3: Bill had 3 dogs and 2 dogpens. He had to decide where to house the dogs.)

Teaching page 36

Have students work this page independently, using counters if they choose.

Extra Credit   *Sets*

Play a game of set dominoes. Cut heavy paper into 4 inch by 8 inch cards, one for each student. Make sets of dots from one through ten on each half of the cards. Vary the arrangement of the dots on each section. Make one double card with equivalent sets on each end. Distribute one card to each child and divide the class into two teams. Place the double card on the floor to begin. Each team takes a turn placing a card with a matching set next to the end card. The first team to use all its cards wins.

Two students can play by picking 4 cards while the rest are face down. Place the double card face up, and students take turns matching the equivalent sets. If students do not have a matching card they draw from the pile, ending their turn. Play continues until one student has no cards remaining.

Fact Families
Sums of 8 and 9

pages 37-38

Objectives

To discover fact families for sums of 8 and 9
To add vertically for sums of 8 and 9

Materials

9 counters
Sheet of paper

Mental Math

What numbers come before:
1. 7 (6, 5, 4, 3, 2, 1, 0)
2. 1
3. 3
4. 5
5. 2
6. 8
7. 6
8. 9

Skill Review

Write on the board in the order given: **3 + 3, 7 + 0, 4 + 3, 2 + 5, 0 + 6, 1 + 5, 2 + 4, 3 + 4, 6 + 0, 0 + 7, 5 + 1, 1 + 6, 5 + 2, 4 + 2, 6 + 1.** Draw 2 houses on the board and write **6** on one roof and **7** on the other. Have students put each fact under its correct roof.

Write the facts.

$$8 + \underline{0} = 8 \qquad 9 + \underline{0} = 9$$
$$7 + \underline{1} = 8 \qquad 8 + \underline{1} = 9$$
$$6 + \underline{2} = 8 \qquad 7 + \underline{2} = 9$$
$$5 + \underline{3} = 8 \qquad 6 + \underline{3} = 9$$
$$4 + \underline{4} = 8 \qquad 5 + \underline{4} = 9$$
$$3 + \underline{5} = 8 \qquad 4 + \underline{5} = 9$$
$$2 + \underline{6} = 8 \qquad 3 + \underline{6} = 9$$
$$1 + \underline{7} = 8 \qquad 2 + \underline{7} = 9$$
$$0 + \underline{8} = 8 \qquad 1 + \underline{8} = 9$$
$$0 + \underline{9} = 9$$

Discovering fact families, sums of 8 and 9

(thirty-seven) **37**

Teaching page 37

Have students find the fact family for 8. (0 + 8, 1 + 7, 2 + 6, 3 + 5, 4 + 4, 5 + 3, 6 + 2, 7 + 1, 8 + 0) Allow students to use counters if they choose. Ask how many facts are in the fact family for 8. (9) Repeat for the 9 fact family. (0 + 9, 1 + 8, 2 + 7, 3 + 6, 4 + 5, 5 + 4, 6 + 3, 7 + 2, 8 + 1, 9 + 0) Ask how many facts are in the fact family for 9. (10)

Have students complete the page by writing the facts in the families of 8 and 9.

Add.

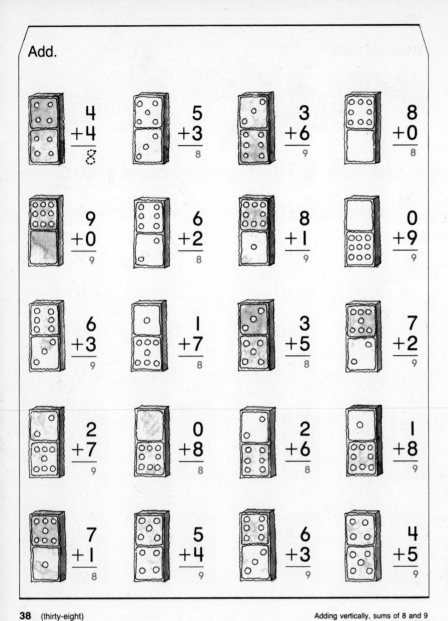

$\begin{array}{r}4\\+4\\\hline 8\end{array}$	$\begin{array}{r}5\\+3\\\hline 8\end{array}$	$\begin{array}{r}3\\+6\\\hline 9\end{array}$	$\begin{array}{r}8\\+0\\\hline 8\end{array}$
$\begin{array}{r}9\\+0\\\hline 9\end{array}$	$\begin{array}{r}6\\+2\\\hline 8\end{array}$	$\begin{array}{r}8\\+1\\\hline 9\end{array}$	$\begin{array}{r}0\\+9\\\hline 9\end{array}$
$\begin{array}{r}6\\+3\\\hline 9\end{array}$	$\begin{array}{r}1\\+7\\\hline 8\end{array}$	$\begin{array}{r}3\\+5\\\hline 8\end{array}$	$\begin{array}{r}7\\+2\\\hline 9\end{array}$
$\begin{array}{r}2\\+7\\\hline 9\end{array}$	$\begin{array}{r}0\\+8\\\hline 8\end{array}$	$\begin{array}{r}2\\+6\\\hline 8\end{array}$	$\begin{array}{r}1\\+8\\\hline 9\end{array}$
$\begin{array}{r}7\\+1\\\hline 8\end{array}$	$\begin{array}{r}5\\+4\\\hline 9\end{array}$	$\begin{array}{r}6\\+3\\\hline 9\end{array}$	$\begin{array}{r}4\\+5\\\hline 9\end{array}$

Adding vertically, sums of 8 and 9

Correcting Common Errors

Have students who need practice with sums of 8 and 9 work in pairs. Begin with 8 counters. Have one partner take all the counters. Ask, "How many counters do you each have?" (8 and 0) "How many do you both have in all?" (8) Have students write the fact $8 + 0 = 8$. Have the student with no counters take 1 from his partner. Ask them the same questions and have them write the new fact. ($7 + 1 = 8$) Continue until the second partner has all 8 counters. Repeat the activity with 9 counters.

Enrichment

1. For sums through 10, find fact families having a fact which is built with one number. (ex. 1 = 1 + 1)
2. Use dominoes to play "Concentration". Turn all dominoes face down. Draw 2. A match of 2 facts in the same family earns another turn. Play until all dominoes have been matched.

Teaching page 38

Have students count the dots on the dominoes to find the sums. Allow the use of counters as long as the students need them. Have students complete the page independently.

Extra Credit   *Applications*

Music is a mathematical aspect of life. Begin by introducing long and short notes. Do not refer to quarter notes and eighth notes. Let the students feel, by clapping, that some notes are longer than others. Begin by clapping these rhythms and have students repeat your rhythm like an echo:

♩♩♫♩   ♫♩♫♩♩   ♩♩♩♫♫

Now have volunteers clap a rhythm and have the class repeat their rhythms. Eventually, you can use common phrases to show students that even their speech has a rhythm. Have them clap and say:

SEE YOU LATER ALLIGATOR   and   FEE FI FO FUM.

♫♫♫♫♫♫   ♩♩♩♩

Ask students to tell which are long notes, which are short.

Fact Families Sums of 10

pages 39-40

Objectives

To discover fact family for sums of 10
To add vertically for sums through 10

Materials

10 counters
Sheet of paper
*Set of addition fact cards for sums through 9

Mental Math

What fact family has:
1. 3 facts (2)
2. 0 + 9 (9)
3. 1 fact (0)
4. 2 + 2 (4)
5. 7 + 1 and 1 + 7 (8)
6. 2 facts (1)
7. 10 facts (9)

Skill Review

Shuffle fact cards. Show an addition fact card and have a student give the fact family as quickly as possible. Allow for each student to have several turns.

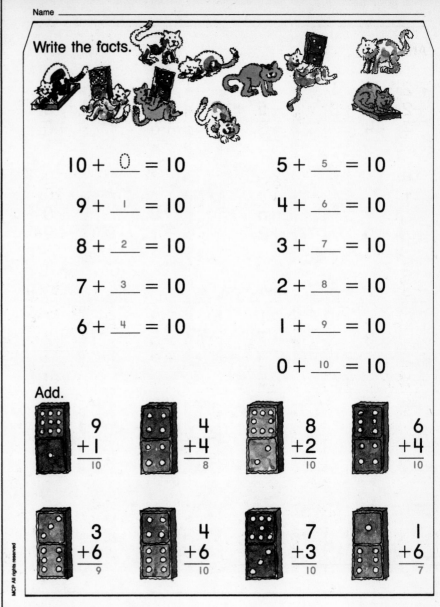

Name _____

Write the facts.

$10 + \underline{0} = 10$ $5 + \underline{5} = 10$

$9 + \underline{1} = 10$ $4 + \underline{6} = 10$

$8 + \underline{2} = 10$ $3 + \underline{7} = 10$

$7 + \underline{3} = 10$ $2 + \underline{8} = 10$

$6 + \underline{4} = 10$ $1 + \underline{9} = 10$

     $0 + \underline{10} = 10$

Add.

$\begin{array}{r} 9 \\ +1 \\ \hline 10 \end{array}$ $\begin{array}{r} 4 \\ +4 \\ \hline 8 \end{array}$ $\begin{array}{r} 8 \\ +2 \\ \hline 10 \end{array}$ $\begin{array}{r} 6 \\ +4 \\ \hline 10 \end{array}$

$\begin{array}{r} 3 \\ +6 \\ \hline 9 \end{array}$ $\begin{array}{r} 4 \\ +6 \\ \hline 10 \end{array}$ $\begin{array}{r} 7 \\ +3 \\ \hline 10 \end{array}$ $\begin{array}{r} 1 \\ +6 \\ \hline 7 \end{array}$

Discovering fact families, sums of 10   (thirty-nine) **39**

Teaching page 39

Have students find the facts in the family of 10. (0 + 10, 1 + 9, 2 + 8, 3 + 7, 4 + 6, 5 + 5, 6 + 4, 7 + 3, 8 + 2, 9 + 1, 10 + 0) Ask how many facts are in the fact family for 10. (11)

Have students write the facts in the 2 columns at the top of the page. Then tell students to complete the page by writing answers for each fact.

Add.

2 +2 4	1 +8 9	5 +2 7	1 +4 5	4 +3 7	2 +3 5
4 +1 5	5 +5 10	3 +2 5	6 +4 10	0 +7 7	5 +3 8
3 +3 6	1 +5 6	4 +4 8	2 +4 6	6 +3 9	3 +7 10
2 +5 7	4 +6 10	3 +5 8	8 +2 10	2 +7 9	2 +8 10
3 +6 9	1 +9 10	5 +4 9	1 +7 8	4 +5 9	7 +3 10

Adding vertically, sums through 10

Correcting Common Errors

Have students who need practice with sums of 10 work in pairs with 10 counters and 2 pieces of paper. Have them put all 10 counters on one piece of paper. Tell the students to write the number fact shown on the two pieces of paper. (10 + 0 = 10) Have the students take 1 counter from the first piece of paper and place it on the second. Tell them to write the new fact. (9 + 1 = 10) Have the students take another counter from the first piece of paper and place it on the second, writing the new fact. (8 + 2 = 10) Have them continue until all counters are on the second piece of paper and they have written 11 facts.

Enrichment

1. Make "Addition Fact Families Books" with one page for each number through 10. Write all facts for each family on its proper page.
2. Using a spinner containing numbers 0 through 9, give a fact for the number spun.
3. Play "Addition Fact Family" in 2 teams. Take turns and give another fact in the same family as the fact card shown.

Teaching page 40

Have students work the first fact and trace the 4. Students may wish to set up each problem with counters before writing the answers. Tell them to complete the page.

Extra Credit   *Counting*

Construct a set of picture puzzles that will help the students practice their counting and matching skills. For each puzzle use a rectangular piece of oak tagboard, approximately four inches by seven inches in size.

Draw the same number of objects on each half of a pair, but vary the illustration and the arrangement. Laminating the pieces will increase their durability. Cut each rectangle to make two matching puzzle pieces. Start with a set of puzzles for quantities through ten. Add to the set as students learn to count to 20.

Sums through 10

pages 41-42

Objective
To learn sums through 10

Materials
10 counters
Sheet of paper

Mental Math
How much is:
1. 3 and 2 more (5)
2. 2 plus 4 (6)
3. 8 and 1 more (9)
4. 0 plus 9 (9)
5. 6 and 0 more (6)
6. 5 and 2 more (7)
7. 0 plus 0 (0)

Skill Review
Write on the board:
2 and 8 more is 10
3 and 6 more is 9
4 and 4 more is 8
5 and 0 more is 5
0 and 7 more is 7
1 and 5 more is 6
0 and 0 more is 0
Have a student come to the board and write the first sentence a shorter way. (2 + 8 = 10) Have another student write the same sentence vertically. Continue until all the sentences are written both horizontally and vertically.

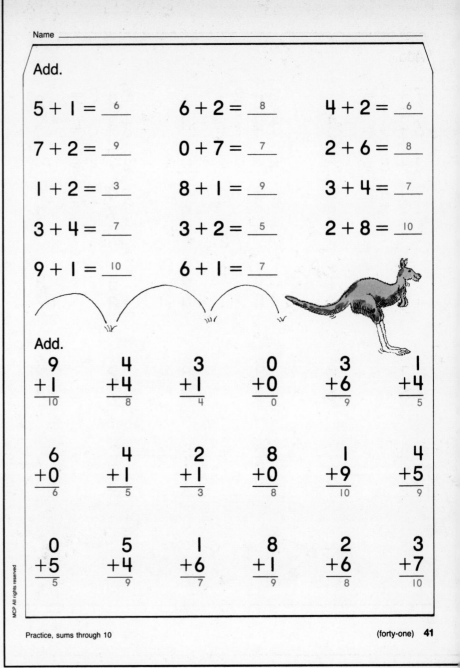

Name _____

Add.

$5 + 1 = \underline{6}$ $6 + 2 = \underline{8}$ $4 + 2 = \underline{6}$

$7 + 2 = \underline{9}$ $0 + 7 = \underline{7}$ $2 + 6 = \underline{8}$

$1 + 2 = \underline{3}$ $8 + 1 = \underline{9}$ $3 + 4 = \underline{7}$

$3 + 4 = \underline{7}$ $3 + 2 = \underline{5}$ $2 + 8 = \underline{10}$

$9 + 1 = \underline{10}$ $6 + 1 = \underline{7}$

Add.

9	4	3	0	3	1
+1	+4	+1	+0	+6	+4
10	8	4	0	9	5

6	4	2	8	1	4
+0	+1	+1	+0	+9	+5
6	5	3	8	10	9

0	5	1	8	2	3
+5	+4	+6	+1	+6	+7
5	9	7	9	8	10

Practice, sums through 10   (forty-one) **41**

Teaching page 41
Have students write the answers to each problem.
Allow students to use counters as long as they choose.
For students needing more practice, use flash cards to build speed of recall.

Add.

$7 + 2 = \underline{9}$ $3 + 2 = \underline{5}$ $2 + 3 = \underline{5}$

$6 + 4 = \underline{10}$ $7 + 1 = \underline{8}$ $3 + 0 = \underline{3}$

$2 + 5 = \underline{7}$ $4 + 2 = \underline{6}$ $3 + 4 = \underline{7}$

$1 + 2 = \underline{3}$ $1 + 1 = \underline{2}$ $5 + 1 = \underline{6}$

$5 + 2 = \underline{7}$ $6 + 1 = \underline{7}$

1 +5 — 6	7 +3 — 10	1 +3 — 4	5 +5 — 10	4 +0 — 4	2 +7 — 9
4 +3 — 7	3 +5 — 8	8 +2 — 10	2 +2 — 4	6 +3 — 9	3 +1 — 4
4 +6 — 10	7 +0 — 7	0 +9 — 9	5 +3 — 8	0 +3 — 3	1 +8 — 9

Practice, sums through 10

Correcting Common Errors

If some students have difficulty with sums to 10, have them practice with partners using the "count on" strategy. For a fact such as 7 + 3, they should start with 7 and count on 3 more: 7 . . . 8, 9, 10. The sum is 10. When students use this strategy, have them turn some of the addends around so the first addend is the greater number; e.g., to do 2 + 6, they should start with 6 and count on 2 more: 6 . . . 7, 8.

Enrichment

1. Arrange 66 addition fact cards for sums through 10 into families 0 through 9.
2. Line up for lunch, etc. by naming a fact in a particular family.
3. Carry an addition fact card for sums through 10. Move to stand with other students carrying facts in the same family.

Teaching page 42

Have students complete the page independently.

Extra Credit   *Applications*

Collect examples of three common magnetic objects, such as paper clips, pins, etc. Assign each type of object a number value 1 through 3, and write this on the board. Also collect various non-magnetic items made of wood, plastic, etc., to mix with the magnetic objects. Place all the items on a desk top and announce "fishing" time. Prepare a magnetic "fishing pole" by attaching a magnet to the end of a pencil or ruler, with a string. Allow each student to make one fishing pass over the pile of objects. Then have the student refer to the number value list, list the value of each of the magnetic items "caught," and the total. The student who "catches" the highest total, wins. Students can fish several times to try to better their scores. Discuss what objects were not picked up by the fishing pole, and why.

Sums through 10¢

pages 43-44

Objective

To add pennies for sums through 10¢

Materials

10 real or punchout pennies
1 paper cup

Mental Math

Count to 10 from:
1. 2 (2, 3, 4, 5, 6, 7, 8, 9, 10)
2. 6
3. 1
4. 8
5. 4

Skill Review

Draw on the board:

7 5 8 3 4

Ask students to come to the board and write a fact under each fact family box. Continue for all facts.

7	5	8	3	4
(0 + 7)	(0 + 5)	(0 + 8)	(0 + 3)	(0 + 4)
(1 + 6)	(1 + 4)	(1 + 7)	(1 + 2)	(1 + 3)
(2 + 5)	(2 + 3)	(2 + 6)	(2 + 1)	(2 + 2)
(3 + 4)	(3 + 2)	(3 + 5)	(3 + 0)	(3 + 1)
(4 + 3)	(4 + 1)	(4 + 4)		(4 + 0)
(5 + 2)	(5 + 0)	(5 + 3)		
(6 + 1)		(6 + 2)		
(7 + 0)		(7 + 1)		
		(8 + 0)		

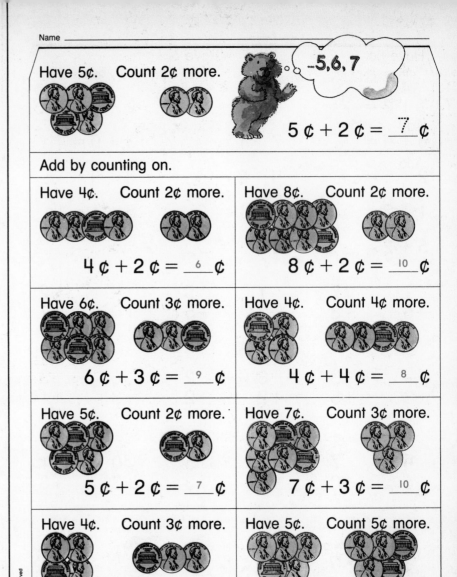

Adding pennies by counting

Teaching page 43

Draw on the board:

Tell students that to find the number of pennies in all, we say 3¢ and then add 1¢ one at a time. Count for the students as you point to each: **3¢, 4¢, 5¢, 6¢.** Tell students to put 4 pennies in their cups and lay 5 pennies beside the cup. Tell students we start with the greater number and then count on. Ask which number is greater, 4¢ or 5¢. (5¢) Have students count with you to find how many pennies in all. Write **9¢** on the board and remind students that we must use the **¢** sign to mean money. Write **2 + 5 = __ ¢** on the board.

Have students count aloud to find how many pennies in all. (5¢, 6¢, 7¢) Repeat procedure for 6 + 3 and 4 + 6. Be sure students are starting with the greater number.

Have student look at the bear and the pennies at the top of the page. Tell students the bear starts with the 5 pennies because 5 is greater than 2 and adds on by saying "5¢, 6¢, 7¢". Have students complete the page by counting on from the greater number.

43

Have 8¢.
Add 1¢ more.

$$\begin{array}{r} 8\text{¢} \\ +1\text{¢} \\ \hline 9\text{¢} \end{array}$$

Have 6¢.
Add 2¢ more.

$$\begin{array}{r} 6\text{¢} \\ +2\text{¢} \\ \hline 8\text{¢} \end{array}$$

Add.

$$\begin{array}{r} 5\text{¢} \\ +3\text{¢} \\ \hline 8\text{¢} \end{array}$$

$$\begin{array}{r} 4\text{¢} \\ +6\text{¢} \\ \hline 10\text{¢} \end{array}$$

$$\begin{array}{r} 3\text{¢} \\ +5\text{¢} \\ \hline 8\text{¢} \end{array}$$

$$\begin{array}{r} 6\text{¢} \\ +2\text{¢} \\ \hline 8\text{¢} \end{array}$$

$$\begin{array}{r} 2\text{¢} \\ +7\text{¢} \\ \hline 9\text{¢} \end{array}$$

$$\begin{array}{r} 4\text{¢} \\ +5\text{¢} \\ \hline 9\text{¢} \end{array}$$

$$\begin{array}{r} 6\text{¢} \\ +4\text{¢} \\ \hline 10\text{¢} \end{array}$$

$$\begin{array}{r} 3\text{¢} \\ +7\text{¢} \\ \hline 10\text{¢} \end{array}$$

Adding money, sums through 10¢

Correcting Common Errors

If students have difficulty adding with money, have them place coins or play money next to each addend and count to find the sum.

Enrichment

1. Play in 2 teams. Use cards numbered 1 to 9. A member of each team draws a card. Student having the greater number counts on to 10.
2. Act out purchasing an item for 7¢. Have 5¢ in hand and 4 pennies in pocket. Count on for correct amount.

Teaching page 44

Tell students that the greater number is not always the first number on this page. Have students tell which number is greater in each problem. Remind students to begin with the greater number and then count on. Have students complete the page.

Extra Credit *Applications*

Demonstrate long and short notes with your students. Clap these rhythms and have them respond like an echo: ♪♪♪♩ ♪♩♪♩ ♩♩♪♪

Ask students to identify the long and short notes in a rhythm.

Now write these sentences on the board. Use the names of your students in the sentences:

♩♩♩♩
MY NAME IS CLAIRE.
♩♩♩♪♩
MY NAME IS JEFFREY.

Ask students to clap and say each phrase in the rhythm you have written. Continue, adding the names of other students. Explain that each name has a different rhythm.

Column Addition

pages 45-46

Objective

To add in columns for sums through 10

Materials

10 counters
Sheet of paper
Worksheet

Mental Math

What 2 numbers can be added together to make:
1. 4 (2,2; 1,3; 4,0)
2. 0 (0,0)
3. 7 (4,3; 7,0; 2,5; 6,1)
4. 8 (3,5; 2,6; 1,7; 0,8; 4,4)
5. 5 (5,0; 1,4; 2,3)
6. 3 (3,0; 2,1)

Skill Review

Write on the board:
4 3 (4 + 3 = 7, 3 + 4 = 7)
2 4 (2 + 4 = 6, 4 + 2 = 6)
3 7 (3 + 7 = 10, 7 + 3 = 10)
6 2 (6 + 2 = 8, 2 + 6 = 8)
0 9 (0 + 9 = 9, 9 + 0 = 9)
Have a student come to the board and write an addition number sentence using the 2 numbers. Ask another student to write the same problem vertically.
$\left(\begin{array}{r} 4 \\ +3 \\ \hline 7 \end{array}\right)$

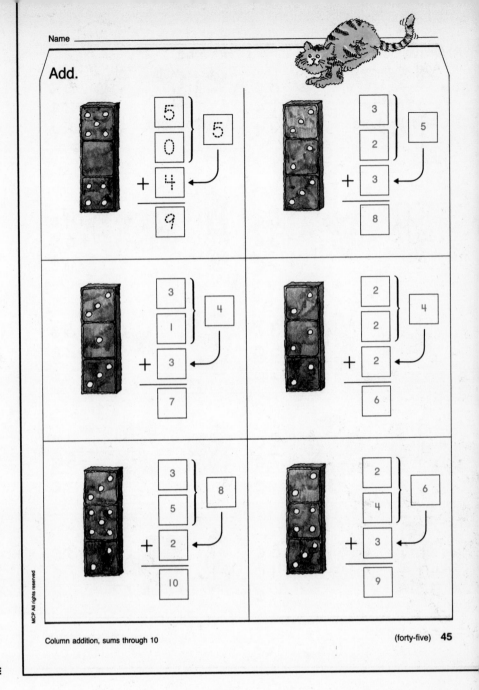

Name _____

Add.

Column addition, sums through 10

(forty-five) **45**

Teaching page 45

Have students work in pairs with 5 counters and the following blank worksheet:

Sums of 5		
(2)	(3)	(0)
(1)	(4)	(0)
(3)	(2)	(0)
(0)	(3)	(2)
(0)	(4)	(1)
(4)	(1)	(0)

Tell students to find 3 numbers that, when added together, make a sum of 5. Allow use of counters. Have students write each group of 3 numbers across the worksheet as illustrated. Give additional worksheets

as needed to allow recording of all possible combinations. Repeat for sums of 4. Have students find the 3-part domino in the first box. Tell students to count the dots at the top of the domino (5) and trace the 5. Continue for the next 2 sections of the domino. Tell students to add the 5 and 0 (5) and trace the 5. Have students then add the 5 and 4 (9) and trace the 9. Work similarly through the second problem and then ask students to complete the page.

Add.

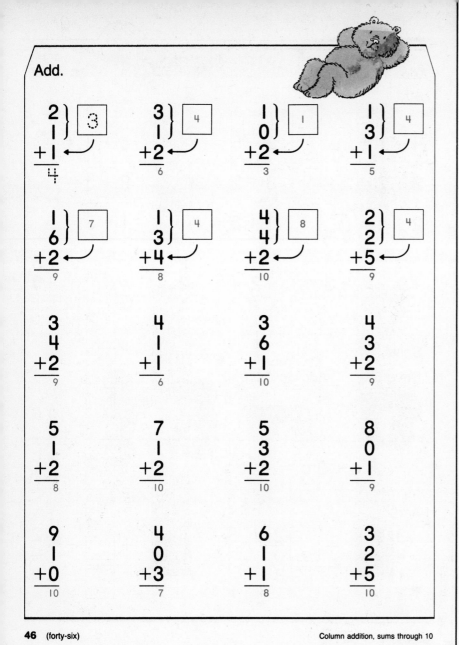

2 1 +1 4 → 3	3 1 +2 6 → 4	1 0 +2 3 → 1	1 3 +1 5 → 4
1 6 +2 9 → 7	1 3 +4 8 → 4	4 4 +2 10 → 8	2 2 +5 9 → 4
3 4 +2 9	4 1 +1 6	3 6 +1 10	4 3 +2 9
5 1 +2 8	7 1 +2 10	5 3 +2 10	8 0 +1 9
9 1 +0 10	4 0 +3 7	6 1 +1 8	3 2 +5 10

Column addition, sums through 10

Correcting Common Errors

Watch for students who have difficulty finding the sum of three numbers because they cannot remember the sum of the first two numbers when they add the third number. Have them write the sum of the first two numbers next to the two addends, and then add this sum and the third addend to find the final sum.

Enrichment

1. Cut and paste a picture of 4 objects in 3 groups. (ex. 2 toys, 1 toy, 1 toy)
2. Tell a story wherein the numbers 2, 3 and 1 are added together to make 6. (ex. Mom needed 6 eggs for breakfast. She took 2 eggs from the refrigerator. Dad carried 3 eggs and I carried 1 egg.)

Teaching page 46

Have students count or add the 2 and 1 (3) and trace the 3. Tell students to add the 3 and 1 (4) and trace the 4. Help students with more problems. Have students complete the page.

Extra Credit *Sets*

Students can take an outdoor excursion, and carry small bags to collect sets. Small groups of students can gather sets of nuts and seeds, leaves from a variety of trees, or rocks, etc. Ask them how many different ways they can group their collections. To conclude the activity, discuss why things are grouped into sets. Encourage them to look for other sets on their way home and share their discoveries with the class.

Chapter Review

pages 47-48

Objective

To review addition sums through 10

Materials

10 counters
Sheet of paper

Mental Math

How much is:
1. 4¢ plus 5¢ (9¢)
2. 1 more than 2 (3)
3. nothing plus nothing (0)
4. the sum of 1 and 7 (8)
5. 6 pennies and 1 more (7¢)
6. 1 eye plus 1 eye (2 eyes)
7. 4 plus 0 (4)

Skill Review

Write on the board:
2¢ + 4¢ + 1¢ = (7¢)
1 + 1 + 1 = (3)
5 + 4 + 0 = (9)
1 + 6 + 1 = (8)
2¢ + 1¢ + 7¢ = (10¢)
0 + 0 + 6 = (6)
Have students write the problems vertically on the board and write the answers.

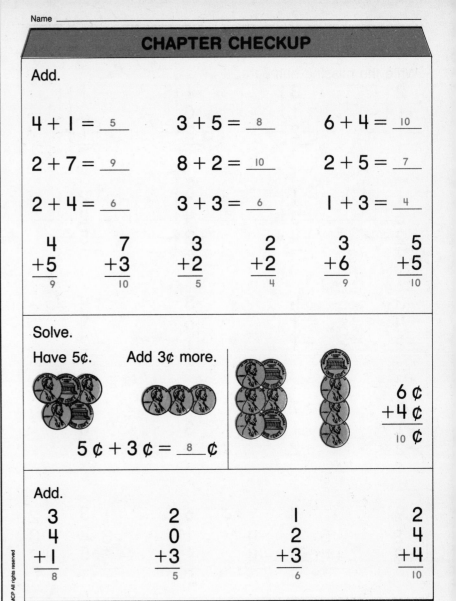

CHAPTER CHECKUP

Add.

$4 + 1 =$ _5_ $3 + 5 =$ _8_ $6 + 4 =$ _10_

$2 + 7 =$ _9_ $8 + 2 =$ _10_ $2 + 5 =$ _7_

$2 + 4 =$ _6_ $3 + 3 =$ _6_ $1 + 3 =$ _4_

$\begin{array}{r} 4 \\ +5 \\ \hline 9 \end{array}$
$\begin{array}{r} 7 \\ +3 \\ \hline 10 \end{array}$
$\begin{array}{r} 3 \\ +2 \\ \hline 5 \end{array}$
$\begin{array}{r} 2 \\ +2 \\ \hline 4 \end{array}$
$\begin{array}{r} 3 \\ +6 \\ \hline 9 \end{array}$
$\begin{array}{r} 5 \\ +5 \\ \hline 10 \end{array}$

Solve.

Have 5¢.   Add 3¢ more.

$5 ¢ + 3 ¢ =$ _8_ ¢

$\begin{array}{r} 6\ ¢ \\ +4\ ¢ \\ \hline 10\ ¢ \end{array}$

Add.

$\begin{array}{r} 3 \\ 4 \\ +1 \\ \hline 8 \end{array}$
$\begin{array}{r} 2 \\ 0 \\ +3 \\ \hline 5 \end{array}$
$\begin{array}{r} 1 \\ 2 \\ +3 \\ \hline 6 \end{array}$
$\begin{array}{r} 2 \\ 4 \\ +4 \\ \hline 10 \end{array}$

Chapter review

Teaching page 47

Tell students that this page has some problems with 2 numbers to add, some problems adding pennies and some problems with 3 numbers to add. Ask students to find the problems with 2 numbers to add. (top third of page) Ask students to point to the problems with pennies. (middle boxes) Ask students to find the problems with 3 numbers to add. (bottom) Have students complete the page.

ROUNDUP REVIEW

Write the missing numbers.

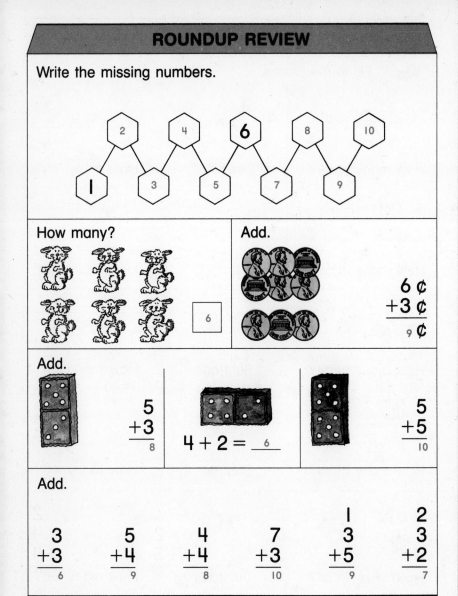

How many?

6

Add.

6 ¢
+3 ¢
9 ¢

Add.

5
+3
8

4 + 2 = 6

5
+5
10

Add.

3
+3
6

5
+4
9

4
+4
8

7
+3
10

1
3
+5
9

2
3
+2
7

Cumulative review

Enrichment

1. Use Bingo cards as illustrated:

BINGO		
0	4	2
9	6	3
5	7	1

A set of 2 numbers 1 through 9 is called out. Players are to find the sum and cover that number on their cards.

2. Use 3 sets of number cards 0 through 3. Draw 3 cards and add the numbers together.

3. Practice number recognition by dialing a play telephone.

Teaching page 48

Have students complete the page independently. This page reviews writing numbers in sequence, counting objects and money, and adding sums through 10.

48

Subtraction

pages 49-50

Objective

To understand the concept of subtraction as taking away

Materials

5 counters
Sheet of paper

Mental Math

Name the number that:
1. is 3 more than 6 (9)
2. is 5 more than 3 (8)
3. comes after 6 (7)
4. comes after 8 (9)
5. comes between 6 and 8 (7)
6. comes between 4 and 6 (5)

Skill Review

Write on the board:

8   6   7

Have students write addition sentences under each number. (Sentences may have 2 or 3 addends)

Name _____

3 SUBTRACTION, MINUENDS THROUGH 10

Fill in the blanks.

 △ △ ◁ _3_ How many in all?	 △ _1_ Subtract.	_2_ How many left?
 ▢ ▢ ▢ ▢ _4_ How many in all?	 ▢ ▢ _2_ Subtract.	_2_ How many left?
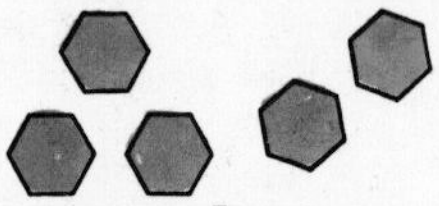 ⬡ ⬡ ⬡ ⬡ ⬡ _5_ How many in all?	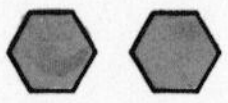 ⬡ ⬡ _2_ Subtract.	_3_ How many left?
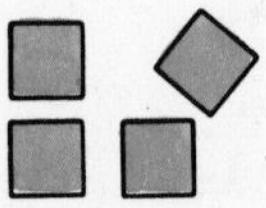 ▢ ▢ ▢ ▢ _4_ How many in all?	▢ _1_ Subtract.	_3_ How many left?
 ★ ★ ★ _3_ How many in all?	 ★ _1_ Subtract.	_2_ How many left?

Understanding subtraction

(forty-nine) **49**

MCP All rights reserved

Teaching page 49

Have students watch carefully as you hold up two hands. Ask students how many hands they see in all. (2) Put one hand behind you. Ask how many hands are hidden. (1) Ask how many hands are left. (1) Repeat the concept using counters. Have students place 5 counters on a sheet of paper. Tell them to move 3 counters off the paper and tell the number they have left. Repeat for other subtraction combinations, having students identify the numbers started with, taken away and left. Have students look at the first problem on the page. Have them trace over the number answers as you reinforce the questions. Students may use counters to demonstrate that $3 - 1 = 2$. Read the next problem with students. Tell students to complete the page.

49

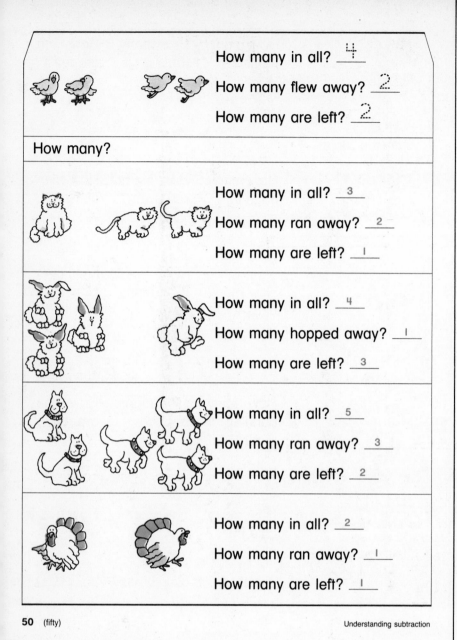

How many in all? __4__
How many flew away? __2__
How many are left? __2__

How many?

How many in all? __3__
How many ran away? __2__
How many are left? __1__

How many in all? __4__
How many hopped away? __1__
How many are left? __3__

How many in all? __5__
How many ran away? __3__
How many are left? __2__

How many in all? __2__
How many ran away? __1__
How many are left? __1__

50 (fifty)

Understanding subtraction

Correcting Common Errors

Some students may have difficulty deciding how many are left. Have them work with partners with counters and a pad. Direct them to place a number of counters on the pad. When you tell them how many to take away, have them count those that remain on the pad to find how many are left. Encourage them to verbalize the modeled fact. Then have them use the pad and counters to model the problems in this lesson.

Enrichment

1. Draw a picture that tells 5 take away 1 leaves 4.
2. Draw a picture showing take away where 2 is left.
3. Using a spinner having numbers 1 through 5, tell a subtraction story for a number spun. (ex. for 4: There were 4 dogs playing in our yard but 2 ran off. Then there were 2 dogs in our yard.)

Teaching page 50

Have students tell what the birds in the first problem are doing. (Some birds are sitting and some are flying away.) Ask how many birds in all. (4) Have students trace the 4. Complete the next two questions in the same way. Then have a student use these numbers to tell the story of the birds. (There were 4 birds in all. 2 birds flew away and 2 birds were left.) Help students complete the next problem before they finish the page independently.

Extra Credit *Applications*

Provide students with old magazines. Ask them to cut out pictures of groups of 4, 5, and 6 things or people. Have them paste the pictures to precut pieces of tagboard. The students can use the cards to group the pictures in sets. Use the cards to play a simple game of "Concentration." Mix and spread all the cards picture side down. Place them into rows. Take turns in turning up any two cards. If the two pictures match (the same number of things or people), the player keeps the matching cards. As long as a player selects two matching cards his or her turn continues. If the two pictures do not match the pictures are turned face down again and the other player takes a turn. The player with the most cards wins.

Minuends through 5

Objective

To write subtraction sentences using
− and = correctly

Materials

5 counters per student
Sheet of paper per student

Mental Math

Name the number that:
1. is left in 4 take away 2 (2)
2. is 4 more than 3 and 2 (9)
3. is the sum of 4, 2 and 1 (7)
4. is 4¢ take away 3¢ (1¢)
5. is the sum of 3 and 6 (9)
6. is the sum of 2, 0 and 4 (6)

Skill Review

Say: Five little monkeys
jumping on the bed;
One fell off and
broke his head.
Mama called the doctor
and the doctor said,
"How many monkeys
are left on the bed?" (4)
Continue stanzas, subtracting one
more monkey each time. Stop when
one monkey is left. Tell students to
place counters on their papers to tell
this poem's story as you say it again.

Name _____

	How many hamsters in all?	How many ran away?	How many are left?
	5	− 1	= 4

Write the facts.

	How many dogs in all?	How many ran away?	How many are left?
	4	− 1	= 3

	How many birds in all?	How many flew away?	How many are left?
	2	− 1	= 1

	How many bunnies in all?	How many hopped away?	How many are left?
	5	− 4	= 1

	How many cats in all?	How many ran away?	How many are left?
	3	− 1	= 2

Writing subtraction sentences   (fifty-one) **51**

Teaching page 51

Write on the board: **5 take away 3 equals 2.** Ask
students to read it. Tell students there is a shorter way
to write this sentence. Write **5 − 3 = 2** under the first
sentence. Tell students that this sentence is read "5
minus 3 equals 2." Ask what the 5 tells us. (how many
in all) Tell students the minus sign tells us to take
away. Ask what the 3 tells us. (how many to take
away) Ask what the 2 tells us. (how many are left) Tell
students the equals sign means "is the same as".
Repeat procedure for 4 − 1 = 3.

Have students find the hamsters at the top of the page.
Ask how many hamsters are there in all. (5) Tell
students to trace the 5. Ask how many ran away. (1)
Tell students to trace the 1. Ask students how many
hamsters are left. (4) Have students trace the 4. Read

through the second problem and have students
complete the page.

51

$3 - 1 = \underline{2}$

$5 - 1 = \underline{4}$

Subtract.

$5 - 3 = \underline{2}$

$4 - 2 = \underline{2}$

$2 - 1 = \underline{1}$

$3 - 2 = \underline{1}$

$3 - 1 = \underline{2}$

$5 - 2 = \underline{3}$

$4 - 3 = \underline{1}$

$5 - 4 = \underline{1}$

Subtraction facts, minuends through 5

Correcting Common Errors

Some students may need additional help understanding the − sign and the = sign. Have 5 students stand together. Ask, "How many students?" (5) Pull 2 of the students aside. Ask, "How many were taken away?" (2) "How many are left?" (3) Write the following on the chalkboard.

> 5 take away 2 equals 3
> $5 - 2 = 3$

Repeat the activity for other minuends of 5.

Enrichment

1. Use hand puppets to act out the poem "Five Little Monkeys". Make subtraction sentence cards to help tell the story.
2. Name and list situation when we use subtraction. (ex. I had 3 crayons and Jim borrowed 2. Now I have 1.)

Teaching page 52

Ask students to tell the story of the dogs. (There are 3 dogs in all but 1 is running away and 2 are left.) Write $3 - 1 = 2$ on the board. Point to each part as you ask students what it tells us. (the 3, how many dogs in all; the minus sign, to take away; the 1, how many dogs ran away; the equals sign, is the same as; the 2, how many dogs are left) Have students trace the numbers. Repeat the process for the fish story and have students complete the page independently.

Extra Credit   *Applications*

Explain that many things prepared in a kitchen come partly prepared by a manufacturer. In order to make the food, we must follow directions on the package. Give each group of students a partly thawed can of frozen juice and a large pitcher or jar. Have students find the spot on the container that gives directions for preparing the juice. Read the directions aloud and have a student explain what they mean. (They must empty the contents of the can into a large container. Then they must fill the container with water 3 times, each time emptying the water into the container of juice.) Open the cans and have students follow directions. When each batch is well stirred, let students drink the juice.

Minuends through 5

pages 53-54

Objectives

To subtract with zeroes
To subtract from minuends
through 5

Materials

5 counters
Sheet of paper

Mental Math

Give the addition sentence for:
1. 2 and 2 (2 + 2 = 4)
2. 1 and 0 and 1 (1 + 0 + 1 = 2)
3. 7 and 2 (7 + 2 = 9)
4. 3 plus 5 and 1 more
   (3 + 5 + 1 = 9)
5. 1 and 9 (1 + 9 = 10)
6. 1 plus 8 (1 + 8 = 9)
7. 1 plus 2 plus 3 (1 + 2 + 3 = 6)

Skill Review

Write on the board:
5 take away 4 equals 1
Have a student come to the board
and write the sentence using the
minus and equals signs. (5 − 4 = 1)
Continue for 4 − 1 = 3, 2 − 1 = 1,
5 − 3 = 2, 4 − 3 = 1.

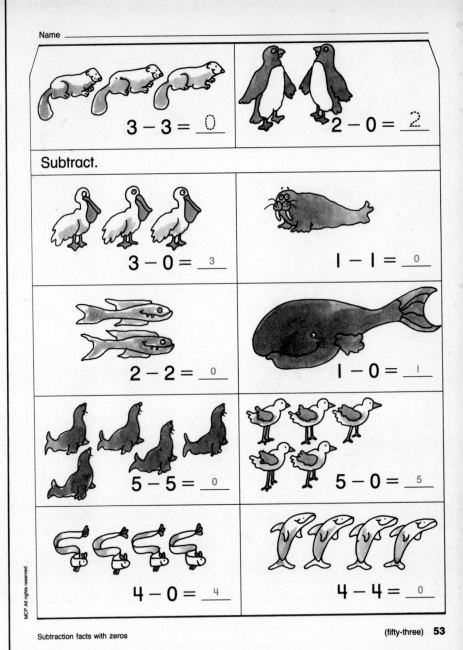

Name _____

$3 - 3 = 0$

$2 - 0 = 2$

Subtract.

$3 - 0 = 3$

$1 - 1 = 0$

$2 - 2 = 0$

$1 - 0 = 1$

$5 - 5 = 0$

$5 - 0 = 5$

$4 - 0 = 4$

$4 - 4 = 0$

Subtraction facts with zeros

(fifty-three) **53**

MCP All rights reserved

Teaching page 53

Have students place 3 counters in their hands and tell
how many counters in all.(3) Tell students to take 3
counters away and tell how many are left in their
hands. (none) Have a student write **3 − 3 = 0** on the
board. Tell students to put 3 counters in their hands
again and take none away. Ask how many counters in
their hands. (3) Have a student write this subtraction
sentence on the board. (3 − 0 = 3) Repeat more
examples if needed for students to understand what
happens when "all" and "no" objects are taken away.

Have students tell a story about what could happen in
the first box, to match the problem. (ex: 3 sea otters
are swimming away.) Ask students to read the sentence
3 − 3 = 0 and trace the 0. Ask students to tell what is
happening in the picture of the penguins. (2 penguins

are there and no penguins are going away.) Have
students read the sentence, 2 − 0 = 2, and trace the 2.
Tell students to look at each picture and complete its
subtraction sentence.

53

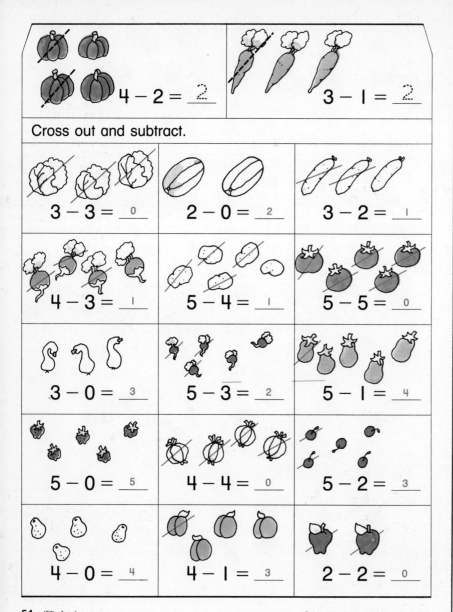

$4 - 2 = \underline{2}$

$3 - 1 = \underline{2}$

Cross out and subtract.

$3 - 3 = \underline{0}$

$2 - 0 = \underline{2}$

$3 - 2 = \underline{1}$

$4 - 3 = \underline{1}$

$5 - 4 = \underline{1}$

$5 - 5 = \underline{0}$

$3 - 0 = \underline{3}$

$5 - 3 = \underline{2}$

$5 - 1 = \underline{4}$

$5 - 0 = \underline{5}$

$4 - 4 = \underline{0}$

$5 - 2 = \underline{3}$

$4 - 0 = \underline{4}$

$4 - 1 = \underline{3}$

$2 - 2 = \underline{0}$

54 (fifty-four)

Subtraction facts, minuends through 5

Correcting Common Errors

Some students may be confused about the role of zero in subtraction. Have four students stand in front of the class. Ask, "How many students in all?" (4) Tell 4 students to sit down. Ask, "How many students went away?" (4) "How many are left in front of the class?" (0) Write $4 - 4 = 0$ on the chalkboard. Next, have 4 students come to the front of the class again. Ask, "Suppose zero students sit down. How many would be left in front of the class?" (4) Write $4 - 0 = 4$ on the chalkboard. Repeat the activity for other minuends through 5.

Enrichment

1. Use the code below to solve these problems: $G - A = G$; $C - C = A$; $E - A = E$; $F - D = B$.

   A B C D E F G
   0 1 2 3 4 5 6

2. Make subtraction fact cards with minuends through 5.

Teaching page 54

Have students tell how many pumpkins are in the first box. (4) Ask how many are crossed out. (2) Ask students to read the sentence (4 minus 2 equals 2) and trace the 2. Repeat the procedure for the second example. Tell students to count the number of objects in all, take away the number of objects crossed out and write the number left for each problem.

Extra Credit *Geometry*

Have the class make several sets of "Concentration" cards using the four basic shapes. Give each pair of students scissors, glue, and 16 unlined 3 × 5 cards. Also, give the group a sheet of red paper and blue paper with two circles, two squares, two rectangles, and two triangles traced on each. Ask students to cut out the shapes and glue one shape onto each card. There are several games they can play. Have one student arrange 8 red shapes facedown. Ask the other student to match identical shapes, looking at the cards two at a time and turning them face down if unmatched or keeping them if matched. Have them count the number of turns it takes to match all the cards. Now add the eight blue cards and allow students to match for shape alone, i.e. a red circle can match a blue circle or another red circle. Finally let them use all 16 cards.

54

Vertical Subtraction

pages 55-56

Objective

To subtract vertically from minuends through 5

Materials

5 counters
Sheet of paper

Mental Math

Which is greater?
1. 2 + 2 or 4 + 1 (4 + 1)
2. 1 + 0 or 0 + 0 (1 + 0)
3. 4 + 0 or 4 + 4 (4 + 4)
4. 0 + 6 + 1 or 2 + 7 (2 + 7)
5. 2 + 2 + 2 or 2 + 2 + 1
   (2 + 2 + 2)
6. 5 + 1 or 2 + 1 (5 + 1)
7. 6 + 2 or 4 + 3 (6 + 2)

Skill Review

Have students watch what you do and then write the subtraction sentence on the board to describe your action. Pick up 5 books and lay them down again. (5 − 5 = 0) Gather 3 pencils and keep them. (3 − 0 = 3) Continue with several more actions.

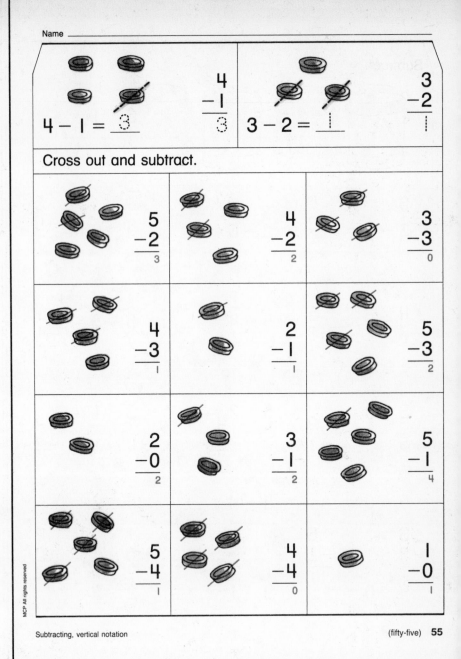

Subtracting, vertical notation

Teaching page 55

Write **4 − 1 = __** on the board. Ask how many in all. (4) Ask a student to draw 4 circles on the board. Ask how many are to be taken away. (1) Tell students we can cross out one circle to show it is taken away. Ask how many are left (3) and have a student write 3 in the blank. Repeat for 5 − 4 = __ and 4 − 2 = __.
Now write **4 − 1 = 3** on the board and **4** under it.
$$\begin{array}{r} 4 \\ -1 \\ \hline 3 \end{array}$$

Tell students that the latter is the "up and down" way to write this problem. Tell students that the top number tells us how many in all, the minus sign tells us to subtract and we write the number left under the line. Tell students we read both problems as "4 minus 1 equals 3". Give several examples of the horizontal

and vertical problems until the students are comfortable with them written either way.

Ask students to tell how many checkers are there, in all, in the first box. (4) Ask how many are taken away or crossed out. (1) Ask how many are left. (3) Have students trace the 3 in both problems. Repeat for the second example. Tell students that any 2 of the 3 checkers could have been crossed out to show that 1 checker was taken away. Have students cross out the checkers that are to be taken away in each problem and write the number left.

55

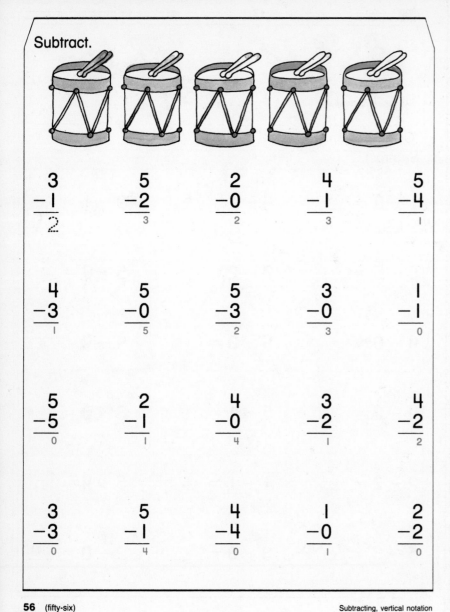

Subtract.

3 −1 = 2	5 −2 = 3	2 −0 = 2	4 −1 = 3	5 −4 = 1
4 −3 = 1	5 −0 = 5	5 −3 = 2	3 −0 = 3	1 −1 = 0
5 −5 = 0	2 −1 = 1	4 −0 = 4	3 −2 = 1	4 −2 = 2
3 −3 = 0	5 −1 = 4	4 −4 = 0	1 −0 = 1	2 −2 = 0

56 (fifty-six)

Subtracting, vertical notation

Correcting Common Errors

Some students may need extra practice subtracting vertically. Have students work in pairs with a worksheet that has a variety of subtraction problems in vertical form with minuends through 5. Have students draw large dots for the number indicated by the minuend. Then, they should cross out the dots represented by the number to be subtracted as indicated by the subtrahend. They can then count to find how many are left.

Enrichment

1. Draw a picture for this story: Mary had 2 dolls but 1 is hiding. How many dolls does she see?
2. Use fact cards for minuends through 5, to group according to fact families.
3. Tape a subtraction fact to each student's back. Have students give each other the answer to the facts as clues to guessing their facts.

Teaching page 56

Have students work the first problem and trace the 2. Allow the use of counters as needed. Tell students to complete the page.

Extra Credit   *Numeration*

Draw a simple tree on a piece of tagboard or on the board. Cut cherries from red paper, and cut 11 baskets from brown paper. On each cherry write a math fact whose answer is 0 through 10. Label each basket with numbers from 0 through 10. A student picks a cherry from the tree, orally answers the math fact and then places the cherry on top of the correct basket. This can be a large group or a small group activity.

Minuends through 5

pages 57-58

Objective

To practice subtraction facts for minuends through 5

Materials

5 counters
Sheet of paper

Mental Math

Which is less?
1. 5 + 2 or 5 + 3 (5 + 2)
2. 4 + 1 or 4 + 0 (4 + 0)
3. 3 + 3 or 4 + 3 (3 + 3)
4. 5 + 4 or 5 + 5 (5 + 4)
5. 2 + 1 or 1 + 1 (1 + 1)
6. 2 + 1 or 2 + 2 (2 + 1)
7. 4 + 1 or 3 + 3 (4 + 1)

Skill Review

Ask students to watch closely as you place 4 books in a stack. Now take 3 books away. Ask a student to write a subtraction problem on the board for what you did. (4 − 3 = 1) Have another student write the problem vertically. Act out other situations and have students write the problems both vertically and horizontally.

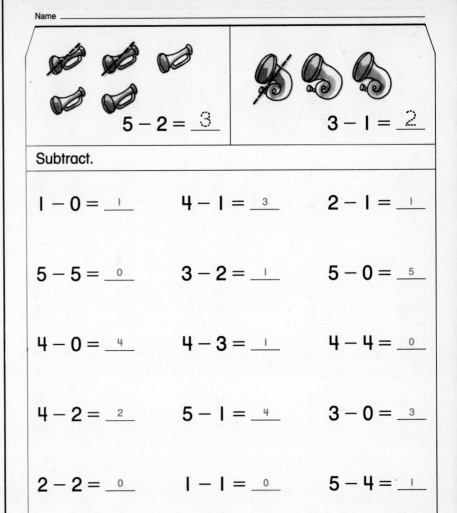

Name _____

$5 - 2 = \underline{3}$

$3 - 1 = \underline{2}$

Subtract.

$1 - 0 = \underline{1}$ $4 - 1 = \underline{3}$ $2 - 1 = \underline{1}$

$5 - 5 = \underline{0}$ $3 - 2 = \underline{1}$ $5 - 0 = \underline{5}$

$4 - 0 = \underline{4}$ $4 - 3 = \underline{1}$ $4 - 4 = \underline{0}$

$4 - 2 = \underline{2}$ $5 - 1 = \underline{4}$ $3 - 0 = \underline{3}$

$2 - 2 = \underline{0}$ $1 - 1 = \underline{0}$ $5 - 4 = \underline{1}$

$5 - 3 = \underline{2}$ $3 - 3 = \underline{0}$ $2 - 0 = \underline{2}$

Practice, minuends through 5   (fifty-seven) **57**

Teaching page 57

Have students tell what 5 minus 2 is (3) and trace the 3. Repeat for 3 − 1 = 2. Have students complete the page, using counters if desired.

Subtract.

4 −1 ___ 3	5 −3 ___ 2	2 −1 ___ 1	4 −3 ___ 1	3 −0 ___ 3
5 −0 ___ 5	3 −1 ___ 2	5 −5 ___ 0	1 −0 ___ 1	5 −1 ___ 4
2 −2 ___ 0	4 −0 ___ 4	1 −1 ___ 0	5 −2 ___ 3	3 −3 ___ 0
4 −4 ___ 0	3 −2 ___ 1	4 −2 ___ 2	2 −0 ___ 2	5 −4 ___ 1

Practice, minuends through 5

Correcting Common Errors

Students may have difficulty learning the subtraction facts with minuends through 5. Have them practice by using fact cards with the facts without the answers on one side and the facts with the answers on the other. Have them work in pairs quizzing each other using these fact cards.

Enrichment

1. In pairs use cards:

0	5	4
3	1	2

   One partner shows a subtraction fact for minuends through 5. The other lays a counter or marker on the answer.

2. Act out 5 Little Mice.
   5 little mice
   went out to play,
   picking up bread crumbs
   along the way.
   Along came a tomcat
   sleek and black,
   and 4 scared mice
   came running back.

   Continue to subtract one mouse for each new stanza until no mice are left.

Teaching page 58

Work the first two problems with students and have them complete the page independently.

Extra Credit *Counting*

Students can complete this simplified scavenger hunt independently or in pairs. Have only a small group of students work on the "hunt" at one time. Prior to class, assemble between five and ten "counting boxes." In each, place a different number of objects, up to ten. Items could include crayons, paper clips, pine cones, buttons, etc. Place the boxes around the room so that they are inconspicuous, but not totally hidden. To begin, provide students with a tally sheet picturing each of the objects they will be counting. Tell students that they will be going on a special hunt to find these objects. Students are to find each box, count the items, write the correct amount next to the matching picture on their paper, and replace the items. When the activity is completed bring the boxes together in front of the class, choose students to count the objects aloud, and have the others check their answers.

Minuends of 6 and 7

pages 59-60

Objective

To subtract from minuends through 7

Materials

35" Yarn ring
7 counters
Sheet of paper
Coat hanger and 7 clothespins per pair of students

Mental Math

Give the addition fact family for:

1. 2 + 2 (4)
2. 0 + 1 (1)
3. 5 + 0 (5)
4. 0 + 0 (0)
5. 1 + 1 (2)
6. 2 + 1 (3)

Skill Review

Say, "5 tired children came through the door; 1 fell asleep, then there were (4)." And "4 big elephants running from a bee; 1 fell behind, then there were (3)." Have students help make up silly stanzas for 3 − 1 = 2 (3 little girls with nothing to do; 1 found her work, then there were (2).) and 5 − 4 = 1 (5 purple cows grazing in the sun; 4 stopped eating, then there was (1).)

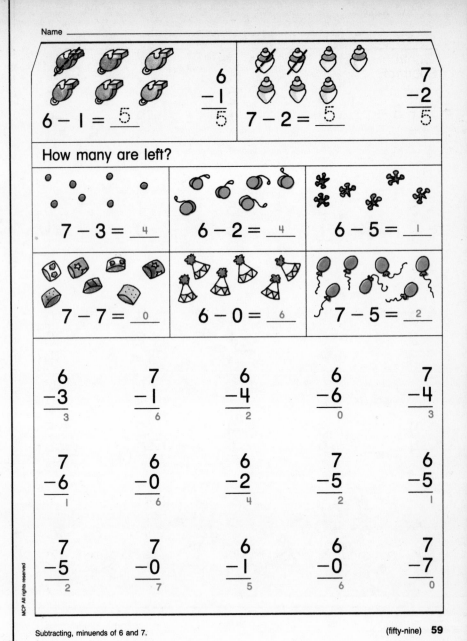

Name _____

$6 - 1 = \underline{5}$ $\begin{array}{r} 6 \\ -1 \\ \hline 5 \end{array}$ $7 - 2 = \underline{5}$ $\begin{array}{r} 7 \\ -2 \\ \hline 5 \end{array}$

How many are left?

$7 - 3 = \underline{4}$ $6 - 2 = \underline{4}$ $6 - 5 = \underline{1}$

$7 - 7 = \underline{0}$ $6 - 0 = \underline{6}$ $7 - 5 = \underline{2}$

$\begin{array}{r} 6 \\ -3 \\ \hline 3 \end{array}$ $\begin{array}{r} 7 \\ -1 \\ \hline 6 \end{array}$ $\begin{array}{r} 6 \\ -4 \\ \hline 2 \end{array}$ $\begin{array}{r} 6 \\ -6 \\ \hline 0 \end{array}$ $\begin{array}{r} 7 \\ -4 \\ \hline 3 \end{array}$

$\begin{array}{r} 7 \\ -6 \\ \hline 1 \end{array}$ $\begin{array}{r} 6 \\ -0 \\ \hline 6 \end{array}$ $\begin{array}{r} 6 \\ -2 \\ \hline 4 \end{array}$ $\begin{array}{r} 7 \\ -5 \\ \hline 2 \end{array}$ $\begin{array}{r} 6 \\ -5 \\ \hline 1 \end{array}$

$\begin{array}{r} 7 \\ -5 \\ \hline 2 \end{array}$ $\begin{array}{r} 7 \\ -0 \\ \hline 7 \end{array}$ $\begin{array}{r} 6 \\ -1 \\ \hline 5 \end{array}$ $\begin{array}{r} 6 \\ -0 \\ \hline 6 \end{array}$ $\begin{array}{r} 7 \\ -7 \\ \hline 0 \end{array}$

Subtracting, minuends of 6 and 7.   (fifty-nine) **59**

Teaching page 59

Have students form a yarn ring and place 6 counters inside. Ask how many counters in all. (6) Tell students to take 1 away and tell how many are left. (5) Ask a student to write the subtraction sentence on the board. (6 − 1 = 5) Have another student write the problem vertically. Repeat procedure for 6 counters take away 3 counters, 6 − 4, 6 − 6, 6 − 5, 6 − 0, 6 − 2. Give students a seventh counter and continue the procedure for 7 − 6, etc. Tell students to look at the 6 whistles. Ask how many are crossed out. (1) Ask how many are left. (5) Have students trace the 5's. Repeat for 7 tops and have students complete the page.

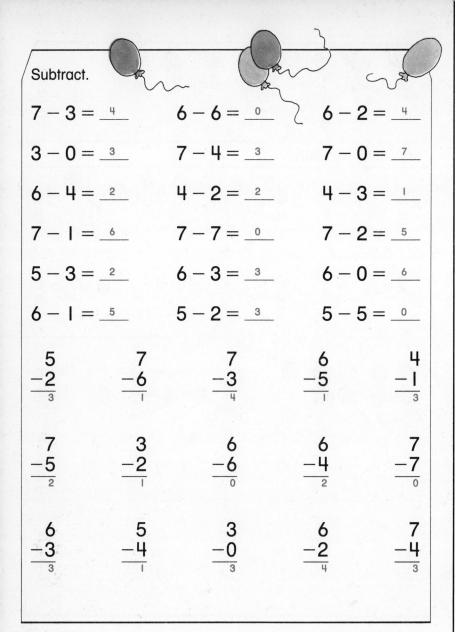

Subtract.

$7 - 3 = \underline{4}$ $6 - 6 = \underline{0}$ $6 - 2 = \underline{4}$

$3 - 0 = \underline{3}$ $7 - 4 = \underline{3}$ $7 - 0 = \underline{7}$

$6 - 4 = \underline{2}$ $4 - 2 = \underline{2}$ $4 - 3 = \underline{1}$

$7 - 1 = \underline{6}$ $7 - 7 = \underline{0}$ $7 - 2 = \underline{5}$

$5 - 3 = \underline{2}$ $6 - 3 = \underline{3}$ $6 - 0 = \underline{6}$

$6 - 1 = \underline{5}$ $5 - 2 = \underline{3}$ $5 - 5 = \underline{0}$

| $\begin{array}{r}5\\-2\\\hline 3\end{array}$ | $\begin{array}{r}7\\-6\\\hline 1\end{array}$ | $\begin{array}{r}7\\-3\\\hline 4\end{array}$ | $\begin{array}{r}6\\-5\\\hline 1\end{array}$ | $\begin{array}{r}4\\-1\\\hline 3\end{array}$ |

| $\begin{array}{r}7\\-5\\\hline 2\end{array}$ | $\begin{array}{r}3\\-2\\\hline 1\end{array}$ | $\begin{array}{r}6\\-6\\\hline 0\end{array}$ | $\begin{array}{r}6\\-4\\\hline 2\end{array}$ | $\begin{array}{r}7\\-7\\\hline 0\end{array}$ |

| $\begin{array}{r}6\\-3\\\hline 3\end{array}$ | $\begin{array}{r}5\\-4\\\hline 1\end{array}$ | $\begin{array}{r}3\\-0\\\hline 3\end{array}$ | $\begin{array}{r}6\\-2\\\hline 4\end{array}$ | $\begin{array}{r}7\\-4\\\hline 3\end{array}$ |

Subtracting, minuends through 7

Correcting Common Errors

For students who need practice subtracting from minuends through 7, have them work with partners and use counters. For each fact, they use the counters to represent the minuend and then take away the number that is indicated. They count those that remain to find the answer to how many are left. Be sure that the students write and read aloud each fact that they model.

Enrichment

1. Make subtraction fact cards for minuends of 6 and 7.
2. Draw a picture showing $6 - 4 = 2$.
3. Write all subtraction and addition facts which have sums or minuends of 7.

Teaching page 60

Have students complete each subtraction problem. Allow use of counters as needed.

Extra Credit   *Logic*

Bring in the following: five pictures of a breed of dog each student would recognize, five pictures of other breeds, and five pictures of mammals (but not dogs). You may want to paste each picture on a piece of heavy paper. Ask students to sort the pictures. Eventually you want them to arrange three piles, but let them do it in any logical way at first. When they have arrived at three categories, label the string loops for example: collies, dogs, animals. Have students arrange the pictures in the proper loops. Now take a collie and put it in with the dogs. Ask if the labels have to be changed. (no) Put the collie in with the animals and ask if the labels should be changed. (no) Replace the collie. Take one of the animals and put it in with the dogs. Ask if the label is still correct. (no) Replace the animal. Take one of the dogs and put it in with the collies. Ask if the label is correct. (no)

60

Minuends of 8 and 9

pages 61-62

Objective

To subtract from minuends of 8 and 9

Materials

Coat hanger and 9 clothespins per pair of students
9 counters
35 inches of yarn
Sheet of paper

Mental Math

Name the number that is:
1. 1 more than 4 − 3 (2)
2. 1 plus 2 take away 3 (0)
3. 2 minus 1 plus 3 (4)
4. 1 less than 10 (9)
5. 0 minus 0 (0)
6. 0 plus 0 (0)

Skill Review

Draw on the board:

Tell students the trucks need cargo. The 7 truck carries subtraction facts for 7 and the 6 truck carries subtraction facts for 6. Ask students to prepare cargo for the trucks by writing subtraction facts under the trucks. (7: 7 − 0 = 7, 8 − 1 = 7, 9 − 2 = 7, 10 − 3 = 7; 6: 6 − 0 = 6, 7 − 1 = 6, 8 − 2 = 6, 9 − 3 = 6, 10 − 4 = 6)

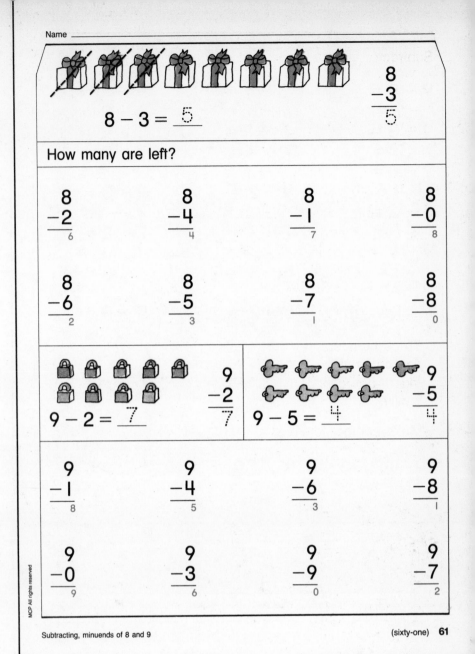

Name _____

$8 - 3 = 5$

$\begin{array}{r} 8 \\ -3 \\ \hline 5 \end{array}$

How many are left?

$\begin{array}{r} 8 \\ -2 \\ \hline 6 \end{array}$ $\begin{array}{r} 8 \\ -4 \\ \hline 4 \end{array}$ $\begin{array}{r} 8 \\ -1 \\ \hline 7 \end{array}$ $\begin{array}{r} 8 \\ -0 \\ \hline 8 \end{array}$

$\begin{array}{r} 8 \\ -6 \\ \hline 2 \end{array}$ $\begin{array}{r} 8 \\ -5 \\ \hline 3 \end{array}$ $\begin{array}{r} 8 \\ -7 \\ \hline 1 \end{array}$ $\begin{array}{r} 8 \\ -8 \\ \hline 0 \end{array}$

$9 - 2 = 7$ $\begin{array}{r} 9 \\ -2 \\ \hline 7 \end{array}$ $9 - 5 = 4$ $\begin{array}{r} 9 \\ -5 \\ \hline 4 \end{array}$

$\begin{array}{r} 9 \\ -1 \\ \hline 8 \end{array}$ $\begin{array}{r} 9 \\ -4 \\ \hline 5 \end{array}$ $\begin{array}{r} 9 \\ -6 \\ \hline 3 \end{array}$ $\begin{array}{r} 9 \\ -8 \\ \hline 1 \end{array}$

$\begin{array}{r} 9 \\ -0 \\ \hline 9 \end{array}$ $\begin{array}{r} 9 \\ -3 \\ \hline 6 \end{array}$ $\begin{array}{r} 9 \\ -9 \\ \hline 0 \end{array}$ $\begin{array}{r} 9 \\ -7 \\ \hline 2 \end{array}$

Subtracting, minuends of 8 and 9   (sixty-one) **61**

Teaching page 61

Group students in pairs giving each a coat hanger and 8 clothespins. Have students place 8 clothespins toward the left side of the hanger and tell how many in all. (8) Have students move 1 pin to the far right and tell how many were taken away. (1) Ask how many pins are left. (7) Have a student write the sentence on the board (8 − 1 = 7) and another student write it vertically. Repeat the procedure for 8 − 5, 8 − 4, 8 − 3, 8 − 2, 8 − 6, 8 − 7, 8 − 8. Give each pair a ninth clothespin and repeat the procedure for 9 − 1, etc.

Have students find the boxes at the top of the page and tell how many in all. (8) Ask how many are to be taken away. (3) Tell students to cross out 3 boxes. Ask how many are left. (5) Have students trace the 5's and

complete the subtraction facts for 8. Go through the padlocks problem similarly. Help students complete the keys problem. Tell students to complete the page.

61

Subtract.

$9 - 0 = \underline{9}$ $8 - 7 = \underline{1}$ $8 - 5 = \underline{3}$

$9 - 3 = \underline{6}$ $9 - 4 = \underline{5}$ $9 - 6 = \underline{3}$

$9 - 8 = \underline{1}$ $9 - 7 = \underline{2}$ $8 - 2 = \underline{6}$

$8 - 2 = \underline{6}$ $9 - 5 = \underline{4}$ $8 - 4 = \underline{4}$

$9 - 9 = \underline{0}$ $9 - 3 = \underline{6}$ $9 - 8 = \underline{1}$

FIELD TRIP

Three numbers can be used to make a number family.

$\begin{matrix} 3 & 2 \\ & 5 \end{matrix}$

$3 + 2 = 5$ $5 - 2 = 3$

$2 + 3 = 5$ $5 - 3 = 2$

Make number families.

$\begin{matrix} 4 & 2 \\ & 6 \end{matrix}$

$\underline{4} + \underline{2} = 6$ $\underline{6} - \underline{2} = 2$

$\underline{2} + \underline{4} = 6$ $\underline{6} - \underline{4} = 4$

$\begin{matrix} 4 & 3 \\ & 7 \end{matrix}$

$\underline{4} + \underline{3} = 7$ $\underline{7} - \underline{4} = 3$

$\underline{3} + \underline{4} = 7$ $\underline{7} - \underline{3} = 4$

Subtracting, minuends of 8 and 9

Correcting Common Errors

For students who need more practice subtracting from minuends of 8 and 9, have them work in pairs. Have them use a piece of yarn to make a ring on their work area and place 8 counters inside. Ask, "How many counters are inside the ring?" (8) Tell students to take 1 counter away. Ask, "How many counters are left inside the ring?" (7) Have students write the subtraction fact $8 - 1 = 7$. Have students continue the procedure starting with 8 counters inside the ring and then taking away 2, 3, 4, 5, 6, 7, and 8 counters, writing the subtraction fact each time. Then have them start with 9 counters and repeat the activity.

Enrichment

1. Make subtraction fact cards for minuends of 8 and 9.
2. Draw a picture to show some objects taken away from 8.
3. Group subtraction fact cards in families for 8 and 9.

Teaching page 62

Have students work the problems in the 3 columns at the top of the page.

Field Trip

Tell students the numbers 3, 5 and 2 can be used to make a number family of 2 addition and 2 subtraction sentences. Have students trace the numbers in the examples and read the 4 sentences. Encourage them to complete the number facts for the set of three numbers in each cloud. Perhaps some students may want to create their own fact families illustrating them with markers.

Extra Credit *Sets*

Take a field trip to a grocery store. Point out how foods are grouped into sets. Ask students what subsets are in the dairy section? the meat section? Show students foods that are packaged in sets, such as hot dogs, eggs, hamburger buns, etc. Ask stockers to tell about their work, especially how the foods are shipped and priced in sets.

If possible, purchase several foods from each food group such as crackers, cheese, fruit and lunch meats. Students can help assemble a snack tray in the classroom.

Minuends
6 through 9

pages 63-64

Objective

To subtract from minuends 6
through 9

Materials

9 counters
Sheet of paper
Yarn ring
Number cards 1 through 9

Mental Math

What is:
1. 7 take away 3 (4)
2. 8 minus 5 (3)
3. 6 take away 6 (0)
4. 4 take away 2 (2)
5. 9 minus 8 (1)
6. 5 minus 1 (4)
7. 0 minus 0 (0)

Skill Review

Write **7 − 3 =** ___ on the board. Ask
students how many in all (7) and
have them place 7 counters in their
yarn rings. Ask how many do we
take away? (3) Ask students to show
their number card to tell how many
are left. (4) Continue for 6 − 4,
8 − 7, 9 − 2, 8 − 5, 9 − 1. Allow
use of counters as needed.

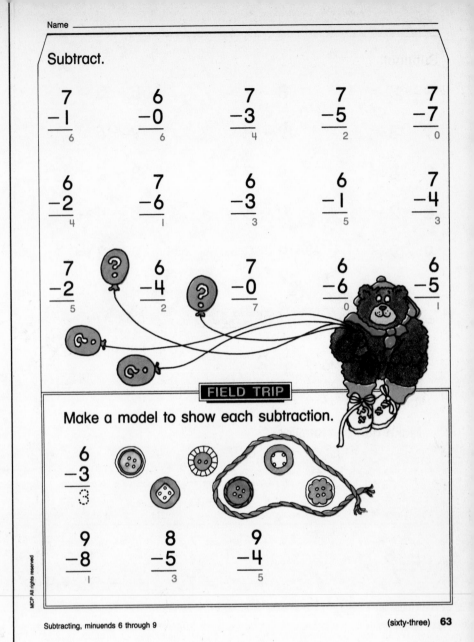

Subtract.

7	6	7	7	7
−1	−0	−3	−5	−7
6	6	4	2	0

6	7	6	6	7
−2	−6	−3	−1	−4
4	1	3	5	3

7	6	7	6	6
−2	−4	−0	−6	−5
5	2	7	0	1

FIELD TRIP

Make a model to show each subtraction.

6
−3
3

9	8	9
−8	−5	−4
1	3	5

Subtracting, minuends 6 through 9   (sixty-three) **63**

Teaching page 63

Have students complete each problem on the top half
of the page.

Field Trip

Discuss with the students the paper model which
illustrates the fact 6 − 3 = 3. Be sure they understand
the meaning of the whole array of markers (the
minuend) the circled subset (the subtrahend), and
uncircled subset (the difference). Encourage them to
model each of the subtractions using actual markers
and a piece of yarn.

63

Subtract.

$9 - 2 = \underline{7}$ $9 - 6 = \underline{3}$ $8 - 6 = \underline{2}$

$8 - 4 = \underline{4}$ $8 - 7 = \underline{1}$ $9 - 4 = \underline{5}$

$9 - 4 = \underline{5}$ $8 - 5 = \underline{3}$ $8 - 3 = \underline{5}$

$9 - 1 = \underline{8}$ $9 - 7 = \underline{2}$ $9 - 9 = \underline{0}$

$8 - 0 = \underline{8}$ $9 - 5 = \underline{4}$ $9 - 8 = \underline{1}$

FIELD TRIP

Write a fact for each model.

| 5 | 4 | 9 |

$\begin{array}{r} 5 \\ +\ 4 \\ \hline 9 \end{array}$ $\begin{array}{r} 4 \\ +\ 5 \\ \hline 9 \end{array}$ $\begin{array}{r} 9 \\ -\ 4 \\ \hline 5 \end{array}$ $\begin{array}{r} 9 \\ -\ 5 \\ \hline 4 \end{array}$

Subtracting, minuends 6 through 9

Correcting Common Errors

For those students who continue to have difficulty subtracting from minuends of 6 through 9, have them practice using the "count back" strategy. For a fact such as $8 - 3$, have them start with 8 and count back three: 8 . . . 7, 6, 5. The answer is 5. This strategy is especially helpful when they are subtracting 1, 2, or 3.

Enrichment

1. Group fact cards for minuends 6 through 9 in families.
2. Show a fact card for minuends 6 through 9. Have a partner tell another subtraction fact in the same family.
3. Act out a subtraction fact for friends to guess.

Teaching page 64

Have students complete the problems on the top half of the page.

Field Trip

Encourage students to discover that 9 markers are adequate for modeling all 4 facts of the fact family of 5, 4, and 9. Be sure to discuss each of the models in the sample in terms of addends, sums, minuends, subtrahends, and differences. Encourage students to create their own models of other facts.

Extra Credit   *Applications*

Help the students learn important phone numbers and use the telephone in emergencies. Provide the students with toy telephones and the phone numbers of the local fire and police departments. Ask them to read the numbers and to copy them. Have them write their own phone numbers and addresses. Discuss with them how to make an emergency phone call. Have them practice making emergency calls and allow them to take turns being the police or firefighter, and the caller. Remind them to be sure to give all the information needed for the authorities to find their house.

Minuends through 10

pages 65-66

Objective

To subtract from minuends through 10

Materials

10 counters
Sheet of paper
Coat hanger and 10 clothespins per pair of students

Mental Math

Which equals 1?
1. 10 − 9 or 7 − 4 (10 − 9)
2. 0 − 0 or 2 − 1 (2 − 1)
3. 6 − 4 or 6 − 5 (6 − 5)
4. 5 − 4 or 6 − 2 (5 − 4)
5. 8 − 8 or 8 − 7 (8 − 7)
6. 3 − 1 or 3 − 2 (3 − 2)

Skill Review

Group students in pairs giving each a coat hanger and 9 clothespins. Have students place 9 clothespins toward the left side of the hanger and tell how many in all. (9) Have students move 3 pins to the far right and tell how many were taken away. (3) Ask how many pins are left. (6) Have a student write the sentence on the board (9 − 3 = 6) and another student write it vertically. Repeat the procedure for other facts for 8 and 9.

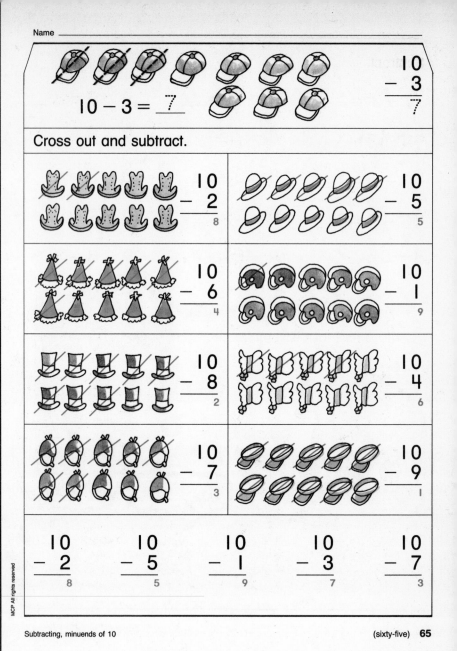

Subtracting, minuends of 10

(sixty-five) **65**

Teaching page 65

Ask students if they've ever been bowling or played a toy bowling game. Allow for several bowling stories to be shared. Draw on the board the regular, triangular formation of bowling pins.
Tell students the goal of bowling is to knock down the 10 pins. Ask students how many pins would have been knocked down if 6 were left. (4) Write
10 − 6 = 4 on the board. Tell students it is easiest in a bowling game to count the pins left standing and subtract that number from 10. Allow students to use counters to help figure the number of pins knocked down if 5 are left, if 9 are left, etc.

Have students count the baseball caps (10) and tell how many are to be taken away. (3) Have students trace the 3 baseball caps to be crossed out. Have students trace the 7's to show that 7 are left. Tell students to subtract the number of hats crossed out and write the number left in each box. Have students work the next 8 problems the same way. Then have students write the answers to the row of facts at the bottom of the page.

65

Subtract.

$7 - 1 = \underline{6}$ $\qquad$ $10 - 2 = \underline{8}$ $\qquad$ $9 - 5 = \underline{4}$

$8 - 2 = \underline{6}$ $\qquad$ $9 - 4 = \underline{5}$ $\qquad$ $8 - 6 = \underline{2}$

$9 - 2 = \underline{7}$ $\qquad$ $7 - 3 = \underline{4}$ $\qquad$ $10 - 8 = \underline{2}$

$10 - 3 = \underline{7}$ $\qquad$ $10 - 0 = \underline{10}$ $\qquad$ $7 - 5 = \underline{2}$

$7 - 4 = \underline{3}$ $\qquad$ $10 - 6 = \underline{4}$ $\qquad$ $9 - 6 = \underline{3}$

9	7	9	10	10
-8	-2	-0	-1	-4
1	5	9	9	6

10	8	9	7	8
-7	-3	-7	-6	-4
3	5	2	1	4

8	10	8	7	10
-7	-5	-5	-0	-9
1	5	3	7	1

Subtracting, minuends through 10

Correcting Common Errors

For students who have difficulty subtracting from 10, have them use their fingers to model the problems. For $10 - 4$, for example, they should hold up 10 fingers, fold down 4, and then count the fingers still up.

Enrichment

1. Draw a picture of bowling pins, some standing, some knocked down. Write number facts to tell what happened.
2. Trace around your hands on a sheet of paper and decorate all but 7 fingers with rings.

Teaching page 66

Have students write the correct number to complete each problem.

Extra Credit *Sets*

Have students cut pictures from magazines of things that belong in sets. Some possible sets are: jungle animals, pets, farm animals, cars, and snack foods, etc. Have students paste the pictures on poster board labeled with the identifying name of the set, and hang them in the classroom. As an extension of this activity, distribute a checklist for children to count any sets they can find at home. Include a list of common household items such as: chairs, beds, sinks, people, clocks, and pets. The next day discuss and compare the results of the checklists.

Minuends through 10¢

pages 67-68

Objective

To subtract from minuends through 10¢

Materials

10 real or punch-out pennies

Mental Math

How many?
1. 5 apples and 2 more (7)
2. 3 pears minus 1 pear (2)
3. 2 toys plus 2 more (4)
4. 2 pennies and 2 more (4¢)
5. 7 cars and 2 more (9)
6. 4 shirts minus 1 (3)
7. 3 cats but 3 run away (0)

Skill Review

Draw 3 circles on the board. Ask students how many in all. (3) Now write **1¢** in each circle and ask students how many cents in all. (3¢) Ask students what 3¢ means. (3 pennies) Write **3¢** on the board. Draw another penny and ask a student to write how many in all. (4¢) Draw 1 more penny and ask a student to write how many pennies in all. (5¢) Leave the 5 pennies on the board.

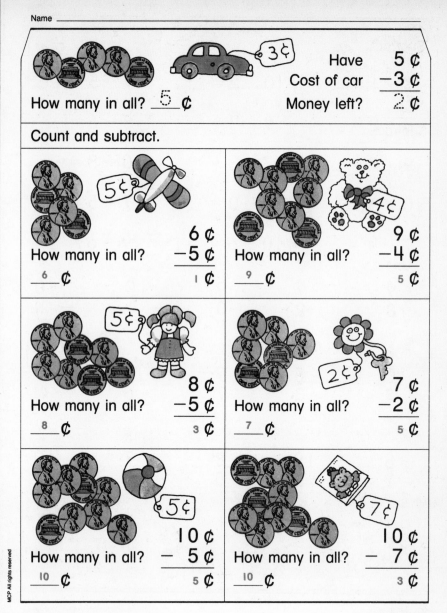

Name _____

How many in all? 5 ¢

Have 5 ¢
Cost of car −3 ¢
Money left? 2 ¢

Count and subtract.

How many in all? 6 ¢ −5 ¢
6 ¢ — 1 ¢

How many in all? 9 ¢ −4 ¢
9 ¢ — 5 ¢

How many in all? 8 ¢ −5 ¢
8 ¢ — 3 ¢

How many in all? 7 ¢ −2 ¢
7 ¢ — 5 ¢

How many in all? 10 ¢ − 5 ¢
10 ¢ — 5 ¢

How many in all? 10 ¢ − 7 ¢
10 ¢ — 3 ¢

Subtracting money, minuends through 10¢ (sixty-seven) **67**

Teaching page 67

Draw 5 more pennies on the board. Tell students to look at the first 5 pennies and count on from 5¢ and tell how many cents in all. (10¢) Tell students to suppose that Zeke had 10¢ and then gave 5¢ to his sister. Ask a student to cross out 5 of the pennies to show they were taken away. Ask how much money Zeke would have left. (5¢)

Write **10¢ − 5¢ = 5¢** and **10¢** on the board.

$$\begin{array}{r} 10¢ \\ -\ 5¢ \\ \hline 5¢ \end{array}$$

Now tell students another story of Susan shopping with 9¢ and buying some gum for 5¢. Ask a student to write the problem on the board. (9¢ − 5¢ = 4¢) Have another student write the problem vertically. Tell other stories and have students write the problems on the board.

Tell students to count the pennies available to buy the car at the top of the page. (5¢) Tell students to trace the 5 to tell how many pennies in all. Ask how much the car costs. (3¢) Ask how much would be left if we had 5¢ and bought the car for 3¢. (2¢) Have students trace the 2. Go through the next problem with students and then have them complete the page independently.

67

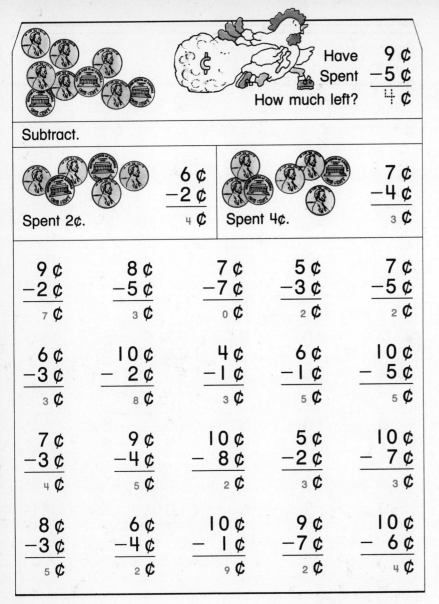

Have   9 ¢
Spent   −5 ¢
How much left?   4 ¢

Subtract.

Spent 2¢.
6 ¢
−2 ¢
4 ¢

Spent 4¢.
7 ¢
−4 ¢
3 ¢

9 ¢	8 ¢	7 ¢	5 ¢	7 ¢
−2 ¢	−5 ¢	−7 ¢	−3 ¢	−5 ¢
7 ¢	3 ¢	0 ¢	2 ¢	2 ¢

6 ¢	10 ¢	4 ¢	6 ¢	10 ¢
−3 ¢	− 2 ¢	−1 ¢	−1 ¢	− 5 ¢
3 ¢	8 ¢	3 ¢	5 ¢	5 ¢

7 ¢	9 ¢	10 ¢	5 ¢	10 ¢
−3 ¢	−4 ¢	− 8 ¢	−2 ¢	− 7 ¢
4 ¢	5 ¢	2 ¢	3 ¢	3 ¢

8 ¢	6 ¢	10 ¢	9 ¢	10 ¢
−3 ¢	−4 ¢	− 1 ¢	−7 ¢	− 6 ¢
5 ¢	2 ¢	9 ¢	2 ¢	4 ¢

68 (sixty-eight)

Subtracting money, minuends through 10¢

Correcting Common Errors

If students have difficulty subtracting with money, have them use pennies or play money to represent the minuend in each problem. They should remove the number of coins indicated by the subtrahend and count to find the amount left.

Enrichment

1. Use 10 pennies to purchase an item in the classroom store and tell how much money is left.
2. Purchase an item in the classroom store for less than 10¢. Count on to 10¢ when checking your change.
3. Start with 10 pennies with heads up. Turn 5 pennies tails up to show 10¢ − 5¢ = 5¢. Do other problems with heads and tails.

Teaching page 68

Ask students how many pennies are in the first box. (9¢) Ask how many are spent. (5¢) Have students tell how many are left. (4¢) Have students trace the 4. Go through the next 2 boxes with the students and have them write the number to tell how many pennies are left. Remind students that the cent sign is used to show we are talking about money. Have students use pennies, if they choose, to work the problems to the end of the page.

Extra Credit *Numeration*

Have a group of students make a fishing game for the class by cutting out fish from construction paper, and writing a math fact on each fish. Place the fish in a bowl. One student draws a fish from the bowl and orally gives the fact. Have a student at the board write down the fact, the answer and all the related facts (ex: 2 + 7 = 9, 7 + 2 = 9, 9 − 2 = 7, 9 − 7 = 2). The game continues until all the fish are caught.

68

Subtraction Practice

pages 69-70

Objective

To practice adding and subtracting for sums and minuends through 10

Materials

10 counters
Sheet of paper
*Fact cards for sums and minuends through 10

Mental Math

Name the number that equals:
1. 4 + 4 (8)
2. 6 − 4 (2)
3. 0 + 9 (9)
4. 8 − 0 (8)
5. 9 − 2 (7)
6. 5 + 5 (10)
7. 7 − 4 (3)

Skill Review

Draw 6 circles on the board and write **1¢** in each. Ask how much money in all. (6¢) Ask students to count on as you draw 3 more pennies. Ask how much money in all. (9¢) Ask students how much of this money would be needed to buy a toy that costs 4¢. (4¢) Ask a student to cross out 4 pennies and tell how many pennies are left. (4)

Subtract.

$$8 - 2 = \underline{6} \qquad 10 - 3 = \underline{7} \qquad 4 - 3 = \underline{1}$$

$$9 - 5 = \underline{4} \qquad 7 - 6 = \underline{1} \qquad 6 - 1 = \underline{5}$$

$$5 - 2 = \underline{3} \qquad 9 - 2 = \underline{7} \qquad 8 - 6 = \underline{2}$$

$$8 - 7 = \underline{1} \qquad 3 - 1 = \underline{2} \qquad 10 - 2 = \underline{8}$$

$$6 - 0 = \underline{6} \qquad 7 - 4 = \underline{3} \qquad 8 - 5 = \underline{3}$$

$$9 - 6 = \underline{3} \qquad 4 - 2 = \underline{2} \qquad 9 - 1 = \underline{8}$$

| $\begin{array}{r} 7 \\ -5 \\ \hline 2 \end{array}$ | $\begin{array}{r} 10 \\ -8 \\ \hline 2 \end{array}$ | $\begin{array}{r} 4 \\ -1 \\ \hline 3 \end{array}$ | $\begin{array}{r} 7 \\ -3 \\ \hline 4 \end{array}$ | $\begin{array}{r} 5 \\ -5 \\ \hline 0 \end{array}$ | $\begin{array}{r} 10 \\ -1 \\ \hline 9 \end{array}$ |

| $\begin{array}{r} 8 \\ -1 \\ \hline 7 \end{array}$ | $\begin{array}{r} 10 \\ -9 \\ \hline 1 \end{array}$ | $\begin{array}{r} 8 \\ -4 \\ \hline 4 \end{array}$ | $\begin{array}{r} 10 \\ -4 \\ \hline 6 \end{array}$ | $\begin{array}{r} 8 \\ -3 \\ \hline 5 \end{array}$ | $\begin{array}{r} 9 \\ -3 \\ \hline 6 \end{array}$ |

| $\begin{array}{r} 10 \\ -5 \\ \hline 5 \end{array}$ | $\begin{array}{r} 9 \\ -7 \\ \hline 2 \end{array}$ | $\begin{array}{r} 6 \\ -3 \\ \hline 3 \end{array}$ | $\begin{array}{r} 10 \\ -7 \\ \hline 3 \end{array}$ | $\begin{array}{r} 7 \\ -7 \\ \hline 0 \end{array}$ | $\begin{array}{r} 10 \\ -4 \\ \hline 6 \end{array}$ |

Practice, minuends through 10

(sixty-nine) **69**

Teaching page 69

Have students read the first problem in the first column. (8 − 2 = __) Tell students to write the answers for each problem. Allow use of counters if needed.

Add.

3	5	0	4	4	6
+3	+5	+7	+6	+4	+1
6	10	7	10	8	7

2	7	2	2	5	8
+8	+2	+5	+4	+3	+1
10	9	7	6	8	9

5	1	6	3	3	1
+4	+9	+2	+4	+7	+7
9	10	8	7	10	8

Subtract.

8	5	10	8	6	5
−3	−1	− 5	−6	−3	−5
5	4	5	2	3	0

10	6	7	4	9	9
− 6	−5	−2	−2	−1	−7
4	1	5	2	8	2

7	10	6	9	10	7
−7	− 3	−1	−5	− 9	−3
0	7	5	4	1	4

Practice, adding and subtracting

Correcting Common Errors

Some students may need additional practice with addition and subtraction facts. With partners have them practice with mixed addition and subtraction fact cards. Have them take turns quizzing each other using the cards. Each responder should say all three numbers in the fact as the answer; e.g., for 8 − 3 = □, the student should say, "8 minus 3 equals 5," and not just "5."

Enrichment

1. Tell stories using numbers 0 through 10. Tell if the problem requires you to add or subtract. (ex. Mary had 6 rings but lost 2−subtract)
2. Play "What's My Number?" with addition and subtraction facts for sums and minuends through 10. Tell the number that is the sum of 8 and 2, etc.
3. Work timed tests on addition and subtraction facts for sums and minuends through 10.

Teaching page 70

Tell students that the top 3 rows of problems ask them to add, while they will be subtracting in the bottom 3 rows. Have students complete the page independently.

Extra Credit *Applications*

Discuss with students how playground games depend on counting: playing hopscotch, jumping rope, bouncing a ball. Team games require counting in order to keep score. Board games require counting squares or the dots on the dice. Mark off one section of the chalkboard and ask students to list as many games as they can think of that require counting. Let the list grow for at least a day, allowing students time to think of the ways their games require counting. Then ask students to put their name beside one of the games. Have each student demonstrate how that game is played and how counting is used. Encourage them to bring games from home. See if anyone can think of a game that does not use counting.

Chapter Review

pages 71-72

Objectives

To review subtraction facts for minuends through 10
To maintain skills learned in Chapters 1 and 2

Materials

10 counters
Sheet of paper
Set of subtraction fact cards per 2 students

Mental Math

Count on from:
1. 6¢ to 8¢ (6¢, 7¢, 8¢)
2. 5¢ to 10¢
3. 1¢ to 4¢
4. 3¢ to 9¢
5. 5¢ to 9¢
6. 2¢ to 5¢
7. 7¢ to 10¢

Skill Review

Group students in pairs with subtraction fact cards for minuends through 10. Have one student flash cards for second student to give the answer as quickly as possible.

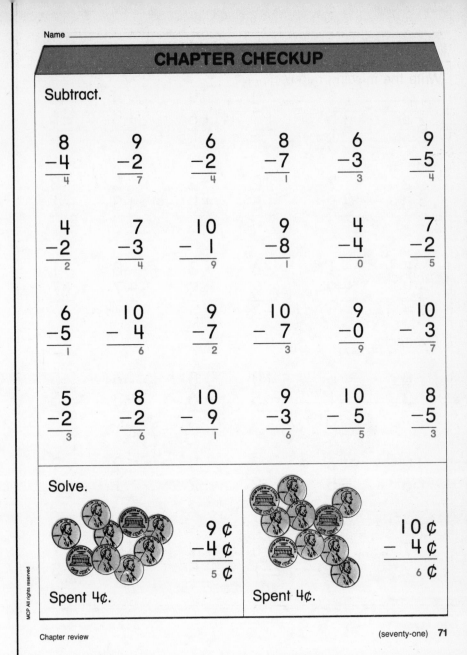

CHAPTER CHECKUP

Subtract.

8 −4 = 4	9 −2 = 7	6 −2 = 4	8 −7 = 1	6 −3 = 3	9 −5 = 4
4 −2 = 2	7 −3 = 4	10 −1 = 9	9 −8 = 1	4 −4 = 0	7 −2 = 5
6 −5 = 1	10 −4 = 6	9 −7 = 2	10 −7 = 3	9 −0 = 9	10 −3 = 7
5 −2 = 3	8 −2 = 6	10 −9 = 1	9 −3 = 6	10 −5 = 5	8 −5 = 3

Solve.

9 ¢
−4 ¢
5 ¢

Spent 4¢.

10 ¢
− 4 ¢
6 ¢

Spent 4¢.

Chapter review

(seventy-one) **71**

Teaching page 71

Have students write the number left in each problem. In the 2 problems at the bottom of the page, have students cross out the number of pennies spent, and write the amount of money left.

ROUNDUP REVIEW

Write the missing numbers.

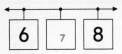

| 6 | 7 | 8 |

| 8 | 9 | 10 |

| 4 | 5 | 6 |

Add.

$$\begin{array}{r} 3 \\ +3 \\ \hline 6 \end{array} \qquad \begin{array}{r} 6 \\ +2 \\ \hline 8 \end{array} \qquad \begin{array}{r} 1 \\ +3 \\ \hline 4 \end{array} \qquad \begin{array}{r} 7 \\ +3 \\ \hline 10 \end{array} \qquad \begin{array}{r} 2 \\ +1 \\ \hline 3 \end{array} \qquad \begin{array}{r} 3 \\ +4 \\ \hline 7 \end{array}$$

Subtract.

$10 - 8 = \underline{2}$ $8 - 3 = \underline{5}$ $9 - 6 = \underline{3}$

$7 - 3 = \underline{4}$ $7 - 7 = \underline{0}$ $6 - 4 = \underline{2}$

$10 - 5 = \underline{5}$ $5 - 0 = \underline{5}$ $7 - 4 = \underline{3}$

Solve.

How much money? __7__ ¢

How much money? __5__ ¢

$$\begin{array}{r} 6 ¢ \\ +3 ¢ \\ \hline 9 ¢ \end{array}$$

Spent 4¢.

$$\begin{array}{r} 8 ¢ \\ -4 ¢ \\ \hline 4 ¢ \end{array}$$

72   (seventy-two)

Cumulative review

Enrichment

1. Fill in the missing numbers:

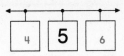

| 8 | +0 | 8 | −1 | (7) | +2 | (9) | −1 | (8) |

2. Work in pairs with a die. Throw the die and subtract the number thrown from 10.

3. Work in pairs. Throw two dice and tell which number is greater. Variations: Tell which number is less, and subtract the smaller number from larger.

Teaching page 72

Tell students to fill in the missing numbers at the top of the page. Then have students complete the page.

This page reviews writing numbers in sequence; addition and subtraction facts through 10; and counting, adding and subtracting money.

72

Fact Families

pages 73-74

Objective

To recognize addition fact pairs for sums through 6 and related subtraction facts for minuends through 6

Materials

6 counters
Sheet of paper
Paper cup

Mental Math

What number equals:
1. 7 + 2 (9)
2. 9 − 2 (7)
3. 5 + 4 (9)
4. 9 − 5 (4)
5. 3 + 2 (5)
6. 5 − 3 (2)

Skill Review

Draw on the board three circles with spokes and a center hub. Put the number 6, 7, 8 in each hub. Ask students to write subtraction facts between the spokes of the wheels to equal the number on the hub.

(10 − 4)	(10 − 3)	(10 − 2)
(9 − 3)	(9 − 2)	(9 − 1)
(8 − 2)	(8 − 1)	(8 − 0)
(7 − 1)	(7 − 0)	
(6 − 0)		

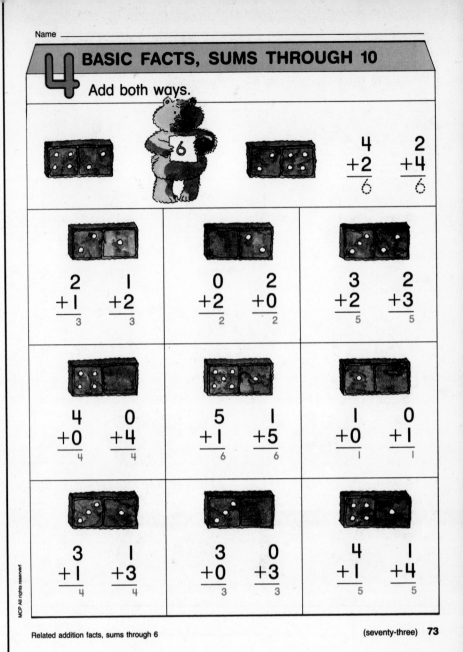

Related addition facts, sums through 6

(seventy-three) **73**

Teaching page 73

Have students fold their papers in half. Tell students to open the paper and draw a line along the crease. Tell students to count out 5 counters and lay some of the 5 on one side of the line and some on the other side. Now write **2 + 3 = 5** on the board and tell students that this sentence is one way to show 5. Ask if any students made 5 with a 2 and a 3. If a student does not volunteer that 3 + 2 = 5 also, write the latter on the board under 2 + 3 = 5 and tell students that these are both names for 5. Ask if anyone found yet another way to add 2 numbers to make 5. Repeat this question until all possible "addend pairs" have been discovered and written horizontally and vertically on the board. (5 + 0 = 5, 0 + 5 = 5, 4 + 1 = 5, 1 + 4 = 5)

Ask students to tell what the bear wants to know. (which domino matches his number 6) Ask students to answer the bear's question. (both equal 6) Have students read both problems and trace the 6's. Now tell students to look at each domino and write the sums for the problems under each.

73

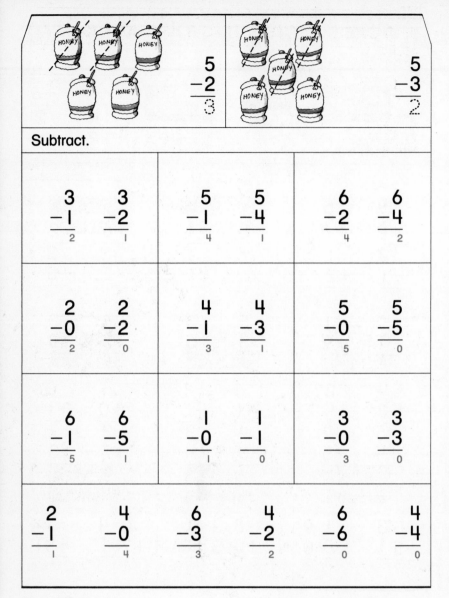

Subtract.

3 -1 2	3 -2 1	5 -1 4	5 -4 1	6 -2 4	6 -4 2
2 -0 2	2 -2 0	4 -1 3	4 -3 1	5 -0 5	5 -5 0
6 -1 5	6 -5 1	1 -0 1	1 -1 0	3 -0 3	3 -3 0
2 -1 1	4 -0 4	6 -3 3	4 -2 2	6 -6 0	4 -4 0

Related subtraction facts, minuends through 6

Correcting Common Errors

Some students may have difficulty recognizing addition-fact pairs. Have them work with partners using 6 counters and 2 cups. Have them put some of the 6 counters in one cup and the rest in the other cup and write the addition fact for what they did. Then have them reverse the cups and write the new fact. Have them continue to write other addition-fact pairs for 6, and then use 5, 4, and 3 counters to continue the activity with different sums.

Enrichment

1. Show why any 2 of 6 clothespins can be removed from a coat hanger to show $6 - 2 = 4$.
2. For sums or minuends through 6, find all facts that equal 5. Repeat for 0, 1, 2, 3, 4, 6.
3. Name situations where you might need to know several ways to make 5. (ex. A family of 5 people wants to ride the Ferris wheel together, but one car holds no more than 4 people)

Teaching page 74

Have students read the problem in the first box. (5 minus 2 equals 3) Tell students to trace the lines through the 2 honey jars to show that 2 are taken away and then trace the 3 to show that 3 are left. Repeat for $5 - 3 = 2$. Have students complete the problems in each box and the last row of problems.

Extra Credit *Numeration*

Give every student five addition flashcards and five subtraction flashcards with answers 0 through 10. Give an answer, such as three. The students who have a card such as $1 + 2$, $2 + 1$, $4 - 1$, $10 - 7$ etc., will bring you the flashcard in exchange for a ticket. Proceed in this manner until all students have received at least one ticket. Continue the activity through the week, allowing students more chances to win tickets. As a variation, a student who is having trouble with the facts, could use flashcards with the correct answer on the back.

Minuends 6 through 10

pages 75-76

Objective

To review addition facts for sums 6 through 10 and related subtraction facts for minuends 6 through 10

Materials

Paper cup
10 popsicle sticks

Mental Math

Name the number that equals:
1. 6 − 1 (5)
2. 5 + 1 (6)
3. 4 − 3 (1)
4. 3 + 1 (4)
5. 5 − 2 (3)

Skill Review

Have students hold up their left hands with knuckles toward them. Ask how many fingers in all. (5) Tell students to hold their fingers together and spread their thumbs out. Ask what number sentence their hands show. (4 + 1 = 5) Tell students to turn their hands so their palms face them with thumbs out and fingers together. Ask what number sentence is now shown. (1 + 4 = 5) Explore sums of 5 with fingers spread in other ways.

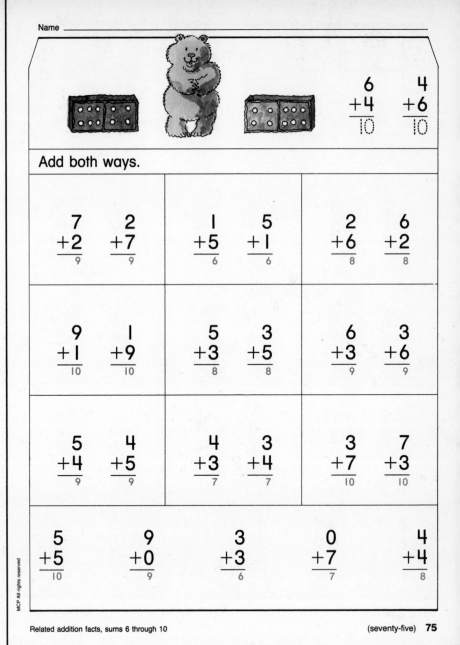

Name _____

Add both ways.

7 +2 ___ 9	2 +7 ___ 9	1 +5 ___ 6	5 +1 ___ 6	2 +6 ___ 8	6 +2 ___ 8
9 +1 ___ 10	1 +9 ___ 10	5 +3 ___ 8	3 +5 ___ 8	6 +3 ___ 9	3 +6 ___ 9
5 +4 ___ 9	4 +5 ___ 9	4 +3 ___ 7	3 +4 ___ 7	3 +7 ___ 10	7 +3 ___ 10

5
+5
___
10   9
+0
___
9   3
+3
___
6   0
+7
___
7   4
+4
___
8

Related addition facts, sums 6 through 10   (seventy-five) **75**

Teaching page 75

Have students place 6 popsicle sticks in their cups. Tell students to put 4 more sticks into their cups and tell how many in all. (10) Write **6 + 4 = 10** on the board vertically and horizontally. Have students remove all the sticks from their cups and then replace 4 sticks. Tell students to put 6 more sticks in their cups and tell how many in all. (10) Write **4 + 6 = 10** on the board vertically and horizontally. Have students remove 4 sticks and tell how many are left. (6) Write **10 − 4 = 6** on the board. Have students put all 10 sticks in their cups again and then remove 6. Ask how many sticks are left. (4) Write **10 − 6 = 4** on the board. Have students read each fact from the board. Repeat for 4 + 5 = 9, 5 + 3 = 8, 2 + 5 = 7, 2 + 4 = 6.

Have students find the bear at the top of the page. Ask what the bear needs to know. (which domino equals 10) Ask students to tell which domino equals 10. (both) Ask students why both dominoes equal 10. (6 + 4 = 10 and 4 + 6 = 10) Have students trace both 10's and then complete the page.

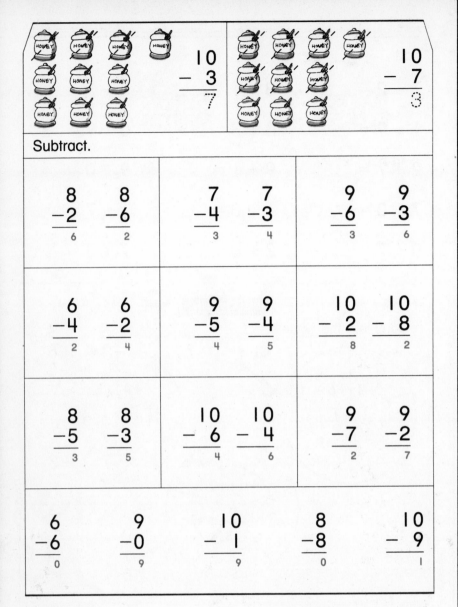

Subtract.

8 −2 6	8 −6 2	7 −4 3	7 −3 4	9 −6 3	9 −3 6
6 −4 2	6 −2 4	9 −5 4	9 −4 5	10 − 2 8	10 − 8 2
8 −5 3	8 −3 5	10 − 6 4	10 − 4 6	9 −7 2	9 −2 7
6 −6 0	9 −0 9	10 − 1 9	8 −8 0	10 − 9 1	

76 (seventy-six)   Related subtraction facts, minuends 6 through 10

Correcting Common Errors

For those students who need practice recognizing related subtraction facts, write 0, 1, 2, 3, 4, 5, 6, 7, 8, 9, and 10 on the chalkboard. Then, to illustrate how to find the answer to $10 - 4 = \square$, start at 10 and count back 4 until you reach 6. Have students write the fact $10 - 4 = 6$. Then illustrate $10 - 6 = \square$ by starting at 10 and counting back 6 until you reach 4. Have students write the fact $10 - 6 = 4$. Repeat with other pairs of facts.

Enrichment

1. Use a number line 0 through 10. Find 2 addition facts for the sum of 6 and 2 subtraction facts with a minuend of 6.
2. Fold a sheet of paper into 4 parts and open it flat. Write $1 + 8 = 9$ in one section. Using the numbers 1, 8 and 9, write three different subtraction or addition facts, one in each section left.

Teaching page 76

Have students trace the dotted lines through the honey pots in the first example and trace the number 7. Continue with second example. Tell students to complete the page independently.

Extra Credit   *Probability*

Play a game called "Zapped"! You will need 13 small objects, such as bottlecaps or erasers. Challenge your students to play the game with you, one at a time, letting the others observe. Place the 13 objects in a line. You and the student take turns taking away one or two objects at a time, until one object is left. The one who is forced to take the last object is Zapped! As the students observe, let them predict whether it is better to go first or second. Ask them to explain how they can avoid getting Zapped! Keep a chart of wins and losses for all players.

To the teacher: Always let your opponent go first. You must draw one object if they draw two. Draw two objects if they draw one and so until they get Zapped!

Facts through 10

pages 77-78

Objective

To review addition facts for sums through 10 and related subtraction facts for minuends 6 through 10

Materials

Sheet of paper
10 counters
*Set of addition and subtraction fact cards for sums through 10

Mental Math

Name another addition fact using these numbers:

1. 6 + 2 = 8 (2 + 6 = 8)
2. 0 + 1 = 1 (1 + 0 = 1)
3. 9 + 1 = 10 (1 + 9 = 10)
4. 4 + 5 = 9 (5 + 4 = 9)
5. 3 + 4 = 7 (4 + 3 = 7)
6. 2 + 1 = 3 (1 + 2 = 3)
7. 2 + 4 = 6 (4 + 2 = 6)

Skill Review

Divide students into 2 teams. Practice speed of recall of addition and subtraction facts for sums through 10.

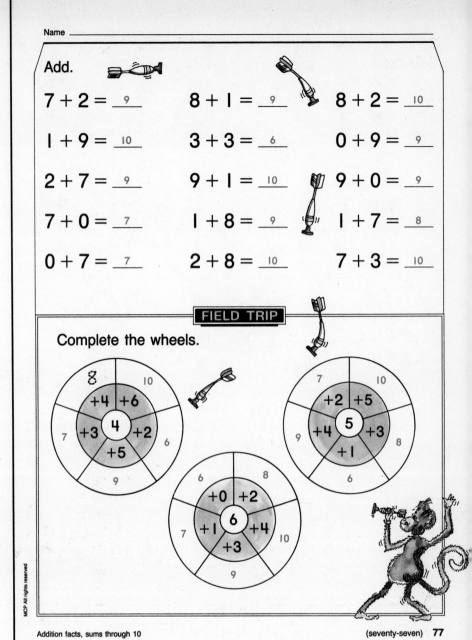

Add.

$7 + 2 = \underline{9}$ $8 + 1 = \underline{9}$ $8 + 2 = \underline{10}$

$1 + 9 = \underline{10}$ $3 + 3 = \underline{6}$ $0 + 9 = \underline{9}$

$2 + 7 = \underline{9}$ $9 + 1 = \underline{10}$ $9 + 0 = \underline{9}$

$7 + 0 = \underline{7}$ $1 + 8 = \underline{9}$ $1 + 7 = \underline{8}$

$0 + 7 = \underline{7}$ $2 + 8 = \underline{10}$ $7 + 3 = \underline{10}$

FIELD TRIP

Complete the wheels.

Addition facts, sums through 10

(seventy-seven) **77**

Teaching page 77

Have students complete the 3 columns of addition facts.

Field Trip

Draw a wheel on the board similar to those on page 77. Write +2 in the center and the numbers 5, 9, 8, 4 and 6 around it. Ask students to tell the sum of 5 plus 2. (7) Write 7 in the outer rim next to 5. Continue asking the sums of each number +2 to complete the wheel.

Tell students they are to complete the 3 wheels on this page. Ask what number is to be added to each number in the first wheel. (4) Ask students the sum of 4 + 4. (8) Tell students to trace the 8. Talk through the rest of the problems in the first wheel. Then tell students to complete the other 2 wheels.

77

Subtract.

$10 - 7 = \underline{3}$　　　　$6 - 1 = \underline{5}$　　　　$8 - 7 = \underline{1}$

$8 - 1 = \underline{7}$　　　　$9 - 9 = \underline{0}$　　　　$7 - 5 = \underline{2}$

$6 - 3 = \underline{3}$　　　　$10 - 3 = \underline{7}$　　　　$9 - 1 = \underline{8}$

$10 - 5 = \underline{5}$　　　　$8 - 4 = \underline{4}$　　　　$7 - 2 = \underline{5}$

$9 - 8 = \underline{1}$　　　　$7 - 6 = \underline{1}$　　　　$6 - 5 = \underline{1}$

$7 - 1 = \underline{6}$　　　　$8 - 0 = \underline{8}$　　　　$7 - 7 = \underline{0}$

FIELD TRIP

Complete the tables.

Subtract 5	
7	2
5	0
10	5
8	3
9	4
6	1

Subtract 2	
10	8
7	5
6	4
8	6
5	3
9	7

Subtract 4	
8	4
10	6
7	3
6	2
9	5
5	1

Subtract 3	
9	6
6	3
5	2
7	4
10	7
8	5

　　　　Related subtraction facts, minuends 6 through 10

Correcting Common Errors

For those students who need more review and practice, have them work with partners. For each fact shown in the lesson, one partner can tell a story using the numbers, and the other partner can use counters to model the problem and give the answer.

Enrichment

1. Fold paper in half and lay flat. Draw a picture on one side that shows an addition fact. Use the same 3 numbers in a subtraction fact and draw a picture on the other side. Write the facts under the pictures.
2. In pairs, play with scrambled addition and subtraction fact cards for sums through 10. Draw 2 cards. Player tells whether the two facts are related, i.e. use the same numbers.

Teaching page 78

Have students complete the 3 columns of subtraction facts.

Field Trip

Tell students they are to subtract 5 from each number in the first table. Ask students to tell the number left when 5 is subtracted from 7.(2) Have students trace the 2 and complete the first table. Ask students what number is to be subtracted in each of the next 3 tables.(2,4,3) Tell students to complete the tables.

Extra Credit　*Logic*

Write simple story problems on the chalk-board by listing 3 nouns or noun phrases, and a question for each one. Include one irrelevant item that is not necessary to solve the problem.
Example: 5 mothers
　　　　3 peanuts
　　　　1 boy
　　　　HOW MANY PEOPLE?

Ask the class to name the information needed to solve the problem and what mathematical operation will be used. After several examples, pass out small cards with other simple problems printed on them for small groups of children to solve. As the student's logical thinking skills improve, they can make up their own story problems to share with the class.

Practice of Facts

pages 79-80

Objective

To practice addition and subtraction facts related to sums through 10

Materials

10 counters
Sheet of paper
*Set of addition and subtraction fact cards for sums through 10

Mental Math

Name the number that:
1. is 1 more than 9 (10)
2. means nothing (0)
3. comes after 6 (7)
4. rhymes with late (8)
5. comes before 1 (0)
6. tells about your toes (10)
7. rhymes with twine (9)
8. is 2 more than 7 (9)

Skill Review

Write on the board:
9 − 1 = 8   8 + 1 = 9
9 − 2 = 7   7 + 2 = 9
9 − 3 = 6   6 + 3 = 9
Have a student come to the board and write the next set of related facts. (9 − 4 = 5, 5 + 4 = 9)
Continue the procedure through 9 − 9 = 0, 0 + 9 = 9. Repeat for 8 − 1 = 7, 7 + 1 = 8.

Name _____

Add or subtract.

$7 + 2 = \underline{9}$ $6 + 2 = \underline{8}$ $5 + 0 = \underline{5}$

$4 - 1 = \underline{3}$ $6 - 2 = \underline{4}$ $7 - 2 = \underline{5}$

$7 + 1 = \underline{8}$ $4 + 2 = \underline{6}$ $9 - 3 = \underline{6}$

$3 + 2 = \underline{5}$ $9 - 6 = \underline{3}$ $6 + 3 = \underline{9}$

$4 - 4 = \underline{0}$ $10 - 2 = \underline{8}$ $5 - 4 = \underline{1}$

$5 + 2 = \underline{7}$ $8 - 2 = \underline{6}$ $1 + 2 = \underline{3}$

3 −2 __ 1	9 −7 __ 2	10 − 5 __ 5	9 −1 __ 8	3 +7 __ 10	10 − 7 __ 3
2 +2 __ 4	10 − 3 __ 7	9 +1 __ 10	2 +7 __ 9	8 +2 __ 10	6 −3 __ 3
0 +7 __ 7	6 −4 __ 2	2 +1 __ 3	6 −5 __ 1	4 +5 __ 9	2 +3 __ 5

Practice, addition and subtraction facts

(seventy-nine) **79**

Teaching page 79

Shuffle the addition and subtraction fact cards. Show the cards one at a time, and ask if we add or subtract. Have a student give the sum or number left for each fact. Continue until each student has given several responses.

Have students look at the first problem and tell if they are to add or subtract. (add) Go through the next 3 problems asking the same question for each. Then ask students if they are to add or subtract for each of the vertical problems in the first row. Tell students they are to first decide if they are to add or subtract for each problem on this page and then write the answer. Have students complete the page. Check to see that students are watching the signs.

79

Add or subtract.

$0 + 3 = \underline{3}$ $9 - 0 = \underline{9}$ $4 + 4 = \underline{8}$

$2 + 5 = \underline{7}$ $4 - 3 = \underline{1}$ $7 - 3 = \underline{4}$

$10 - 6 = \underline{4}$ $4 + 6 = \underline{10}$ $5 + 3 = \underline{8}$

$7 - 4 = \underline{3}$ $3 - 1 = \underline{2}$ $1 + 4 = \underline{5}$

$1 + 7 = \underline{8}$ $4 + 3 = \underline{7}$ $7 - 6 = \underline{1}$

$8 - 1 = \underline{7}$ $9 - 4 = \underline{5}$ $0 + 5 = \underline{5}$

2	6	8	3	5	9
+4	−6	−3	+3	−3	−8
6	0	5	6	2	1

3	1	8	7	2	8
+4	+5	−7	−5	+6	−5
7	6	1	2	8	3

2	5	8	3	5	7
+8	−2	−6	+5	−0	+3
10	3	2	8	5	10

Practice, addition and subtraction facts

Correcting Common Errors

Some students may confuse addition and subtraction when working with a mixed set of problems. Have these students use one color crayon to circle all the addition signs on the page and another color to circle all the subtraction signs. These should provide signals as students move from one problem to the next. You also may want them to go through the set doing all the addition problems first and then doing all the subtraction problems.

Enrichment

1. Solve the problems $4 + 1$ and $4 - 1$. Tell how they differ. Make up similar pairs of problems for a friend to work.
2. Act out a story where someone subtracted instead of adding. (ex. Jamie got 2 toys from Grandma and 1 toy from his aunt. Show the one toy being taken away from Jamie instead of being given to him.)

Teaching page 80

Have students tell if they are to add or subtract each of the first 3 horizontal problems and the first several vertical problems. Then have students complete the page independently. Check to see that students are watching the signs.

Extra Credit   Sets

Distribute one-half of an egg carton (six sections) and a handful of assorted buttons to each child. Allow students enough time to group their buttons into sets. Have students tell by what characteristics they grouped their buttons. (Answers will vary.) Collect the buttons, mix them, and redistribute them to students to sort again into other sets. Have them count the buttons in each set to compare with each other. To conclude the activity, ask students to place all metal buttons in a small plastic bag. Continue to package the wooden buttons, buttons with round tops, etc. Have them count the members in each bag and list them on a chart from the most members to the fewest.

Problem Solving

pages 81-82

Objective

To solve money problems using addition facts to sums through 10 and related subtraction facts

Materials

10 real or punch-out pennies
*Flannel board and felt toys, animals and price tags

Mental Math

Do you add or subtract for:
1. 2 plus 4 (add)
2. 4 take away 2 (subtract)
3. 6 minus 4 (subtract)
4. 5 and 2 more (add)
5. 7 plus 1 (add)
6. 2 minus 2 (subtract)
7. 3 and 6 more (add)
8. 8 take away 0 (subtract)

Skill Review

Write on the board:

6¢ + 1¢ = (7¢)	**9 − 4 = (5)**
3 + 2 = (5)	**7 + 1 = (8)**
6 − 1 = (5)	**3¢ − 2¢ = (1¢)**
8 − 0 = (8)	**6 − 5 = (1)**
2¢ + 7¢ = (9¢)	**9 − 3 = (6)**

Have a student circle the sign that tells to add or subtract and then write the answer to the first problem. Continue through all the problems.

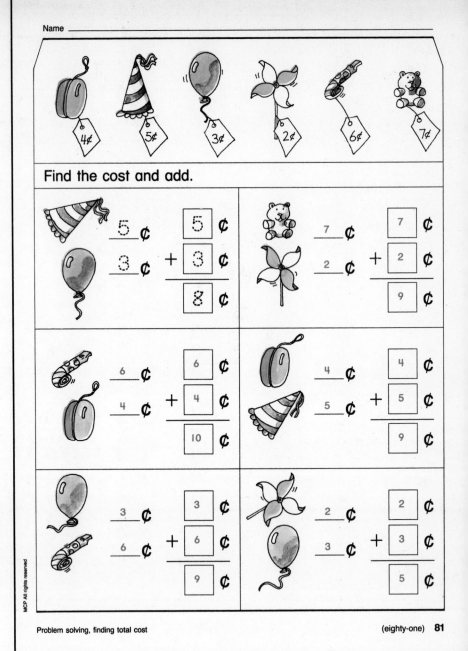

Name _____

Find the cost and add.

Problem solving, finding total cost

(eighty-one) **81**

Teaching page 81

Display on the flannel board 2 felt items with prices of 2¢ and 6¢. Tell students it would take 2 pennies and 6 more pennies, or 8¢, to buy the 2 toys. Write **2¢ + 6¢ = 8¢** on the board and also in vertical form. Continue pretending to buy other pairs of items costing a total of 10¢ or less. Be sure to stress that we add the 2 prices together to find the total cost. Have students tell the number sentence for each purchase. Write their responses on the board vertically and horizontally.

Tell students to look at the pictures of toys at the top of the page. Identify each item and its cost. Ask students to tell how many pennies are needed to buy the 2 items in each box. Tell students to find how much the hat costs by looking at its price tag. (5¢) Tell

students to trace the 5 in the blank beside the hat. Have students find the cost of the balloon. Now have students trace the 3 and 8 to show that 5¢ plus 3¢ equals 8¢. Repeat the procedure for the next problem. Have students complete the page.

81

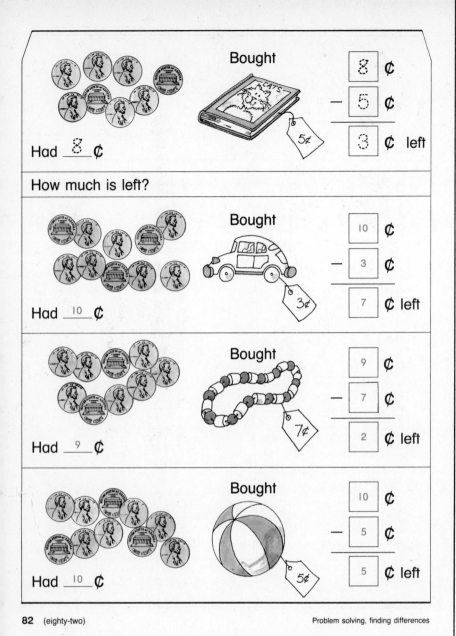

Bought

8	¢	
− 5	¢	
3	¢ left	

Had __8__ ¢

How much is left?

Bought

10	¢	
− 3	¢	
7	¢ left	

Had __10__ ¢

Bought

9	¢	
− 7	¢	
2	¢ left	

Had __9__ ¢

Bought

10	¢	
− 5	¢	
5	¢ left	

Had __10__ ¢

82 (eighty-two)   Problem solving, finding differences

Correcting Common Errors

Some students may need additional practice adding and subtracting money because they are unsure of their basic addition and subtraction facts. To provide additional practice for these students, change the prices of the items on pages 81 and 82 so that they have additional problems to do.

Enrichment

1. Use pennies to practice buying items from the flannel board or from a classroom store.
2. Work in pairs with 10 pennies in a bag. One names an item costing up to 10¢. Other student grabs a handful of pennies, and tells if there is enough money to buy the item.

Teaching page 82

Put an item with a price tag of 6¢ on the flannel board. Draw 8 circles on the board and write **1¢** in each. Tell students how many pennies would be left if they had these 8 pennies and spent 6 of them to buy this item. Ask a student to cross out the pennies to be spent for the item. Write the vertical problem **8¢ − 6¢ = 2¢** on the board as you say, "We write 8¢ minus 6¢ for an answer of 2¢ left." Repeat the procedure for several more examples.

Ask students to count the pennies in the first problem and trace the 8. Ask students to tell how many pennies the book costs. (5¢) Have students trace the 8 to show they had 8¢, the 5 to show they spent 5¢ and the 3 to show they had 3¢ left. Go over the next example similarly and have students complete the page.

Extra Credit *Sets*

Fill a small paper bag with a set of objects with similar attributes. Sets might include a small group of toy vehicles, crayons, pens, pencils or a set of salty snacks. Introduce the set as a "Mystery Set." Give students clues and encourage them to guess the set as you list the clues on the chalkboard. Begin with clues such as, "My set does not have members that are green," or "My set does not have members made of metal." Gradually, give more specific clues until someone guesses what is in the bag. Students can bring their own "Mystery Bag" from home. Discuss various sets that could be assembled to avoid duplication. Sets might include soft things, objects of one color, coins, objects used for sewing, etc. Choose several children each day to share their "Mystery Bag."

Column Addition Problem Solving

pages 83-84

Objectives

To review column addition for sums through 10

To solve problems for sums through 10

Materials

3 paper cups and 10 popsicle sticks for each pair of students

Mental Math

How many all together?
1. 2 plus 6 and 1 more (9)
2. 1 plus 1 and 2 more (4)
3. 5 and 0 and 3 more (8)
4. 2 plus 7 and 0 more (9)
5. 4 and 4 and 2 more (10)
6. 1 plus 2 and 4 more (7)

Skill Review

Give subtraction story problems such as "I had 8 cents and I spent 2¢. How much do I have left?" Ask a student to work the problem on the board.

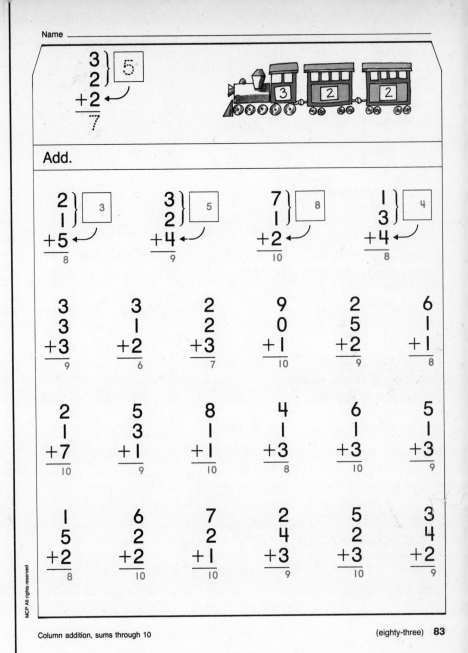

Column addition, sums through 10

(eighty-three) **83**

Teaching page 83

Review column addition by writing on the board:
2 + 6 + 1 = 9 in column form. Remind students that we add the 2 and the 6 for a sum of 8 and then add 8 and 1 for a sum of 9. Do several other examples. Have students find the problem 3 plus 2 plus 2 equals 7 at the top of the page. Tell students to look at the train as you say, "3 plus 2 is 5 plus 2 more is 7." Have students trace the 5 and the 7. Now tell students to do each problem in the next 2 rows. Check to see that students are writing the sum of the first 2 numbers before writing the answer. Tell students to complete the page.

83

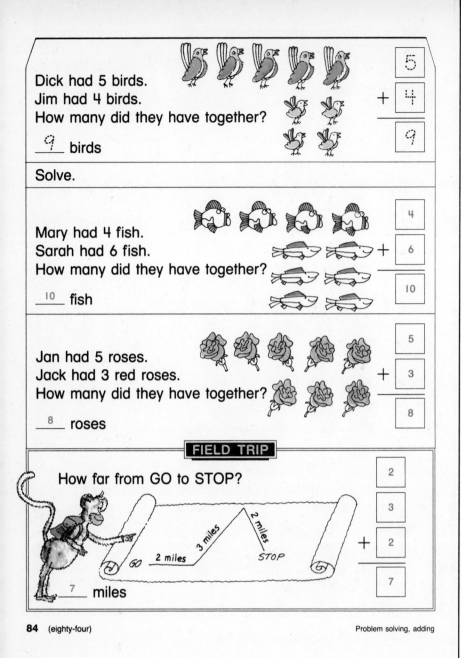

Dick had 5 birds.
Jim had 4 birds.
How many did they have together?

___9___ birds

5
+ 4
___
9

Solve.

Mary had 4 fish.
Sarah had 6 fish.
How many did they have together?

___10___ fish

4
+ 6
___
10

Jan had 5 roses.
Jack had 3 red roses.
How many did they have together?

___8___ roses

5
+ 3
___
8

FIELD TRIP

How far from GO to STOP?

2 miles
3 miles
2 miles
GO
STOP

___7___ miles

2
3
+ 2
___
7

84   (eighty-four)   Problem solving, adding

Correcting Common Errors

Some students may have difficulty finding the sum of three numbers because they cannot remember the sum of the first two numbers when they are ready to add the third number. Have them continue to write the sum of the first two numbers next to the addends. Then they can add this number to the third addend to find the final sum.

Enrichment

1. Find out how many cats you and 2 friends have altogether. How many dogs? How many birds?
2. If you have 10¢ and can buy 3 items, what might each item cost? (Hint: find all the ways to add 3 numbers to make 10)

Teaching page 84

Ask students to find Dick's 5 birds and Jim's 4 birds as you read the problem. Tell students the words "how many in all" tell us to add. Have students trace the 5 for Dick's birds and the 4 for Jim's birds. Ask students how many birds in all. (9) Tell students to trace the 9. Read each problem similarly with students and ask them to tell what numbers go in each box.

Field Trip

Tell students to find the total number of miles from the word GO to the word STOP. Ask students how to find this distance. (add the numbers) Ask what numbers should be added. (2, 3, 2) Tell students to write those numbers in the boxes and find their sum. (7) Tell students to find the blank line before the word miles and write the sum of the problem on that line. (7)

Extra Credit   *Logic*

Have students bring in shoe boxes labeled with their name, and a small toy to put into the box. Put all the boxes in the front of the room, and ask students to come up one by one and put their toys in the boxes. Count the number of students and tell the class how many are in the room. Now ask someone to explain how many shoeboxes there are. (as many as there are students in the room) Ask how many toys are in the boxes. (as many as there are students) Have students draw a picture that shows themselves, their boxes, and their toys each on a separate piece of paper. Put the names of the students in a column, the pictures of their boxes in another, and pictures of their toys in another column on the board in mixed order. Help students to trace the connection from their name, to their box, to their toy on the board.

Chapter Review

pages 85-86

Objective

To review addition and subtraction facts related to sums through 10

Materials

10 counters
Sheet of paper

Mental Math

Name the fact family for:
1. 4 − 2 (2)
2. 3 + 6 (9)
3. 5 + 0 (5)
4. 6 − 3 (3)
5. 5 + 5 (10)
6. 7 − 6 (1)

Skill Review

Read the following problems and ask students to write the addition or subtraction sentence for each on the board.
1. Joe had lost 2 teeth, then 1 tooth and now has lost 1 more. How many teeth has he lost in all? (2 + 1 + 1 = 4)
2. Marcia's family had 4 people in it until the new baby was born. How many people are in her family now? (4 + 1 = 5)
3. Paula has 9 pennies. She buys a comb for 5¢. How much money is left? (9¢ − 5¢ = 4¢)

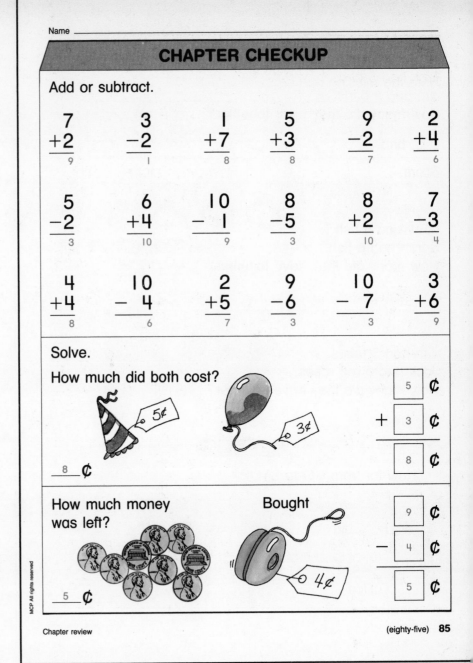

Name _____

CHAPTER CHECKUP

Add or subtract.

7 +2 9	3 −2 1	1 +7 8	5 +3 8	9 −2 7	2 +4 6
5 −2 3	6 +4 10	10 −1 9	8 −5 3	8 +2 10	7 −3 4
4 +4 8	10 −4 6	2 +5 7	9 −6 3	10 −7 3	3 +6 9

Solve.

How much did both cost?

5¢   3¢

8 ¢

```
  5 ¢
+ 3 ¢
  8 ¢
```

How much money was left?   Bought

4¢

5 ¢

```
  9 ¢
− 4 ¢
  5 ¢
```

Teaching page 85

Tell students to look at the sign in each problem in the first 3 rows and write the answer. Tell students to solve the 2 story problems and find the sums of the column addition problems. Have students complete the page independently.

85

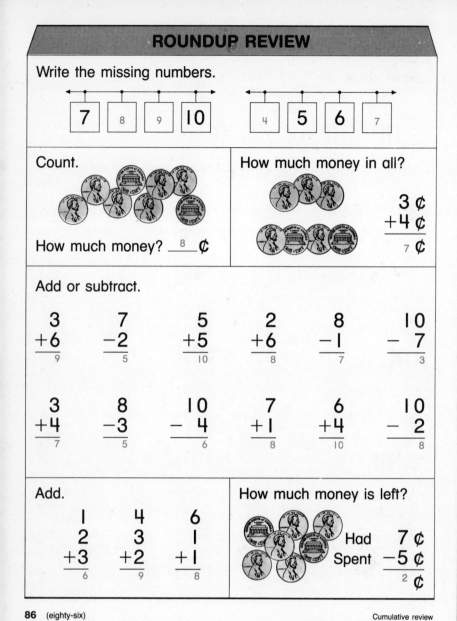

ROUNDUP REVIEW

Write the missing numbers.

7 8 9 10   4 5 6 7

Count.

How much money? __8__ ¢

How much money in all?

3 ¢
+4 ¢
7 ¢

Add or subtract.

3	7	5	2	8	10
+6	−2	+5	+6	−1	− 7
9	5	10	8	7	3

3	8	10	7	6	10
+4	−3	− 4	+1	+4	− 2
7	5	6	8	10	8

Add.

1	4	6
2	3	1
+3	+2	+1
6	9	8

How much money is left?

Had   7 ¢
Spent −5 ¢
2 ¢

86 (eighty-six)

Cumulative review

Enrichment

1. Be a store clerk. Draw 10 items you will sell. Price each item from 1¢ through 10¢. Have a friend bring 10¢ to buy 1 or 2 items.
2. Make a number line for 0 through 10. Write only 3 of the numbers on the line and have a friend complete the number line.
3. Work in groups of 4. By moving around, show all the ways to make sums of 4 using 2 groups. Then show all the ways to make sums of 4 with 3 groups.

Teaching page 86

Tell students to carefully examine each problem on this page to decide how to solve it. Have students complete the page.

Extra Credit *Numeration*

Have students run a "Subtraction Race." Make copies of a page of vertical subtraction problems. Separate students into teams of four or five. Give each team a sheet of problems. Each student must work a problem and pass the sheet to the next member of the team, who works another problem. The race continues until one team completes all the problems. The team with the most correct problems wins.

Place Value through 19

pages 87-88

Objective

To recognize numbers 10 through 19 as 1 group of 10 and 0 through 9 ones

Materials

19 popsicle sticks
Rubber band
Paper cup

Mental Math

How much?
1. 2¢ + 4¢ − 1¢ (5¢)
2. 9 − 2 + 3 (10)
3. 7 pins from 10 pins (3 pins)
4. Had 10¢, spent 2¢ (8¢)
5. 4 − 2 + 3 (5)
6. Have 5 and get 4 more (9)
7. 3 take away 0 (3)

Skill Review

Act out the poem:
    Five tiny seeds,
    Five tiny seeds,
    3 will sprout flowers
    but __ will sprout weeds. (2)
Repeat for the following:
10 − 5 = 5, 8 − 2 = 6, 7 − 3 = 4,
10 − 1 = 9.

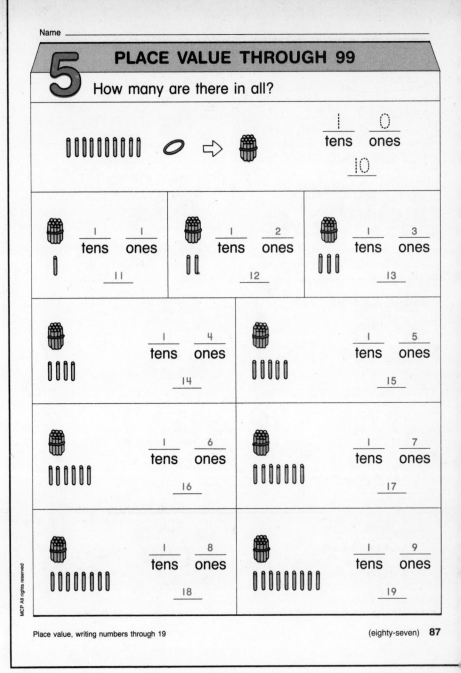

Name _____

5 PLACE VALUE THROUGH 99

How many are there in all?

Place value, writing numbers through 19

(eighty-seven) **87**

Teaching page 87

Count out 10 sticks and hold them in 1 hand. Ask students what would happen if you dropped the 10 sticks. (They would scatter over the floor.) Tell students the sticks would be 10 separate sticks. Now put a rubber band around the 10 sticks and ask students what would happen if you dropped them. (They would stay together in a bundle.) Write **1 ten** on the board. Say, "We call this bundle 1 ten." Write **10** on the board. Remind students that they have already learned to write 10 to mean 10 things. Say, "The symbol 10 means 1 ten and 0 ones." Tell students to count out 10 sticks and use the rubberband to make a bundle. Tell students to lay their bundle down beside 1 single stick. Say, "Now you have 1 ten and 1 one." Write **11** on the board and tell students this is how we

write 1 ten and 1 one. Tell students to put one more single stick beside the bundle. Say, "Now you have 1 ten and 2 ones," as you write **12** on the board. Continue this procedure to develop the numbers 13 through 19.

Have students count the sticks at the top of the page and tell what the picture shows. (putting a band around 10 sticks to make 1 bundle of 10) Have students trace the 1, 0, and 10. Go through the first problem similarly and have students complete the page.

87

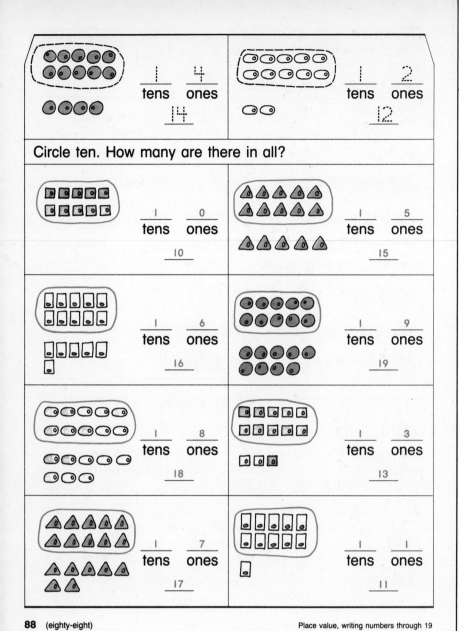

tens ones
1   4
14

tens ones
1   2
12

Circle ten. How many are there in all?

tens ones
1   0
10

tens ones
1   5
15

tens ones
1   6
16

tens ones
1   9
19

tens ones
1   8
18

tens ones
1   3
13

tens ones
1   7
17

tens ones
1   1
11

Place value, writing numbers through 19

Correcting Common Errors

Some students may have difficulty grouping and counting tens and ones. Have them work with partners with 19 tongue depressors and 2 cups. Have them count out 10 sticks and put them in one cup. Ask, "How many groups of ten?" (1) Write 1 ten. Ask, "How many are left?" (9) Write 9 ones. Then write 1 ten 9 ones = 19. Repeat with other numbers from 11 through 18.

Enrichment

1. Find out how many eggs are in a carton. (12) Give the number in tens and ones.
2. Make pages in "Number Books" for numbers 11 through 19. Draw the correct number of objects on each page.

Teaching page 88

Tell students to trace the circle around 10 objects. Next, have them trace the 1 for 1 ten, the 4 for 4 ones and the 14 for 14 objects in all. Repeat for the second example. Have students complete the page. Check to be sure students are circling the group of 10 in each problem and writing their responses on the correct lines.

Extra Credit *Sets*

Pass out 2 cards from a deck of playing cards to each student. Ask them to name several ways to group the cards into sets. (by color, suit, number) Have one student select one category and let small groups place their cards into the appropriate pile on a table. After various sets have been demonstrated, ask students which set has the most members. Which has the fewest? Have the class name sets to which the deck of cards *would not* belong. (cards with yellow numerals, cards with triangles, etc.)

10 through 19

pages 89-90

Objective
To read and write numbers through 19

Materials
19 sticks
Rubberband

Mental Math
Give 2 addition or subtraction facts that equal:
1. 6 (3 + 3, 7 − 1, etc.)
2. 9
3. 10
4. 8
5. 0

(Allow any correct fact of 2 or 3 numbers.)

Skill Review
Draw 15 sticks on the board. Have a student circle a group of 10. Have another student tell how many tens and how many ones and write the number. Repeat for other numbers 10 through 19.

Name _____

ten 10

Read and write the number.

eleven __11__

twelve __12__

thirteen __13__

fourteen __14__

fifteen __15__

sixteen __16__

seventeen ____

eighteen __18__

nineteen __19__

How many are there in all?

12	15	13
19	17	16

Reading and writing numbers 10 through 19

(eighty-nine) **89**

Teaching page 89

Draw 10 x's on the board and ask students how many x's. (10) Have a student circle the 10 x's to show 1 ten. Write **1 ten 0 ones** and the number **10** on the board. Now write the word **ten** on the board and tell students this is the word for 10. Draw another group of 10 x's, circle them and add 1 single x. Ask students how many tens and ones. (1, 1) Write **1 ten 1 one**, Write **11** and **eleven** on the board. Point to each as you read them. Tell students that **eleven** is the word for 11. Continue similarly writing the same through 19, so that students see the development of 10 through 19.

Have students look at the group of glue jars at the top of the page. Ask how many tens. (1) Tell students to find the word for 10 and then trace the number. Have students tell how many tens are in the second line. (1) Ask how many ones. (1) Tell students to look at the word eleven and write an 11 on the line. Tell students to now look at the boxes at the bottom of the page. Read the words "How many are there in all?" Tell students they are to find how many tens and ones and write the numbers. Have students work the page independently.

89

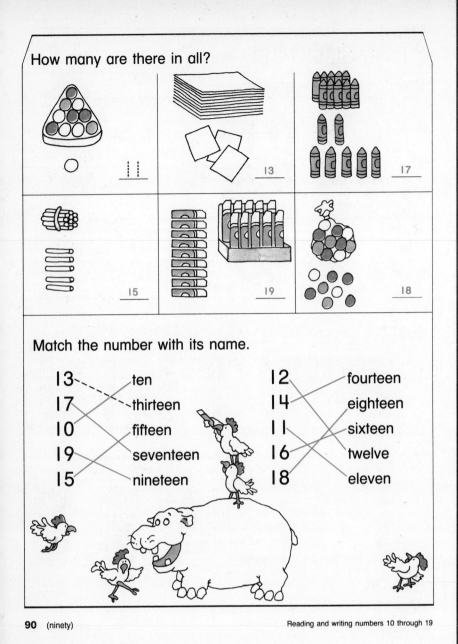

How many are there in all?

11	13	17
15	19	18

Match the number with its name.

13 - - - ten
17 - - thirteen
10 fifteen
19 seventeen
15 nineteen

12 fourteen
14 eighteen
11 sixteen
16 twelve
18 eleven

Reading and writing numbers 10 through 19

Correcting Common Errors

If students have difficulty associating the number with the number name, have them work with partners with number cards from 11 through 19 and the matching number-name cards. Both sets should be shuffled and kept separate. The partners work with both sets until they have matched each number with its number name. Then they use counters to model each number.

Enrichment

1. Make number and number-name cards for numbers 10 through 19.
2. Write the numbers that tell the ages of all teenagers. (13 through 19)

Teaching page 90

Write the numbers 10 through 19 on the board. Write each number's name beside it. Have students read the number names as you point randomly to them. Tell students they are to find the number of tens and ones in each box at the top of the page and write the number. Now have students look at the columns of numbers and words. Tell students they are to draw a line from the 13 to its word. Have students trace the dotted line for 13. Have students complete the page.

Extra Credit   *Probability*

Play a probability game called "See-Saw". Pair off the class. Each pair gets six markers and three dice. Name one player See and the other Saw, and tell them See represents even numbers and Saw is odd numbers. The players take turns rolling the dice. If 11 is the sum of the dice, See gives a marker to Saw. If 14 is the sum, Saw gives a marker to See. Students continue to roll the dice and the first player to collect all of the markers is the winner. Have students play again. This time let them predict whether it is better to be See or Saw. Play once more to test their predictions.

Place Value through 49

pages 91-92

Objective

To write numbers 10 through 49

Materials

49 sticks and
4 rubberbands per pair of students

Mental Math

What is the number?

1. 1 ten and 0 ones (10)
2. 1 ten and 5 ones (15)
3. 0 tens and 9 ones (9)
4. 1 ten and 9 ones (19)
5. 1 ten and 2 ones (12)
6. 0 tens and 6 ones (6)
7. 1 ten and 7 ones (17)

Skill Review

Write numbers 0 through 19 on the board with each number's name under it. Point to each in order and have students count with you. Now ask a student to begin at 9 and count to 13. Continue to have each student count from one specified number to another. Have all students count from 0 through 19 as you point to the number names.

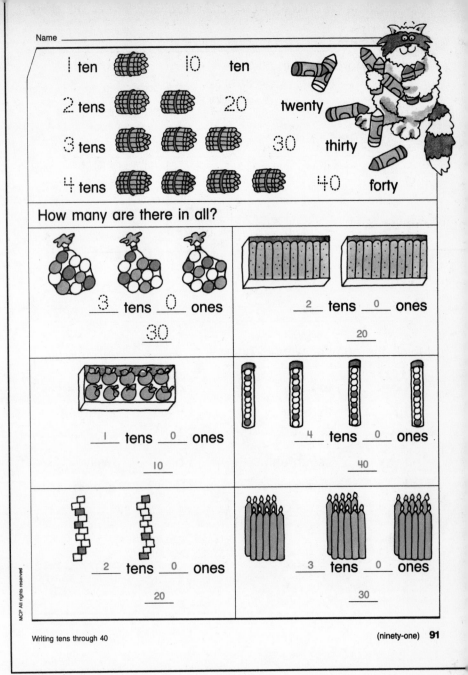

Writing tens through 40

(ninety-one) **91**

Teaching page 91

Have students work in pairs with 19 sticks and 4 rubber bands. Tell students to count their sticks and put a band around each 10 sticks. Ask students how many tens they have in all.(1) Ask how many ones.(9) Write **19, 1 ten 9 ones,** and **nineteen** on the board. Give pairs of students 1 more stick and ask them if they have enough to make another bundle of 10.(yes) Have students bundle the 10 and tell how many tens in all.(2) Ask how many ones.(0) Write **20, 2 tens 0 ones** and **twenty** on the board. Read each to the students. Give each pair of students 1 more stick and ask how many tens and ones.(2,1) Write **21** and **two tens 1 one** on the board. Note: only the words twenty, thirty, and forty will be introduced in this lesson. Continue to give 1 more stick to develop each number through 29. When students have enough sticks

to make a third bundle, write **30, 3 tens 0 ones** and **thirty** on the board. Proceed similarly through 49, writing the word **forty** for 4 tens 0 ones.

Have students look at the bundle of crayons at the top of the page. Ask how many bundles of 10 and how many ones.(1,0) Have students trace the number 10. Have students look at the bundles for 20, 30 and 40. Have students trace each number as you read it. Go through the first problem and have them trace the 3 and 0. Have students complete the page.

91

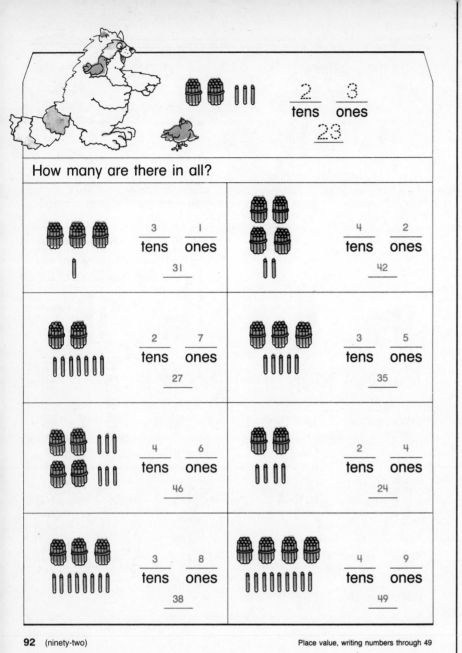

How many are there in all?

3 tens, 1 ones — 31	4 tens, 2 ones — 42
2 tens, 7 ones — 27	3 tens, 5 ones — 35
4 tens, 6 ones — 46	2 tens, 4 ones — 24
3 tens, 8 ones — 38	4 tens, 9 ones — 49

Place value, writing numbers through 49

Correcting Common Errors

Some students may count 2 groups of ten and 2 ones by saying, "10, 20, 30, 40," instead of saying, "10, 20, 21, 22." Have them pause and take a breath after counting the tens and before they count the ones.

Enrichment

1. Write the age of each member of your family in tens and ones.
2. Collect toothpicks from home and bundle the tens to have 49 in all.

Teaching page 92

Draw 24 sticks on the board. Circle the first 10 sticks and then circle the next 10 sticks. Ask students how many tens and ones. (2,4) Write **24** on the board. Now draw 24 sticks again and circle the last 10. Draw another circle around the next 10, leaving the first 4 sticks separate. Ask students how many tens and ones there are. (2 tens 4 ones) Write **24** on the board. Tell students we always say the number of tens first and then the number of ones. Draw 18 sticks and repeat the procedure to be sure students understand that the first number tells how many tens.

Have students look at the raccoon counting the sticks. Ask students to tell how many tens and ones. (2,3) Have students trace the 2 and the 3 and then trace 23. Have students complete the page independently.

Extra Credit *Numeration*

Cut balloon shapes from construction paper. On each balloon write a different number from 0 through 49. Place the balloons in random groups of three on the board. One student picks a set of balloons, and all the students write the numbers from smallest to largest on paper. The volunteer who picked the balloons at the board, rearranges them at the board. Select another volunteer and repeat the exercise.

20 through 49

pages 93-94

Objective

To read and write numbers 20 through 49 in sequence

Materials

Four 10-sticks
Ten 1-squares
4 rubberbands

Mental Math

Count on to 19 from:
1. 9 (9 . . . . 19)
2. 13
3. 10
4. 6
5. 11
6. 0

Skill Review

Write on the board:

42   25   11   38   16

Have students tell how many tens and ones for each number. Ask individual students to draw sticks on the board for each number and circle the tens.

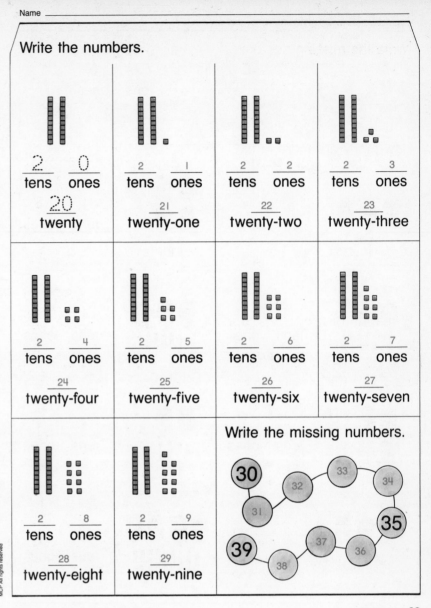

Name _____

Write the numbers.

2 0	2 1	2 2	2 3
tens ones	tens ones	tens ones	tens ones
20	21	22	23
twenty	twenty-one	twenty-two	twenty-three
2 4	2 5	2 6	2 7
tens ones	tens ones	tens ones	tens ones
24	25	26	27
twenty-four	twenty-five	twenty-six	twenty-seven

2 8	2 9	Write the missing numbers.
tens ones	tens ones	
28	29	
twenty-eight	twenty-nine	

Reading and writing 20 through 39 in sequence   (ninety-three) **93**

Teaching page 93

Have students place 2 10-sticks in front of them. Ask how many tens and ones are shown.(2,0) Write **20** and **twenty** on the board. Tell students to put 1 1-square with the 2 10-sticks. Ask how many tens and ones.(2,1) Tell students the word for this number is "twenty-one." Write **21** and **twenty-one** on the board under 20 and twenty. Continue this procedure to develop numbers through 29. Now ask what will happen if 1 more is added to the 29.(2 tens and 10 ones) Ask students to take the 10 1-squares away and put a 10-stick in its place. Ask how many tens and ones.(3,0) Write **30** and **thirty** on the board and tell students this is the number 30. Continue to 39 and have students again remove the 10 ones and replace with a 10-stick for 40. Continue through 49.

Have students look at the 2 10-sticks in the first box and tell how many tens and ones.(2,0) Have students trace the 2, the 0 and the 20. Work through each of the 9 problems with the students. Now have students look at the number chain at the bottom of the page. Tell students they are to write the numbers in order from 30 to 39. Read each number word in order as students write the numbers.

93

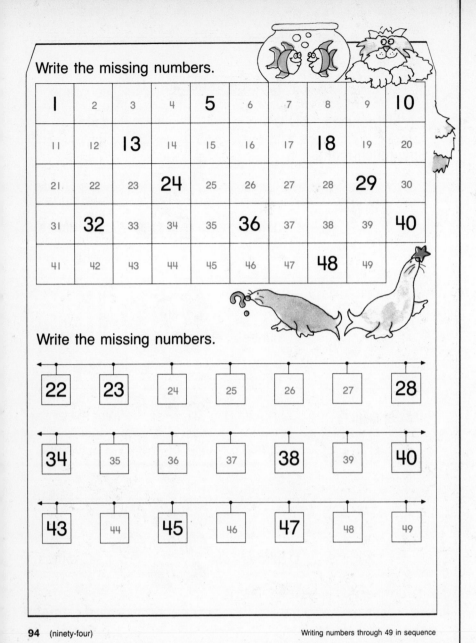

Write the missing numbers.

1	2	3	4	5	6	7	8	9	10
11	12	13	14	15	16	17	18	19	20
21	22	23	24	25	26	27	28	29	30
31	32	33	34	35	36	37	38	39	40
41	42	43	44	45	46	47	48	49	

Write the missing numbers.

| 22 | 23 | 24 | 25 | 26 | 27 | 28 |

| 34 | 35 | 36 | 37 | 38 | 39 | 40 |

| 43 | 44 | 45 | 46 | 47 | 48 | 49 |

Writing numbers through 49 in sequence

Correcting Common Errors

Some students may write digits in the wrong place. Discuss how the tens place is always to the left and the ones place is to the right. It also would help if students discuss any patterns they find after they complete the chart at the top of page 94. For example, in each row, the tens are the same and the ones increase by 1; in each column, the tens increase by 1 ten and the ones are the same.

Enrichment

1. Draw a number line from 0 through 49. Write your name under the number for your age. Do the same for each member of your family.
2. Make a calendar for this month.

Teaching page 94

Tell students to look at the rows of boxes and find the 1 and the 10. Ask students to fill in the numbers that come between 1 and 10. Tell students they are to fill in the rest of the numbers through 49. Tell students they are to write the missing numbers on each of the 3 numbers lines at the bottom of the page. Have students complete the page independently.

Extra Credit   *Numeration*

Students can work together in pairs. One student flashes a set of math fact flashcards, while the other student gives answers. The student responding keeps any card answered correctly. If the given answer is incorrect, the student flashing the cards keeps the card. At the end of the pile, the student with the correctly answered cards counts them and records the total. The students reverse roles using all the flashcards. The object is to see who can accumulate the most correct answers. A tally could be made to keep track of daily totals, and which student has the highest weekly total.

Numbers through 19

pages 95-96

Objective

To read and write numbers 10 through 90 by tens

Materials

Nine 10-sticks and 9 real or punch-out dimes per pair of students 10 real or punch-out pennies

Mental Math

Name the number that comes:
1. before 12 (11)
2. after 16 (17)
3. before 19 (18)
4. between 10 and 12 (11)
5. after 11 (12)
6. before 13 (12)

Skill Review

Write on the board:

10	.... **26**	**23**	.... **42**
35	.... **48**	**12**	.... **31**
11	.... **33**	**19**	.... **49**

Have students begin with the first number and count on to the second number.

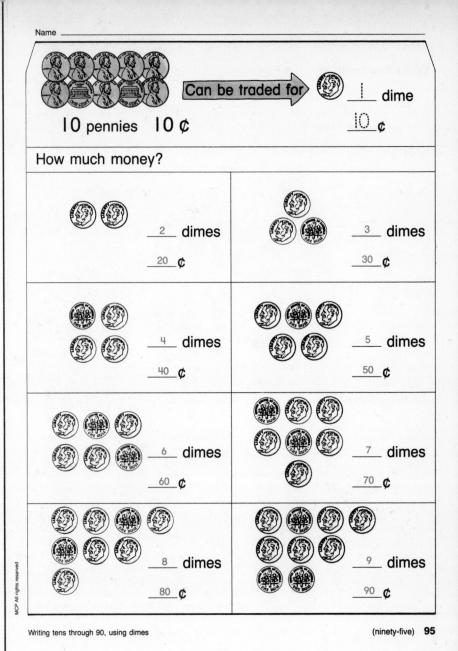

Name _____

10 pennies   10 ¢   Can be traded for   _1_ dime   _10_ ¢

How much money?

	2 dimes / 20 ¢		3 dimes / 30 ¢
	4 dimes / 40 ¢		5 dimes / 50 ¢
	6 dimes / 60 ¢		7 dimes / 70 ¢
	8 dimes / 80 ¢		9 dimes / 90 ¢

Writing tens through 90, using dimes

(ninety-five) **95**

Teaching page 95

Have each pair of students lay out 1 10-stick to show 1 ten and 0 ones. Write **10** and **ten** on the board. Tell them to add another 10-stick. Ask how many tens and ones. (2,0) Write **20** and **twenty** on the board. Continue to add 1 10-stick each time to build and record the decade numbers through 90. Have students count by 10's as you point to the numbers and number-names. Now point randomly to the numbers 10 through 90 and ask students how many tens and ones. Show a dime and tell students the coin is called a **dime** and has a value of 10¢. Ask how many tens and ones in a dime. (1,0) Show students 10 pennies and 1 dime. Write **10¢** on the board and tell students that 10¢ can mean 10 pennies or 1 dime. Show 2 dimes and write **20¢** on the board. Tell students that 2 dimes is written as **20¢**. Show 3 dimes and ask how to

write this new amount. (30¢) Write **30¢** on the board. Continue to add 1 more dime to develop 40¢, 50¢, 60¢, 70¢, 80¢ and 90¢. Have students count the dimes by 10's. (10¢ . . . 90¢)

Have students find the 10 pennies at the top of the page. Ask how many dimes are the same as 10 pennies. (1) Read, "10 pennies or 10¢ can be traded for 1 dime or 10¢." Have students trace the 1 and the 10. Go through the next problem with the students and then have them complete the page.

95

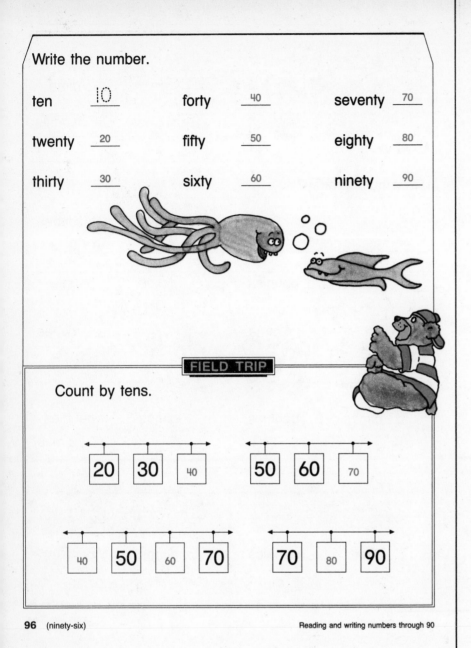

Write the number.

ten	10	forty	40	seventy	70
twenty	20	fifty	50	eighty	80
thirty	30	sixty	60	ninety	90

FIELD TRIP

Count by tens.

20	30	40		50	60	70

40	50	60	70		70	80	90

Reading and writing numbers through 90

Correcting Common Errors

Some students may have difficulty associating a number of tens with its number name. Have them work with partners and 9 bundles of ten sticks. One partner lays out a group of bundles and the other partner counts them by saying the number word names—ten, twenty, thirty, and so on—and then writes the number name for the total. The partners take turns as they continue the activity with different numbers of bundles.

Enrichment

1. Write 10 through 90 by tens and draw bundles of sticks to show each.
2. Take a handful of dimes from a bag of 9 dimes. Count your money by tens.

Teaching page 96

Have the students look for the word ten and its number at the top of the page. Tell students to trace the 10. Tell students they are to count by 10's through 90 and write the numbers in the blanks. Tell students there are some numbers written on each number line but some are missing. Tell them they are to count by 10's and fill in the missing numbers.

Field Trip

Before students complete the number lines in this Field Trip, encourage them to create models of groups of ten markers up through 90. Have them take turns counting the individual markers and then skip counting by ten to see the faster way.

Extra Credit   *Statistics*

Bring a picture of each of these items to class: pants, overalls, dress, skirt. On a large sheet of paper draw a large circle on the left. Glue the pictures in a vertical column on the right. During the class have students write their names in the large circle. At the end of class, draw a line from each name to the appropriate item of clothing. If you use a different color marker for each category, it will be easier for students to distinguish the lines going to the pants from those to the skirt, those from overalls from those to the dress. Question students about the results indicated. For example, ask if more students are wearing overalls or skirts.

96

Counting Money

pages 97-98

Objective

To recognize value of dimes and pennies

Materials

9 real or punch-out pennies
9 real or punch-out dimes

Mental Math

Add 2 to the sum of each two numbers:
1. 2 and 3 (7)
2. 0 and 5 (7)
3. 6 and 1 (9)
4. 3 and 5 (10)
5. 1 and 3 (6)
6. 3 and 3 (8)
7. 1 and 0 (3)

Skill Review

Use dimes to review counting by 10's to 90. Ask students how many tens are in each number 10 through 90. Then ask how many dimes are in each number 10 through 90.

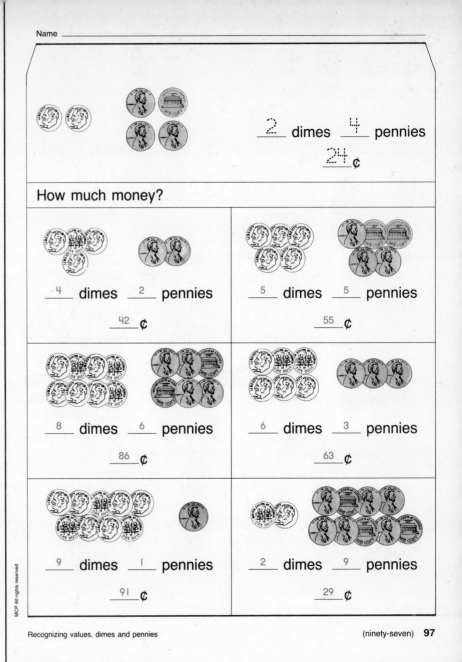

Name _____

_2_ dimes _4_ pennies

_24_ ¢

How much money?

_4_ dimes _2_ pennies

_42_ ¢

_5_ dimes _5_ pennies

_55_ ¢

_8_ dimes _6_ pennies

_86_ ¢

_6_ dimes _3_ pennies

_63_ ¢

_9_ dimes _l_ pennies

_91_ ¢

_2_ dimes _9_ pennies

_29_ ¢

Recognizing values, dimes and pennies

(ninety-seven) **97**

Teaching page 97

Ask students to count out 9 pennies. Ask students to count by 10's to count out 9 dimes. Tell students they are now going to put some dimes and pennies together and count them. Tell students to lay out 4 dimes and 3 pennies. Count, 10, 20, 30, 40, 41, 42, 43. Tell students they have laid out 43¢ in all. Tell students to lay out 6 dimes and 9 pennies and tell how much money they have.(69¢) Repeat for 27¢, 55¢, 92¢ and 17¢.

Have students tell how many dimes are shown at the top of the page.(2) Ask how much money that is.(20¢) Ask how many pennies are shown and how much money that is.(4,4¢) Have students trace the 2, 4 and the 24. Go through the first problem with the students and have them complete the page independently.

97

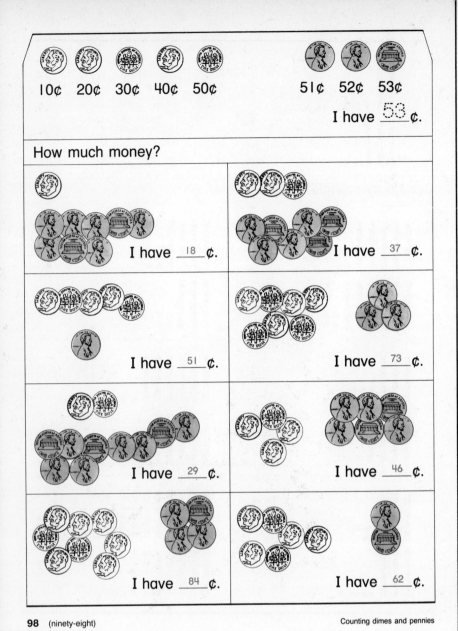

10¢ 20¢ 30¢ 40¢ 50¢   51¢ 52¢ 53¢

I have __53__ ¢.

How much money?

I have __18__ ¢.

I have __37__ ¢.

I have __51__ ¢.

I have __73__ ¢.

I have __29__ ¢.

I have __46__ ¢.

I have __84__ ¢.

I have __62__ ¢.

98 (ninety-eight)   Counting dimes and pennies

Correcting Common Errors

Some students may continue to count by tens as they move from counting dimes to counting pennies. Have them pause after counting all the dimes and before they continue to count the pennies.

Enrichment

1. Place 9 dimes and 9 pennies in a bag. Pick a handful of coins and tell how much money you have.
2. Draw dimes and pennies to make 92¢, 48¢, 17¢ and 38¢.
3. Pretend you are going shopping. Tell how much money you have with you. Then tell that amount in dimes and pennies.

Teaching page 98

Have students count the dimes by 10's and count on by 1's for the pennies, to tell how much money in all. (53¢) Have students trace the 53. Tell students they are to count the money in each box and write the amount on the line. Have students complete the page.

Extra Credit *Applications*

Tell students to fold their papers in half. Have them list half the alphabet on one side and half on the other. Have the students select one textbook from their desks. Direct them to make a tally mark on their papers every time one of the letters appears on the title page. When finished, tell the students to add the number of tallies found for each letter. Students can also report to the class the letters that were not used on the page. As a variation, the students can record the letters that appear on the blackboard.

Comparing Numbers

pages 99-100

Objective

To find the greater or lesser amount for numbers through 99

Materials

Nine 10-sticks
Nine 1-squares

Mental Math

Count to 10 backwards by 10's from:
1. 40 (30, 20, 10)
2. 90
3. 60
4. 50
5. 20
6. 80
7. 70
8. 30

Skill Review

Write on the board:

92¢	(9,2)	**25¢**	(2,5)
83¢	(8,3)	**70¢**	(7,0)
16¢	(1,6)	**58¢**	(5,8)
64¢	(6,4)	**12¢**	(1,2)

Have students tell how many tens and ones for each amount. Ask how many dimes and pennies in each.

Name _____

32 is greater than 23.

23

(32)

Circle the number that is greater.

52

(64)

(45)

34

35

(41)

(62)

55

28

(33)

(81)

72

Comparing numbers, greater than

(ninety-nine) **99**

Teaching page 99

Show 33 and 24 with 10-sticks and 1-squares. Ask a student to write on the board the number for each group. Ask a second student to write how many tens and ones in each.(3,3; 2,4) Ask students which number has the most tens.(33) Ask which number is greater.(33) Repeat for more sets of 2 numbers having different tens amounts. Now show 34 and 36 and ask how many tens in each.(3) Ask if one number has more tens than the other.(no) Tell students they must now compare the number of ones in each number to find the greater number. Ask which number has more ones.(36) Repeat for more examples where the ones are different. Now give 67 and 76, 54 and 45, 46 and 41, 35 and 53, 79 and 74, 53 and 59 so that students develop the habit of first comparing the tens.

Have students count to find the numbers in the example at the top of the page. Ask students which number has more tens.(32) Tell students to trace the circle around 32 to show that 32 is greater than 23. Go through the next problem with the students and ask, "Which number is greater?" Remind students they are to circle the number that is greater in each problem on this page. Have students complete the page.

99

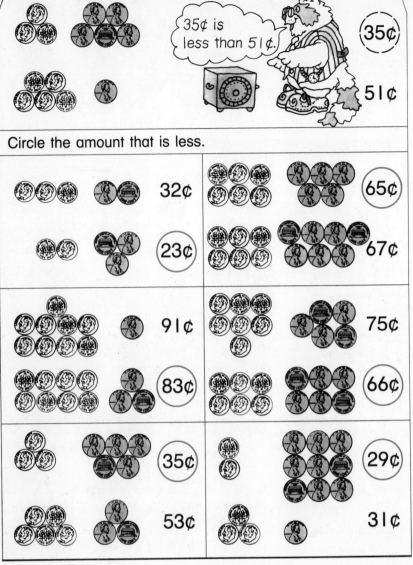

Circle the amount that is less.

Comparing amounts, less than

Teaching page 100

Show 36¢ and 24¢ with 10-sticks and 1-squares. Ask students how many tens and ones in 36¢.(3,6) Ask how many dimes and pennies in 36¢.(3,6) Now ask the same questions for 24¢.(2,4) Ask which number is greater.(36¢) Ask which number is less.(24¢) Ask which is more money (36¢) and which is less.(24¢) Repeat for more examples.

Have students look at the raccoon at the top of the page. Tell them to count the dimes and pennies in each row and help the raccoon decide which is less money. Have students trace the circle around 35¢ to show that 35¢ is less than 51¢. Tell students they are to decide which amount of money is less and circle that amount in each problem on the page.

Extra Credit *Applications*

Bring in a number of old magazines and newspapers. Give each student a magazine or section of the newspaper and ask them to find the page numbers. Have a volunteer explain where the page numbers are found. Ask if anyone knows what the page numbers are for. (to help you find an article or feature) Show students the table of contents page in one of the magazines. See if they can find the table of contents page in their own magazine. Now give each student scissors, paper, and glue. Ask them to cut out twenty consecutive page numbers and paste them, in order, on the paper. Point out that they can be the numbers 1 through 20 or they might use the numbers 10 through 30 or 25 through 45. Any series of numbers will do. Display their number sequences on the board.

100

Ordinal Numbers

pages 101-102

Objective

To use ordinal numbers first through tenth

Materials

Set of ordinal word cards first through tenth
Set of ordinal number cards 1st through 10th

Mental Math

How many tens and ones?
1. 44 (4, 4)
2. 79 (7, 9)
3. 26 (2, 6)
4. 10 (1, 0)
5. 54 (5, 4)
6. 38 (3, 8)
7. 45 (4, 5)

Skill Review

Write 2 numbers from 0 through 99 on the board. Ask which number is greater. Ask which is less. Ask students to tell how we know which of the 2 numbers is greater and which is less. (compare number of tens and ones) Repeat for several examples of 2 numbers.

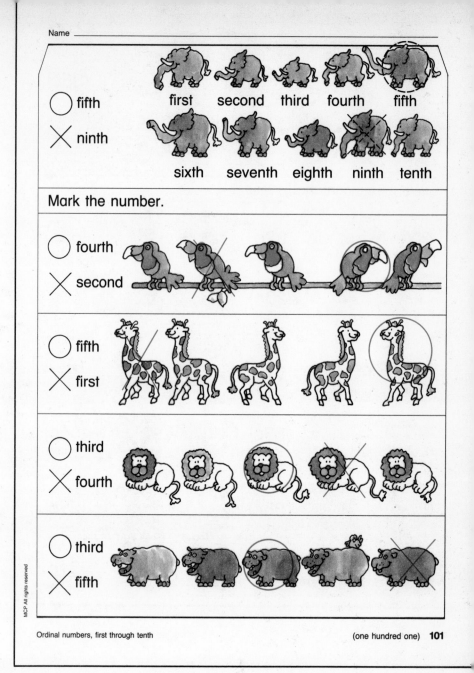

Name _____

○ fifth
✗ ninth

first   second   third   fourth   fifth

sixth   seventh   eighth   ninth   tenth

Mark the number.

○ fourth
✗ second

○ fifth
✗ first

○ third
✗ fourth

○ third
✗ fifth

Ordinal numbers, first through tenth

(one hundred one) **101**

Teaching page 101

Have 3 students line up at the pencil sharpener. Ask students who is 1st in line, 2nd in line and 3rd. Have 4 students line up at the door. Ask who is 1st, 2nd, 3rd and 4th. Continue to add 1 more student until ordinal numbers through tenth have been introduced. Now write the words **first** through **tenth** across the board. Have 1 student stand in front of each word. Ask who is 1st, 2nd, etc. through 10th. Write ordinal numbers **1st** through **10th** under the word for each. Have 4 students line up along a wall or window. Tell students we could start at either end of the line to tell who is 1st, etc. Start at one end of the line and name students by 1st, 2nd, 3rd, 4th. Then start at the other end and do the same. Have 10 students line up at the chalkboard. Ask each to tell their ordinal number in the line. Have the 10th student lead the line to the

door. Have each student now tell their ordinal number. Find the elephants at the top of the page. Beginning with the first elephant, have students count to the fifth elephant, saying the ordinal numbers. Draw a circle around it. Have students find the ninth elephant and draw an X across it. Help students with the next problem and have them complete the page.

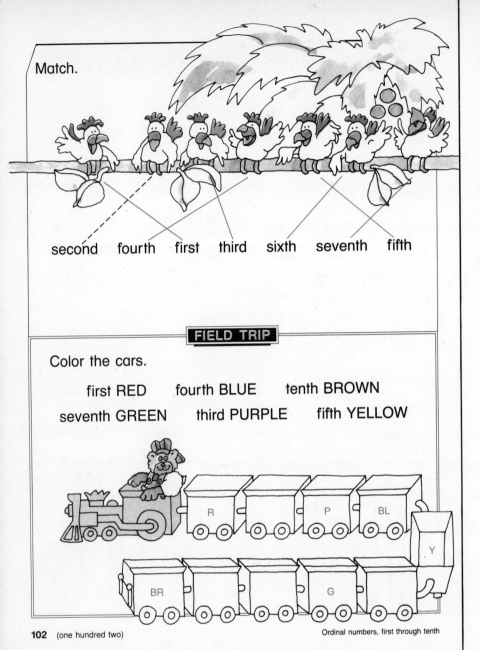

Match.

second fourth first third sixth seventh fifth

FIELD TRIP

Color the cars.

first RED   fourth BLUE   tenth BROWN

seventh GREEN   third PURPLE   fifth YELLOW

102 (one hundred two)   Ordinal numbers, first through tenth

Some students may need a review of the ordinal numbers. Write the numbers 1 through 10 in a row on the chalkboard. Ask students which is the first number. (1) Write first under the number. Continue in this manner through 10, the tenth number. Encourage students to compare and discuss the names for the first ten ordinal and cardinal numbers. When the students are in line, have them count off using the ordinal numbers occasionally.

Enrichment

1. Shuffle a set of ordinal number cards, first through tenth, and put them in order.
2. Draw 10 circles in a row. Color the 4th circle red, the 7th circle blue, the 2nd circle orange and the 9th circle green.

Teaching page 102

Have students look at the birds and draw a line from the first bird to the word first and a line from the second bird to the word second. Have students match all the birds to their ordinal words.

Field Trip

Ask students to point to the first car on the train. Have students point to each of the cars as you say the ordinal numbers in order. Now have students point to cars as you say their ordinal numbers at random. Tell students to follow the directions that tell them what color each car should be.

Ask students what color they will color the fourth car. (blue) Continue through all the directions at random. Ask students if they will color all the cars. (no) Tell students to finish the train independently.

Extra Credit   *Numeration*

As a timed numeration activity, announce a decade number and have the students write it on their papers. At a given signal, tell them to write the next ten numbers in sequence before time is called. Have the students then read the numbers orally. The teacher may also call out a number and have students write a decreasing number sequence in a given amount of time. Repeat the activity asking a volunteer to pick a number.

Chapter Review

pages 103-104

Objectives

To review place value for 11 through 99
To maintain previously learned skills

Materials

9 dimes and 9 pennies
Nine 10-sticks
Nine 1-squares

Mental Math

Which is greater?
1. 7 or 17 (17)
2. 26 or 62 (62)
3. 44 or 35 (44)
4. 89 or 96 (96)
5. 35 or 53 (53)
6. 29 or 21 (29)
7. 92 or 29 (92)
8. 63 or 83 (83)

Skill Review

If students are seated in rows, ask who is 1st, 2nd, etc. in each row. Now go to the opposite end of the rows and ask who is 1st, 2nd, etc.
Or, as an alternative, have students line up in rows of 10 or less and ask them similar questions.

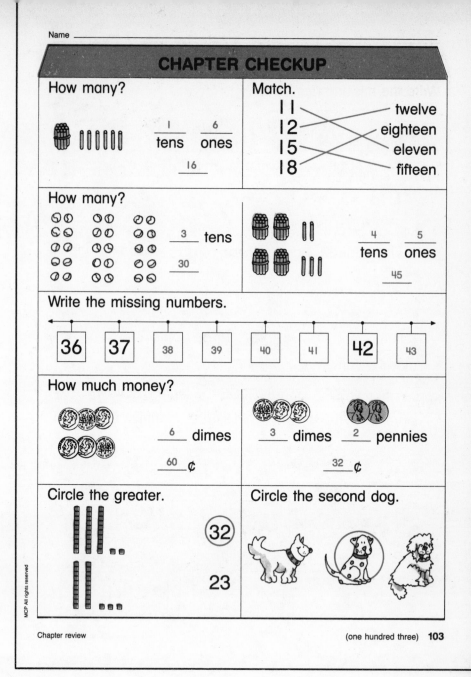

Teaching page 103

Tell students that this page asks them to do several different things. Have students look at the first box and tell what is to be done. (write the number of tens and ones and the number) Continue to ask what is to be done in each box. Have students complete the page.

103

ROUNDUP REVIEW

Write the missing numbers.

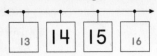

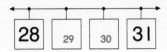

Add or subtract.

3 +4 = 7	6 +3 = 9	1 +7 = 8	2 +4 = 6	5 +2 = 7	9 +1 = 10
5 +3 = 8	4 +6 = 10	3 +2 = 5	4 +4 = 8	2 +2 = 4	3 +3 = 6
8 −3 = 5	9 −5 = 4	7 −4 = 3	5 −3 = 2	8 −4 = 4	10 − 5 = 5
6 −2 = 4	10 − 3 = 7	9 −2 = 7	8 −6 = 2	7 −2 = 5	10 − 4 = 6

3 + 3 = 6   10 − 6 = 4   4 + 5 = 9

7 + 2 = 9   9 − 4 = 5   8 − 2 = 6

104   (one hundred four)   Cumulative review

Enrichment

1. Draw a picture of your family in order by ages. Write the ordinal number under each person to show who was born first, second, etc.
2. Tell a story of several things that happened to you in one week. Tell which happened first, second, third, etc.
3. Work in small groups. Make cards that read "I am a ten" and "I am a one." Hold cards to act out numbers 11 through 99.

Teaching page 104

Tell students this page also asks them to do several different things. Go through each set of problems asking students what is to be done. Remind students that the problems at the bottom of the page ask them to first look at the sign. Go through each of the 6 addition and subtraction problems, and have students tell what is to be done as they circle the + or − sign. Have students complete the page independently.

This page reviews writing numbers in sequence and addition and subtraction facts.

Practice Sums through 10

pages 105-106

Objective

To review addition facts for sums through 10

Materials

2 paper cups and 10 popsicle sticks for each pair of students

Mental Math

Give the fact family for:
1. 7 plus 2 (9)
2. 6 minus 1 (5)
3. 4 take away 2 (2)
4. 6 and 1 more (7)
5. 8 plus 2 (10)
6. 10 take away 3 (7)
7. 3 and 6 more (9)
8. 7 minus 7 (0)

Skill Review

Show the 5 + 3 = 8 fact card. Ask students to give the related addition fact. (3 + 5 = 8) Continue with other fact cards for sums through 10.

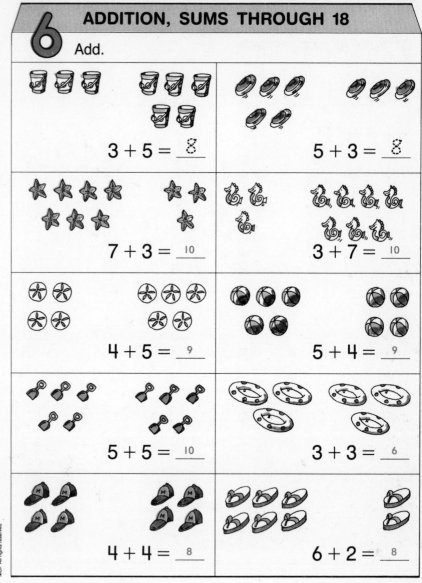

6 ADDITION, SUMS THROUGH 18

Add.

$3 + 5 = 8$

$5 + 3 = 8$

$7 + 3 = 10$

$3 + 7 = 10$

$4 + 5 = 9$

$5 + 4 = 9$

$5 + 5 = 10$

$3 + 3 = 6$

$4 + 4 = 8$

$6 + 2 = 8$

Reviewing addition, sums through 10

(one hundred five) **105**

Teaching page 105

Draw 7 circles in a row on the board. Draw a vertical line between the 2nd and 3rd circles. Ask students to tell the addition sentence. (2 + 5 = 7) Write **2 + 5 = 7** on the board. Ask students to tell another addition sentence using 2 and 5. (5 + 2 = 7) Write this sentence on the board. Now erase the line and draw a line between the 4th and 5th circles. Ask students to tell the 2 addition sentences. (4 + 3 = 7, 3 + 4 = 7) Erase the line and have a student come and draw a line between the 5th and 6th circles and write the 2 addition sentences shown. (5 + 2 = 7, 2 + 5 = 7) Continue until 3 + 4 = 7, 4 + 3 = 7, 1 + 6 = 7 and 6 + 1 = 7 have been shown. Now draw a line before the first circle and write **0 + 7 = 7** and **7 + 0 = 7.** Erase all work and repeat for 5 circles drawn on the board.

Have students look at the first two examples on the page and tell what is shown. (2 ways to make 8) Tell students to trace the 8 in each. Have students complete the page.

105

Add.

9 + 0 = _9_   4 + 3 = _7_   6 + 0 = _6_

2 + 8 = _10_   1 + 4 = _5_   7 + 2 = _9_

1 + 2 = _3_   4 + 2 = _6_   4 + 6 = _10_

2 + 4 = _6_   1 + 9 = _10_   3 + 2 = _5_

3 + 4 = _7_   8 + 2 = _10_   5 + 0 = _5_

8 + 1 = _9_   5 + 1 = _6_   7 + 1 = _8_

6 + 4 = _10_   1 + 7 = _8_   2 + 3 = _5_

3 + 6 = _9_   6 + 3 = _9_   9 + 1 = _10_

2 + 7 = _9_   2 + 5 = _7_   0 + 4 = _4_

1 + 6 = _7_   1 + 8 = _9_   5 + 2 = _7_

106 (one hundred six)   Reviewing addition facts, sums through 10

Correcting Common Errors

Some students may need additional practice with sums through 10. Have them work with partners and write all the addition facts for a sum. For example, for 9 they would write:

9 + 0 = 9	8 + 1 = 9
7 + 2 = 9	6 + 3 = 9
5 + 4 = 9	4 + 5 = 9
3 + 6 = 9	2 + 7 = 9
1 + 8 = 9	0 + 9 = 9

When they finish, they should try to find models of as many of the facts as possible around the classroom.

Enrichment

1. Work in pairs with addition fact cards for sums through 10. Deal 7 cards to each player and place rest of deck face down. Players try to match related facts by drawing a card and placing pairs on the table. First player with no cards left wins.
2. Draw 10 dominoes. Write 2 addition sentences for each of the dominoes.

Teaching page 106

Tell students to work each addition problem to the end of the page.

Extra Credit   *Numeration*

Have each student make number cards from 0 through 9. Place the cards at the top of the desk. Ask the students to form various numbers that you call out such as 85, 126, etc., by putting number cards next to each other to form numbers. To extend this activity, ask the students to make the number that comes before a given number, or after a given number. The teacher could also call out two numbers, have students tell which is larger or smaller.

Practice Sums through 10

pages 107-108

Objective

To practice recall of addition facts for sums through 10

Materials

10 counters
Sheet of paper

Mental Math

Which is less?
1. 42 or 24 (24)
2. 76 or 61 (61)
3. 55 or 75 (55)
4. 16 or 67 (16)
5. 12 or 11 (11)
6. 34 or 43 (34)
7. 28 or 27 (27)
8. 19 or 69 (19)

Skill Review

Have 6 students stand together. Tell students to arrange themselves to show one of the 7 facts in the 6 family. Now have them arrange themselves for another fact of 6. Have other students take turns writing the facts on the board as shown. Repeat for 8 students and 9 students.

Name _____

Add.

$$\begin{array}{r} 5 \\ +3 \\ \hline 8 \end{array} \qquad \begin{array}{r} 4 \\ +5 \\ \hline 9 \end{array}$$

$$\begin{array}{r} 7 \\ +2 \\ \hline 9 \end{array} \qquad \begin{array}{r} 9 \\ +1 \\ \hline 10 \end{array}$$

$$\begin{array}{r} 6 \\ +3 \\ \hline 9 \end{array} \qquad \begin{array}{r} 4 \\ +6 \\ \hline 10 \end{array}$$

$$\begin{array}{r} 2 \\ +6 \\ \hline 8 \end{array} \qquad \begin{array}{r} 5 \\ +5 \\ \hline 10 \end{array}$$

$$\begin{array}{r} 3 \\ +4 \\ \hline 7 \end{array} \qquad \begin{array}{r} 8 \\ +2 \\ \hline 10 \end{array}$$

$$\begin{array}{r} 7 \\ +3 \\ \hline 10 \end{array} \qquad \begin{array}{r} 3 \\ +5 \\ \hline 8 \end{array}$$

Reviewing addition, sums through 10   (one hundred seven) **107**

Teaching page 107

Draw a large domino on the board for 4 + 3 = 7. Have students tell the 2 facts. (4 + 3 = 7, 3 + 4 = 7) Draw another domino for 5 + 2 = 7 and have students tell the facts. (5 + 2 = 7, 2 + 5 = 7) Continue to draw dominoes for 7 to show 6 + 1, 1 + 6, 7 + 0 and 0 + 7. Now draw dominoes for facts with sums of 8.

Have students look at the first domino and tell its number sentence. (5 + 3 = 8) Tell students they are to look at each domino and its addition sentence, and write the answer. Have students complete the page independently.

Add.

8 +1 9	5 +4 9	6 +2 8	4 +3 7	3 +2 5	5 +2 7	9 +0 9
3 +3 6	7 +1 8	2 +5 7	3 +6 9	6 +4 10	2 +8 10	5 +1 6
2 +4 6	4 +2 6	8 +0 8	4 +4 8	3 +7 10	2 +7 9	2 +3 5

FIELD TRIP.

Complete the tables.

Add 3	
2	5
6	9
3	6
5	8
7	10
4	7

Add 4	
3	7
0	4
6	10
4	8
2	6
5	9

Add 5	
1	6
5	10
0	5
2	7
4	9
3	8

108 (one hundred eight)

Reviewing addition facts, sums through 10

Correcting Common Errors

Have students practice sums through 10 by working with partners. Assign them a sum such as 7 and ask them to find all the addition facts, writing them in related pairs.

7 + 0 = 7	6 + 1 = 7
0 + 7 = 7	1 + 6 = 7
5 + 2 = 7	4 + 3 = 7
2 + 5 = 7	3 + 4 = 7

Enrichment

1. Work in 2 teams. When a number 0 through 10 is said, a team member writes an addition fact from that number's fact family on the board. The other team tells if the fact is correct.
2. Work in pairs. Flash addition cards for sums through 10. Work to increase your speed.
3. Make your own domino cards. Play with a friend.

Teaching page 108

Tell students they are to complete the four rows of addition problems.

Field Trip

Tell students they are to add 3 to each number in the first table. Tell students to give the sum of 2 plus 3 and trace the 5. Now ask students what they are to do in the next two tables. (add 4, add 5) Tell students to complete the 3 tables.

Extra Credit   *Statistics*

Give each student a piece of plain paper, two inches square. Ask each to draw a picture of either slacks, overalls, a dress, or a skirt. Tack up a sheet of paper with the heading: CLOTHING GRAPH. Draw a horizontal line near the bottom, beneath it labeling the four columns: slacks, overalls, dress, skirt.

Ask students to come up during the class and glue their picture in the appropriate column. Ask them to put them in a straight column, one above the other. At the end of class, show students the completed graph. Ask if it is easy to tell what most students are wearing from the graph. (yes)

Sums through 12

pages 109-110

Objective

To add for sums 11 and 12

Materials

12 counters
Sheet of paper

Mental Math

Name the number that:
1. comes after 48 (49)
2. comes before 39 (38)
3. is 6 tens and 4 ones (64)
4. is 0 tens and 0 ones (0)
5. comes between 21 and 23 (22)
6. is 1 ten and 2 ones (12)
7. is 8 tens and 0 ones (80)

Skill Review

Tell the story, "4 cows were grazing in the field when the farmer sent 6 more cows to join them." Ask how many cows in all. (10) Have students act out the story with 1 student being the farmer. Now have the farmer arrange the cows in 2 other groups to show a different addition fact for 10. Write the facts on the board as acted out. Continue until all facts are written on the board. Repeat the activity for 8 elephants in a circus, with one student being the elephant trainer.

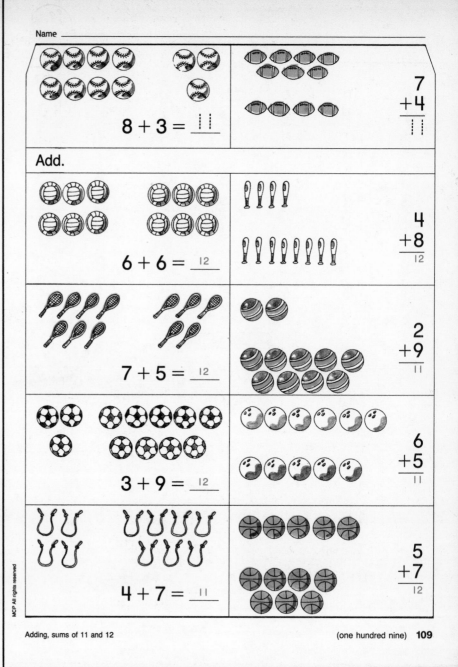

Adding, sums of 11 and 12   (one hundred nine) **109**

Teaching page 109

Have students lay out 11 counters. Tell students to separate the counters into 2 piles. Tell students each pile must have no less than 2 counters. Draw on the board:

11	
(5)	(6)
(4)	(7)
(3)	(8)

Have a student come to the board and write 2 numbers on the first line to show 11. Tell the student to write an addition sentence on the board for those numbers. Continue having students write their numbers and sentences until all addition sentences are shown for 11 using 1-digit numbers. Note that 10 + 1 and 11 + 0 are not basic facts for 11. Repeat the procedure for 12.

Have students look at the first box on the page. Ask how many in all. (11) Have students read 8 + 3 = 11 and trace the 11. Repeat for the vertical fact for 11 in the second box. Tell students to complete the page.

109

$$
\begin{array}{ccccccc}
9 & 7 & 6 & 8 & 7 & 8 & 5 \\
+2 & +3 & +6 & +2 & +5 & +3 & +5 \\
\hline
11 & 10 & 12 & 10 & 12 & 11 & 10
\end{array}
$$

$$
\begin{array}{ccccccc}
8 & 4 & 3 & 5 & 4 & 6 & 3 \\
+4 & +5 & +9 & +6 & +8 & +4 & +8 \\
\hline
12 & 9 & 12 & 11 & 12 & 10 & 11
\end{array}
$$

$$
\begin{array}{ccccccc}
5 & 3 & 4 & 9 & 6 & 4 & 2 \\
+7 & +6 & +7 & +3 & +5 & +6 & +9 \\
\hline
12 & 9 & 11 & 12 & 11 & 10 & 11
\end{array}
$$

FIELD TRIP

Complete the wheels.

110 (one hundred ten)

Adding, sums through 12

Correcting Common Errors

Some students may need a visual model for sums of 11 and 12. Have 11 students stand side-by-side in a row. Ask, "How many in all?" (11) Tell students that they are going to use the numbers 2 through 9 to find addition facts for 11. Move 2 students apart from the rest and ask, "What fact does this show?" (9 + 2 = 11) Write the fact on the chalkboard. Continue to move 1 more student each time to develop the facts for 11 through 2 + 9 = 11. Then add a 12th student and in a similar manner develop the facts for 12 from 9 + 3 = 12 through 3 + 9 = 12.

Enrichment

1. Make addition fact cards for sums of 11 and 12.
2. Draw 11 balloons. Color them 2 different colors to show an addition fact for 11.
3. Draw dimes and pennies to show 11¢ and 12¢.

Teaching page 110

Tell students they are to find the sum in each problem. Have students complete the 3 rows independently.

Field Trip

Tell students they are to complete the addition wheels on this page. Ask what number is to be added to each number in the first wheel. (3) Ask students to give the sum of 7 plus 3. (10) Have students trace the 10. Ask students what number is to be added to each number in the second wheel. (5) Tell students to complete both wheels.

Extra Credit   *Statistics*

This activity is designed to help students see that there are different ways to display the same information. Write a list of your students' names on a long piece of graph paper. Along the top of the page put these headings:

Student name   pants   overalls   dress   skirt

Ask members of the class to make an X after their names in the column that describes what they are wearing. At the end of the day, show students the paper. Explain that this is one way of illustrating the results of a survey. Question students about the results of the survey. Are more students wearing pants or dresses, for example?

110

Sums through 14

pages 111-112

Objective

To add for sums through 14

Materials

14 counters
Sheet of paper

Mental Math

Name the amount that is:

1. 8 dimes (80¢)
2. 0 dimes and 1 penny (1¢)
3. 5 dimes and 5 pennies (55¢)
4. 7 dimes and 9 pennies (79¢)
5. 3 dimes and 2 pennies (32¢)
6. 6 dimes and 0 pennies (60¢)
7. 4 dimes and 2 pennies (42¢)
8. 2 dimes and 1 penny (21¢)

Skill Review

Draw a large domino for 6 + 5 = 11. Have students tell the fact. (6 + 5 = 11 or 5 + 6 = 11) Draw another domino for 4 + 7 = 11 and have students tell the fact. (4 + 7 = 11 or 7 + 4 = 11) Continue to draw dominoes to show 3 + 8, 8 + 3, 2 + 9, 9 + 2. Now draw dominoes for facts with sums of 12.

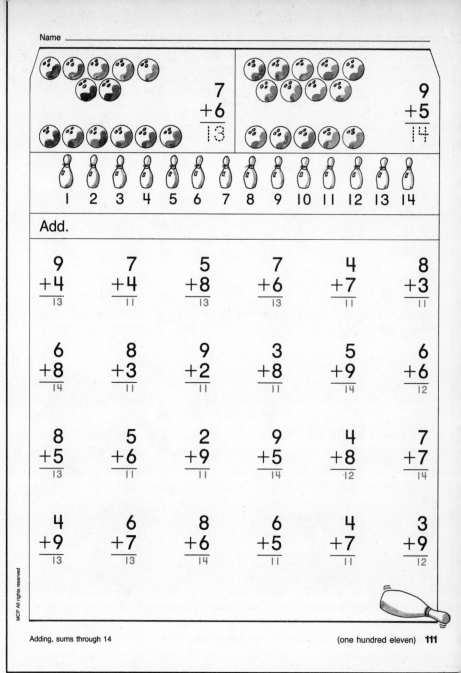

Name _____

$$\begin{array}{r} 7 \\ +6 \\ \hline 13 \end{array}$$

$$\begin{array}{r} 9 \\ +5 \\ \hline 14 \end{array}$$

1 2 3 4 5 6 7 8 9 10 11 12 13 14

Add.

$\begin{array}{r}9\\+4\\\hline 13\end{array}$	$\begin{array}{r}7\\+4\\\hline 11\end{array}$	$\begin{array}{r}5\\+8\\\hline 13\end{array}$	$\begin{array}{r}7\\+6\\\hline 13\end{array}$	$\begin{array}{r}4\\+7\\\hline 11\end{array}$	$\begin{array}{r}8\\+3\\\hline 11\end{array}$
$\begin{array}{r}6\\+8\\\hline 14\end{array}$	$\begin{array}{r}8\\+3\\\hline 11\end{array}$	$\begin{array}{r}9\\+2\\\hline 11\end{array}$	$\begin{array}{r}3\\+8\\\hline 11\end{array}$	$\begin{array}{r}5\\+9\\\hline 14\end{array}$	$\begin{array}{r}6\\+6\\\hline 12\end{array}$
$\begin{array}{r}8\\+5\\\hline 13\end{array}$	$\begin{array}{r}5\\+6\\\hline 11\end{array}$	$\begin{array}{r}2\\+9\\\hline 11\end{array}$	$\begin{array}{r}9\\+5\\\hline 14\end{array}$	$\begin{array}{r}4\\+8\\\hline 12\end{array}$	$\begin{array}{r}7\\+7\\\hline 14\end{array}$
$\begin{array}{r}4\\+9\\\hline 13\end{array}$	$\begin{array}{r}6\\+7\\\hline 13\end{array}$	$\begin{array}{r}8\\+6\\\hline 14\end{array}$	$\begin{array}{r}6\\+5\\\hline 11\end{array}$	$\begin{array}{r}4\\+7\\\hline 11\end{array}$	$\begin{array}{r}3\\+9\\\hline 12\end{array}$

Adding, sums through 14   (one hundred eleven) **111**

Teaching page 111

Have students lay out 13 counters. Tell students to separate the counters into 2 piles. Tell students each pile must have at least 2 counters. Draw on the board:

13	
(6)	(7)
(5)	(8)
(4)	(9)

Have a student come to the board and write 2 numbers on the first line to show 13. Tell the student to write an addition sentence on the board for those numbers. Continue having students write their numbers and sentences until all addition sentences are shown for 13, using 1-digit numbers. Note that 12 + 1 and 13 + 0 are not basic facts for 13. Repeat the procedure for 14.

Have students look at the bowling balls in the first box at the top of the page. Ask students how many in all. (13) Ask student what 2 numbers have been added to make 13. (7, 6) Tell students to trace the 13. Repeat the procedure for the second box of 14 bowling balls. Now tell students they can use the 14 bowling pins to help them add. Tell students if they wanted to add 9 and 4 they would start at 9 and count 4 pins over to 13. Have students practice this for 5 + 8 = 13 and 7 + 7 = 14. Tell students to complete the page.

111

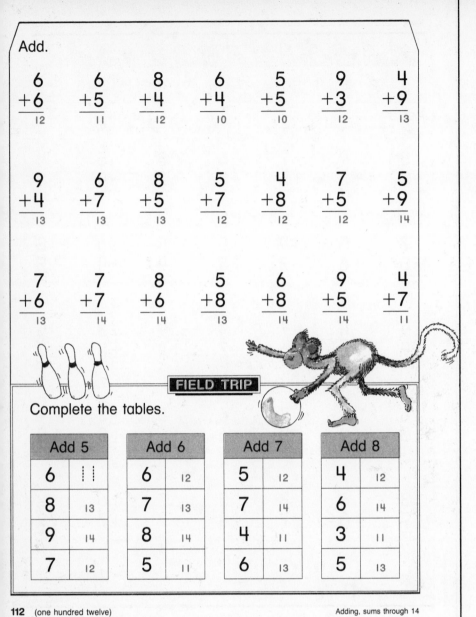

Add.

6 +6 = 12	6 +5 = 11	8 +4 = 12	6 +4 = 10	5 +5 = 10	9 +3 = 12	4 +9 = 13
9 +4 = 13	6 +7 = 13	8 +5 = 13	5 +7 = 12	4 +8 = 12	7 +5 = 12	5 +9 = 14
7 +6 = 13	7 +7 = 14	8 +6 = 14	5 +8 = 13	6 +8 = 14	9 +5 = 14	4 +7 = 11

FIELD TRIP

Complete the tables.

Add 5	
6	11
8	13
9	14
7	12

Add 6	
6	12
7	13
8	14
5	11

Add 7	
5	12
7	14
4	11
6	13

Add 8	
4	12
6	14
3	11
5	13

Adding, sums through 14

Correcting Common Errors

Have students who have difficulty with sums of 13 and 14 work in pairs with counters and 2 cups. Have them start with 13 counters and put some of them in each cup, but not more than 9 in any one cup. Have them write the related addition facts that this models. For example, if they put 9 counters in one cup and 4 in the other, then they would write 9 + 4 = 13 and 4 + 9 = 13. Have them continue to move one counter at a time from one cup to another, to write facts for 13. Then have them do the same with 14 counters.

Enrichment

1. For sums through 14, write the addition facts that are a number plus itself. (ex. 3 + 3 = 6)
2. Write all the addition facts for sums through 14 that have a 7 in them.
3. Make addition fact cards for sums of 13 and 14.

Teaching page 112

Have students write the sums for the 3 rows of problems.

Field Trip

Tell students they are to add 5 to each number in the first table and write the number. Ask students to give the sum of 6 plus 5 and trace the 11. Ask students what they are to do in each of the next tables. (add 6, add 7, add 8) Have students complete the 4 tables.

Extra Credit   *Numeration*

Select two teams of 10 students each. Give each team a set of number cards (0 through 9). Give one card to each student. The leader calls a number from 10 through 99. If the number called is 37, the players on the team who have the numbers 3 and 7 must arrange themselves facing everyone, holding their cards so that the correct number is shown. The team whose members make the correct number first, scores a point.

112

Practice Sums through 14

pages 113-114

Objective

To practice sums through 14

Materials

14 counters
Sheet of paper
*Set of addition fact cards for sums through 14

Mental Math

Name the number that tells:
1. your age
2. your address
3. your telephone number
4. how many in your family
5. how many pets you have
6. how many in your class

Skill Review

Write **8 + 4 = 12** on the board. Ask students to use the numbers 3 through 9 to give another addition fact for 12. Continue until all facts for 12 are written on the board. Repeat for facts for 11, 13 and 14.

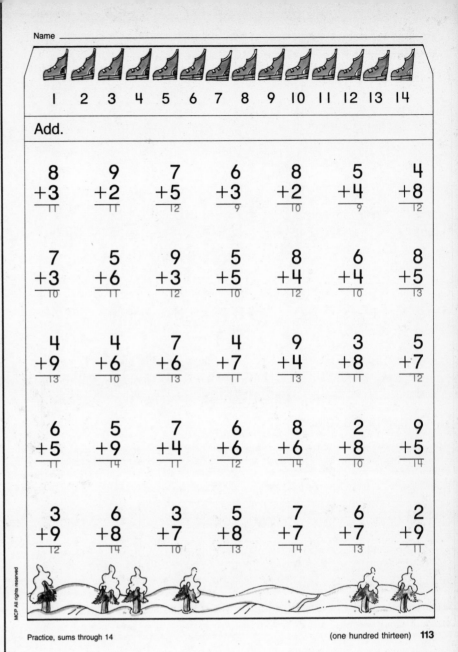

Name _____

1 2 3 4 5 6 7 8 9 10 11 12 13 14

Add.

8 +3 11	9 +2 11	7 +5 12	6 +3 9	8 +2 10	5 +4 9	4 +8 12
7 +3 10	5 +6 11	9 +3 12	5 +5 10	8 +4 12	6 +4 10	8 +5 13
4 +9 13	4 +6 10	7 +6 13	4 +7 11	9 +4 13	3 +8 11	5 +7 12
6 +5 11	5 +9 14	7 +4 11	6 +6 12	8 +6 14	2 +8 10	9 +5 14
3 +9 12	6 +8 14	3 +7 10	5 +8 13	7 +7 14	6 +7 13	2 +9 11

Practice, sums through 14

(one hundred thirteen) **113**

Teaching page 113

Draw 14 circles in a row across the board and write the numbers 1 through 14 under them. Write **9 + 4 = ___** on the board. Tell a student to find the answer to the problem by starting at the 9th circle and counting over 4 more circles. Have the student write the answer in the space. (13) Now write **4 + 9 = ___**. Tell a student to start with the larger number and count over for the smaller number. Have the student write the answer. (13) Give more examples for students to learn to start with the larger number.

Tell students they are to write the sums for all the facts on this page. Tell students the boots can be helpful in counting over to find the sums.

113

Complete the tables.

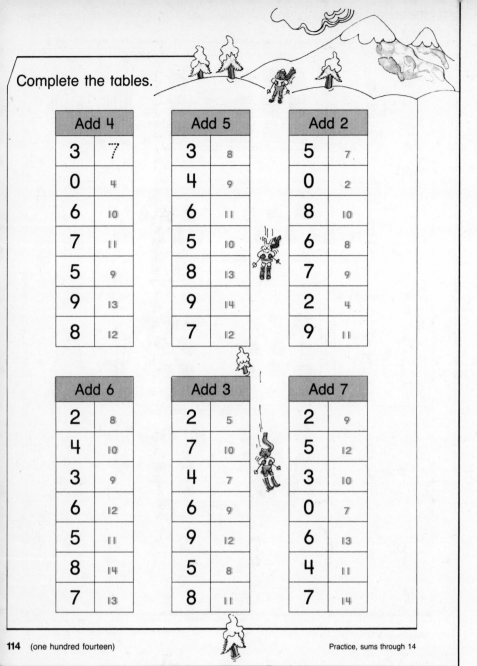

Add 4	
3	7
0	4
6	10
7	11
5	9
9	13
8	12

Add 5	
3	8
4	9
6	11
5	10
8	13
9	14
7	12

Add 2	
5	7
0	2
8	10
6	8
7	9
2	4
9	11

Add 6	
2	8
4	10
3	9
6	12
5	11
8	14
7	13

Add 3	
2	5
7	10
4	7
6	9
9	12
5	8
8	11

Add 7	
2	9
5	12
3	10
0	7
6	13
4	11
7	14

Practice, sums through 14

Correcting Common Errors

Have students who need more practice work with partners and counters. One partner should say a sum of 14 or less. The other partner can write an addition fact, such as 8 + 6 = 14. The first partner then should write the related fact 6 + 8 = 14. Lastly, both partners should work together with counters to confirm their answers. They can continue taking turns saying a sum to get each round started.

Enrichment

1. Make and complete a table titled "Add 7". Write numbers down the side to be added to 7.
2. Draw a picture showing an addition fact for the sum of 14.
3. Draw a ladder with 6 rungs. Write an addition fact for the sum of 13 on each rung.

Teaching page 114

Tell students to find the words **Add 4** at the top of the page. Tell students this is called a **table.** Tell students they are to add 4 to each of the numbers down the column and write the answer next to the number. Ask, "How much is 3 plus 4?" (7) Tell students to trace the 7. Ask what 0 + 4 is. (4) Tell students to write the 4. Now tell students to look at the next table where they are to add 5 to each number. Help students with the first 2 answers. Help students with the first 2 answers of the next table also. Have students complete the page independently.

Extra Credit *Statistics*

Show students how to keep a tally of a number of objects, making a mark for each object and a crossmark when they get to every fifth object.

Now divide the class into several small teams. Explain that each team is to keep track of the number of cars they see passing in the street outside. They should use the tally you have just shown them. At the end of the announced period (five to fifteen minutes, depending on how busy the street is) have teams compare their results.

114

Sums through 16

pages 115-116

Objective

To add for sums of 15 and 16

Materials

16 counters
Sheet of paper

Mental Math

What is the next number?
1. 11 (12)
2. 29 (30)
3. 46 (47)
4. 34 (35)
5. 79 (80)
6. 80 (81)
7. 12 (13)

Skill Review

Write **1 + 1 = 2** on the board. Ask students to tell another addition fact where 1 number is added to itself. Help students list on the board all these facts through sums of 14: 2 + 2 = 4, 3 + 3 = 6, 4 + 4 = 8, 5 + 5 = 10, 6 + 6 = 12, 7 + 7 = 14.

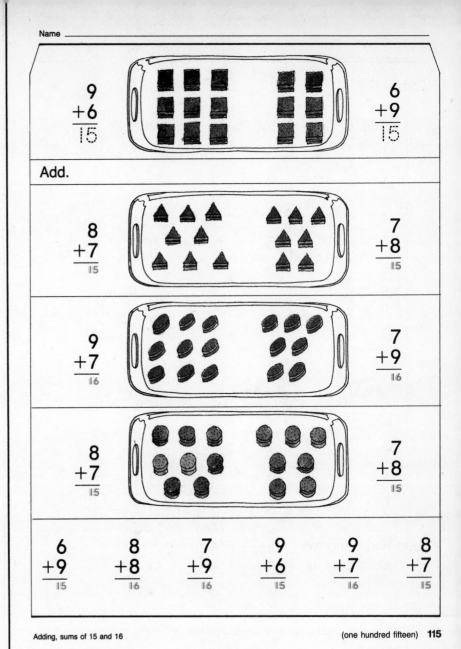

Name _____

Add.

$$\begin{array}{r}9\\+6\\\hline 15\end{array} \qquad \begin{array}{r}6\\+9\\\hline 15\end{array}$$

$$\begin{array}{r}8\\+7\\\hline 15\end{array} \qquad \begin{array}{r}7\\+8\\\hline 15\end{array}$$

$$\begin{array}{r}9\\+7\\\hline 16\end{array} \qquad \begin{array}{r}7\\+9\\\hline 16\end{array}$$

$$\begin{array}{r}8\\+7\\\hline 15\end{array} \qquad \begin{array}{r}7\\+8\\\hline 15\end{array}$$

$$\begin{array}{r}6\\+9\\\hline 15\end{array} \quad \begin{array}{r}8\\+8\\\hline 16\end{array} \quad \begin{array}{r}7\\+9\\\hline 16\end{array} \quad \begin{array}{r}9\\+6\\\hline 15\end{array} \quad \begin{array}{r}9\\+7\\\hline 16\end{array} \quad \begin{array}{r}8\\+7\\\hline 15\end{array}$$

Adding, sums of 15 and 16   (one hundred fifteen) **115**

Teaching page 115

Tell students the above facts can be called **doubles.** Now write **1 + 2 = 3** on the board. Tell students this problem can be thought of as a double plus 1 because 1 has been added to 1 to make 2. Write **2 + 2 = 4** and ask students what the double plus 1 fact would be. (2 + 3 = 5) Continue to find the double plus 1 for each of the doubles. (3 + 4 = 7, 4 + 5 = 9, 5 + 6 = 11, 6 + 7 = 13) Write **7 + 7 = 14** on the board and ask students to tell the double plus 1. (7 + 8) Ask students what 7 plus 8 equals. (15) Ask students to tell other facts for sums of 15. Remind students that basic facts are made with 1-digit numbers as you develop 9 + 6 = 15, 8 + 7 = 15 and 6 + 9 = 15. Write **8 + 7 = 15** on the board and ask students what 8 plus 8 would equal. (16) Ask students to name other basic facts for 16. (9 + 7, 7 + 9)

Have students look at the problem 9 + 6 = 15 at the top of the page. Tell students to count the objects and write the sum for each problem. Have students complete the page.

115

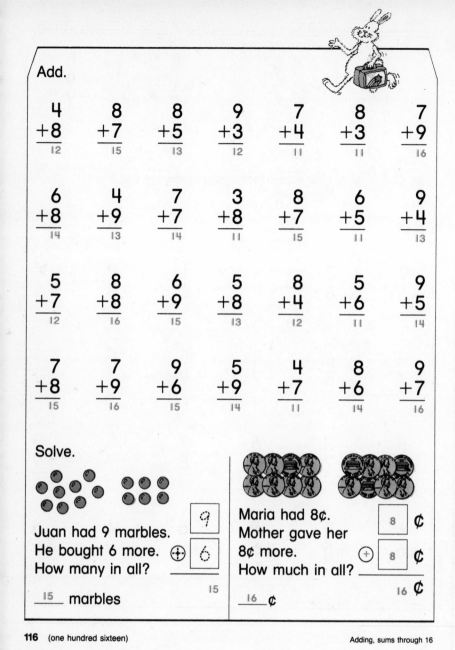

Add.

4	8	8	9	7	8	7
+8	+7	+5	+3	+4	+3	+9
12	15	13	12	11	11	16

6	4	7	3	8	6	9
+8	+9	+7	+8	+7	+5	+4
14	13	14	11	15	11	13

5	8	6	5	8	5	9
+7	+8	+9	+8	+4	+6	+5
12	16	15	13	12	11	14

7	7	9	5	4	8	9
+8	+9	+6	+9	+7	+6	+7
15	16	15	14	11	14	16

Solve.

Juan had 9 marbles.
He bought 6 more. ⊕ [9] [6]
How many in all? ___
15

__15__ marbles

Maria had 8¢.
Mother gave her
8¢ more. ⊕ [8] ¢ [8] ¢
How much in all? ___
16 ¢

__16__ ¢

Adding, sums through 16

Correcting Common Errors

Some students may need additional practice with sums of 15 and 16. Draw 15 circles on the chalkboard and write the numbers from 1 through 15 under them. Write 8 + 7 = ☐ on the board. Start at 8 and count over 7 more circles. Ask, "What does 8 plus 7 equal?" (15) Write 6 + 9 = ☐ on the board. Ask, "If you start with the larger number being added, which number would you start with?" (9) Have a volunteer come to the chalkboard, start at 9 and count over 6 circles and write the sum, 15. Continue to develop all sums of 15 using 1-digit numbers. Have students draw and number their own circles on paper to develop the facts for 16 in the same way.

Enrichment

1. Make addition fact cards for sums of 15 and 16.
2. Draw dimes and pennies to show 15¢ and 16¢.
3. Write all facts that use the addend 9, through sums of 16.

Teaching page 116

Have students write the sum for each problem in all 4 rows. Now have students look at the first story problem as you read it. Have students trace the 9 to show how many marbles Juan had and trace the 6 to show he got 6 more. Ask students if we should add or subtract to show how many marbles in all. (add) Have students trace the plus sign. Ask students how many in all. (15) Have students write 15 under the problem and again beside the word marbles. Work similarly with students through the next story problem.

Extra Credit *Numeration*

Prepare approximately 35 cards that name numbers by values of tens and ones. (ex: 5 tens and 6 ones, 8 tens and 3 ones) Put the cards into a box. Have students take turns choosing a card from the box, reading the card and showing it to the class. Then have all the students write the number on their papers. To extend this activity, have students also write the number that comes before and the number that follows the number they have written.

116

Sums through 18

pages 117-118

Objective

To add for sums through 18¢

Materials

18 counters
Sheet of paper

Mental Math

Name the number that comes before:

1. 40 (39)
2. 12 (11)
3. 80 (79)
4. 76 (75)
5. 48 (47)
6. 92 (91)
7. 71 (70)
8. 55 (54)

Skill Review

Write **1 + 1 = 2** and **1 + 2 = 3** on the board and tell students this is a double and its double plus 1. Have a student write the 2 double under 1 + 1 = 2. (2 + 2 = 4) Ask another student to write the double plus 1 fact under 1 + 2 = 3. (2 + 3 = 5) Continue having students write the doubles through 8 + 8 = 16 in the doubles column, and the corresponding double plus 1 through 8 + 9 = 17.

$$\begin{array}{r} 9 \\ +8 \\ \hline 17 \end{array} \qquad \begin{array}{r} 8 \\ +9 \\ \hline 17 \end{array}$$

$$\begin{array}{r} 9 \\ +9 \\ \hline 18 \end{array}$$

Add.

$\begin{array}{r} 9 \\ +6 \\ \hline 15 \end{array}$	$\begin{array}{r} 3 \\ +6 \\ \hline 9 \end{array}$	$\begin{array}{r} 2 \\ +9 \\ \hline 11 \end{array}$	$\begin{array}{r} 1 \\ +8 \\ \hline 9 \end{array}$	$\begin{array}{r} 9 \\ +8 \\ \hline 17 \end{array}$	$\begin{array}{r} 7 \\ +5 \\ \hline 12 \end{array}$
$\begin{array}{r} 9 \\ +7 \\ \hline 16 \end{array}$	$\begin{array}{r} 6 \\ +8 \\ \hline 14 \end{array}$	$\begin{array}{r} 4 \\ +7 \\ \hline 11 \end{array}$	$\begin{array}{r} 5 \\ +9 \\ \hline 14 \end{array}$	$\begin{array}{r} 9 \\ +3 \\ \hline 12 \end{array}$	$\begin{array}{r} 9 \\ +9 \\ \hline 18 \end{array}$
$\begin{array}{r} 5 \\ +6 \\ \hline 11 \end{array}$	$\begin{array}{r} 3 \\ +7 \\ \hline 10 \end{array}$	$\begin{array}{r} 6 \\ +4 \\ \hline 10 \end{array}$	$\begin{array}{r} 7 \\ +8 \\ \hline 15 \end{array}$	$\begin{array}{r} 5 \\ +7 \\ \hline 12 \end{array}$	$\begin{array}{r} 8 \\ +9 \\ \hline 17 \end{array}$
$\begin{array}{r} 6 \\ +6 \\ \hline 12 \end{array}$	$\begin{array}{r} 9 \\ +5 \\ \hline 14 \end{array}$	$\begin{array}{r} 8 \\ +5 \\ \hline 13 \end{array}$	$\begin{array}{r} 5 \\ +5 \\ \hline 10 \end{array}$	$\begin{array}{r} 6 \\ +9 \\ \hline 15 \end{array}$	$\begin{array}{r} 8 \\ +8 \\ \hline 16 \end{array}$

Adding, sums through 18

(one hundred seventeen) **117**

Teaching page 117

Write on the board: **9 + 8 = ___, 8 + 9 = ___, 9 + 9 = ___.** Tell students these are the last 3 addition facts they will learn. Tell students to lay out 9 counters and add 8 more to find the sum of 9 + 8. (17) Repeat for 8 + 9 and 9 + 9. (17 and 18)

Have students count the objects at the top of the page. (17) Tell students to trace the 17 in each problem to show that 9 + 8 = 17 and 8 + 9 = 17. Now have students count the objects in the next example and trace the 18 to show that 9 + 9 = 18. Have students complete the page independently.

Add.

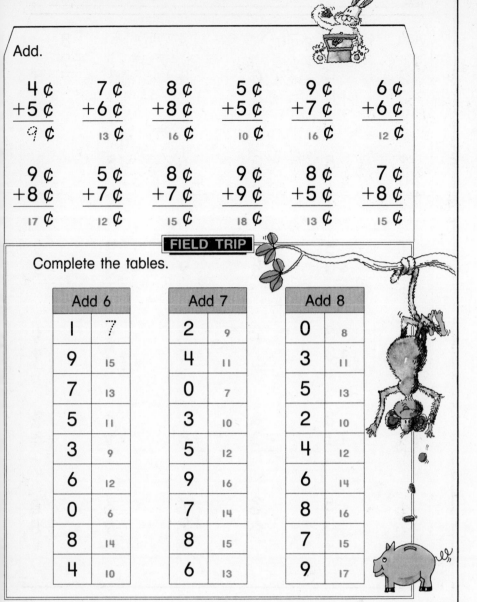

4¢	7¢	8¢	5¢	9¢	6¢
+5¢	+6¢	+8¢	+5¢	+7¢	+6¢
9¢	13¢	16¢	10¢	16¢	12¢

9¢	5¢	8¢	9¢	8¢	7¢
+8¢	+7¢	+7¢	+9¢	+5¢	+8¢
17¢	12¢	15¢	18¢	13¢	15¢

FIELD TRIP

Complete the tables.

Add 6	
1	7
9	15
7	13
5	11
3	9
6	12
0	6
8	14
4	10

Add 7	
2	9
4	11
0	7
3	10
5	12
9	16
7	14
8	15
6	13

Add 8	
0	8
3	11
5	13
2	10
4	12
6	14
8	16
7	15
9	17

Adding, money sums through 18¢

Correcting Common Errors

Students may need practice with the three new facts of 9 + 8, 8 + 9, and 9 + 9. Start with 9 + 9 = 18. Help students discover that 9 + 8 and 8 + 9 each have an addend that is 1 less than 9. Therefore, each sum must be 1 less than 18, or 9 + 8 = 17 and 8 + 9 = 17.

Enrichment

1. Make a table of all addition facts for sums through 18.
2. Make addition fact cards for sums of 17 and 18.
3. Cut and paste pictures from magazines or catalogs to show doubles and doubles plus 1. Write the fact for each.

Teaching page 118

Have students write the sums for the 2 rows of money problems at the top of the page.

Field Trip

Tell students they are to add 6 to each number in the first table and write the sum. Ask students to give the sum of 1 plus 6 (7) and trace the 7. Tell students they are to add 7 to each number to complete the second table and then add 8 to each number in the last table.

Extra Credit   *Counting*

This counting activity can provide day-long suspense. Count out at least 30 small items such as buttons, beads, or ice cream sticks. Place these together in a box. Provide another box, taped shut, with a slit-type opening. Throughout the day have each student count the items in the first box, write the amount and their name on a piece of paper and drop the paper into the second box. At the end of the day, count the items together in class. Then reach into the answer box and draw out one paper. If the answer is correct announce the person's name and allow the student to count out items for the next day's play, or perhaps to choose a favorite story, song or poem to end the day.

118

Practice Sums through 18

pages 119-120

Objective

To practice sums through 18

Materials

18 counters
Sheet of paper
*Set of addition fact cards for sums through 18

Mental Math

How much?
1. 9 take away 4 (5)
2. 9 minus 0 (9)
3. 8 minus 7 (1)
4. 6 take away 1 (5)
5. 9 take away 9 (0)
6. 8 minus 2 (6)
7. 7 minus 5 (2)

Skill Review

Make up story problems for addition facts. Have students write the facts on the board. Remind students that the words **how many in all** and **how many altogether** are clues telling them to add.

Name _____

Add.

2 +2 ___ 4	4 +4 ___ 8	0 +5 ___ 5	4 +2 ___ 6	1 +1 ___ 2	3 +0 ___ 3
3 +4 ___ 7	5 +1 ___ 6	2 +3 ___ 5	6 +1 ___ 7	3 +2 ___ 5	1 +8 ___ 9
1 +2 ___ 3	5 +0 ___ 5	5 +4 ___ 9	0 +9 ___ 9	4 +3 ___ 7	2 +5 ___ 7
5 +2 ___ 7	3 +3 ___ 6	2 +7 ___ 9	6 +2 ___ 8	4 +5 ___ 9	1 +4 ___ 5
2 +4 ___ 6	3 +1 ___ 4	6 +3 ___ 9	1 +5 ___ 6	8 +1 ___ 9	3 +5 ___ 8
1 +7 ___ 8	5 +3 ___ 8	3 +6 ___ 9	7 +2 ___ 9	2 +6 ___ 8	7 +1 ___ 8

Practice, sums through 9

(one hundred nineteen) **119**

Teaching page 119

Use addition fact cards to flash drill for sums through 9.

Have students complete the problems to the end of the page.

119

Add.

7 +3 10	9 +2 11	4 +8 12	6 +5 11	3 +8 11	7 +5 12
8 +4 12	5 +5 10	5 +8 13	9 +8 17	5 +6 11	4 +9 13
6 +7 13	6 +4 10	8 +8 16	4 +7 11	9 +4 13	6 +6 12
9 +6 15	7 +7 14	8 +5 13	8 +7 15	4 +6 10	6 +9 15
7 +8 15	9 +3 12	7 +6 13	5 +9 14	7 +9 16	6 +8 14
8 +9 17	9 +5 14	9 +7 16	5 +7 12	8 +6 14	9 +9 18

Practice, sums of 10 through 18

Correcting Common Errors

Have students who need more practice make their own addition tables. Each student will need a piece of grid paper. Have the student write a + sign in a box near the top and left edges. Then have the student write the numbers 0 through 9 across the row to the right of the + sign and 0 through 9 down the column below the + sign. Then have the students complete the table by filling in all the sums from $0 + 0 = 0$ to $9 + 9 = 18$. Encourage students to look for patterns after their grids are finished.

Enrichment

1. Tell a story problem for the addition fact $9 + 7 = 16$.
2. Make a talking addition fact chain. First student says an addition fact. Next student gives the answer and names another addition fact for next student to answer. Continue through all students.
3. Write answers to addition facts when dictated.

Teaching page 120

Have students complete the page independently.

Extra Credit   *Counting*

Provide students with a hand-printed list of first and last names of each child in the class. Draw an answer box following each complete name. Students are to count the number of letters in each name and write the correct numerals in the boxes. Circulate among the children as the activity is being completed. Ask them to recount slowly any that you see are incorrect. The project can be extended by listing the names on the chalkboard in order from fewest to most letters. Try this idea another time with reading words, or names of the city, school, principal and teachers, etc.

120

Missing Addends

pages 121-122

Objective

To write missing addends in facts for sums 11 through 18

Materials

None

Mental Math

Name the number that is 1 more than:

1. 4 + 4 (9)
2. 6 + 6 (13)
3. 5 + 5 (11)
4. 2 + 2 (5)
5. 8 + 8 (17)
6. 3 + 3 (7)
7. 7 + 7 (15)
8. 0 + 0 (1)

Skill Review

Group students into 4 teams. Draw on the board 4 ladders with 10 rungs each. Write 1 number from 6 through 9 at the top of each ladder. Have each team start at the bottom rung and write the addition facts in order for the number. The facts should start with the number plus 0.

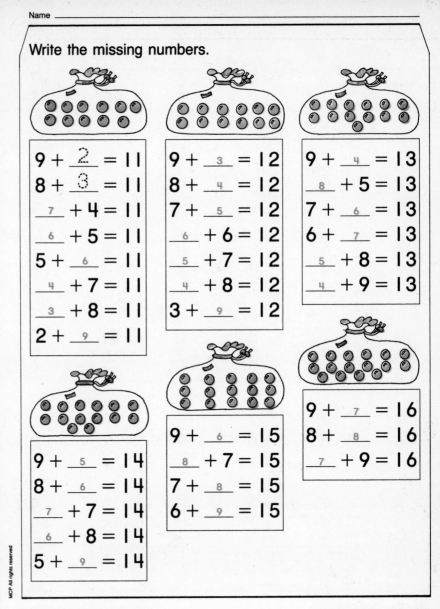

Write the missing numbers.

$9 + 2 = 11$
$8 + 3 = 11$
$7 + 4 = 11$
$6 + 5 = 11$
$5 + 6 = 11$
$4 + 7 = 11$
$3 + 8 = 11$
$2 + 9 = 11$

$9 + 3 = 12$
$8 + 4 = 12$
$7 + 5 = 12$
$6 + 6 = 12$
$5 + 7 = 12$
$4 + 8 = 12$
$3 + 9 = 12$

$9 + 4 = 13$
$8 + 5 = 13$
$7 + 6 = 13$
$6 + 7 = 13$
$5 + 8 = 13$
$4 + 9 = 13$

$9 + 5 = 14$
$8 + 6 = 14$
$7 + 7 = 14$
$6 + 8 = 14$
$5 + 9 = 14$

$9 + 6 = 15$
$8 + 7 = 15$
$7 + 8 = 15$
$6 + 9 = 15$

$9 + 7 = 16$
$8 + 8 = 16$
$7 + 9 = 16$

Writing the missing addends in fact families

(one hundred twenty-one) **121**

Teaching page 121

Write **8 + 4 = 12** on the board. Cover the 4 and ask students what must be added to 8 to make 12. (4) Now cover the 8 and ask what number plus 4 equals 12. (8) Repeat the procedure for several more examples.

Have students count the marbles in the first bag. (11) Tell students to read the first fact for 11. (9 + 2 = 11) Ask students what number is added to 9 to make 11. (2) Have students trace the 2. Repeat for the next problem. Work through all the facts for 11 with the students. Tell students they may use the marbles in each bag to help them find the missing numbers. Tell students to complete the page.

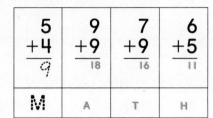

FIELD TRIP

Find the secret message.
Use the sums to break the code.

5 +4 9	9 +9 18	7 +9 16	6 +5 11
M	A	T	H

6 +4 10	8 +5 13
I	S

6 +6 12	9 +8 17	8 +7 15
F	U	N

8 +8 16	5 +9 14
T	O

3 +5 8	7 +7 14
D	O

Code

8	9	10	11	12	13	14	15	16	17	18
D	M	I	H	F	S	O	N	T	U	A

122 (one hundred twenty-two)

Practice, sums through 18

Correcting Common Errors

Have students practice with partners to find missing addends using counters. They can place on their work area the number of counters indicated by the given addend. Next, they should add enough counters to have a total equal to the given sum. Be sure that they understand that the number of counters they had to add is the missing addend.

Enrichment

1. Work with friends to act out a fact for a sum of 15, 16, 17 or 18.
2. Draw a picture showing a doubles plus 1 fact. Tell the story your picture shows.
3. Tell the double that helps to find the sums of $5 + 6$, $4 + 3$, $8 + 9$, $9 + 8$ and $6 + 7$.

Teaching page 122

Field Trip

Tell students they are to write the sum of each problem. Have students verify and trace the 9 in the first problem. Tell students to find the 9 in the code at the bottom of the page. Ask students to tell the alphabet letter under the 9 in the code. (M) Tell students to trace the M under the problem. Have students find and record the letter for each sum and read the word. Tell students to find the rest of the sums to decode the next 4 words. Have students read the sentence when all students have finished.

Extra Credit   *Statistics*

Ask students if they made their bed before they left for school. On the board, draw a picture of a tidy bed and next to it a picture of a messy bed. Have students come up and write their name under the one that looks most like their bed at home. When all have written their name in one column or the other, ask a volunteer to explain whether more have made their bed or not made it. Ask how they could tell. (by looking to see which column had more names in it) Have a student count the names in each list and write the number at the bottom of the column.

122

Column Addition, Problem Solving

pages 123-124

Objectives

To add in columns for sums through 18
To solve problems for sums through 18

Materials

18 counters
Sheet of paper

Mental Math

What number plus:
1. 2 equals 4 (2)
2. 3 equals 6 (3)
3. 5 equals 10 (5)
4. 8 equals 16 (8)
5. 9 equals 18 (9)
6. 7 equals 14 (7)

Skill Review

Have 9 students stand together. Tell students you need 16 students in all. Ask how many more students need to come stand with the 9. (7) Have 7 more students join the 9. Tell students to count all the students to see if 9 + 7 = 16. Repeat for more examples of addition facts through sums of 18.

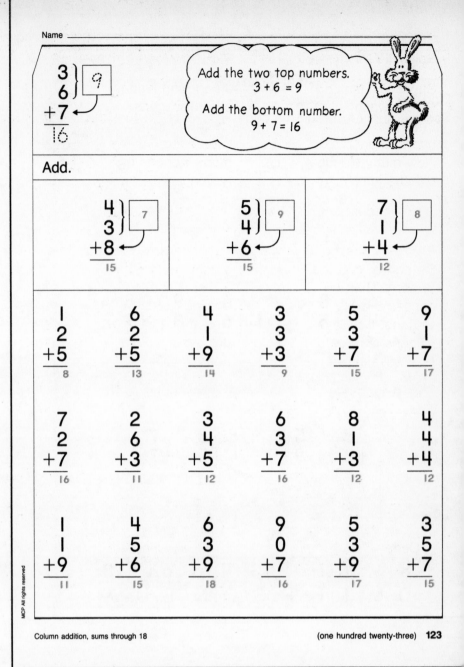

Name _____

Add the two top numbers.
3 + 6 = 9
Add the bottom number.
9 + 7 = 16

$$\begin{array}{r} 3 \\ 6 \\ +7 \\ \hline 16 \end{array}$$ 9

Add.

$$\begin{array}{r} 4 \\ 3 \\ +8 \\ \hline 15 \end{array}$$ 7 $$\begin{array}{r} 5 \\ 4 \\ +6 \\ \hline 15 \end{array}$$ 9 $$\begin{array}{r} 7 \\ 1 \\ +4 \\ \hline 12 \end{array}$$ 8

1	6	4	3	5	9
2	2	1	3	3	1
+5	+5	+9	+3	+7	+7
8	13	14	9	15	17
7	2	3	6	8	4
2	6	4	3	1	4
+7	+3	+5	+7	+3	+4
16	11	12	16	12	12
1	4	6	9	5	3
1	5	3	0	3	5
+9	+6	+9	+7	+9	+7
11	15	18	16	17	15

Column addition, sums through 18   (one hundred twenty-three) **123**

Teaching page 123

Have students count out 14 counters. Write on the board:

3	6	2	4	5	7
4	1	7	5	2	2
+5	+7	+4	+9	+8	+5
(12)	(14)	(13)	(18)	(15)	(14)

Tell students to make 3 stacks of counters to match the addends in the first problem. (3,4,5) Say, "3 plus 4 equals 7 and 7 plus 5 equals 12," as you point to the addends. Repeat the procedure for the other problems.

Have students look at the example at the top of the page as you read the words. Have students trace the 9 and 16. Repeat the written instructions as students work the next 3 problems. Tell students to complete the page.

123

Solve.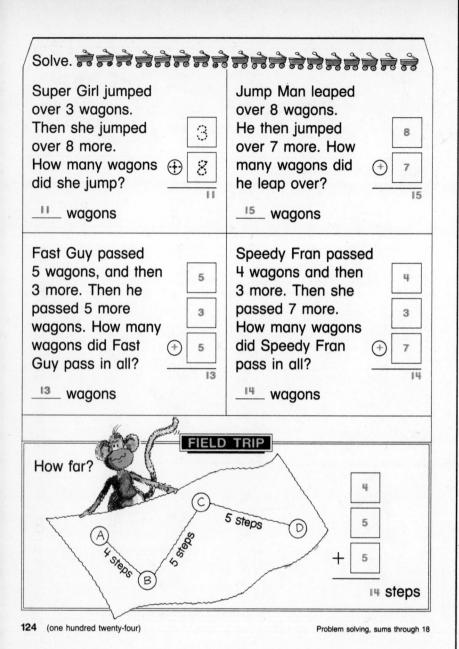

Super Girl jumped
over 3 wagons.
Then she jumped
over 8 more.
How many wagons
did she jump?

3
⊕ 8
___
11

__11__ wagons

Jump Man leaped
over 8 wagons.
He then jumped
over 7 more. How
many wagons did
he leap over?

8
+ 7
___
15

__15__ wagons

Fast Guy passed
5 wagons, and then
3 more. Then he
passed 5 more
wagons. How many
wagons did Fast
Guy pass in all?

5
3
+ 5
___
13

__13__ wagons

Speedy Fran passed
4 wagons and then
3 more. Then she
passed 7 more.
How many wagons
did Speedy Fran
pass in all?

4
3
+ 7
___
14

__14__ wagons

FIELD TRIP

How far?

4 steps
5 steps
5 steps

4
5
+ 5
___
14 steps

Problem solving, sums through 18

Correcting Common Errors

Some students may have difficulty
finding the sum of three numbers
because they cannot remember the
sum of the first two numbers when
they go to add it to the third
number. Have them continue to
write the sum of the first two
numbers next to the addends. Then
they can add this number to the third
addend to find the final sum.

Enrichment

1. Tell a story problem where 4, 5
and 9 are added together.
2. Use number cards 0 through 9.
Place 0, 1, 2 and 3 face down
in one pile. Place 4, 5 and 6
face down in a second pile and
7, 8 and 9 in a third pile. Draw
a card from the first and second
piles and add together. Then
add to a card drawn from the
third pile. Give the sum.

Teaching page 124

Have students look at the wagons. Tell them they may
use these to help them solve the problems. Read the
first problem with the students. Ask what is to be done.
(add 3 + 8) Tell students to trace the 3, the plus sign
and the 8. They should write the answer below the
problem and again on the blank. (11) Read through
each of the next 3 problems with the students and ask
them to fill in the numbers and signs.

Extra Credit *Numeration*

Create a counting-by-tens activity for small groups. At
the top of the blackboard, within student reach, draw a
dog. At the bottom of the board draw a doghouse.
Between the two, create a winding path of sequenced
numbers, counting by tens up to 100. Put in every
other number, and leave blanks for the missing
numbers. Tell students to take turns filling in the
missing tens so the dog can follow the path to reach
its house. After one group finishes, erase the path and
set up a different fill-in sequence for the next group.

Problem Solving

pages 125-126

Objective

To solve story problems for sums through 18¢

Materials

Small toys with price tags of 1¢ through 9¢
18 pennies per student

Mental Math

Which number comes first?
1. 28 or 36 (28)
2. 82 or 57 (57)
3. 19 or 11 (11)
4. 99 or 9 (9)
5. 6 or 64 (6)
6. 72 or 17 (17)

Skill Review

Tell students a story about Demetrius who had 2 soccer balls, 1 basketball and 9 tennis balls. Ask students how many sporting balls the boy had in all. (12) Ask a student to write the problem on the board and tell how to find the sum of 12. (2 plus 1 equals 3 plus 9 equals 12) Repeat for more story problems of 3 addends for sums through 18. Be sure the first sum is less than 10.

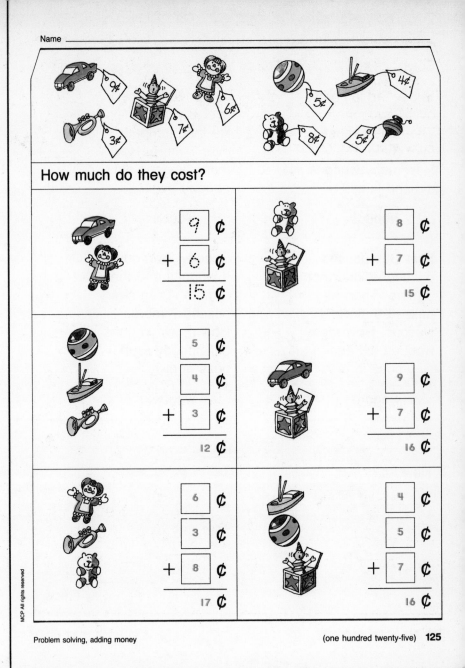

Name _____

How much do they cost?

car + doll	9 ¢ + 6 ¢ 15 ¢	bear + jack-in-box	8 ¢ + 7 ¢ 15 ¢
ball + boat + trumpet	5 ¢ 4 ¢ + 3 ¢ 12 ¢	car + jack-in-box	9 ¢ + 7 ¢ 16 ¢
doll + trumpet + bear	6 ¢ 3 ¢ + 8 ¢ 17 ¢	boat + ball + jack-in-box	4 ¢ 5 ¢ + 7 ¢ 16 ¢

Problem solving, adding money

(one hundred twenty-five) **125**

Teaching page 125

Show students 2 priced toys as you tell a story about buying the toys. Write the problem on the board. Ask students to tell the total cost. Now show 3 items and ask students to tell a story about buying toys. Write the 3-addend problem on the board and have a student tell how to find the sum by adding the first 2 numbers and then the last. Write **16¢** on the board. Ask which 2 items one could buy with 16¢. Write the problem on the board. Now ask which 3 items could be purchased and have a student write the problem and tell how to find the sum.

Have students name the toys and their prices at the top of the page. Have students tell the price of the car in the first problem and then trace the 9. Ask the price of the doll and have students trace the 6. Tell students

to trace the 15 to show that the car and doll together would cost 15¢. Go through the next problem with the students and then have them complete the page independently.

125

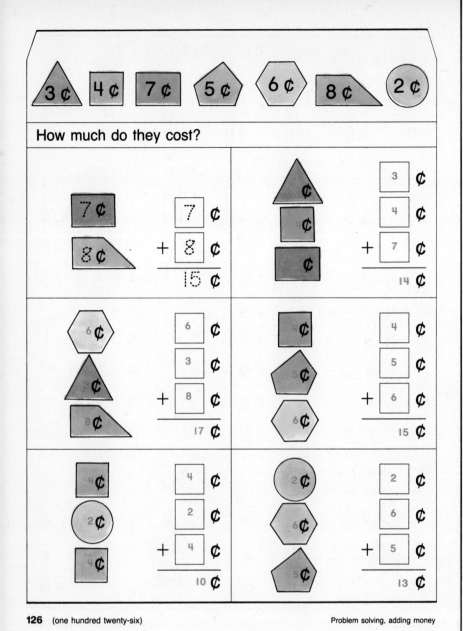

3¢ 4¢ 7¢ 5¢ 6¢ 8¢ 2¢

How much do they cost?

Problem 1:
7¢
8¢
$$7 ¢ + 8 ¢ = 15 ¢$$

Problem 2:
◯¢
◯¢
◯¢
$$3 ¢ \quad 4 ¢ + 7 ¢ = 14 ¢$$

Problem 3:
6¢
3¢
8¢
$$6 ¢ \quad 3 ¢ + 8 ¢ = 17 ¢$$

Problem 4:
◯¢
◯¢
◯¢
$$4 ¢ \quad 5 ¢ + 6 ¢ = 15 ¢$$

Problem 5:
4¢
2¢
4¢
$$4 ¢ \quad 2 ¢ + 4 ¢ = 10 ¢$$

Problem 6:
2¢
6¢
5¢
$$2 ¢ \quad 6 ¢ + 5 ¢ = 13 ¢$$

Problem solving, adding money

Correcting Common Errors

If students have difficulty adding amounts of money, have them use pennies to model each problem and count to find the sum.

Enrichment

1. Draw and price three objects you could buy in a store for a total cost of 18¢.
2. Draw 3 groups of pennies to show 16¢.
3. Take 17¢ to the classroom store. Buy 2 items so that you still have 4¢ left.

Teaching page 126

Have students read the prices of each shape across the top of the page. Tell students to look at the 2 shapes in the first problem and tell their costs. (7¢, 8¢) Tell students to check in the row across the top of the page to see that those prices are correct. Tell students to trace the prices in the 2 shapes and then trace these prices in the problem. Tell students to trace the 15 to show that 15¢ is the total cost of these 2 shapes. Tell students they are to find the prices of each shape, write each price in the shape and then write the problem and find the sum. Work through the next problem with the students and then have them complete the page.

Extra Credit   *Counting*

Cut 30 large balloon-shapes from colored paper. Write a series of 3 consecutive prices, up to 19¢, on each set of 3 balloons. Attach the balloons in sets of 3 on the chalkboard or bulletin board, turning over either the middle or the first and third balloons to show their blank sides. Attach or draw strings tying each set of 3 together. Provide students with a duplicated page showing ten sets of blank balloons. Have them write the prices of the posted balloons and fill in the missing numbers in each series. At the end of the activity, turn the blank balloons over to reveal the missing prices. Make your activity reusable by writing the prices on blank cards and taping them to the balloons. Use this activity again to challenge students when counting up to 50, 100, etc.

126

Chapter Review

pages 127-128

Objectives

To review addition for sums
through 18 and 18¢
To maintain skills previously learned

Materials

None

Mental Math

Name the number that is:
1. 4 tens and 2 ones (42)
2. 0 tens and 9 ones (9)
3. 7 dimes and 3 pennies (73¢)
4. 9 tens and 4 ones (94)
5. 8 tens and 0 ones (80)
6. 1 ten and 2 ones (12)
7. 2 dimes and 6 pennies (26¢)
8. 3 dimes (30¢)

Skill Review

Write **17¢** on the board. Ask a
student to write a 3-addend problem
whose sum is 17¢. Have the student
write the cent signs in the problem.
Ask another student to write another
problem of 3 prices that equal 17¢.
Continue to develop more problems.
Now write **19¢** and repeat the
procedure.

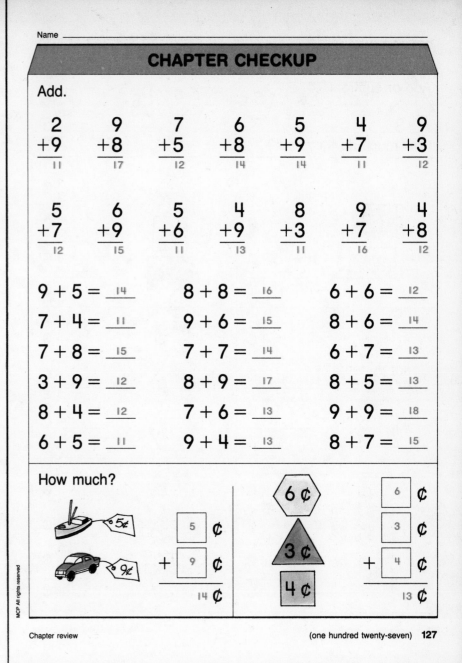

Teaching page 127

Have students complete the page independently by
finding the sums.

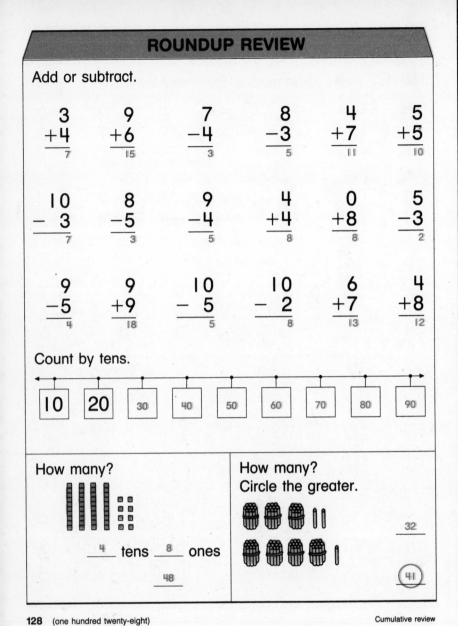

ROUNDUP REVIEW

Add or subtract.

3	9	7	8	4	5
+4	+6	−4	−3	+7	+5
7	15	3	5	11	10

10	8	9	4	0	5
− 3	−5	−4	+4	+8	−3
7	3	5	8	8	2

9	9	10	10	6	4
−5	+9	− 5	− 2	+7	+8
4	18	5	8	13	12

Count by tens.

10	20	30	40	50	60	70	80	90

How many?

_4_ tens _8_ ones

_48_

How many?
Circle the greater.

32

(41)

128 (one hundred twenty-eight)   Cumulative review

Teaching page 128

Have students look at the top row of problems. Tell students to circle the sign in each problem that tells whether to add or subtract. Tell students to continue this for the next 2 rows of problems, and then write the answer. Then tell students they are to count by 10's and write the missing numbers in the blanks on the number line. Go through both problems at the bottom of the page with the students as they write the answers.

This page reviews addition and subtraction facts, skip counting by 10's, place value and comparing numbers.

Minuends through 10

pages 129-130

Objective

To review subtraction for minuends through 10

Materials

10 counters
Yarn ring

Mental Math

How many digits:
1. in your telephone number
2. in your address
3. in 99 (2)
4. on a clock (15)
5. in 82 (2)
6. on a telephone (10)
7. from 0 through 9 (10)
8. from 13 through 16 (8)

Skill Review

Tell students you will say an addition fact and they are to say another addition fact using the same 2 addends. Say, "2 + 3 = 5."(3 + 2 = 5) Give enough facts for each student to give at least 2 responses.

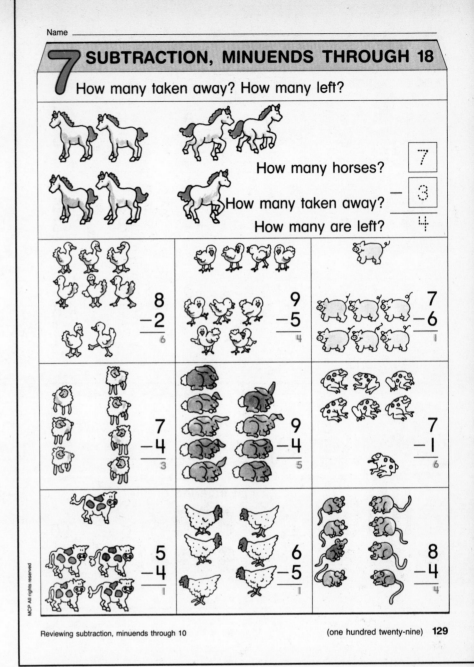

How many taken away? How many left?

How many horses?
How many taken away?
How many are left?

$$\begin{array}{r} 7 \\ -\ 3 \\ \hline 4 \end{array}$$

$$\begin{array}{r} 8 \\ -2 \\ \hline 6 \end{array}$$

$$\begin{array}{r} 9 \\ -5 \\ \hline 4 \end{array}$$

$$\begin{array}{r} 7 \\ -6 \\ \hline 1 \end{array}$$

$$\begin{array}{r} 7 \\ -4 \\ \hline 3 \end{array}$$

$$\begin{array}{r} 9 \\ -4 \\ \hline 5 \end{array}$$

$$\begin{array}{r} 7 \\ -1 \\ \hline 6 \end{array}$$

$$\begin{array}{r} 5 \\ -4 \\ \hline 1 \end{array}$$

$$\begin{array}{r} 6 \\ -5 \\ \hline 1 \end{array}$$

$$\begin{array}{r} 8 \\ -4 \\ \hline 4 \end{array}$$

Reviewing subtraction, minuends through 10

(one hundred twenty-nine) **129**

Teaching page 129

Tell students to lay 7 counters in the yarn ring. Tell students to take away 4 counters and tell how many are left.(3) Write **7 − 4 = 3** on the board. Ask students to tell the parts of 7.(4 and 3) Ask a student to write 2 subtraction sentences on the board to show these 2 parts of 7.(7 − 4 = 3, 7 − 3 = 4)

Now tell students to place 7 counters in the yarn ring and remove 1 counter. Ask how many are left.(6) Ask a student to write the 2 subtraction sentences using these parts of 7.(7 − 1 = 6, 7 − 6 = 1) Continue to develop 7 − 2 = 5 and 7 − 5 = 2 in the same way. Make a table on the board as illustrated:

7 in all	
1	6
2	5
3	4

Repeat the procedure for the parts of 8.

Have students look at the horses at the top of the page and tell how many in all.(7) Tell students to trace the 7. Ask how many are going away.(3) Tell students to trace the 3. Ask how many are left.(4) Tell students to trace the 4. Have the students complete the page.

129

How many taken away? How many left?

$\begin{array}{r} 2 \\ -1 \\ \hline \vdots \end{array}$	$\begin{array}{r} 4 \\ -2 \\ \hline 2 \end{array}$	$\begin{array}{r} 5 \\ -2 \\ \hline 3 \end{array}$
$\begin{array}{r} 5 \\ -3 \\ \hline 2 \end{array}$	$\begin{array}{r} 7 \\ -2 \\ \hline 5 \end{array}$	$\begin{array}{r} 8 \\ -3 \\ \hline 5 \end{array}$
$\begin{array}{r} 9 \\ -2 \\ \hline 7 \end{array}$	$\begin{array}{r} 6 \\ -2 \\ \hline 4 \end{array}$	$\begin{array}{r} 4 \\ -1 \\ \hline 3 \end{array}$
$\begin{array}{r} 5 \\ -5 \\ \hline 0 \end{array}$	$\begin{array}{r} 7 \\ -5 \\ \hline 2 \end{array}$	$\begin{array}{r} 6 \\ -4 \\ \hline 2 \end{array}$
$\begin{array}{r} 8 \\ -6 \\ \hline 2 \end{array}$	$\begin{array}{r} 9 \\ -3 \\ \hline 6 \end{array}$	$\begin{array}{r} 10 \\ -1 \\ \hline 9 \end{array}$

Reviewing subtraction, minuends through 10

Correcting Common Errors

Some students may need additional practice with minuends through 10 Have them work with partners and write all the subtraction facts for a given minuend. For example, for the minuend 9, they would write these subtraction facts:

$9 - 0 = 9$	$9 - 1 = 8$
$9 - 2 = 7$	$9 - 3 = 6$
$9 - 4 = 5$	$9 - 5 = 4$
$9 - 6 = 3$	$9 - 7 = 2$
$9 - 8 = 1$	$9 - 9 = 0$

When they finish, encourage them to find examples of as many of these facts as possible around the classroom.

Enrichment

1. Draw a picture to show 2 parts of 6. Write 2 number sentences that tell about the picture.
2. Write 2 number sentences for 5, if one part is 2.
3. Make subtraction fact cards for minuends through 10.

Teaching page 130

Tell students they are to again cross out the objects to be taken away and then write the answer. Have students trace the 1 in the first problem and then complete the page independently.

Extra Credit *Statistics*

One essential element of statistics is the survey. Have students conduct a survey. Give them the following questions and tell them to ask the questions of at least five people and bring the results back to school the next day.

1. Do you like vanilla ice cream? ___ yes ___ no
2. Have you ever been to a baseball game? ___ yes ___ no
3. Do you have a brother or sister? ___ yes ___ no
4. Do you know how to swim? ___ yes ___ no

When students bring their results in the next day, divide the class into groups and assign each group a different survey question. Give each group one-inch graph paper, and have them mark one square for each answer. Ask one person in the group to write the survey question at the top of the graph to identify it. Display the graphs so students can compare the results.

Minuends through 10

pages 131-132

Objective

To practice subtraction facts for minuends through 10

Materials

10 counters
Yarn ring
10 × 10 grid paper
Crayons

Mental Math

Give an addition and subtraction sentence for the parts:
1. 2 and 4 (6 − 2 = 4, 6 − 4 = 2, 2 + 4 = 6, 4 + 2 = 6)
2. 3 and 6
3. 4 and 1
4. 7 and 3
5. 5 and 2
6. 8 and 1

Skill Review

Write the number **8** on the board. Now write **4 + 3, 3 + 5, 4 + 4, 2 + 6, 5 + 3, 0 + 8, 3 + 4, 7 + 2** and **1 + 7** on the board. Have students circle the facts which show parts of 8.(3 + 5, 4 + 4, 2 + 6, 5 + 3, 0 + 8, 1 + 7) Repeat the activity for parts of 9.

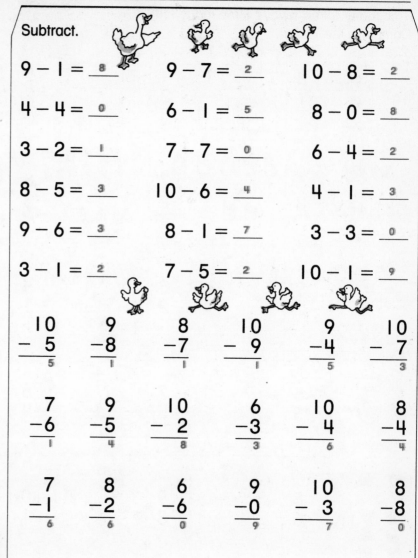

Name _____

Subtract.

9 − 1 = _8_   9 − 7 = _2_   10 − 8 = _2_

4 − 4 = _0_   6 − 1 = _5_   8 − 0 = _8_

3 − 2 = _1_   7 − 7 = _0_   6 − 4 = _2_

8 − 5 = _3_   10 − 6 = _4_   4 − 1 = _3_

9 − 6 = _3_   8 − 1 = _7_   3 − 3 = _0_

3 − 1 = _2_   7 − 5 = _2_   10 − 1 = _9_

10	9	8	10	9	10
− 5	−8	−7	− 9	−4	− 7
5	1	1	1	5	3

7	9	10	6	10	8
−6	−5	− 2	−3	− 4	−4
1	4	8	3	6	4

7	8	6	9	10	8
−1	−2	−6	−0	− 3	−8
6	6	0	9	7	0

Subtraction facts, minuends through 10   (one hundred thirty-one) **131**

Teaching page 131

Write on the board:

10 in all	
(1)	(9)
(2)	(8)
(3)	(7)
(4)	(6)
(5)	(5)

Ask students to lay out counters in yarn rings to name 2 parts of 10 until all 5 sets of numbers are written on the board. Write the 2 subtraction facts for each set of numbers as they are given. (10 − 1 = 9, 10 − 9 = 1, etc.)

Tell students to write the answer for each subtraction fact on this page.

131

Complete the tables.

Subtract 3	
5	2
6	3
10	7
8	5
9	6

Subtract 4	
7	3
10	6
8	4
6	2
9	5

Subtract 5	
6	1
5	0
10	5
9	4
8	3

FIELD TRIP

Subtract. Use the numbers to write another fact.

$9 - 3 = 6$

$9 - 6 = 3$

$4 - 4 = 0$

$4 - 0 = 4$

$8 - 5 = 3$

$8 - 3 = 5$

$10 - 7 = 3$

$10 - 3 = 7$

$10 - 9 = 1$

$10 - 1 = 9$

$7 - 0 = 7$

$7 - 7 = 0$

Subtraction facts, minuends through 10

Correcting Common Errors

For students who need more practice subtracting with minuends through 10, have them work with partners. Give them a minuend, such as 7, and have them find all the subtraction facts, writing them in related pairs.

$7 - 1 = 6$ $7 - 2 = 5$
$7 - 6 = 1$ $7 - 5 = 2$

$7 - 3 = 4$ $7 - 0 = 7$
$7 - 4 = 3$ $7 - 7 = 0$

Enrichment

1. Color an 8×8 grid to show all the ways to make 8 with 2 numbers. Use any colors.
2. Color a 6×6 grid with only 2 colors to show the parts of 6. Look for an interesting pattern in your work.

Teaching page 132

Tell students to find the words **Subtract 3** in the first table. Tell students they are to take away 3 from each number in this table, and write the number left in the box beside the number. Ask what is left if 3 is taken away from 5.(2) Have students complete the **Subtract 3** table. Now tell students they are to subtract 4 from each number in the second table and take away 5 in the last table. Tell students to complete the 2 tables independently.

Field Trip

Remind students that they can use the 3 numbers from one subtraction sentence to write another subtraction sentence. Write **6 − 2 = 4** on the board and ask students to use these same numbers to write another subtraction sentence.(6 − 4 = 2) Have students trace

the number left when 3 is subtracted from 9.(6) Ask students to trace the numbers in the next sentence to show how the same 3 numbers are used for the second subtraction sentence. Tell students to find the number left in the first sentence in each box and then use those 3 numbers to write a second subtraction sentence.

Extra Credit   *Counting*

Take the class to the parking lot. Ask the students the following questions: "How many cars have two doors?" "How many cars have four doors?" "How many cars have five doors (station wagons)?" Ask the students to count the number of blue cars, white cars, etc. Tell the students to count the tires on the cars, counting by two's. Tell the students to count the doors of the cars counting by two's.

132

Minuends 8 through 12

pages 133-134

Objective

To subtract from minuends 11 and 12

Materials

12 counters
Yarn ring

Mental Math

What is the other part of 9 if:

1. 5 is one part (4)
2. 2 is one part (7)
3. 4 is one part (5)
4. 3 is one part (6)
5. 0 is one part (9)
6. 6 is one part (3)
7. 7 is one part (2)
8. 8 is one part (1)

Skill Review

Tell students to write the answers as you dictate 20 subtraction facts through minuends of 10.

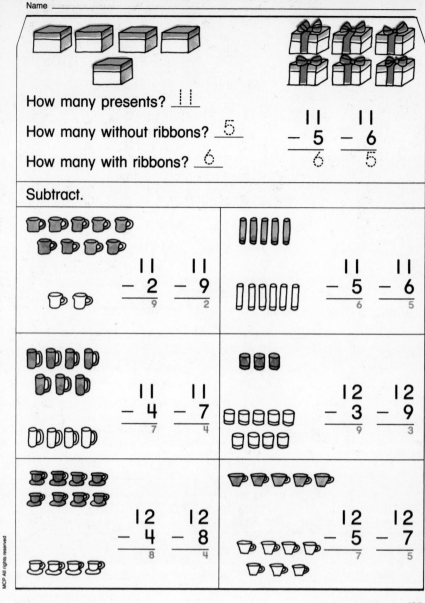

Name _____

How many presents? _11_

How many without ribbons? _5_

How many with ribbons? _6_

$$\begin{array}{r} 11 \\ -\ 5 \\ \hline 6 \end{array} \qquad \begin{array}{r} 11 \\ -\ 6 \\ \hline 5 \end{array}$$

Subtract.

$$\begin{array}{r} 11 \\ -\ 2 \\ \hline 9 \end{array} \qquad \begin{array}{r} 11 \\ -\ 9 \\ \hline 2 \end{array} \qquad\qquad \begin{array}{r} 11 \\ -\ 5 \\ \hline 6 \end{array} \qquad \begin{array}{r} 11 \\ -\ 6 \\ \hline 5 \end{array}$$

$$\begin{array}{r} 11 \\ -\ 4 \\ \hline 7 \end{array} \qquad \begin{array}{r} 11 \\ -\ 7 \\ \hline 4 \end{array} \qquad\qquad \begin{array}{r} 12 \\ -\ 3 \\ \hline 9 \end{array} \qquad \begin{array}{r} 12 \\ -\ 9 \\ \hline 3 \end{array}$$

$$\begin{array}{r} 12 \\ -\ 4 \\ \hline 8 \end{array} \qquad \begin{array}{r} 12 \\ -\ 8 \\ \hline 4 \end{array} \qquad\qquad \begin{array}{r} 12 \\ -\ 5 \\ \hline 7 \end{array} \qquad \begin{array}{r} 12 \\ -\ 7 \\ \hline 5 \end{array}$$

Subtracting, minuends of 11 and 12

(one hundred thirty-three) **133**

Teaching page 133

Write on the board:

11 in all	
(2)	(9)
(3)	(8)
(4)	(7)
(5)	(6)

Ask students to place 11 counters in their rings and then remove 2. Ask how many are left. (9) Have a student fill in the table and write the subtraction sentence on the board. (11 − 2 = 9) Ask students to tell the parts of 11. (2 and 9) Ask a student to write another subtraction sentence using 2 and 9. (11 − 9 = 2) Continue to fill in the table and build other subtraction sentences for 11. Tell students that basic facts are built with parts of 9 or less. Make a similar table and write the sentences for the parts of 12. (12 − 3 = 9, 12 − 9 = 3, 12 − 4 = 8, 12 − 8 = 4, 12 − 5 = 7, 12 − 7 = 5, 12 − 6 = 6)

Have students look at the presents and tell how many in all. (11) Have students trace the 11. Ask how many are without ribbons. (5) Have students trace the 6. Have students read the vertical problems, tell the 2 parts of 11 and the answers. Go through the next problem with the students as they write the answers. Now have students complete the page.

133

Subtract.

$8 - 3 = \underline{5}$ $11 - 2 = \underline{9}$ $9 - 7 = \underline{2}$

$9 - 1 = \underline{8}$ $12 - 4 = \underline{8}$ $10 - 1 = \underline{9}$

$10 - 2 = \underline{8}$ $10 - 3 = \underline{7}$ $8 - 5 = \underline{3}$

$11 - 5 = \underline{6}$ $12 - 5 = \underline{7}$ $10 - 9 = \underline{1}$

$9 - 9 = \underline{0}$ $11 - 9 = \underline{2}$ $11 - 6 = \underline{5}$

$12 - 3 = \underline{9}$ $9 - 3 = \underline{6}$ $10 - 5 = \underline{5}$

9 -2 7	10 -4 6	12 -7 5	9 -6 3	11 -3 8	12 -9 3
8 -2 6	10 -8 2	9 -4 5	11 -8 3	12 -8 4	10 -7 3
11 -4 7	9 -5 4	12 -6 6	11 -7 4	9 -8 1	10 -6 4

Subtracting, minuends 8 through 12

Correcting Common Errors

Some students may have difficulty subtracting from minuends of 11 and 12. For each subtraction fact, have them write a related addition fact and then find the missing addend.
EXAMPLE:

Problem: $12 - 7 = \square$
Write: $\square + 7 = 12$
Think: What number added to 7 equals 12. Answer: 5.
Fact: $12 - 7 = 5$

Enrichment

1. Color a 12×8 grid of 1 inch squares with 2 colors to show the parts of 12 with 2 numbers. Always use the same color first and look for a pattern in your work.
2. Write all the addition and subtraction facts to name 11.

Teaching page 134

Tell students they are to complete all the subtraction problems on this page.

Extra Credit   *Statistics*

Use the results from a previous survey the students have done to help students understand the idea of predicting. For example, hold up the graph made for the question: "Do you have any brothers or sisters?" Ask a volunteer to explain whether there are more people with siblings or without. (with, most likely) Explain that they are going to ask the same question of ten people they have not surveyed before, perhaps students in a neighboring class. Ask your class to predict how many of the students will answer that they have a brother or sister. (answers will vary) Write their prediction on the board. Now survey the ten additional students and write the results of the survey on the board. Ask students how close their prediction was.

Minuends of 13 and 14

pages 135-136

Objective

To subtract from minuends of 13 and 14

Materials

14 counters
Yarn ring
*Set of subtraction fact cards for minuends through 12

Mental Math

How many?
1. pennies in a dime (10)
2. hands on a clock (2)
3. toes on one foot (5)
4. toes on two feet (10)
5. numbers between 12 and 16 (3)
6. tens in 67 (6)
7. ones in 93 (3)

Skill Review

Show subtraction fact cards for minuends through 12 and have students give another fact for each minuend.

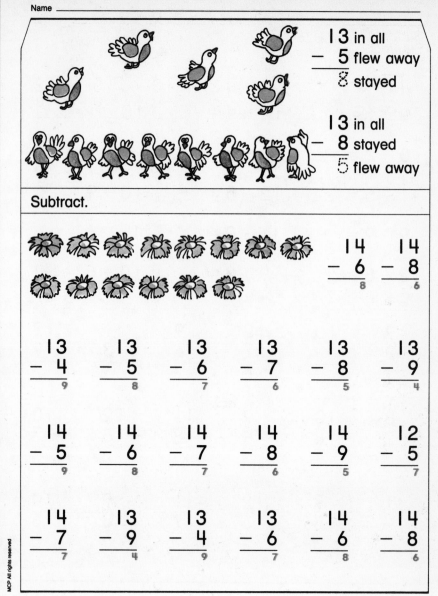

Name _____

$$\begin{array}{r} 13 \text{ in all} \\ -\ 5 \text{ flew away} \\ \hline 8 \text{ stayed} \end{array}$$

$$\begin{array}{r} 13 \text{ in all} \\ -\ 8 \text{ stayed} \\ \hline 5 \text{ flew away} \end{array}$$

Subtract.

$$\begin{array}{r} 14 \\ -\ 6 \\ \hline 8 \end{array} \qquad \begin{array}{r} 14 \\ -\ 8 \\ \hline 6 \end{array}$$

$$\begin{array}{r} 13 \\ -\ 4 \\ \hline 9 \end{array} \quad \begin{array}{r} 13 \\ -\ 5 \\ \hline 8 \end{array} \quad \begin{array}{r} 13 \\ -\ 6 \\ \hline 7 \end{array} \quad \begin{array}{r} 13 \\ -\ 7 \\ \hline 6 \end{array} \quad \begin{array}{r} 13 \\ -\ 8 \\ \hline 5 \end{array} \quad \begin{array}{r} 13 \\ -\ 9 \\ \hline 4 \end{array}$$

$$\begin{array}{r} 14 \\ -\ 5 \\ \hline 9 \end{array} \quad \begin{array}{r} 14 \\ -\ 6 \\ \hline 8 \end{array} \quad \begin{array}{r} 14 \\ -\ 7 \\ \hline 7 \end{array} \quad \begin{array}{r} 14 \\ -\ 8 \\ \hline 6 \end{array} \quad \begin{array}{r} 14 \\ -\ 9 \\ \hline 5 \end{array} \quad \begin{array}{r} 12 \\ -\ 5 \\ \hline 7 \end{array}$$

$$\begin{array}{r} 14 \\ -\ 7 \\ \hline 7 \end{array} \quad \begin{array}{r} 13 \\ -\ 9 \\ \hline 4 \end{array} \quad \begin{array}{r} 13 \\ -\ 4 \\ \hline 9 \end{array} \quad \begin{array}{r} 13 \\ -\ 6 \\ \hline 7 \end{array} \quad \begin{array}{r} 14 \\ -\ 6 \\ \hline 8 \end{array} \quad \begin{array}{r} 14 \\ -\ 8 \\ \hline 6 \end{array}$$

Subtracting, minuends of 13 and 14

(one hundred thirty-five) **135**

Teaching page 135

Write on the board:

13 in all	
(4)	(9)
(5)	(8)
(6)	(7)

Ask students to place 13 counters in their rings and then remove 4. Ask how many are left. (9) Have a student write the subtraction sentence on the board. (13 − 4 = 9) Ask students to tell the parts of 13. (4 and 9) Ask a student to write another subtraction sentence using 4 and 9. (13 − 9 = 4) Continue to build other subtraction sentences for 13. Remind students that basic facts are built with parts of 9 or less. Make a similar

table and write the sentences for the parts of 14. (14 − 7 = 7, 14 − 8 = 6, 14 − 6 = 8)

Have students count the birds and tell how many in all. (13) Ask how many flew away. (5) Ask how many are left. (8) Have students trace the 8. For the next problem ask how many in all (13), how many stayed (8) and how many flew away. (5) Go through the next picture and problem similarly. Then tell students to work the three rows of problems.

Subtract.

$$\begin{array}{r} 11 \\ -\ 3 \\ \hline 8 \end{array} \quad \begin{array}{r} 11 \\ -\ 8 \\ \hline 3 \end{array} \quad \begin{array}{r} 12 \\ -\ 3 \\ \hline 9 \end{array} \quad \begin{array}{r} 12 \\ -\ 9 \\ \hline 3 \end{array} \quad \begin{array}{r} 13 \\ -\ 4 \\ \hline 9 \end{array} \quad \begin{array}{r} 13 \\ -\ 9 \\ \hline 4 \end{array} \quad \begin{array}{r} 12 \\ -\ 4 \\ \hline 8 \end{array}$$

$$\begin{array}{r} 12 \\ -\ 8 \\ \hline 4 \end{array} \quad \begin{array}{r} 13 \\ -\ 5 \\ \hline 8 \end{array} \quad \begin{array}{r} 13 \\ -\ 8 \\ \hline 5 \end{array} \quad \begin{array}{r} 11 \\ -\ 5 \\ \hline 6 \end{array} \quad \begin{array}{r} 11 \\ -\ 6 \\ \hline 5 \end{array} \quad \begin{array}{r} 12 \\ -\ 5 \\ \hline 7 \end{array} \quad \begin{array}{r} 12 \\ -\ 7 \\ \hline 5 \end{array}$$

$$\begin{array}{r} 13 \\ -\ 6 \\ \hline 7 \end{array} \quad \begin{array}{r} 13 \\ -\ 7 \\ \hline 6 \end{array} \quad \begin{array}{r} 14 \\ -\ 5 \\ \hline 9 \end{array} \quad \begin{array}{r} 14 \\ -\ 9 \\ \hline 5 \end{array} \quad \begin{array}{r} 14 \\ -\ 6 \\ \hline 8 \end{array} \quad \begin{array}{r} 14 \\ -\ 8 \\ \hline 6 \end{array} \quad \begin{array}{r} 14 \\ -\ 7 \\ \hline 7 \end{array}$$

FIELD TRIP

Complete the wheels.

Subtracting, minuends of 11 through 14

Teaching page 136

Tell students to write the answers for the subtraction problems.

Field Trip

Have students find the 14 in the center of the first wheel. Ask students what is left if they have 14 and take 7 away. (7) Have students trace the 7. Tell students they are to subtract each number in the wheel from 14 and write the number left. Tell students to find the 13 in the center of the second wheel. Ask what is left when 7 is taken away from 13. (6) Tell students to complete both wheels.

Extra Credit   *Counting*

Hang a piece of clothesline between two chairs at least 3 feet apart. Have available a supply of spring-type clothspins, and 100 index cards numbered from 1 through 100. The line can be used to answer a variety of problems by having a student hang the correct number cards on the line with clothespins. Have problems such as the following printed on paper for the students to complete:

1. count by 10's to 100.
2. count by 5's to 50.
3. start with 1 and continue counting to discover how many cards will fit on the line.
4. start with 79 and count to 100.
5. start with 65 and count backwards to 58.

Students can use the "number line" in teams of two.

136

Minuends through 14

pages 137-138

Objective

To practice subtraction facts for minuends 10 through 14

Materials

*Set of subtraction fact cards for minuends through 14
Grid sheets for 11 through 14 squares across
14 counters
Yarn ring

Mental Math

Who is older?
1. Mary is 38, Tom is 13 (Mary)
2. Ari is 14, Ti is 41 (Ti)
3. Chan is 62, Al is 26 (Chan)
4. Phil is 29, Bo is 92 (Bo)
5. Lin is 18, Lon is 7 (Lin)
6. Mike is 13, Sue is 12 (Mike)
7. Red is 28, Sam is 30 (Sam)
8. Lu is 72, Bart is 70 (Lu)

Skill Review

Show subtraction fact cards for minuends through 14. Have student give another fact for each minuend.

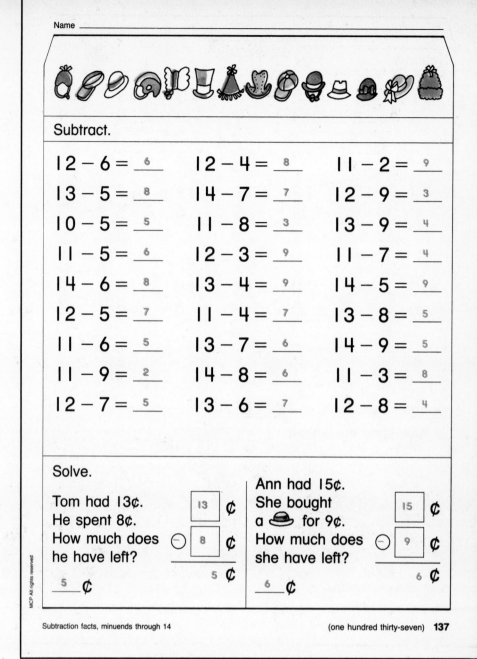

Name _____

Subtract.

$12 - 6 = \underline{6}$ $12 - 4 = \underline{8}$ $11 - 2 = \underline{9}$

$13 - 5 = \underline{8}$ $14 - 7 = \underline{7}$ $12 - 9 = \underline{3}$

$10 - 5 = \underline{5}$ $11 - 8 = \underline{3}$ $13 - 9 = \underline{4}$

$11 - 5 = \underline{6}$ $12 - 3 = \underline{9}$ $11 - 7 = \underline{4}$

$14 - 6 = \underline{8}$ $13 - 4 = \underline{9}$ $14 - 5 = \underline{9}$

$12 - 5 = \underline{7}$ $11 - 4 = \underline{7}$ $13 - 8 = \underline{5}$

$11 - 6 = \underline{5}$ $13 - 7 = \underline{6}$ $14 - 9 = \underline{5}$

$11 - 9 = \underline{2}$ $14 - 8 = \underline{6}$ $11 - 3 = \underline{8}$

$12 - 7 = \underline{5}$ $13 - 6 = \underline{7}$ $12 - 8 = \underline{4}$

Solve.

Tom had 13¢. He spent 8¢. How much does he have left?

13	¢
⊖ 8	¢
5	¢

$\underline{5}$ ¢

Ann had 15¢. She bought a 🎩 for 9¢. How much does she have left?

15	¢
⊖ 9	¢
6	¢

$\underline{6}$ ¢

Subtraction facts, minuends through 14   (one hundred thirty-seven) **137**

Teaching page 137

Write on the board:

14 in all	
(9)	(5)
(8)	(6)
(7)	(7)

Ask students to place 14 counters in their rings and then remove 9. Ask how many are left. (5) Have a student write the subtraction sentence on the board. (14 − 9 = 5) Ask students to tell the parts of 14. (9 and 5) Ask a student to write another subtraction sentence using 9 and 5. (14 − 5 = 9) Continue to build other subtraction sentences for 12, 11 and 13.

Have students tell how many hats are pictured. (14) Tell students they may want to use the hats to help

them work the subtraction problems on this page. Have students do the 3 columns of problems independently. Read each of the story problems with the students as they write the numbers and the minus signs.

FIELD TRIP

Color by answers.

4 brown   6 green
5 blue   7 yellow

$$\begin{array}{r} 14 \\ -\ 9 \\ \hline 5 \end{array}$$

$$\begin{array}{r} 13 \\ -\ 6 \\ \hline 7 \end{array}$$

$$\begin{array}{r} 12 \\ -\ 5 \\ \hline 7 \end{array}$$

$$\begin{array}{r} 13 \\ -\ 9 \\ \hline 4 \end{array}$$

$$\begin{array}{r} 11 \\ -\ 4 \\ \hline 7 \end{array}$$

$$\begin{array}{r} 14 \\ -\ 7 \\ \hline 7 \end{array}$$

$$\begin{array}{r} 11 \\ -\ 6 \\ \hline 5 \end{array}$$

$$\begin{array}{r} 12 \\ -\ 8 \\ \hline 4 \end{array}$$

$$\begin{array}{r} 10 \\ -\ 6 \\ \hline 4 \end{array}$$

$$\begin{array}{r} 12 \\ -\ 7 \\ \hline 5 \end{array}$$

$$\begin{array}{r} 12 \\ -\ 6 \\ \hline 6 \end{array}$$

$$\begin{array}{r} 11 \\ -\ 7 \\ \hline 4 \end{array}$$

$$\begin{array}{r} 13 \\ -\ 8 \\ \hline 5 \end{array}$$

$$\begin{array}{r} 14 \\ -\ 8 \\ \hline 6 \end{array}$$

$$\begin{array}{r} 11 \\ -\ 5 \\ \hline 6 \end{array}$$

$$\begin{array}{r} 13 \\ -\ 7 \\ \hline 6 \end{array}$$

138 (one hundred thirty-eight)   Subtraction facts, minuends 10 through 14

Correcting Common Errors

Have students who need more practice work with partners and counters to model the problems. They can use the counters to show the minuend, take away the number indicated by the subtrahend, and count those that are left to find the answer.

Enrichment

1. Make subtraction fact cards for minuends through 14.
2. Write an addition or subtraction fact for the 2 parts of 11, 12, 13 or 14. Have partner write a + or − sign to complete your fact.

Teaching page 138

Field Trip

Ask students to tell what sign is in all the problems in the picture. (−) Ask what they are to do in each problem. (subtract) Tell students they are to work each problem and then find that number in the code. Tell students they are to color each section the color named beside the number in the code. Ask students what color they will use to color a section if the answer is 7. (yellow)

Repeat directions for the other colors and then tell students to complete the page.

Extra Credit *Counting*

Cut apart several old or unused calendars and give each student one month (not February). Instruct students to cut their pages apart on the lines so that they have a set of numbers from 1 to 30. Provide each student with a storage envelope and a calendar-like grid with seven spaces across and five spaces down. The students can complete a wide variety of tasks such as the following:

1. Count from 1 to 30. (Students place their numbers in the correct order on the grid in rows from left to right.) Compare this arrangement with your room calendar.
2. Start with 30 and count backwards to 1.
3. Put 15 in the first space and count to 30.
4. Put 20 in the first space and count backwards to 10.
5. Count by 2's to 20, 5's to 30, or by 10's to 30.

138

Minuends through 16

pages 139-140

Objective

To subtract from minuends of 15 and 16

Materials

16 counters
Yarn ring
Set of subtraction fact cards for minuends through 14

Mental Math

Count on from:
1. 69 to 76 (69, 70, . . . 75)
2. 10 to 17
3. 89 to 95
4. 18 to 26
5. 34 to 42
6. 28 to 40
7. 69 to 81

Skill Review

Give each student 2 fact cards for minuends through 14. Have students place fact cards on the chalk tray as you ask for all facts for 13. Repeat for other numbers. Continue until all fact cards are grouped into families.

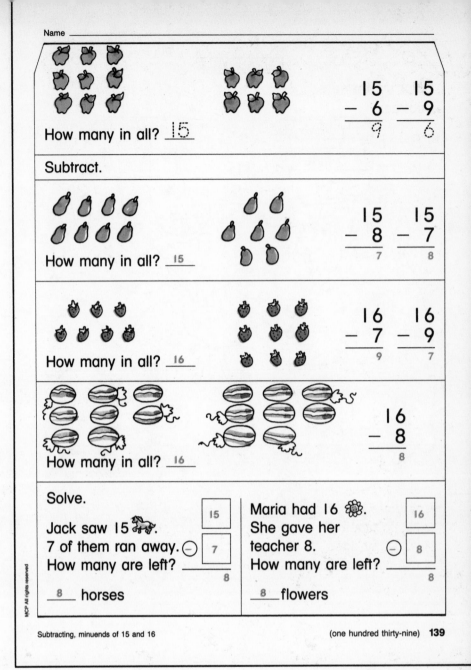

How many in all? 15

$$15 - 6 = 9 \qquad 15 - 9 = 6$$

Subtract.

How many in all? 15

$$15 - 8 = 7 \qquad 15 - 7 = 8$$

How many in all? 16

$$16 - 7 = 9 \qquad 16 - 9 = 7$$

How many in all? 16

$$16 - 8 = 8$$

Solve.

Jack saw 15 🐎.
7 of them ran away. $15 \ominus 7$
How many are left? ___
8

__8__ horses

Maria had 16 🌸.
She gave her teacher 8. $16 \ominus 8$
How many are left? ___
8

__8__ flowers

Subtracting, minuends of 15 and 16

(one hundred thirty-nine) **139**

Teaching page 139

Write on the board:

15 in all	
(6)	(9)
(9)	(6)
(7)	(8)
(8)	(7)

Ask students to place 15 counters in their rings and then remove 6. Ask how many are left. (9) Have a student write the subtraction sentence on the board. (15 − 6 = 9) Ask students to tell the parts of 15. (6 and 9) Ask a student to write another subtraction sentence using 6 and 9. (15 − 9 = 6) Continue to build 15 − 7 = 8 and 15 − 8 = 7. Tell students that since basic facts are built with parts of 9 or less, there are only 4 sentences for parts of

15. Make a similar table and write the sentences for the parts of 16. (16 − 7 = 9, 16 − 9 = 7, 16 − 8 = 8)

Have students tell how many apples are in the picture. (15) Have students trace the 15. Ask how many apples are in each part. (9 and 6) Read the problems to the right of the apples and have students trace the 9 and 6. Have students complete the next 3 problems independently. Read each of the 2 bottom problems and have students complete the problems by writing the numbers and minus signs.

139

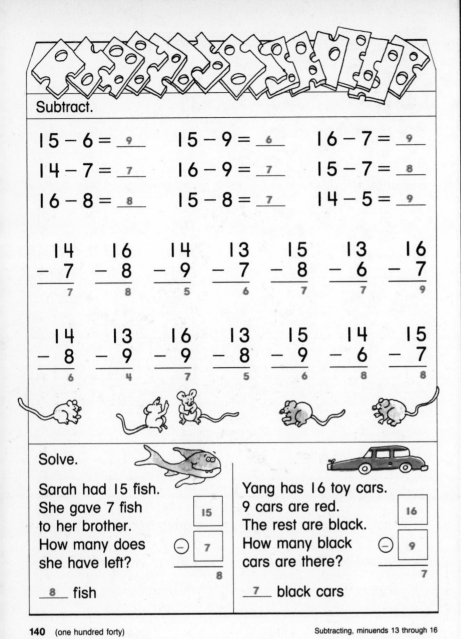

Subtract.

$15 - 6 = \underline{9}$ $15 - 9 = \underline{6}$ $16 - 7 = \underline{9}$

$14 - 7 = \underline{7}$ $16 - 9 = \underline{7}$ $15 - 7 = \underline{8}$

$16 - 8 = \underline{8}$ $15 - 8 = \underline{7}$ $14 - 5 = \underline{9}$

14	16	14	13	15	13	16
− 7	− 8	− 9	− 7	− 8	− 6	− 7
7	8	5	6	7	7	9

14	13	16	13	15	14	15
− 8	− 9	− 9	− 8	− 9	− 6	− 7
6	4	7	5	6	8	8

Solve.

Sarah had 15 fish.
She gave 7 fish
to her brother.
How many does
she have left?

$\boxed{15}$
$\ominus$ $\boxed{7}$
_____
8

$\underline{8}$ fish

Yang has 16 toy cars.
9 cars are red.
The rest are black.
How many black
cars are there?

$\boxed{16}$
$\ominus$ $\boxed{9}$
_____
7

$\underline{7}$ black cars

Subtracting, minuends 13 through 16

Correcting Common Errors

Some students may need more practice subtracting from minuends of 15 and 16. Have students work with partners and counters to follow your directions. Give each pair 15 counters and have them place them in a row on their work area. Say, "Move 6 counters to the right. How many are left?" (9) "What subtraction fact does this show?" (15 − 6 = 9) Have students write the fact. Repeat for other numbers subtracted from 15. Then repeat the activity with 16 counters.

Enrichment

1. Make as many subtraction problems as you can using the numbers 9, 8, 7 and 6 as the parts.
2. Write subtraction sentence pairs for parts of 15 and 16. (ex. 15 − 6 = 9 and 15 − 9 = 6)

Teaching page 140

Have students tell how many pieces of swiss cheese in all. (16) Tell students to count to 13 and cover the remaining 3 pieces of cheese. Now tell students to count off the last 4 pieces and tell how many are left. (9) Repeat for more examples until students can comfortably use the pieces of cheese to do subtraction problems. Tell students to work all the problems in the first 2 sections. Read the 2 story problems and have students write the numbers and minus signs.

Extra Credit   *Geometry*

Give each group of two students a set of 24 "Concentration" cards having pairs of red, blue, and yellow shapes. Ask each group to make as many regular arrays of the 24 cards as they can. For example, they can be arranged in a pattern that is four cards across and six cards down, or three cards across and eight cards down. See how many such arrays they can find. Possibilities include 1 × 24, 2 × 12, 3 × 8, 4 × 6. Some may distinguish 8 × 3 from 3 × 8, 6 × 4 from 4 × 6, and so on. Now have students play "Concentration." Have one student arrange the cards face down while another works alone to identify pairs. Have them match both color and shape and rearrange cards. Have them play with the cards in a 2 × 12 array and then play again with a 4 × 6 array. Ask what makes it easier to remember the location of hidden cards. (Answers will vary.)

140

Minuends through 18

pages 141-142

Objective

To subtract for minuends 17 and 18

Materials

18 counters
Yarn ring

Mental Math

Name the number that is:
1. 14 take away 7 (7)
2. 6 plus 4 (10)
3. 15 take away 9 (6)
4. 7 and 6 more (13)
5. 7 plus 8 (15)
6. 15 minus 8 (7)
7. 6 plus 6 and 1 more (13)

Skill Review

Draw on the board:

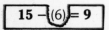

Tell students a mouse ate the other number and they must tell the number. (6) Erase the 9 and write 6. Ask for the missing number. (9) Repeat for other facts for minuends through 16 by changing the minuends and answers.

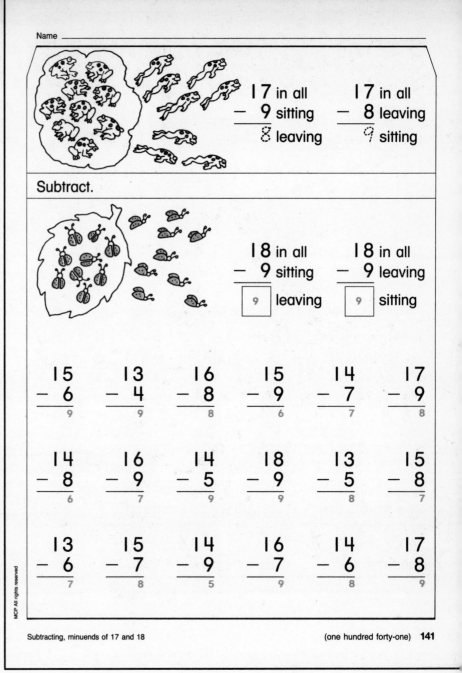

Subtracting, minuends of 17 and 18   (one hundred forty-one) **141**

Teaching page 141

Write **whole − part = part** on the board. Read the sentence to the students, "whole minus part equals part." Place a piece of paper under the word **whole** and say, "a whole piece of paper." Now use scissors to cut a piece of the paper. Put one part under the first **part** and say, "The whole paper minus a part equals a part," as you put the other part under the last word **part**. Repeat this with a whole piece of chalk broken into 2 parts, an armload of books, a box of crayons, etc. Now have 17 students stand in front of the word **whole**. Then move 9 of them to stand in front of the first word **part** and the remaining 8 in front of the second word **part**. Ask students to tell how many are in each part of 17. (9 and 8) Write **17 − 9 = 8** under the words **whole − part = part**. Repeat for 18 − 9 =

9. Encourage the use of counters for students needing them.

Have students tell how many frogs in all. (17) Ask how many are sitting. (9) Ask how many are leaving. (8) Read the 2 problems and have students trace the 8 and 9. Tell students to do the next problem and then write the answers in the 3 rows of facts.

141

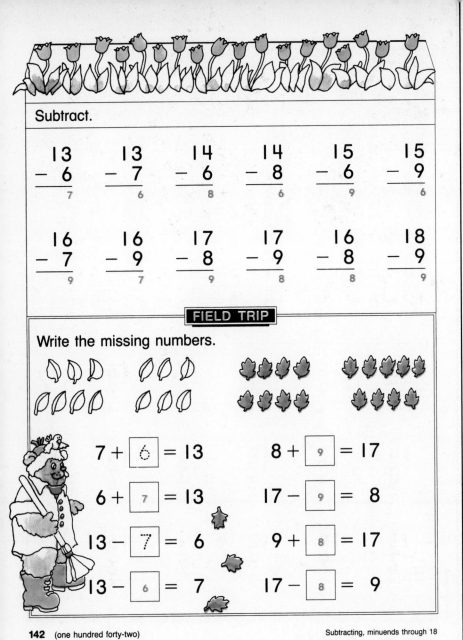

Subtract.

13 − 6 7	13 − 7 6	14 − 6 8	14 − 8 6	15 − 6 9	15 − 9 6
16 − 7 9	16 − 9 7	17 − 8 9	17 − 9 8	16 − 8 8	18 − 9 9

FIELD TRIP

Write the missing numbers.

$7 + \boxed{6} = 13$ $8 + \boxed{9} = 17$

$6 + \boxed{7} = 13$ $17 - \boxed{9} = 8$

$13 - \boxed{7} = 6$ $9 + \boxed{8} = 17$

$13 - \boxed{6} = 7$ $17 - \boxed{8} = 9$

142 (one hundred forty-two)   Subtracting, minuends through 18

Teaching page 142

Tell students to use the flowers at the top of the page to help solve the 2 rows of subtraction facts. Have students complete them independently.

Field Trip

Tell students they are to write the missing number in each box. Ask students what number plus 7 equals 16. (9) Have students trace the 9 and then complete all the problems. Tell students they may count the leaves to help them find the missing numbers.

Extra Credit *Counting*

On a blank sheet of paper the teacher writes the numbers from 1 through 100 in a scattered arrangement. Use one number twice. Duplicate and distribute one sheet to each child. Tell the children that you were counting to 100, but made a mistake and counted one number two times. They are to find the extra number by starting with 1 and circling each number as they go along counting to 100. When they have circled the numbers through 100 (and sometimes before) they will discover the hidden culprit. Tell them to circle that number with a different color.

Minuends 11 through 18

pages 143-144

Objective
To practice subtraction facts for minuends 11 through 18

Materials
None

Mental Math
Count backwards from:
1. 13 to 1 (13, 12, 11 . . . 1)
2. 99 to 89
3. 72 to 64
4. 15 to 6
5. 33 to 20
6. 20 to 10
7. 21 to 1
8. 65 to 54

Skill Review
Group students into 7 groups.
Draw 8 tables on the board:

in all	

Write one number from 11 through 18 at the top of each table and have each group complete its table by writing all parts of the number. Group 7 will complete tables 17 and 18.

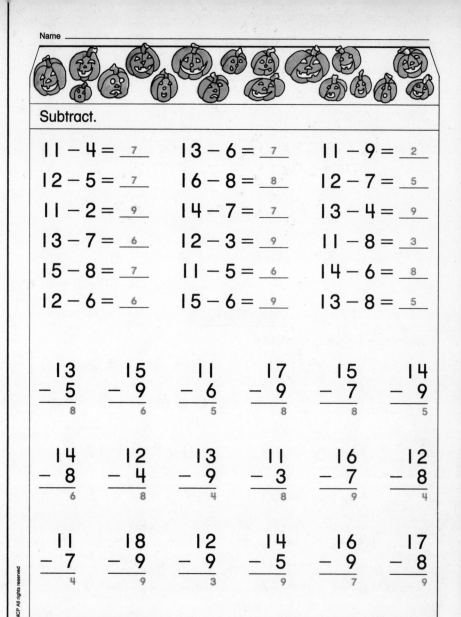

Name _____

Subtract.

$11 - 4 = \underline{7}$ $13 - 6 = \underline{7}$ $11 - 9 = \underline{2}$

$12 - 5 = \underline{7}$ $16 - 8 = \underline{8}$ $12 - 7 = \underline{5}$

$11 - 2 = \underline{9}$ $14 - 7 = \underline{7}$ $13 - 4 = \underline{9}$

$13 - 7 = \underline{6}$ $12 - 3 = \underline{9}$ $11 - 8 = \underline{3}$

$15 - 8 = \underline{7}$ $11 - 5 = \underline{6}$ $14 - 6 = \underline{8}$

$12 - 6 = \underline{6}$ $15 - 6 = \underline{9}$ $13 - 8 = \underline{5}$

13 $-\;5$ 8	15 $-\;9$ 6	11 $-\;6$ 5	17 $-\;9$ 8	15 $-\;7$ 8	14 $-\;9$ 5
14 $-\;8$ 6	12 $-\;4$ 8	13 $-\;9$ 4	11 $-\;3$ 8	16 $-\;7$ 9	12 $-\;8$ 4
11 $-\;7$ 4	18 $-\;9$ 9	12 $-\;9$ 3	14 $-\;5$ 9	16 $-\;9$ 7	17 $-\;8$ 9

Subtraction facts, minuends 11 through 18

(one hundred forty-three) **143**

Teaching page 143
Have students tell how many pumpkins in all. (18) Remind students that they need to cover the 7 extra pumpkins for the first problem since they need only 11 pumpkins. Tell students to count off 4 of the 11 pumpkins and tell how many are left. (7) Tell students to complete the page.

143

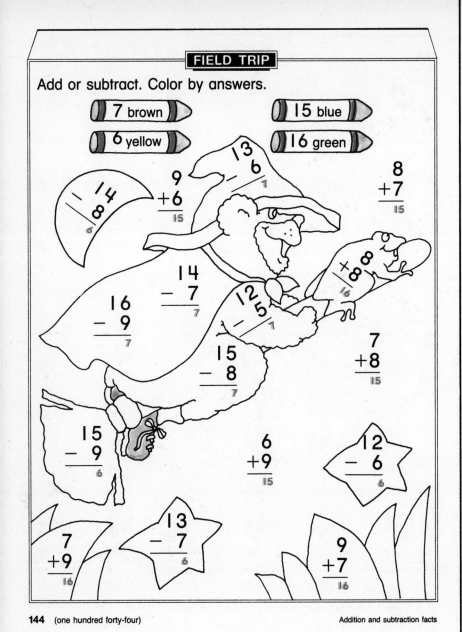

FIELD TRIP

Add or subtract. Color by answers.

7 brown   15 blue
6 yellow   16 green

Addition and subtraction facts

Correcting Common Errors

If some students continue to have difficulty with subtraction facts, have them think of a related addition fact and find the missing addend.
EXAMPLE:

Problem: $15 - 8 = \square$
Think: What number added to 8 equals 15. Answer: 7.
Fact: $15 - 8 = 7$

When students practice facts, they should always say all 3 numbers in the fact. To answer the problem above, for example, they should say "15 minus 8 equals 7," and not just "7."

Enrichment

1. Complete a subtraction table for minuends through 18.
2. Play "Concentration" with facts from minuends through 18. Scatter all fact cards face down. Draw 2 cards. A double, or a match of 2 facts for the same minuend, earns a second turn.

Teaching page 144

Field Trip

Have students look at all the problems in the picture and tell what they are to do. (add and subtract) Tell students they are to work each problem, and then color that section the color named beside that number in the code. Remind students to check the sign in each problem before working it.

Extra Credit *Probability*

Prove the chances of an event happening by doing experiments and keeping charts. Divide the class into groups of five. Supply 1 die to each group and let them examine it. As a class, discover that the die has six sides and that one side is a three. Then present the premise that if you roll a die 6 times, chances are that one time you will get a 3.

Tell a recorder to print the name of each group member in a column along the left side of the paper. Each student in the group takes two turns rolling the die six times. The recorder marks down the number rolled each time and circles every time there was a three rolled. Students compare their results, to the teacher's premise. Students can prove other premises such as: If I toss a coin, the chances are 1 in 2 that I will toss a head.

Subtracting Money

pages 145-146

Objective

To solve money problems for minuends through 18¢

Materials

18 real or punch-out pennies
*Small objects with price tags through 9¢

Mental Math

What is the total cost?
1. 4¢ and 9¢ (13¢)
2. 3¢ and 6¢ (9¢)
3. 9¢ and 8¢ (17¢)
4. 6¢ and 8¢ (14¢)
5. 9¢ and 7¢ (16¢)
6. 4¢ and 8¢ (12¢)
7. 6¢ and 7¢ (13¢)

Skill Review

Ask students to make up a problem about 14 dogs kept in a kennel, until 9 went home. Have a student write the problem on the board. (14 − 9 = 5) Encourage students to tell other stories for minuends through 18, and write the problems on the board.

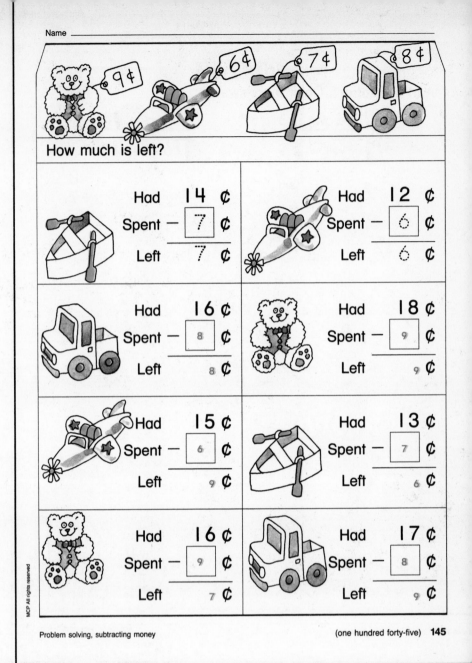

Problem solving, subtracting money

(one hundred forty-five) **145**

Teaching page 145

Write the cent sign on the board and ask students to tell its meaning. (means money) Ask a student to write **14¢** on the board. Use that student's name to tell a story of having 14¢ and spending 9¢. Ask student to write **−9¢** under the 14¢. Ask how much the student would have left. (5¢) Tell other stories using other students. Then have students make up stories of having amounts through 18¢ and spending 9¢ or less.

Have students name the items and their prices at the top of the page. Tell students they are to buy these items and tell how much money is left. Work through the first problem with the students and have them trace the 7 to show 7¢ was spent, and the 7 to show that 7¢ would be left from 14¢. Have students complete the page.

145

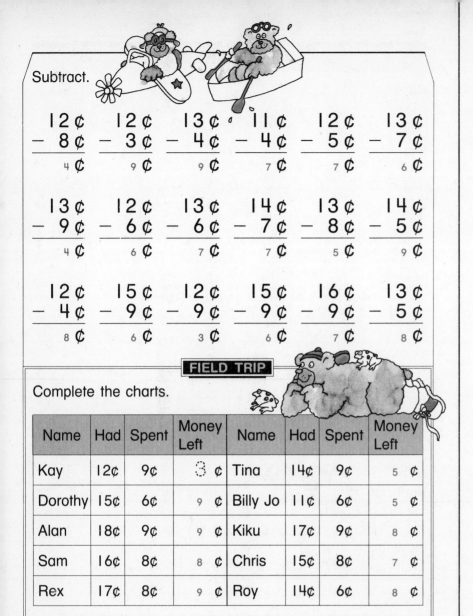

Subtract.

12¢	12¢	13¢	11¢	12¢	13¢
− 8¢	− 3¢	− 4¢	− 4¢	− 5¢	− 7¢
4¢	9¢	9¢	7¢	7¢	6¢

13¢	12¢	13¢	14¢	13¢	14¢
− 9¢	− 6¢	− 6¢	− 7¢	− 8¢	− 5¢
4¢	6¢	7¢	7¢	5¢	9¢

12¢	15¢	12¢	15¢	16¢	13¢
− 4¢	− 9¢	− 9¢	− 9¢	− 9¢	− 5¢
8¢	6¢	3¢	6¢	7¢	8¢

FIELD TRIP

Complete the charts.

Name	Had	Spent	Money Left	Name	Had	Spent	Money Left
Kay	12¢	9¢	3¢	Tina	14¢	9¢	5¢
Dorothy	15¢	6¢	9¢	Billy Jo	11¢	6¢	5¢
Alan	18¢	9¢	9¢	Kiku	17¢	9¢	8¢
Sam	16¢	8¢	8¢	Chris	15¢	8¢	7¢
Rex	17¢	8¢	9¢	Roy	14¢	6¢	8¢

146 (one hundred forty-six)   Problem solving, subtracting money

Chapter Review

pages 147-148

Objectives

To review subtracting from minuends through 18

To maintain skills previously learned

Materials

18 counters

Mental Math

How many tens and ones?
1. 99 (9,9)
2. 87 (8,7)
3. 46 (4,6)
4. 51 (5,1)
5. 11 (1,1)
6. 29 (2,9)
7. 33 (3,3)

Skill Review

Write **4 + 6 = 10** on the board. Ask a student to write on the board a subtraction fact with parts of 4 and 6 and a minuend of 10. (10 − 4 = 6) Ask for another subtraction fact with parts of 4 and 6. (10 − 6 = 4) Repeat for other addition facts with sums through 18.

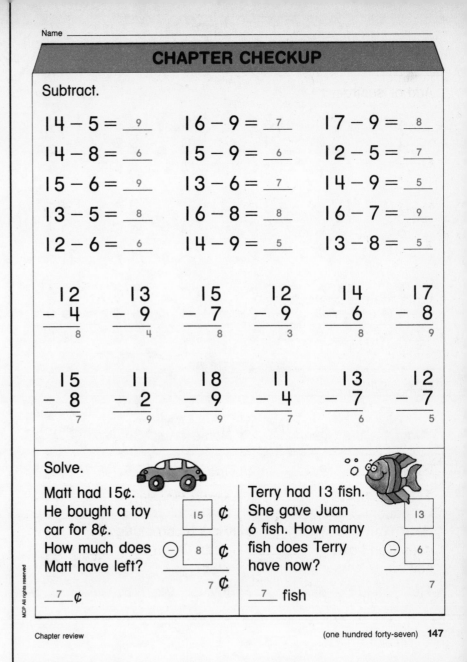

CHAPTER CHECKUP

Subtract.

$14 - 5 = \underline{9}$ $16 - 9 = \underline{7}$ $17 - 9 = \underline{8}$

$14 - 8 = \underline{6}$ $15 - 9 = \underline{6}$ $12 - 5 = \underline{7}$

$15 - 6 = \underline{9}$ $13 - 6 = \underline{7}$ $14 - 9 = \underline{5}$

$13 - 5 = \underline{8}$ $16 - 8 = \underline{8}$ $16 - 7 = \underline{9}$

$12 - 6 = \underline{6}$ $14 - 9 = \underline{5}$ $13 - 8 = \underline{5}$

| $\begin{array}{r}12\\-\ 4\\\hline 8\end{array}$ | $\begin{array}{r}13\\-\ 9\\\hline 4\end{array}$ | $\begin{array}{r}15\\-\ 7\\\hline 8\end{array}$ | $\begin{array}{r}12\\-\ 9\\\hline 3\end{array}$ | $\begin{array}{r}14\\-\ 6\\\hline 8\end{array}$ | $\begin{array}{r}17\\-\ 8\\\hline 9\end{array}$ |

| $\begin{array}{r}15\\-\ 8\\\hline 7\end{array}$ | $\begin{array}{r}11\\-\ 2\\\hline 9\end{array}$ | $\begin{array}{r}18\\-\ 9\\\hline 9\end{array}$ | $\begin{array}{r}11\\-\ 4\\\hline 7\end{array}$ | $\begin{array}{r}13\\-\ 7\\\hline 6\end{array}$ | $\begin{array}{r}12\\-\ 7\\\hline 5\end{array}$ |

Solve.

Matt had 15¢. He bought a toy car for 8¢. How much does Matt have left? _____

15 ¢
⊖ 8 ¢
7 ¢

___7___ ¢

Terry had 13 fish. She gave Juan 6 fish. How many fish does Terry have now?

13
⊖ 6
7

___7___ fish

Chapter review

Teaching page 147

Have students complete the 3 columns and 2 rows of subtraction problems. Read the 2 story problems and have students write the minuends, numbers to be taken away, minus signs and answers. Tell students to write the answer to each problem in the blank also.

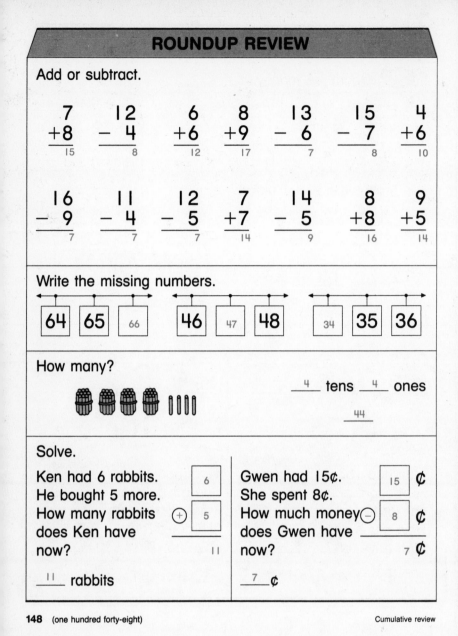

ROUNDUP REVIEW

Add or subtract.

$7 + 8 = 15$ $12 - 4 = 8$ $6 + 6 = 12$ $8 + 9 = 17$ $13 - 6 = 7$ $15 - 7 = 8$ $4 + 6 = 10$

$16 - 9 = 7$ $11 - 4 = 7$ $12 - 5 = 7$ $7 + 7 = 14$ $14 - 5 = 9$ $8 + 8 = 16$ $9 + 5 = 14$

Write the missing numbers.

64	65	66
46	47	48
34	35	36

How many?

_4_ tens _4_ ones

_44_

Solve.

Ken had 6 rabbits. He bought 5 more. How many rabbits does Ken have now?

6 (+) 5 = 11

_11_ rabbits

Gwen had 15¢. She spent 8¢. How much money does Gwen have now?

15¢ (−) 8¢ = 7¢

_7_ ¢

148 (one hundred forty-eight)   Cumulative review

148

Enrichment

1. Write a fact for a sum or minuend through 18 on a small piece of paper. Fold the paper. Make 9 more with different facts. Place all facts in a bag. With a partner, take turns drawing a fact and giving the answer. A correct answer earns another turn.
2. Write the numbers 0 through 99 in order from memory.
3. Write a number from 1 through 99 on a small piece of paper. Repeat for 9 more different numbers. Turn face down and draw 3. Place them in order as they would appear on a number line from 1 through 99.

Teaching page 148

Tell students this page asks them to work different kinds of problems. Tell students that they must look at the sign in each problem in the first two rows to see if they are to add or subtract. Ask what is to be done on the number lines.(write the missing numbers) Ask students what they are to do in the next problems. (count tens and ones and write the numbers) Read the 2 story problems as students write the numbers and minus signs.

This page reviews addition and subtraction facts, number sequences, place value and problem solving.

Counting Money, Nickels

pages 149-150

Objectives

To count by 5's for nickels
To count amounts of nickels and
pennies through 50¢

Materials

*Addition and subtraction fact cards
for sums and minuends through 18
*Real penny and nickel
10 nickels and 10 pennies
1" grid sheet 10 rows across and 5
rows down

Mental Math

Name the number that comes:
1. between 68 and 70 (69)
2. before 1 (0)
3. after 89 (90)
4. before 13 (12)
5. between 49 and 51 (50)
6. before 10 (9)
7. after 79 (80)

Skill Review

Use addition and subtraction fact
cards for sums and minuends
through 18 for speed of recall. Show
card for a second and remove the
card while student answers. Show
card again if needed.

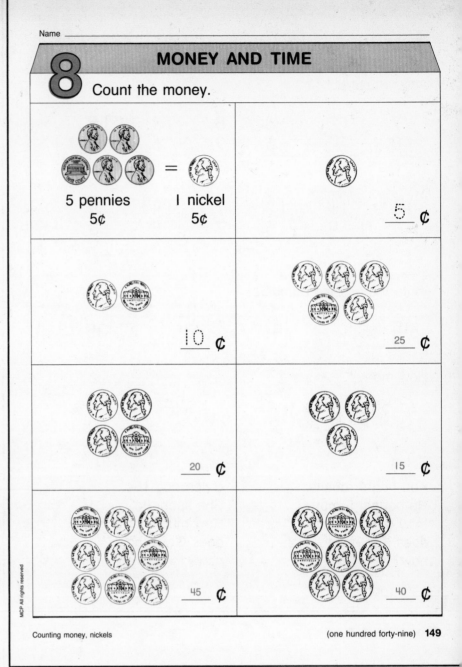

Name _____

MONEY AND TIME

8 Count the money.

5 pennies = 1 nickel
5¢   5¢

_5_ ¢

_10_ ¢

_25_ ¢

_20_ ¢

_15_ ¢

_45_ ¢

_40_ ¢

Counting money, nickels   (one hundred forty-nine) **149**

MCP All rights reserved

Teaching page 149

Draw 5 circles on the board and write **1¢** in each. Ask
students how much money in all.(5¢) Write **5¢** on the
board. Tell students there is a coin that is the same as
5¢. Draw a slightly larger circle on the board and write
5¢ in it. Tell students this coin is called a **nickel** and
has the same value as 5 pennies. Ask students to hold
up 1 nickel. Show students a real penny and real
nickel and ask how they look different.(color and size)
Turn coins to show heads and tails sides of a nickel
and penny. Have them write the numbers 1 through
50 in order with 1 through 10 across the first row.
Now ask students to color all the numbers that end in
5 or 0.(5, 10, 15, 20, . . . 50) Have students count by
5's with you from 5 through 50. Tell students we call
this **counting by 5's**. Ask students to place a nickel
on each colored square. Have students point to each
nickel in order as they count by 5's again.

Tell students to count the pennies and compare them
to the nickel. Now ask students to tell the name of the
coin in the next box (nickel) and trace the 5 to tell its
value of 5 pennies. Ask students the names of the 2
coins in the third box.(nickels) Ask the value of each
nickel.(5¢) Ask students to tell how much money 2
nickels make.(10¢) Ask students how they found the
value of 2 nickels.(count 10 pennies, count by 5's or
add 5 and 5) Go through each of the ways by
counting 5 pennies and then 5 more, by writing
5 + 5 = 10 on the board and by using the grid to
count by 5's. Have students complete the page.

149

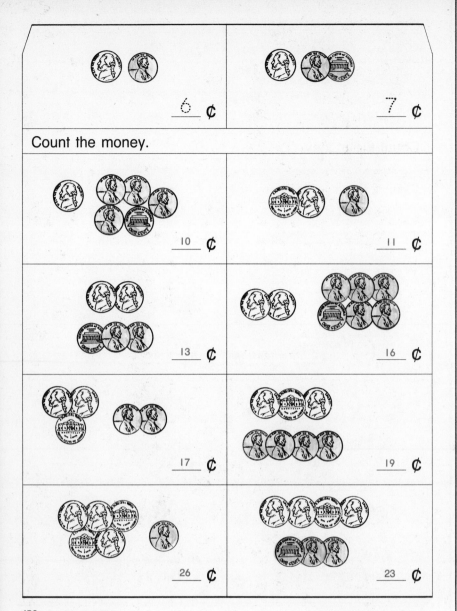

6 ¢

7 ¢

Count the money.

10 ¢

11 ¢

13 ¢

16 ¢

17 ¢

19 ¢

26 ¢

23 ¢

Counting money, nickels and pennies

Correcting Common Errors

Some students may have difficulty equating a nickel with 5 pennies. Have them work with partners and real or play nickels and pennies. One partner should have 25 pennies; the other partner should have 5 nickels. The partner with the pennies should lay down one penny at a time and count. When 5 pennies have been counted, the other partner can pick them up and can lay down a nickel. This continues until all 5 nickels have been used. Partners should count the value of the nickels and compare it with the value of the pennies replaced by the nickels.

Enrichment

1. Tell why you might use a nickel instead of 5 pennies.
2. Draw 46¢ in nickels and pennies. Use as few pennies as possible.

Teaching page 150

Ask students to tell the value of the nickel and the penny and trace the 6. Ask students to tell the value of the coins in the next box, and trace the 7. Tell students to count the money in each box and write the number on the line. Remind students of the 3 ways to find the total amount of money.

Extra Credit *Numeration*

Tell the entire class that they will be able to go for an airplane ride. Allow students to pick a destination on a globe or map. In order to board the plane, they must answer a given math fact correctly. This allows them to remain standing to await the plane. When all have had a turn, tell the standing students to line up behind you, extend their arms, "rev up" their motors and follow you around the classroom. Periodically stop the plane and ask new math facts of all students. If those on board continue to give the right answer, they remain on the plane. New students may come on board if they know the correct answer. When all students have had a ride on the airplane and you have reached your destination, discuss how many hours it would really take to fly to that location.

150

Counting Money, Dimes

pages 151-152

Objectives

To count by 10's for dimes
To count amounts in dimes, nickels and pennies through 60¢

Materials

5 dimes, 10 nickels and 10 pennies
Grid sheet 10 rows across and 5 rows down

Mental Math

Count by 10's from:
1. 40 to 90 (40, 50, . . . 90)
2. 10 to 50
3. 30 to 90
4. 10 to 70
5. 50 to 80
6. 20 to 70

Skill Review

Have students count by 5's as they lay out 10 nickels. Ask how much money in all.(50¢) Now tell students to lay out 30¢. Ask how many nickels make 30¢.(6) Tell students to lay out 36¢. Ask what coins they've used.(7 nickels, 1 penny) Continue to give amounts through 50¢ for students to show with nickels and pennies.

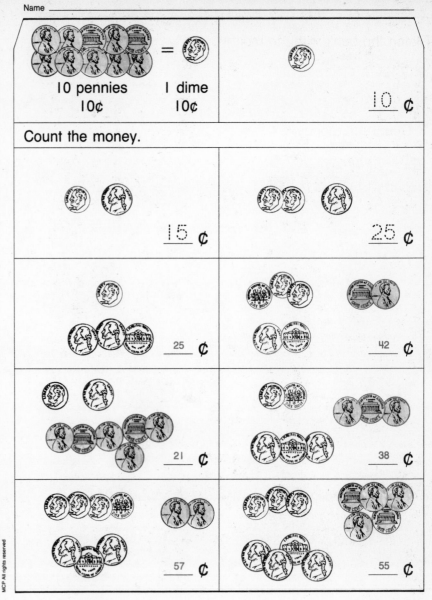

Name _____

10 pennies   1 dime
10¢   10¢

10 ¢

Count the money.

15 ¢   25 ¢

25 ¢   42 ¢

21 ¢   38 ¢

57 ¢   55 ¢

Counting money, dimes, nickels and pennies   (one hundred fifty-one) **151**

Teaching page 151

Have students lay out 10¢ 2 different ways. Ask what coins they used.(2 nickels, 10 pennies) Tell students a dime has the same value as 10¢. Tell students they could exchange 2 nickels for 1 dime or 10 pennies for 1 dime. Give each student 6 dimes and tell them to put a dime in place of the 10 pennies and another dime in place of the 2 nickels. Ask how much money in all.(20¢) Tell students to lay out 3 more dimes and count by 10's to tell how much money in all.(50¢) Now tell students to lay out 1 dime, 1 nickel and 1 penny. Tell students to count by saying, "10, 15, 16¢ in all." Have students lay out 3 dimes, 2 nickels and 4 pennies. Tell students to count by saying, "10, 20, 30, 35, 40, 41, 42, 43, 44¢." Give more examples until students are counting dimes first, then nickels and then pennies.

Have students tell how many pennies are the same as 1 dime.(10) Tell students to trace the 10 to show the value of 1 dime. Tell students to count the dime and nickel in the first box and trace the 15. Repeat for 25¢. Have students count the money in each box and write the amount.

151

Match the bank with the money.

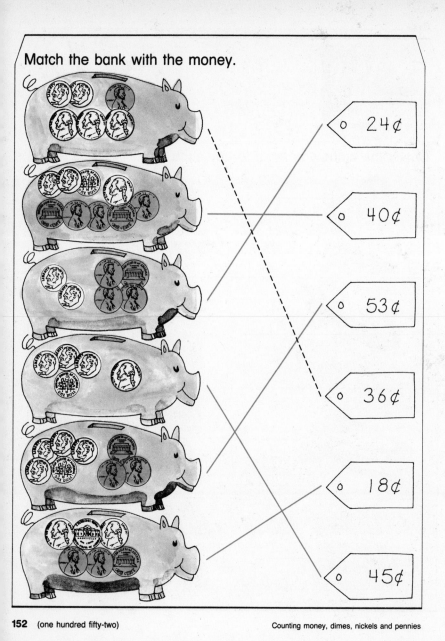

24¢

40¢

53¢

36¢

18¢

45¢

Counting money, dimes, nickels and pennies

Correcting Common Errors

Some students may forget the value of the coins that they are counting. Before they begin, have them identify each coin in the problem by name and by value. Then, as they count all the coins in the problem, have them pause briefly after counting each type of coin to remind themselves that the next coin to be counted has a different value.

Enrichment

1. Draw 48¢ 2 ways.
2. Make money cards by drawing coins to show 42¢, 35¢, 26¢, 17¢, and 48¢. Make another card for each by using different coins. Match the cards.

Teaching page 152

Count the money in the first bank with the students. (10, 20, 25, 30, 35, 36¢) Tell students to trace the line from the bank to the 36¢ tag. Tell students to count the money in each bank, find that amount on the price tag and draw a line to connect the money to its tag. Have students complete the page.

Extra Credit   *Logic*

Bring to class a collection of pencils, pens, chalk, Tinkertoy sticks, match sticks, paper towel tubes, and other objects that are cylinders. Distribute them to the class. Hold up one object, a pencil for example. Now ask students to find another that is both longer and fatter. Allow them time to look through the objects. Then take a piece of chalk and ask them to find an object that is both longer and thinner. Use as many attributes as you can. Hold up one object and ask them to find one that is longer and a toy; or fatter and comes with paper on it. Involve students in this activity. Ask volunteers to choose an object, and then ask the class to find one that is different in a way they describe.

152

Counting Money, Dimes

pages 153-154

Objective

To count dimes, nickels and pennies through 60¢

Materials

*Items priced 36¢, 42¢ and 53¢
5 dimes, 10 nickels and 10 pennies
Grid sheet with 10 rows across and 9 rows down

Mental Math

How much money?
1. 1 nickel (5¢)
2. 2 nickels (10¢)
3. 1 nickel and 1 penny (6¢)
4. 1 nickel and 4 pennies (9¢)
5. 2 nickels and 1 penny (11¢)
6. 3 nickels (15¢)
7. 4 nickels (20¢)

Skill Review

Give students a grid sheet and ask them to write the numbers 1 through 50. Now ask students to place a dime on each number they say as they count by 10's to 50. Now have a student write 10 on the board. Have another student write 20 and continue through 90.

Name _____

Check the coins you need to buy each toy.

33¢

49¢

57¢

51¢

26¢

Counting money, dimes, nickels and pennies

(one hundred fifty-three) **153**

Teaching page 153

Draw on the board a ball with a price tag of 29¢. Tell students to lay out 2 dimes. Ask what other coins are needed to buy the ball.(1 nickel, 4 pennies) Count the coins with the students, "10, 20, 25, 26, 27, 28, 29¢." Change the ball's price to 32¢ and ask students to lay out 32¢ in coins. Accept all correct ways to show 32¢. Change the ball's price to 46¢, 52¢ and 38¢.

Have students tell the cost of the baseball glove.(33¢) Tell students to trace the check marks on the coins to show which are needed to make 33¢. Go over the next problem with the students and then have them complete the page independently.

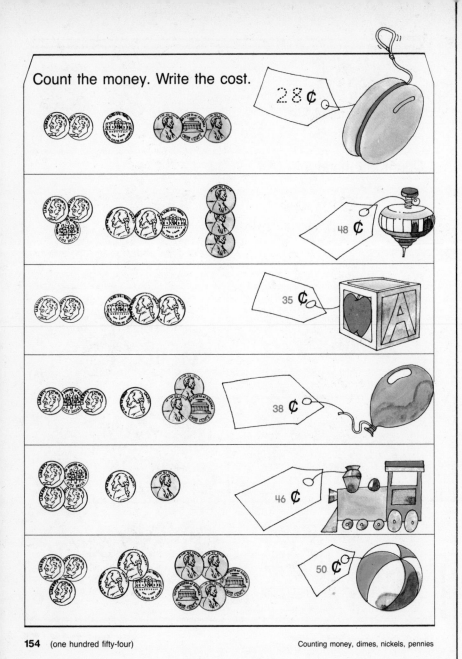

Count the money. Write the cost.

28 ¢

48 ¢

35 ¢

38 ¢

46 ¢

50 ¢

Counting money, dimes, nickels, pennies

Correcting Common Errors

Some students may need more practice determining the coins that make a given amount. Show an item costing 36¢. Ask, "How much does this item cost?" (36¢) "How many dimes are in 36¢?" (3) Have a student count out 3 dimes. Ask students to tell the value of the 3 dimes. (30¢) Ask, "How much more do you need to make 36¢?" (6¢) "How can you make 6¢?" (6 pennies or 1 nickel and 1 penny) Have another student count out these coins and count the amount of all the coins. Repeat the activity with other amounts.

Enrichment

1. Draw 8 coins to make 57¢.
2. Cut from advertisements 5 items costing 10¢ through 60¢. Draw the coins to purchase each.
3. Pull some coins from a bag of 6 dimes, 10 nickels and 10 pennies. Tell how much money you have.

Teaching page 154

Tell students they are to count the money it would take to buy each item and then write that amount on the item's price tag.

Extra Credit   *Probability*

Experiment with probability by drawing marbles from a bag. You will need 10 black and 10 white marbles for each group. Begin as a whole class activity. Ask a student to place 1 black marble and 10 white marbles in a bag. One student will be assigned to keep track of the draws on the chalkboard. Pass the bag around the room, letting each student draw out 1 marble. They announce a black or white draw, replace the marble, and pass the bag to the next person. After 10 draws, discuss the results and give reasons for the outcome. Now divide the class into groups and let them experiment with the marbles to find ways of improving their chances of getting a black draw. (for example, replacing one of the white marbles with another black one) The students continue to make ten draws for each experiment, record the draws, and predict their chances of getting a black draw in any experiment.

154

Counting Money, Quarters

pages 155-156

Objective

To count quarters, dimes, nickels and pennies through 99¢

Materials

1 quarter
5 dimes, 10 nickels and 10 pennies
*Items priced through 99¢

Mental Math

How much money?
1. 1 dime and 2 pennies (12¢)
2. 1 nickel and 4 pennies (9¢)
3. 3 nickels (15¢)
4. 2 dimes (20¢)
5. 2 dimes and 1 penny (21¢)
6. 3 dimes (30¢)
7. 2 dimes and 1 nickel (25¢)

Skill Review

Have a student write a 5 on the board. Ask other students to write the numbers for counting by 5's through 95. (5, 10, 15, . . . 95) Have students circle the numbers they'd say when counting by 10's. (10, 20, 30, . . . 90) Have students count by 5's and 10's and then count backwards by 5's and 10's from 95 and 90.

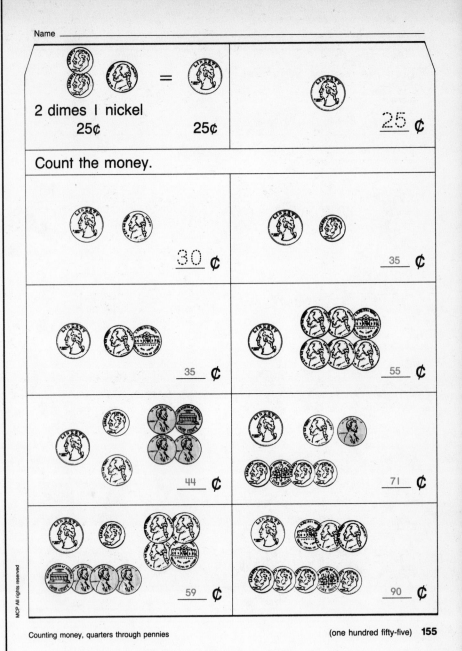

Name _____

2 dimes 1 nickel
25¢   25¢   _25_ ¢

Count the money.

_30_ ¢   _35_ ¢

_35_ ¢   _55_ ¢

_44_ ¢   _71_ ¢

_59_ ¢   _90_ ¢

Counting money, quarters through pennies

(one hundred fifty-five) **155**

Teaching page 155

Show students a quarter. Tell students a quarter is the same as 25 pennies. Ask students another way to make 25 pennies. (2 dimes and 1 nickel, 5 nickels) Tell students to use a quarter and lay out coins to show 28¢. (1 quarter, 3 pennies) Have students use one quarter and other coins to show 82¢, 47¢, 36¢ and 73¢.

Ask students how many dimes and nickels make a quarter. (2 dimes, 1 nickel) Tell students to trace the 25 to show that a quarter is worth 25¢. Tell students they are to tell how much 1 quarter and 1 nickel are worth. Tell students to count 25 and add 5 more or count by 5's from 25 to 30. Have students trace the 30. Tell students to complete the page.

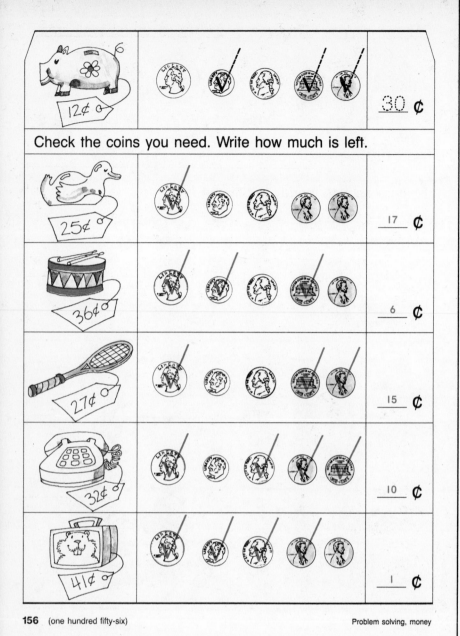

		30 ¢
12¢		

Check the coins you need. Write how much is left.

		17 ¢
25¢		
36¢		6 ¢
27¢		15 ¢
32¢		10 ¢
41¢		1 ¢

Problem solving, money

Correcting Common Errors

Some students may have difficulty understanding the value of a quarter. Have them work with partners with pennies, nickels, and dimes. Have them make different groups of coins totaling a value of 25¢. Have them write and count aloud the combinations that they find; for example, 1 dime 2 nickels 5 pennies as "10, 15, 20, 21, 22, 23, 24, 25 cents."

Enrichment

1. Cut from advertisements 5 items costing 99¢ or less each. Paste them on paper and draw the coins you need to buy each.
2. Write different amounts of money through 99¢ on 10 envelopes. Draw an envelope from the stack and place coins inside to equal the amount written.

Teaching page 156

Have students lay out 43¢. Show students an item costing less than 43¢. Tell students to pick up the coins needed to buy the item and then tell how much money is left. Repeat for more examples of telling how much money is left after buying an item. Have students write the amount left on the board.

Tell students they are to put a check mark on each coin needed to buy the item and then write the amount of money left. Tell students to trace the check marks on dime and 2 pennies to show that 12¢ is needed to buy the item. Ask which coins are left. (quarter and nickel) Ask how much money a quarter and nickel make. (30¢) Tell students to trace the 30. Have students complete the page.

Extra Credit *Sets*

Set up a science table with small shoeboxes labeled with various characteristics such as: float, sink, heavy, light, metal, rough and smooth. Students bring objects from home and place them in the appropriate boxes. Ask if some objects belong to more than one set. Which set has the most members? Which object belongs to the most sets? Children can test some of the characteristics by placing the float objects in water and testing the metal objects with a magnet. Have a box of unidentified objects in a separate box for children to place in correct sets, when class work is complete.

156

Problem Solving, Money

pages 157-158

Objective

To solve money problems

Materials

*Items priced through 99¢
1 quarter
6 dimes, 10 nickels and 10 pennies

Mental Math

What coins do we count:
1. by 1's (pennies)
2. by 10's (dimes)
3. by 5's (nickels)
4. 10, 20, 30, 40 (dimes)
5. 1, 2, 3, 4, 5 (pennies)
6. 5, 10, 15, 20 (nickels)

Skill Review

Draw 1 quarter, 2 dimes, 1 nickel and 1 penny on the board. Ask students how much money in all. (51¢) Draw other amounts through 99¢ using 1 quarter. Ask students to count the money and tell how much in all.

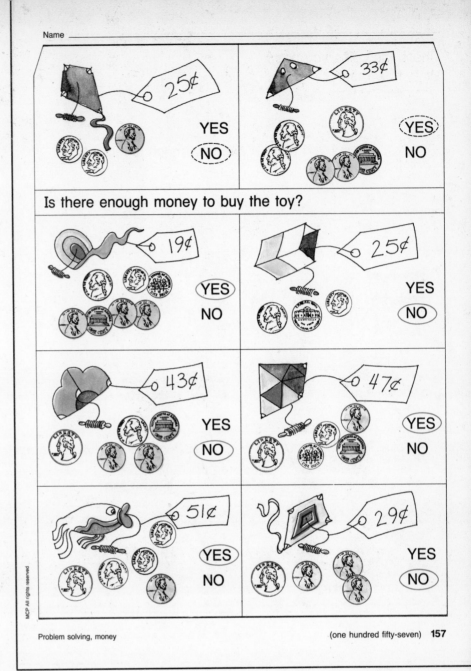

Name _____

Is there enough money to buy the toy?

Problem solving, money

(one hundred fifty-seven) **157**

Teaching page 157

Tell students to lay out 1 quarter, 1 dime, 1 nickel and 1 penny. Show an item priced 45¢. Ask students if they have enough money to buy the item. (no) Ask students how much money they have. (41¢) Ask students if 41¢ is more or less than 45¢. (less) Give more examples for students to compare their money with an item's cost. Now tell students to lay out 1 quarter, 1 dime, 1 nickel and 1 penny. Show students an item costing 35¢. Ask if they have enough money to buy the item. (yes) Ask how much money they have. (41¢) Ask if 41¢ is greater or less than 35¢. (greater) Ask how much more. (6¢) Give more examples for students to tell how much money they will have left.

Have students count the money in the first box. (21¢) Ask if there is enough money to buy the 25¢ kite. (no) Tell students to trace the circle around the word no. Go through the next problem with students and then have them complete the page.

157

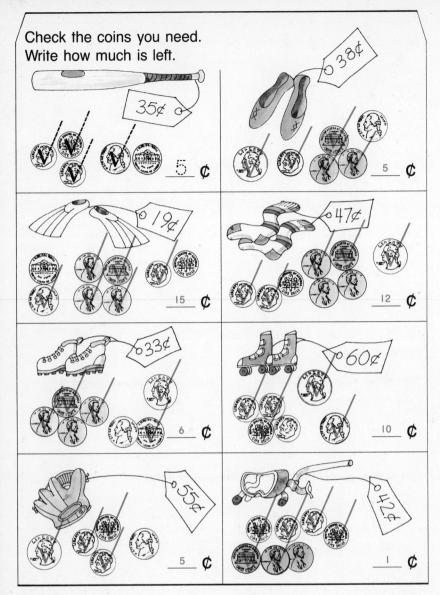

Check the coins you need.
Write how much is left.

35¢ — _5_ ¢

38¢ — _5_ ¢

19¢ — _15_ ¢

47¢ — _12_ ¢

33¢ — _6_ ¢

60¢ — _10_ ¢

55¢ — _5_ ¢

42¢ — _1_ ¢

Problem solving, money

Some students may have difficulty deciding if they have enough money to buy a toy. Have them first count the coins they have and write the amount. Then have them compare the amount to the cost and tell if it is less than or greater than the cost. If less than, then they circle NO. If greater than, then they circle YES. Remind students that they must have at least as much as the object costs in order to buy it.

Enrichment

1. Draw an object priced at 28¢. Draw coins to show that you will have 10¢ left after buying the item.
2. Work with a partner. Each writes an amount of money through 99¢. Tell which is more. Tell how much more.
3. Write the amount of money you would have left if you have 99¢ and buy a toy for 60¢ and gum for 15¢.

Teaching page 158

Tell students they are to count the money in each box, check the coins needed to buy the item and then tell how much money is left. Ask students to read the price tag on the baseball bat. (35¢) Tell students to trace the check marks on the coins to show that 35¢ is needed to buy the baseball bat. Ask students how much money is left. (5¢) Tell students to trace the 5 to show that 5¢ is left. Go through the next problem with the students and have them complete the page.

Extra Credit *Applications*

Ask students to bring in empty food boxes and jars to use in a classroom grocery store. Explain that when you have enough "groceries" you will open the store for business. Before you begin the activity, price the items: 5¢, 10¢, 15¢, 20¢, and 25¢ and distribute play money to students. Appoint one student to be the shopkeeper. Allow the others to go through the shop with their play money, choose one item, and pay the shopkeeper for it. Help students read the prices and find the correct coins. This activity can be repeated many times. You will want to make the prices more difficult as students get better.

Time to the Hour

pages 159-160

Objectives

To recognize the hour and minute hands
To tell and write time to the hour

Materials

*Demonstration clock
Crayons

Mental Math

How much money is:
1. 1 quarter (25¢)
2. 2 dimes (20¢)
3. 2 dimes and 4 pennies (24¢)
4. 2 dimes and 2 nickels (30¢)
5. 2 dimes minus 1 penny (19¢)
6. 8 dimes (80¢)
7. 8 nickels (40¢)

Skill Review

Tell a story of having 92¢ and spending 26¢. Ask a student to draw 92¢ on the board, circle the coins spent and tell how much money is left. Repeat for other stories of amounts through 99¢.

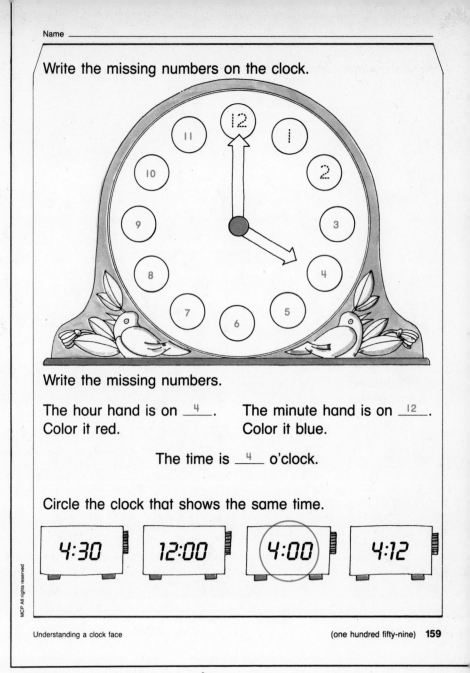

Name _____

Write the missing numbers on the clock.

Write the missing numbers.

The hour hand is on __4__.   The minute hand is on __12__.
Color it red.   Color it blue.

The time is __4__ o'clock.

Circle the clock that shows the same time.

4:30   12:00   4:00   4:12

Understanding a clock face

(one hundred fifty-nine) **159**

Teaching page 159

Show a clock face. Ask students to read the numbers clockwise from 12 through 11. Tell students the 2 hands are a long hand and a short hand. Point to each hand as you ask which is longer and shorter. Tell students the long or big hand points to the minute and the short or little hand points to the hour so we call the hands the minute hand and hour hand. Point to each hand several times as you ask which is the hour hand and which is the minute hand. Now move both hands to the 12 and say, "It is 12:00 when both hands are on the 12." Move the hour hand to another number and tell students the hour time. Now repeat for several hour times and ask students to tell where each hand is pointing and the o'clock. Stress that for each o'clock the minute hand is on 12. Write **12:00** on the board and ask a student to place the hands to show 12:00.

Repeat for all the o'clocks in random order.

Tell students to trace the 12, 1 and 2 on the clock face and then write the rest of the numbers on the clock. Read the instructions under the clock and have students write a 4 and color the hour hand red. Have students trace the 12 and color the minute hand blue. Have students write a 4 to tell it is 4 o'clock. Tell students to circle the clock face that says 4 o'clock. (4:00)

159

Write the times. Match the clocks.

___5___ o'clock

___4___ o'clock

___l___ o'clock

___2___ o'clock

___10___ o'clock

___8___ o'clock

160 (one hundred sixty)

Telling time to the hour

Correcting Common Errors

Some students may confuse the hour hand and minute hand on a clock. Have them work with partners and worksheets that show clock faces without the hands. Have them practice drawing times such as 2 o'clock, 5 o'clock, and 11 o'clock. Remind students that the hour hand is the short hand and the minute hand is the long hand.

Enrichment

1. Draw a clock face that shows 6:00 and write the time under the clock.
2. Work with a friend. Take turns telling an o'clock for the partner to show on a clock and write the time.

Teaching page 160

Ask where the minute hand is pointing on the first clock. (12) Ask where the hour hand is pointing. (5) Ask what time the clock shows. (5 o'clock) Tell students to trace the 5. Tell students to write the number under each clock to show what o'clock it is. Now tell students to look at the digital clocks in the middle and read each. (2 o'clock, 5 o'clock, etc.) Tell students to trace the line from the 5 o'clock face to the 5:00. Ask students to find the clock face that says 2 o'clock and draw a line from it to the 2:00. Continue to help students complete the page.

Extra Credit *Statistics*

Give each student paper, crayons, and scissors. Ask them to draw a picture of the socks they are wearing. Discuss with the class what they will draw if they are wearing tights, or if they are wearing no socks because the weather is warm. Have them cut out the socks. Glue the pictures on a large piece of paper. Ask students to guess how many pairs they think there are, then ask a volunteer to count the pairs. Have another count the number of individual socks.

Time to the Half-hour

pages 161-162

Objective

To tell time to the half-hour

Materials

*Demonstration clock
Clock face

Mental Math

Name the number that is:
1. at the top of a clock (12)
2. 1 more than 98 (99)
3. 6 tens and 9 ones (69)
4. 2 more than 64 (66)
5. at the bottom of a clock (6)
6. 1 quarter and 2 dimes (45¢)
7. 6 dimes (60¢)
8. after 11 on the clock (12)

Skill Review

Have a student show 3:00 on the demonstration clock. Ask another student to write 3:00 on the board. Repeat for all the o'clocks. Ask students to tell where each hand is for each o'clock shown.

Name _____

The time is a half-hour after 9 o'clock
or

9:30

Write the times.

7:00   a half-hour later   7:30

1:00   a half-hour later   1:30

6:00   a half-hour later   6:30

12:00   a half-hour later   12:30

Telling time to the half-hour   (one hundred sixty-one) **161**

Teaching page 161

Start at 12:00 on the demonstration clock. Move the minute hand 1 minute past the 12 and tell students the minute hand has moved 1 minute past 12 o'clock. Continue to move 1 minute at a time to 12:30. Have students count with you by 1's to 30 as the hand moves. Tell students the minute hand has now moved 30 minutes past the hour and we say it is 12:30. Write **12:30** on the board. Ask students where the minute hand is at 12:30. (on 6) Ask where the hour hand is. (between 12 and 1) Tell students the hour hand is halfway between 12 and 1 because the minute hand has moved halfway around the clock. Move the minute hand 1 minute at a time on to 12, and have students count from 31 to 60 with you. Now ask what o'clock it is. (1:00) Continue through 1:30, 2:00, 2:30 and 3:00. Ask students to show 3:30 on their clock faces and tell

where each hand is. Have a student write 3:30 on the board. Continue through more hour and half-hour times. Ask what 4:30 means. (30 minutes after 4:00) Now have students show 7:00 and 30 minutes after 7:00 on their clocks. Ask for more times to be shown.

Ask students to tell where the hands are on the first clock. Read, "The time is 30 minutes after 9 o'clock." Ask a student to write 9:30 on the board. Now tell students to trace the 7:00 to show the time on the clock and 7:30 to show 30 minutes later. Help students complete the page.

161

Write the times.

4:30

2:30

7:30

11:30

8:30

5:30

3:30

10:30

12:30

162 (one hundred sixty-two)

Telling time to the half-hour.

Correcting Common Errors

Some students may write the greater hour instead of the lesser hour when they are writing times such as 3:30, being confused because the hour hand is between the 3 and the 4. Remind them that they should select the hour that the hour hand has just passed (the lesser) on its way to the next hour (the greater) that it has not yet reached. Reinforce the hands always move in the same, clockwise direction.

Enrichment

1. Draw a clock showing 7:30 in the morning. Draw what you are doing then.
2. Act out what you are doing at 12:00 noon, 6:30 in the evening and 8:30 at night.

Teaching page 162

Tell students to trace the 4:30 and tell where the hands are pointing. Tell students to write the time under each clock. Have students complete the page independently.

Extra Credit   *Logic*

Give each student a set of at least ten blank 3 × 5 cards. Write on the board: tall, short, blond hair, brown hair, boy, girl. Tell students to draw as many different dolls as possible using these characteristics, putting one doll on each card. Do not tell them how many dolls you expect them to draw. When they have finished the dolls, have volunteers show eight cards showing the following combinations: tall, blond, boy; tall, brown, boy; short, blond, boy; short, brown, boy; tall, blond, girl; tall, brown, girl; short, blond, girl; and short, brown, girl.

162

Time to the Half-hour

pages 163-164

Objective

To practice telling time to the hour and half-hour

Materials

*Demonstration clock
*Two pencils of different lengths

Mental Math

Which is less?
1. 2 dimes or 5 nickels (2 dimes)
2. 14 pennies or 2 nickels (2 nickels)
3. 5 nickels or 4 dimes (5 nickels)
4. 1 quarter or 2 dimes (2 dimes)
5. 6 nickels or 1 quarter (1 quarter)

Skill Review

Show times to the hour and half hour on the demonstration clock. Have students write the time on the board. Now have a student set the clock to show an hour or half-hour. Have the student ask another student to write the time on the board. Have a student write a time for the hour or half-hour and invite another student to place the hands on the clock to show the times.

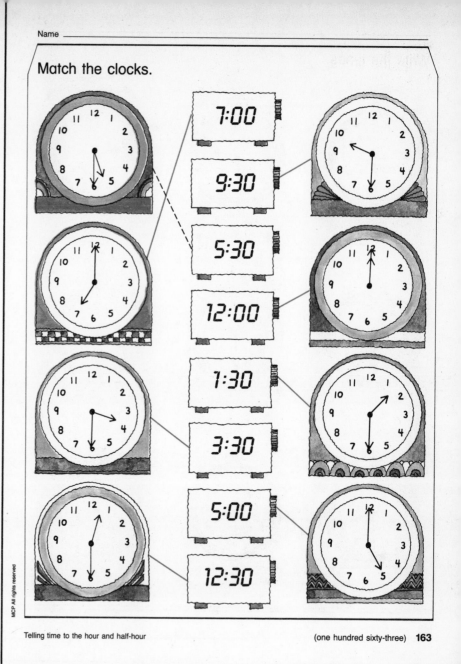

Match the clocks.

7:00
9:30
5:30
12:00
1:30
3:30
5:00
12:30

Telling time to the hour and half-hour

(one hundred sixty-three) **163**

Teaching page 163

On the demonstration clock, start at 12:00 and slowly move the minute hand around the clock. Ask students to tell what the hour hand does as the minute hand moves around the clock face. (moves slowly toward the next number) Tell students the minute hand moves around the clock face 60 minutes while the hour hand moves from one number to the next. Tell students there are 60 minutes in 1 hour.

Ask students to tell where the hour hand is on the first clock. (between 5 and 6) Ask where the minute hand is. (on 6) Ask the time. (5:30) Tell students to find 5:30 in the center column and trace the line from the clock to 5:30. Tell students to draw a line from each clock to its time.

163

Write the times.

1:00

9:30

2:00

10:30

11:00

11:30

8:30

9:00

12:30

4:00

5:30

6:00

Telling time to the hour and half-hour

Correcting Common Errors

If students continue to have difficulty with time to the hour and half-hour, have them work with partners and worksheets that show clock faces without the hands. Have them draw the hands for times in pairs such as 2:00 and 2:30. Before and as they work, ask, "Where does the minute hand point on the hour?" (points at 12) "Where does it point on the half-hour?" (points at 6) "Where is the hour hand on the hour?" (pointing to the number of the hour) "Where is it on the half-hour?" (pointing half-way between the hour and the next hour)

Enrichment

1. Draw a clock face to show 6:30. Write the time as it would look on a digital clock.
2. Draw clock faces to show each of the hours and half hours from 2:00 through 6:00.

Teaching page 164

Ask students to tell the time on the first clock face. (1:00) Tell students to trace the 1:00. Tell students to complete the page by writing the correct time under each clock.

Extra Credit *Applications*

Telling time with a sundial. Provide students with a paper plate and a pencil. Place the plates on the ground in a sunny spot. Put the pencil through the center of the plate, and into the ground. Beginning as early as possible, start to mark on the plate where the shadow of the pencil falls. Begin marking on the hour (ex. 9:00 AM) and continue to mark the shadow every hour. Discuss with the students how a sundial works. What are the problems in telling time with a sundial?

Calendars

pages 165-166

Objective

To understand and make a calendar

Materials

*Demonstration calendar

Mental Math

Name the number that tells the:
1. hour in 4:30 (4)
2. minutes in 6:30 (30)
3. hour in 2:00 (2)
4. minutes in 6:00 (00)
5. hour in 9:00 (9)
6. minutes in 7:30 (30)

Skill Review

Tell students a story of Joe who got up at 7:00 and ate breakfast at 8:00. Ask how much time passed from the time he arose until he ate. (1 hour) Tell other stories which ask students to tell how much time passed between one event and the next. Ask questions which require students to answer in hours and half hours.

Name _____

January

Sunday	Monday	Tuesday	Wednesday	Thursday	Friday	Saturday
				1	2	3
4	5	6	7	8	9	10
11	12	13	14	15	16	17
18	19	20	21	22	23	24
25	26	27	28	29	30	31

Write the answers.

Which month is it? _____January_____

How many days in a week? _7_

How many of each in this month?

Sundays _4_   Mondays _4_   Tuesdays _4_

Wednesdays _4_   Thursdays _5_   Fridays _5_

Saturdays _5_

What is the date?

First Wednesday _7_   Third Tuesday _20_

Second Friday _9_   Fourth Monday _26_

New Year's day _1_

Understanding a calendar   (one hundred sixty-five) **165**

Teaching page 165

Remind students that a clock is used to keep track of time in a day. Show students a calendar as you tell them that a calendar is used to keep track of days. Ask students to say the days of the week in order with you as you point to each. (Sunday, . . . Saturday) Show students the month name, and year numbers on the calendar. Tell students that time is shown in days on a calendar, and days are shown in weeks. Explain that about 4 weeks make a month of time and 12 months make a year. Ask students how many days are in the month shown. Point to each number as you count from 1 to the last day. Show students the Sunday heading and ask them to say the dates of all the Sundays in the month. Repeat for all the days. Ask how many Sundays, Mondays, etc. are in this month. Ask students to give the date of the first Monday, the third Tuesday, etc. Have students tell of important dates such as birthdays and holidays in the month shown and then find the dates on the calendar. Ask students to say the months in order with you. (January, . . . December)

Complete the calendar for this month.

Month .					Year	
Sunday	Monday	Tuesday	Wednesday	Thursday	Friday	Saturday

Write the answers. Answers will vary.

How many days in this month? _____

What date is the first Monday? _____

How many school days? _____

How many Saturdays? _____

How many Sundays? _____

What date is the third Saturday? _____

Making a calendar

Correcting Common Errors

If students have difficulty finding the date for the second Tuesday, for example, have them move their finger across the day names at the top of the calendar and then, when they find the name of the day they want, Tuesday, they can move their finger down the number of boxes indicated by the ordinal given, in this case, 2 boxes or the second box down.

Enrichment

1. Make a calendar of your birthday month this year. Paste a picture of yourself on your day. Display your calendar on the bulletin board.
2. Using the current year's calendar, write the day of the week for each of these dates: January 1, February 14, July 4, December 25 and your birthday.

Teaching page 166

Tell students to look at the demonstration calendar to complete the calendar on this page. Have students write the month and year. Ask students what day of the week the 1 is under. Be sure students place the 1 correctly on the first row. Have students write all the numbers to the last day of the month. Ask students what day of the week is the last day of the month. Have students answer the questions at the bottom as you read them.

Extra Credit   *Logic*

Give each student a handful of assorted buttons and two string loops. Ask students to lay out the string loops on their tables, and put red buttons in one loop and silver buttons in the other. Have them replace those buttons with buttons with two holes in one loop and buttons with four holes in the other. Continue, having them arrange only mutually exclusive groups of buttons. Some students will ask what they should do with the left-over buttons in each case, such as those of a different color, or those with a small ring on the back instead of two or four holes. Hand out a third loop to be used for all other buttons. Ask students to label each loop if they are able. Give them small pieces of paper for this. Write on the board the words they need: red and silver, 2 holes and 4 holes, all other buttons, and so on.

Chapter Review

pages 167-168

Objectives

To review counting money, solving money problems and telling time
To maintain skills learned previously this year

Materials

*Calendar

Mental Math

What day comes after:
1. Monday (Tuesday)
2. Wednesday
3. Friday
4. Sunday
5. Thursday
6. Saturday

Skill Review

Show students the current month on the calendar. Ask the day of the week for the following: 6th, 8th, 1st, 21st, 16th and 27th. Ask students to give the date of the 3rd Sunday, the 2nd Wednesday, etc. Ask students to tell the number of days in the month. Ask the dates of yesterday, tomorrow and the day before yesterday.

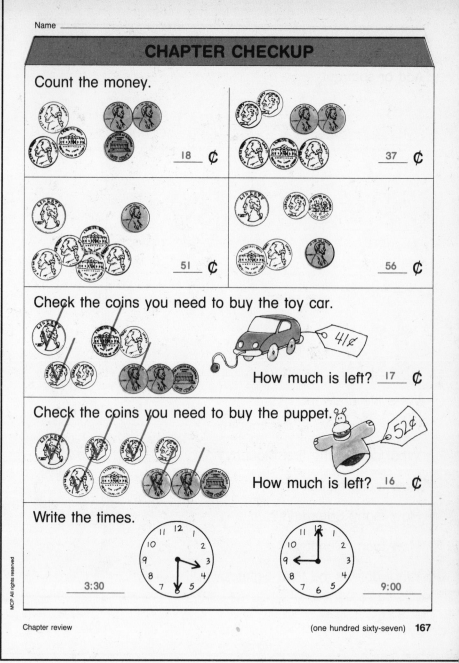

CHAPTER CHECKUP

Count the money.

18 ¢   37 ¢

51 ¢   56 ¢

Check the coins you need to buy the toy car.

41¢

How much is left? 17 ¢

Check the coins you need to buy the puppet.

52¢

How much is left? 16 ¢

Write the times.

3:30   9:00

Chapter review   (one hundred sixty-seven) **167**

Teaching page 167

Tell students they are to count the money in each of the first four problems and write the amount. Read the next 2 problems to the students and ask what they are to do. (write the amount left) Tell students they are to read the clocks and write the times shown. Have students do the page independently.

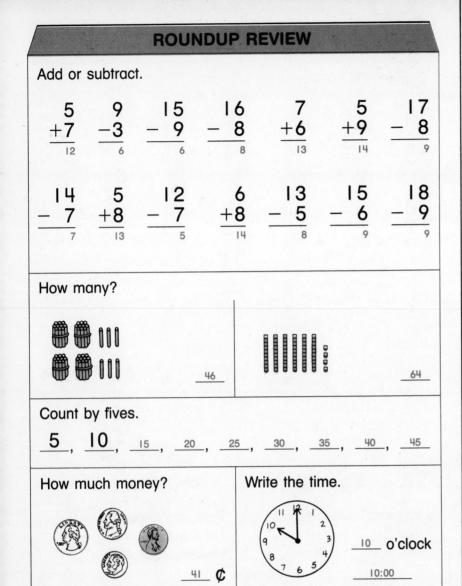

ROUNDUP REVIEW

Add or subtract.

$$\begin{array}{r} 5 \\ +7 \\ \hline 12 \end{array} \quad \begin{array}{r} 9 \\ -3 \\ \hline 6 \end{array} \quad \begin{array}{r} 15 \\ -9 \\ \hline 6 \end{array} \quad \begin{array}{r} 16 \\ -8 \\ \hline 8 \end{array} \quad \begin{array}{r} 7 \\ +6 \\ \hline 13 \end{array} \quad \begin{array}{r} 5 \\ +9 \\ \hline 14 \end{array} \quad \begin{array}{r} 17 \\ -8 \\ \hline 9 \end{array}$$

$$\begin{array}{r} 14 \\ -7 \\ \hline 7 \end{array} \quad \begin{array}{r} 5 \\ +8 \\ \hline 13 \end{array} \quad \begin{array}{r} 12 \\ -7 \\ \hline 5 \end{array} \quad \begin{array}{r} 6 \\ +8 \\ \hline 14 \end{array} \quad \begin{array}{r} 13 \\ -5 \\ \hline 8 \end{array} \quad \begin{array}{r} 15 \\ -6 \\ \hline 9 \end{array} \quad \begin{array}{r} 18 \\ -9 \\ \hline 9 \end{array}$$

How many?

_46_   _64_

Count by fives.

_5_, _10_, _15_, _20_, _25_, _30_, _35_, _40_, _45_

How much money?

_41_ ¢

Write the time.

_10_ o'clock

_10:00_

Cumulative review

Teaching page 168

Tell students they are to watch the signs in the problems in the first 2 rows and write the answers. Ask students to read the 2 words in each of the next 2 problems and tell what they are to do. (write the numbers) Tell students they are to count by 5's in the next row and write in the missing numbers. Ask students what they are to do in the last 2 problems. (count the money and write the amount, read the time and write it 2 ways)

This page reviews addition and subtraction facts, place value, skip-counting by 5's, counting money and telling time.

168

Facts through 10

pages 169-170

Objective

To review addition and subtraction facts for sums through 10

Materials

None

Mental Math

Which is less?
1. 69 or 96 (69)
2. 6 dimes or 50¢ (50¢)
3. 2 days or 2 weeks (2 days)
4. 1 month or 2 weeks (2 weeks)
5. 2 nickels or 9¢ (9¢)
6. 1 month or 1 year (1 month)
7. 10 − 6 or 10 − 7 (10 − 7)

Skill Review

Write the number **9** on the board. Ask students what can be added to 2 to make 9. (7) Write **2 + 7 = 9** on the board. Ask what can be added to 4 to make 9. (5) Write the sentence. Continue to build all sentences for 9. Repeat for 6.

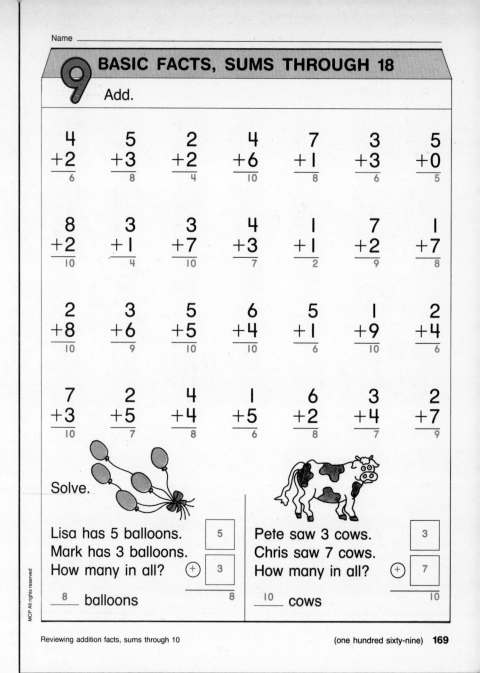

Teaching page 169

Have 4 students stand together. Tell 3 more students to join the 4. Ask a student to write the addition sentence on the board. (4 + 3 = 7) Ask a student to write another addition sentence on the board for this action. (3 + 4 = 7) Tell 3 students to sit down and ask a student to write the subtraction sentence on the board. (7 − 3 = 4) Tell the 3 students to join the group again and then have 4 students sit down. Ask a student to write a subtraction sentence to show this action. (7 − 4 = 3) Have 2 different students stand and ask 5 to join them. Repeat the procedure to develop the sentences 2 + 5 = 7, 5 + 2 = 7, 7 − 2 = 5 and 7 − 5 = 2. Have eight students stand and develop 4 or more sentences for 8.

Tell students they are to look at the sign in each problem and work the problems in all 4 rows. Read the story problems and tell students to write the numbers and signs for each.

169

Subtract.

9 −3 6	10 −1 9	3 −2 1	6 −3 3	7 −5 2	10 −7 3	9 −4 5
6 −5 1	7 −4 3	5 −3 2	8 −7 1	4 −3 1	8 −4 4	10 −9 1
10 −4 6	7 −6 1	9 −5 4	9 −8 1	10 −2 8	7 −3 4	8 −5 3
6 −2 4	8 −3 5	9 −7 2	8 −2 6	10 −6 4	9 −2 7	2 −1 1

Solve.

Jerry saw 9 🐕.
2 🐕 walked away.
How many 🐕
were left?

⬜ 9 ⊖ ⬜ 2
___7

 7 dogs

Mary Lou had 8 🐚.
She gave Danny 3 🐚.
How many 🐚
are left?

⬜ 8 ⊖ ⬜ 3
___5

 5 shells

Reviewing subtraction facts, minuends through 10

Correcting Common Errors

If students need more practice with sums to 10, have them work with partners. Give each pair a number such as 10 and have them list all the pairs of addends having 10 as their sum.

Enrichment

1. Write all the ways to make 9 using 2 numbers from 0 through 10.
2. Draw pictures to tell 2 ways to solve this problem: Chan had 7 soccer balls and kept them in 2 baskets. How many will he put in each basket?

Teaching page 170

Ask students what kind of problems are in the first 4 rows. (subtraction) Tell students they are to write the answers for each problem. Read the 2 story problems and have students write the numbers and the signs in each.

Extra Credit   *Counting*

Tell the students to put both feet in the aisle. Remind them that two of the same item is called a pair. Direct them to write their names on a sheet of paper along with the word mother on the second line, and the word father on the third line. Tell students to count the number of pairs of shoes they own when they go home, and write that number after their names. Next they should do the same for their mothers' and fathers' shoes. The students must then add to find the total pairs of shoes and record this.

Then tell them to count gloves or mittens for each person, and record the information in the same way. Other variations include the counting of shoes for siblings, slippers, eyeglasses, salt and pepper shakers, etc.

Facts through 18

pages 171-172

Objective

To practice addition and subtraction for sums and minuends through 18

Materials

10 counters
Sheet of paper
*Demonstration clock

Mental Math

Count on from:
1. 26 to 42 (26, 27, 28, . . 42)
2. 0 to 21
3. 87 to 99
4. 45 to 60
5. 9 to 29
6. 16 to 30
7. 29 to 40
8. 35 to 52

Skill Review

Show 12:00 on the clock and ask a student to tell the time, write it on the board and tell what activity is usually taking place at that time. (lunch or sleeping) Repeat for waking times, meal times, bus times, etc. that occur on the hour or half-hour.

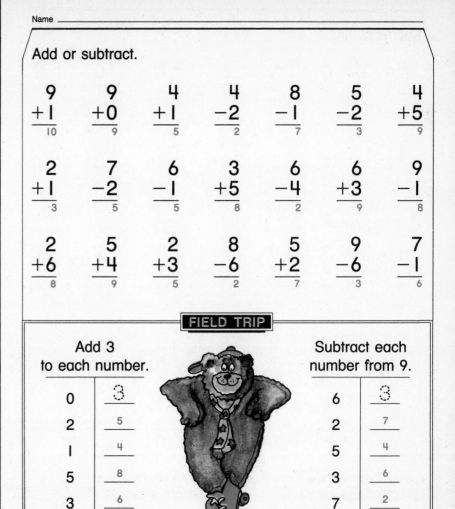

Practice, sums and minuends through 10

(one hundred seventy-one) **171**

Teaching page 171

Tell students to circle the + or − sign in each problem in row 1. Tell students they must first check the sign to know whether to add or subtract. Have students complete the 3 rows of problems independently. Allow use of counters as needed.

Field Trip

Before students complete the T-drills, lead them through oral drills where they add fixed numbers to one-digit numbers given by classmates. If the sums given are correct, the students can then challenge with numbers to subtract from a given minuend. Change addends and minuends occasionally until students feel comfortable with the skills.

171

Add or subtract.

8 +0 ___ 8	6 −2 ___ 4	8 −3 ___ 5	10 − 5 ___ 5	7 +0 ___ 7	1 +2 ___ 3
1 +4 ___ 5	10 − 3 ___ 7	5 −5 ___ 0	6 +0 ___ 6	10 − 8 ___ 2	6 +4 ___ 10

Complete the tables.

Add 4		Subtract 3		Add 5		Subtract 2	
2	6	5	2	1	6	8	6
1	5	7	4	3	8	5	3
3	7	10	7	5	10	7	5
6	10	8	5	4	9	6	4
5	9	6	3	2	7	4	2

Solve.

Mike picked 7 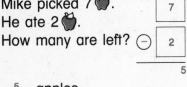.
He ate 2 🍎.
How many are left? ⊖

7
2
___
5

__5__ apples

Diana had 6 🚗.
She bought 4 more.
How many does
she have now? ⊕

6
4
___
10

__10__ cars

Practice, sums and minuends through 10

Students may confuse addition and
subtraction when they are working
on a mixed set of problems. Before
they begin, have them circle all
the + signs in one color and all the
− signs in another color. When they
come to a sign with a different color,
it will remind them to change the
operation.

Enrichment

1. Draw two pictures that show
   adding 2 and 6 and subtracting
   2 from 6.
2. Work with a partner to see
   how quickly you can say the sign
   of + or − and give the answers
   to scrambled addition and
   subtraction facts for sums and
   minuends through 10.

Teaching page 172

Have students circle the + or − sign in each problem
and then complete the problems in the first 2 rows
independently. Have students find the first table in the
middle of the page and tell what they are to do. (add
4 to each number) Have students add 4 to the 2 and
trace the 6. Now have students tell what is to be done
in the second table. (subtract 3 from each number)
Ask students what 5 take away 3 is and have them
trace the 2. Tell students to complete the 4 tables
independently. Now read each of the story problems.
Tell students they are to decide whether to add or
subtract and then write the sign in the problem before
they solve it.

Extra Credit *Geometry*

Give each student one paper, a pencil, and crayons.
Lay out a number of simple objects such as a set of
blocks, several books, some balls, and some dishes.
Ask them to select an object and draw its shape. Some
may trace the object, others simply approximate its
shape in their drawing. When they have finished one
object, have them select another and draw its shape.
When all the students have drawn at least three
shapes, hold some of the drawings up for the rest of
the class. Ask them to guess the object that was used
to make the drawing. Explain that every object has its
own shape and can be identified by it.

172

Facts through 18

pages 173-174

Objective

To practice addition and subtraction for sums and minuends 11 through 18

Materials

18 counters
Sheet of paper

Mental Math

Count on by:
1. 5's from 25 to 60 (25, 30, 35, . . . 60)
2. 10's from 40 to 90
3. 1's from 26 to 42
4. 5's from 65 to 95
5. 10's from 10 to 60
6. 1's from 11 to 21
7. 5's from 5 to 30

Skill Review

Write on the board:

__+1 = 3	2 + 3 = __+2
__+6 = 8	2 + 3 = __+3
4 + __=8	2 + 3 = __+4
5 + __=9	4 + __=2 + 5
__+3 = 9	6 + 3 = 5 + __
2 + __=7	9 + 1 = 4 + __

Have a student work each problem at the board while others work with counters at their seats.

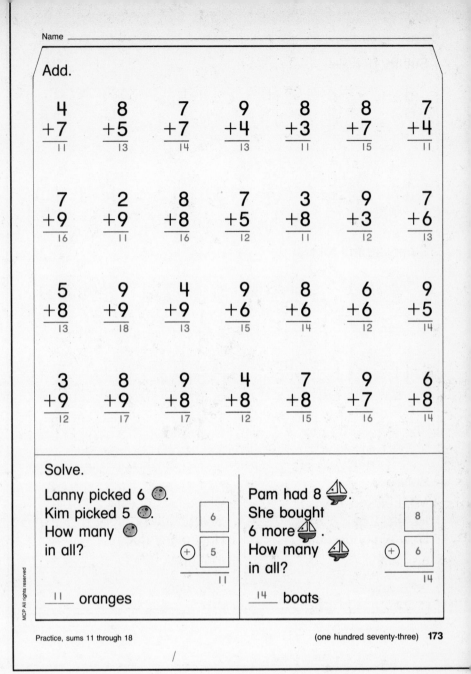

Name _____

Add.

4 +7 = 11	8 +5 = 13	7 +7 = 14	9 +4 = 13	8 +3 = 11	8 +7 = 15	7 +4 = 11
7 +9 = 16	2 +9 = 11	8 +8 = 16	7 +5 = 12	3 +8 = 11	9 +3 = 12	7 +6 = 13
5 +8 = 13	9 +9 = 18	4 +9 = 13	9 +6 = 15	8 +6 = 14	6 +6 = 12	9 +5 = 14
3 +9 = 12	8 +9 = 17	9 +8 = 17	4 +8 = 12	7 +8 = 15	9 +7 = 16	6 +8 = 14

Solve.

Lanny picked 6 🍪.
Kim picked 5 🍪.
How many 🍪 in all?

6
+	5
11

__11__ oranges

Pam had 8 ⛵.
She bought 6 more ⛵.
How many ⛵ in all?

8
+	6
14

__14__ boats

Practice, sums 11 through 18

(one hundred seventy-three) **173**

Teaching page 173

Ask students what sign is in all the problems. (plus) Ask students what they are to do in all these problems. (add) Remind students to write the + signs in the story problems. Offer reading assistance where needed as students complete the page independently. Allow use of counters as needed.

173

Subtract.

13 − 7 <small>6</small>	15 − 6 <small>9</small>	11 − 9 <small>2</small>	16 − 8 <small>8</small>	14 − 5 <small>9</small>	15 − 7 <small>8</small>	13 − 8 <small>5</small>
17 − 9 <small>8</small>	15 − 9 <small>6</small>	11 − 6 <small>5</small>	13 − 9 <small>4</small>	18 − 9 <small>9</small>	11 − 5 <small>6</small>	12 − 7 <small>5</small>
13 − 5 <small>8</small>	12 − 5 <small>7</small>	17 − 8 <small>9</small>	13 − 6 <small>7</small>	14 − 8 <small>6</small>	11 − 4 <small>7</small>	14 − 6 <small>8</small>
11 − 8 <small>3</small>	11 − 7 <small>4</small>	16 − 9 <small>7</small>	12 − 8 <small>4</small>	16 − 7 <small>9</small>	15 − 8 <small>7</small>	14 − 9 <small>5</small>

Solve.

Jim had 11 🚗.
He gave Sue 2 🚙.
How many cars
are left?

⊟ $\begin{array}{r} 11 \\ \ominus\ 2 \\ \hline 9 \end{array}$

_9_ cars

A store had 14 ⚽.
7 balls are sold.
How many balls
are left?

$\begin{array}{r} 14 \\ \ominus\ 7 \\ \hline 7 \end{array}$

_7_ balls

Correcting Common Errors

If students have difficulty with a subtraction fact, have them write the related addition sentence, and use their knowledge of addition facts to find the answer to a subtraction problem.
Example Problem: $15 − 8 = \square$
Students should think: $\square + 8 = 15$
Since $7 + 8 = 15$, then: $15 − 8 = 7$

Enrichment

1. Write all addition and subtraction facts for doubles through sums of 18.
2. Have a partner time you writing answers for all addition facts for sums through 18.
3. Write all subtraction facts for minuends of 15, 16, 17 and 18.

Teaching page 174

Ask students what sign is in all the problems in the 4 rows. (minus) Ask what they are to do in all these problems. (subtract) Offer reading assistance where needed in the story problems. Remind students to write the minus signs in the circles. Have students complete the page independently.

Extra Credit   *Statistics*

Ask another class to cooperate with yours to make a survey of students who will buy lunch and those who have brought their lunch. Pass out 2 different tokens, perhaps some that look like little lunch bags and others that look like coins for buying lunch. Have students in both classes take the token that matches what they will do today for lunch.

Ask volunteers in your class to collect all the tokens and glue them onto a piece of paper, with lunch bags on one side of the paper and school lunch coins on the other. Before looking at the paper have a student tell which group they think is larger. Then ask a volunteer to count the numbers of bags and of school lunches and write the numbers at the bottom of the collage. Explain that this is a survey.

174

Facts through 18

pages 175-176

Objective

To practice addition and subtraction for sums and minuends 11 through 18.

Materials

*Addition and subtraction fact cards for sums and minuends 11 through 18
Clock face

Mental Math

What time is it if the long hand is on:

1. 12 and short hand on 9 (9:00)
2. 6 and short hand is between 2 and 3 (2:30)
3. 12 and short hand on 5 (5:00)
4. 6 and short hand is between 5 and 6 (5:30)
5. 12 and short hand on 8 (8:00)
6. 6 and short hand is between 4 and 5 (4:30)

Skill Review

Show an addition or subtraction fact card and ask what sign is in the problem. Ask if they are to add or subtract in the problem. Flash the cards as students answer the 2 questions for each. Begin again and ask students to tell the sign, the operation and the answer.

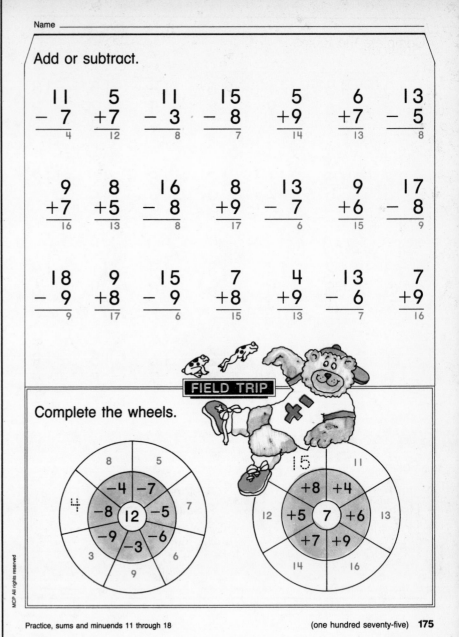

Name _____

Add or subtract.

11 − 7 4	5 +7 12	11 − 3 8	15 − 8 7	5 +9 14	6 +7 13	13 − 5 8
9 +7 16	8 +5 13	16 − 8 8	8 +9 17	13 − 7 6	9 +6 15	17 − 8 9
18 − 9 9	9 +8 17	15 − 9 6	7 +8 15	4 +9 13	13 − 6 7	7 +9 16

FIELD TRIP

Complete the wheels.

Practice, sums and minuends 11 through 18

(one hundred seventy-five) **175**

Teaching page 175

Tell students to circle the + and − signs in all 3 rows of problems. Tell students to say each problem to themselves as 11 take away 7 or 5 plus 7, etc. before working each problem. Have students work the 3 rows of problems independently.

Field Trip

Tell students they are to subtract each number from the number in the center of the wheel and write the number left. Ask students how many in all for each problem. (12) Ask students to take 8 away from 12 and tell the number left. (4) Tell students to trace the 4. Now tell students to look at the second wheel and tell what they are to do. (add 7 to each number and write the sum)

Ask students to add 7 to 8 and tell the sum. (15) Tell students to trace the 15. Tell students to complete both wheels.

175

Complete the tables.

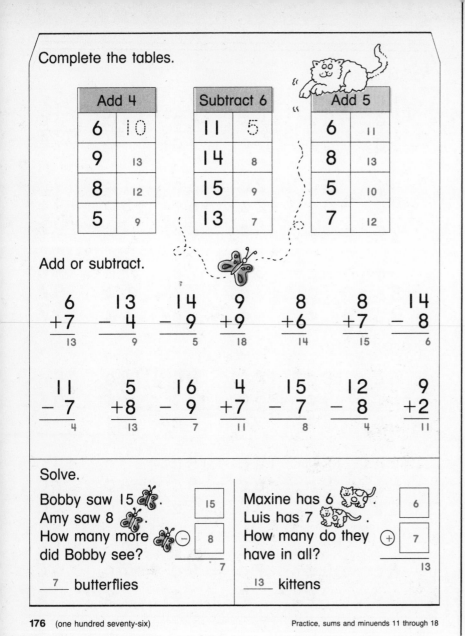

Add 4	
6	10
9	13
8	12
5	9

Subtract 6	
11	5
14	8
15	9
13	7

Add 5	
6	11
8	13
5	10
7	12

Add or subtract.

$$\begin{array}{r} 6 \\ +7 \\ \hline 13 \end{array} \quad \begin{array}{r} 13 \\ -4 \\ \hline 9 \end{array} \quad \begin{array}{r} 14 \\ -9 \\ \hline 5 \end{array} \quad \begin{array}{r} 9 \\ +9 \\ \hline 18 \end{array} \quad \begin{array}{r} 8 \\ +6 \\ \hline 14 \end{array} \quad \begin{array}{r} 8 \\ +7 \\ \hline 15 \end{array} \quad \begin{array}{r} 14 \\ -8 \\ \hline 6 \end{array}$$

$$\begin{array}{r} 11 \\ -7 \\ \hline 4 \end{array} \quad \begin{array}{r} 5 \\ +8 \\ \hline 13 \end{array} \quad \begin{array}{r} 16 \\ -9 \\ \hline 7 \end{array} \quad \begin{array}{r} 4 \\ +7 \\ \hline 11 \end{array} \quad \begin{array}{r} 15 \\ -7 \\ \hline 8 \end{array} \quad \begin{array}{r} 12 \\ -8 \\ \hline 4 \end{array} \quad \begin{array}{r} 9 \\ +2 \\ \hline 11 \end{array}$$

Solve.

Bobby saw 15 🦋.
Amy saw 8 🦋.
How many more 🦋 did Bobby see?

15 Ⓜ 8 ____
7

___7___ butterflies

Maxine has 6 🐱.
Luis has 7 🐱.
How many do they have in all?

6 ⊕ 7 ____
13

___13___ kittens

Practice, sums and minuends 11 through 18

Correcting Common Errors

Some students may continue to have difficulty with addition and subtraction facts. Have them work with partners and use a number line from 0 to 18 on which to model the problems. For addition, they should start at 0, draw an arrow for the first addend, and then continue with another arrow for the second addend. Where the second arrow ends is the sum. For subtraction, have them start at the minuend and draw an arrow back toward 0 the number of spaces indicated by the subtrahend. Where the arrow ends, is the difference.

Enrichment

1. Practice speed in writing answers for all subtraction facts for minuends through 18 by having a partner time you.
2. Write all addition facts for the family of 9.
3. Work with 12 friends to act out all subtraction facts for minuends of 13.

Teaching page 176

Tell students to add 4 and 6 and trace the 10 in the first table. Then tell students to subtract 6 from 11 in the next table and trace the 5. Ask students what is to be done in each table. (add 4, subtract 6, add 5) Tell students to look at each sign before working each problem in the next 2 rows. Tell students they are then to read each story problem and write the sign and numbers. Offer reading assistance if needed. Have students complete the page independently.

Extra Credit   *Statistics*

Explain that the class is going to keep track of the number of school lunches bought and the number of lunches brought from home, for a whole week. Each day, put a sheet of paper by the door. As students come in, ask them to write their name in the column marked with a lunch bag if they have brought their own lunch, or in the column marked with coin if they are going to buy the school lunch. When all the students have signed in, have volunteers count the names and write the total in each column. Post each day's survey and discuss the results at the end of the week. For example, ask which day showed the most lunches bought, and which the most lunches brought from home. Ask students whether they think that more students bring or buy their lunches, and why. (Answers will vary.)

176

Money, Adding and Subtracting

pages 177-178

Objective

To add and subtract for money problems through 18¢

Materials

18 pennies
Clock face
*Digital clock

Mental Math

Name 2 numbers of pennies to make:

1. 18¢ (9 and 9)
2. 16¢ (7 and 9, etc.)
3. 12¢ (6 and 6, etc.)
4. 15¢ (7 and 8, etc.)
5. 13¢ (7 and 6, etc.)
6. 9¢ (5 and 4, etc.)
7. 11¢ (6 and 5, etc.)

Skill Review

Show a digital clock and have students read several hour and half-hour times. Now show an hour or half-hour and have students show the time on their clock faces. Repeat for more hour and half-hour times.

Add.

1¢	7¢	8¢	9¢	8¢	3¢
+1¢	+3¢	+4¢	+2¢	+8¢	+3¢
2¢	10¢	12¢	11¢	16¢	6¢

4¢	5¢	2¢	6¢	1¢	9¢
+9¢	+5¢	+2¢	+6¢	+5¢	+9¢
13¢	10¢	4¢	12¢	6¢	18¢

6¢	5¢	3¢	7¢	7¢	4¢
+8¢	+7¢	+7¢	+7¢	+5¢	+4¢
14¢	12¢	10¢	14¢	12¢	8¢

Subtract.

6¢	10¢	12¢	8¢	16¢	9¢
−5¢	− 4¢	− 5¢	−3¢	− 7¢	−5¢
1¢	6¢	7¢	5¢	9¢	4¢

11¢	13¢	14¢	15¢	8¢	14¢
− 3¢	− 4¢	− 6¢	− 8¢	−6¢	− 7¢
8¢	9¢	8¢	7¢	2¢	7¢

12¢	17¢	10¢	14¢	13¢	11¢
− 8¢	− 9¢	− 7¢	− 9¢	− 7¢	− 6¢
4¢	8¢	3¢	5¢	6¢	5¢

Adding and subtracting money

Teaching page 177

Ask students to look through the first row of problems and tell what they are to do in each problem. (add) Ask students this question for each row of problems on this page. Have students then complete the page independently.

Ed had 10¢.
He bought a ⛵.
How much
was left?

$$10¢ \ominus 7¢ = 3¢$$

3 ¢

Rafer has 8¢.
Karen has 9¢.
How much in all?

$$8¢ \oplus 9¢ = 17¢$$

17 ¢

Solve.

Liz had 8¢.
She found 7¢.
How much in all?

$$8¢ \oplus 7¢ = 15¢$$

15 ¢

Joan had 17¢.
She bought a 🚗 9¢.
How much was
left?

$$17¢ \ominus 9¢ = 8¢$$

8 ¢

Mei Ling has 7¢.
Randy has 5¢.
How much in all?

$$7¢ \oplus 5¢ = 12¢$$

12 ¢

Leah had 9¢.
Uncle Phil gave
her 6¢.
How much in all?

$$9¢ \oplus 6¢ = 15¢$$

15 ¢

Fran had 15¢.
She bought a 🧸 9¢.
How much is
left?

$$15¢ \ominus 9¢ = 6¢$$

6 ¢

Linda has 9¢.
Ro has 9¢.
How much in all?

$$9¢ \oplus 9¢ = 18¢$$

18 ¢

Problem solving, choosing the operation

Correcting Common Errors

Some students may get incorrect
answers when working with amounts
of money because they have not
mastered some of the facts. Have
them work with partners, using coins
as counters to model each problem.

Enrichment

1. Draw 18¢ using dimes, nickels
   or pennies. Draw an item priced
   13¢ and circle the coins you
   would have left after buying it.
2. Write a story problem about
   your having 17¢ and spending
   12¢. Write the problem with a +
   or − sign. Write the answer to
   your problem.

Teaching page 178

Have students read the first problem with you and tell
if they are to add or subtract. (subtract) Tell students to
trace the − sign in the circle. Ask students to tell what
the problem will be. (10¢ − 7¢ = 3¢) Tell students
to trace the numbers 10, 7, 3 and 3. Repeat the
procedure for the next problem. Tell students to
complete the page. Give reading assistance where
needed.

Extra Credit   *Measurement*

Students understand the need for standard units of
measure when they compare measurements made with
unequal units. Have students work in pairs to help
each other cut strings the length of their feet, and open
hand span. Have them measure objects in the room
with these strings. Compare the results. Guide students
in understanding the reason for the differences in their
measurements. Repeat the measuring process with
strings cut to the same length. Compare these results.
Discuss the need for standard measures in different
situations and occupations. Ask what other kinds of
measures need to be standardized.

Problem Solving

pages 179-180

Objectives

To choose adding or subtracting to solve problems

To practice adding and subtracting for sums and minuends through 18

Materials

*Demonstration clock

Mental Math

Will you add or subtract?
1. How many in all? (add)
2. How many are left? (subtract)
3. How many altogether? (add)
4. plus (add)
5. take away (subtract)
6. minus (subtract)
7. and 3 more (add)

Skill Review

Show 6:00 on the demonstration clock. Ask a student to write the time on the board. Ask another student to write the time for 30 minutes after 6:00 (6:30) and show that time on the clock. Repeat for several more hours and half-hours.

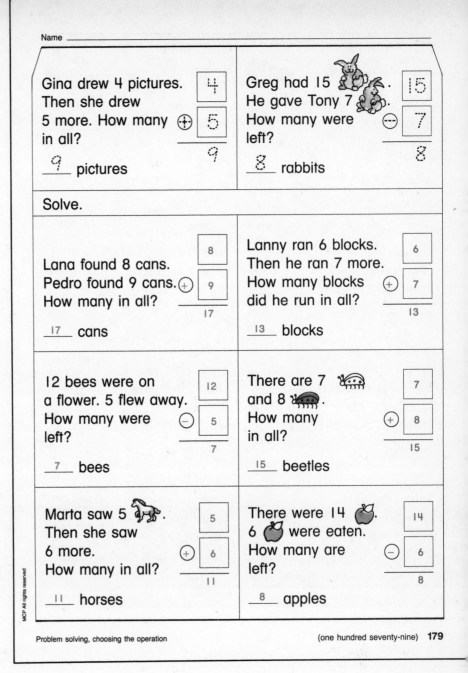

Name _____

Gina drew 4 pictures. Then she drew 5 more. How many in all?

$\boxed{4} \oplus \boxed{5}$
$\overline{\quad 9}$

_9_ pictures

Greg had 15 🐰. He gave Tony 7 🐰. How many were left?

$\boxed{15} \ominus \boxed{7}$
$\overline{\quad 8}$

_8_ rabbits

Solve.

Lana found 8 cans. Pedro found 9 cans. How many in all?

$\boxed{8} \oplus \boxed{9}$
$\overline{\quad 17}$

_17_ cans

Lanny ran 6 blocks. Then he ran 7 more. How many blocks did he run in all?

$\boxed{6} \oplus \boxed{7}$
$\overline{\quad 13}$

_13_ blocks

12 bees were on a flower. 5 flew away. How many were left?

$\boxed{12} \ominus \boxed{5}$
$\overline{\quad 7}$

_7_ bees

There are 7 🐞 and 8 🐛. How many in all?

$\boxed{7} \oplus \boxed{8}$
$\overline{\quad 15}$

_15_ beetles

Marta saw 5 🐴. Then she saw 6 more. How many in all?

$\boxed{5} \oplus \boxed{6}$
$\overline{\quad 11}$

_11_ horses

There were 14 🍎. 6 🍎 were eaten. How many are left?

$\boxed{14} \ominus \boxed{6}$
$\overline{\quad 8}$

_8_ apples

Problem solving, choosing the operation

(one hundred seventy-nine) **179**

Teaching page 179

Tell students they must decide whether to add or subtract for each problem on this page. Read the first problem with the students and ask if they are to add or subtract to find how many pictures Gina drew. (add) Tell students to trace the + sign and then trace the numbers in the problem. Repeat for the second problem, first asking what operation is to be done and tracing its sign. Tell students to complete the page. Offer reading assistance when needed.

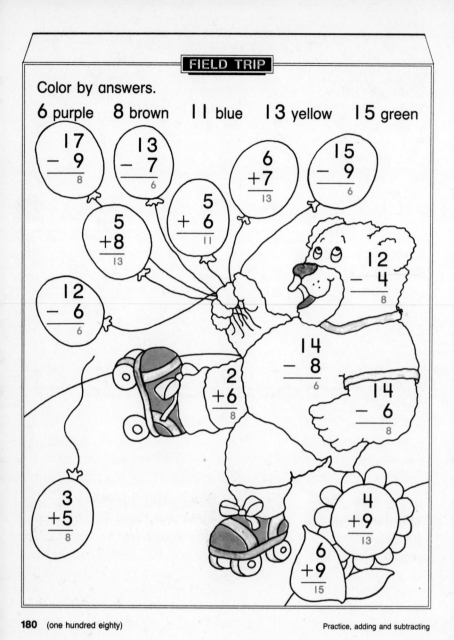

FIELD TRIP

Color by answers.

6 purple   8 brown   11 blue   13 yellow   15 green

$$17 - 9 = 8$$

$$13 - 7 = 6$$

$$6 + 7 = 13$$

$$15 - 9 = 6$$

$$5 + 6 = 11$$

$$5 + 8 = 13$$

$$12 - 6 = 6$$

$$12 - 4 = 8$$

$$14 - 8 = 6$$

$$2 + 6 = 8$$

$$14 - 6 = 8$$

$$3 + 5 = 8$$

$$4 + 9 = 13$$

$$6 + 9 = 15$$

180 (one hundred eighty)

Practice, adding and subtracting

Correcting Common Errors

If students have difficulty with word problems, have them work in pairs where one partner retells the problem in his or her own words, and the second partner uses counters to act out the problem.

Enrichment

1. Write 6 addition or subtraction problems. Trade papers with a friend and write the correct answers.
2. Lay out 18 or less counters in two groups. Have a partner write an addition or subtraction sentence for the groups.

Teaching page 180

Field Trip

Ask students to tell what they are to do on this page. (find the sum or number left and color the section the color beside that number in the code) Have students tell the sign for several of the problems to be sure they note that the problems are mixed. Remind students to look at the sign in each problem before working each. The coloring may be done after all the problems are worked.

Extra Credit   *Measurement*

Students can practice the techniques of measurement using their hands and feet as measuring tools. Demonstrate, stressing that all units must go end to end, starting even with one edge of the item being measured. Explain there can be no gaps between units. Use only hands or feet. Have students measure desks, books, walls and several other items. They can then draw pictures of items that they can measure at home. The next day they record their results next to the picture. Display the papers on a bulletin board about measurement.

180

Chapter Review

pages 181-182

Objectives

To review adding and subtracting for sums and minuends through 18
To maintain skills learned previously this year

Materials

None

Mental Math

Name the number that:
1. comes between 79 and 81 (80)
2. comes before 26 (25)
3. is 8 dimes (80¢)
4. tells 10's in 74 (7)
5. tells nickels in 1 dime (2)
6. is 4 tens and 9 ones (49)
7. comes after 4th (5th)

Skill Review

Draw 10 circles on the board. Ask a student to cross out the 4th circle. Ask other students to cross out other circles as you give the ordinal numbers in random order. Continue until all circles are crossed out. Give ordinal numbers again in random order, and ask students to erase that circle and draw a stick in its place.

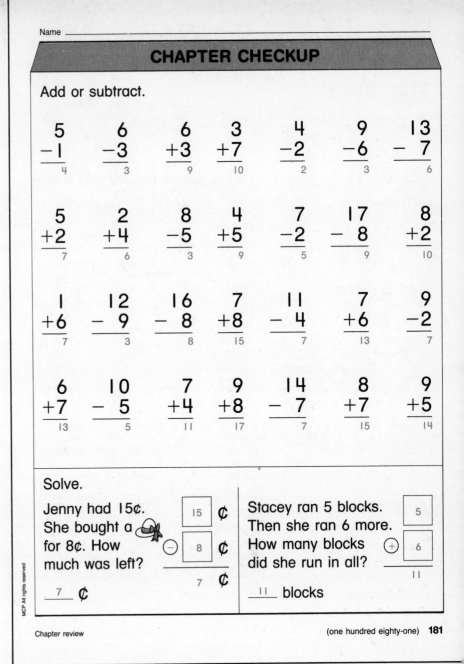

Teaching page 181

Tell students they are to look at the sign in each of the 28 problems and then add or subtract and write the answer. Tell students that the 2 story problems at the bottom of the page need signs in the circles. Tell students to read each problem carefully and look for words that help them know to add or subtract. Have students complete the page independently but offer reading assistance where needed.

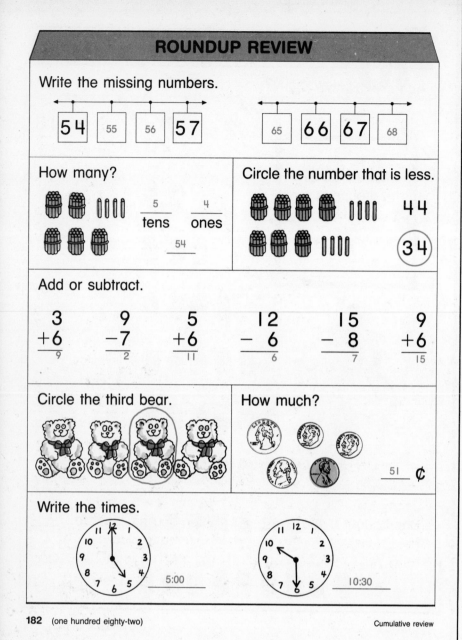

ROUNDUP REVIEW

Write the missing numbers.

5 4 | 55 | 56 | 5 7

65 | 6 6 | 6 7 | 68

How many?

5 tens   4 ones

54

Circle the number that is less.

4 4

(3 4)

Add or subtract.

$$\begin{array}{r} 3 \\ +6 \\ \hline 9 \end{array}$$
$$\begin{array}{r} 9 \\ -7 \\ \hline 2 \end{array}$$
$$\begin{array}{r} 5 \\ +6 \\ \hline 11 \end{array}$$
$$\begin{array}{r} 12 \\ -6 \\ \hline 6 \end{array}$$
$$\begin{array}{r} 15 \\ -8 \\ \hline 7 \end{array}$$
$$\begin{array}{r} 9 \\ +6 \\ \hline 15 \end{array}$$

Circle the third bear.

How much?

51 ¢

Write the times.

5:00

10:30

182 (one hundred eighty-two)

Cumulative review

Teaching page 182

Go through each of the boxes and ask students what they are to do. Tell students to complete the page independently.

This page reviews sequencing numbers, place value, comparing numbers, addition and subtraction facts, ordinal numbers, counting money and telling time.

182

Place Value
Tens and Ones

pages 183-184

Objective

To review place value for tens and ones

Materials

99 counting sticks
9 rubber bands

Mental Math

Count by 1's from:
1. 1 to 30 (1, 2, 3, . . . 30)
2. 10 to 41
3. 0 to 20
4. 11 to 38
5. 42 to 60
6. 15 to 34
7. 78 to 92

Skill Review

Have students work in pairs to count out 25 sticks. Tell students to bundle 10 of the 25. Tell students to bundle another 10 sticks. Ask if they can make a third bundle. (no) Ask how many groups of 10. (2) Ask how many ones. (5) Ask a student to write the number on the board. (25) Repeat this activity for several more numbers through 99. Now repeat the activity for 10, 20, 30, . . . 90.

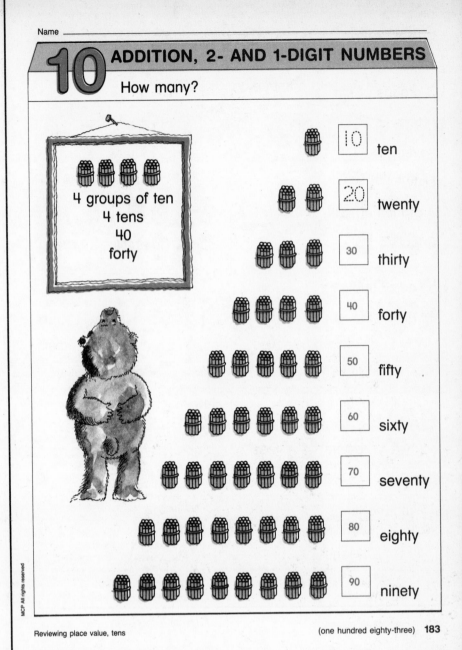

Name _____

10 ADDITION, 2- AND 1-DIGIT NUMBERS
How many?

4 groups of ten
4 tens
40
forty

10	ten	
20	twenty	
30	thirty	
40	forty	
50	fifty	
60	sixty	
70	seventy	
80	eighty	
90	ninety	

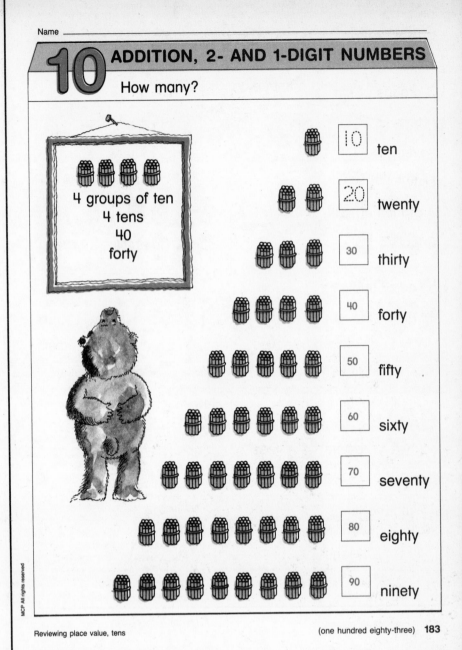

Reviewing place value, tens

(one hundred eighty-three) **183**

Teaching page 183

Ask students how many tens are shown in the 4 bundles. (4) Ask how many ones are in 40. (40) Tell students they are to count the bundles and write how many ones are in that number of bundles. Tell students to write the number beside its number name. Have students complete the page independently.

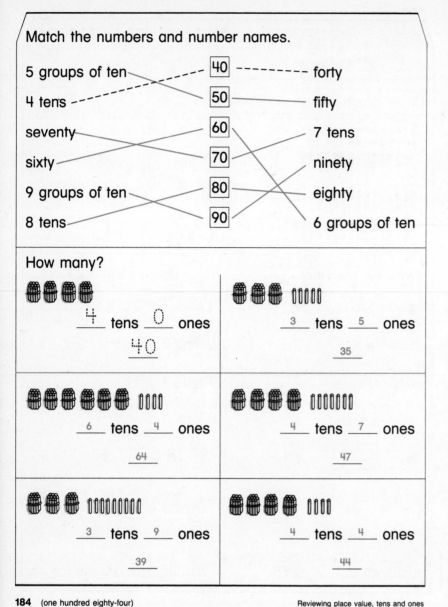

Match the numbers and number names.

5 groups of ten — 40 ----- forty

4 tens ----- 50 — fifty

seventy — 60 — 7 tens

sixty — 70 — ninety

9 groups of ten — 80 — eighty

8 tens — 90 — 6 groups of ten

How many?

___4___ tens ___0___ ones
___40___

___3___ tens ___5___ ones
35

___6___ tens ___4___ ones
64

___4___ tens ___7___ ones
47

___3___ tens ___9___ ones
39

___4___ tens ___4___ ones
44

184 (one hundred eighty-four)   Reviewing place value, tens and ones

Correcting Common Errors

Some students may need additional review with tens. Draw 90 sticks on the chalkboard. Have a student count the first 10 and circle them as a group. Continue to have other students circle groups of 10 until all the sticks have been circled. Ask, "How many groups of 10 in all?" (9) "How many ones is that?" (90) Then, as you point to the groups from left to right, have the students count them by tens, saying "ten, twenty, thirty, ..." Repeat the pointing and have them write the numbers: 10, 20, 30, ...

Enrichment

1. Work with a friend to make a 10's chain. Write the numbers 10, 20, 30, . . . 90 on separate cards. Join the cards in order with string or tape.
2. Use dimes and pennies as tens and ones and show the numbers 84, 63, 58 and 19. Draw each amount.
3. Give a friend 9 dimes to pay for an item costing 10¢. Have your friend count by 10's to give the dimes in change. Buy items costing 20¢, 60¢ and 40¢.

Teaching page 184

Ask students how many ones are in 5 groups of ten. (50) Find that number in the second column and trace the line to 50. Find the number name for 50 in the third column and draw a line from 50 to fifty. Have students complete the top half of the page independently.

Tell students to write the number of tens and ones in each box and write the number. Ask how many tens are in the first box. (4) Ask how many ones. (0) Ask what number is 4 tens and 0 ones. (40) Tell students to trace the numbers. Go through the second box similarly and then have students complete the page.

Extra Credit   *Statistics*

Ask students to come to the board one by one and write their ages. Then ask a volunteer to tell approximately how old everyone in the class is. This will be fairly easy, since most children will be one age, with a few slightly younger and a few slightly older. Explain that the number they arrived at is called the average.

Have your class survey the ages of members of another class, using a class in a different grade if possible. When they have recorded the ages of all the students, ask a volunteer to tell what their average age is. Point out that the average is a number that most correctly tells the age of most of the students in the class.

Number Sequences

pages 185-186

Objectives

To review place value for tens and ones
To review numbers in sequence through 99

Materials

99 counting sticks
9 rubber bands

Mental Math

Count by 1's from:
1. 1 through 10
2. 11 through 20
3. 21 through 30
4. 41 through 50
5. 51 through 60
6. 61 through 70
7. 81 through 90
8. 91 through 99

Skill Review

Write the number words **one** through **nine** on the board in a column. Ask students to read the words. Have a student write the number beside its word. Erase and write the number words again in scrambled order. Have students read the words and then write the number beside each.

Name _____

→ _1_ tens _4_ ones → 14

Circle groups of 10. How many?

→ _2_ tens _5_ ones → 25

→ _3_ tens _3_ ones → 33

Write the numbers.		Write the missing numbers.	
twenty-two	22	4 tens 7 ones → 47	
thirty-five	35	6 tens 2 ones → 62	
sixty-seven	67	9 tens 9 ones → 99	
ninety-seven	97	5 tens 2 ones → 52	
fifty	50	_5_ tens _5_ ones → 55	
forty-three	43	_6_ tens _9_ ones → 69	
seventy-one	71	_3_ tens _4_ ones → 34	
eighty-four	84	_2_ tens _6_ ones → 26	

Reviewing place value, tens and ones

(one hundred eighty-five) **185**

Teaching page 185

Write the number words **ninety-four, eighty-three, seventy-six, sixty-two,** and **forty-six** on the board. Ask students to read these words and write the numbers beside them.

Tell students they are to circle the 10's in the first problem. How many tens are there? (1) Ask how many ones? (4) How many sticks in all? (14) Trace the 1, 4 and 14. Tell students they are to circle the 10's and write how many tens and ones and the number.

Tell students they are to read each number word in the lower left box and write the number beside it. Tell students they are to write the missing numbers. Have students complete the page independently.

Write the missing numbers.

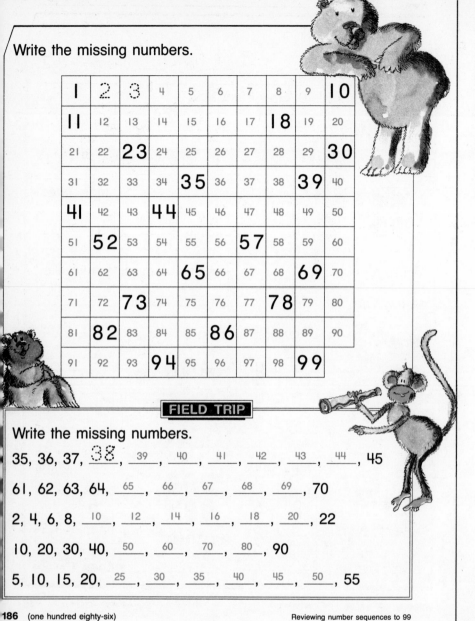

1	2	3	4	5	6	7	8	9	10
11	12	13	14	15	16	17	18	19	20
21	22	23	24	25	26	27	28	29	30
31	32	33	34	35	36	37	38	39	40
41	42	43	44	45	46	47	48	49	50
51	52	53	54	55	56	57	58	59	60
61	62	63	64	65	66	67	68	69	70
71	72	73	74	75	76	77	78	79	80
81	82	83	84	85	86	87	88	89	90
91	92	93	94	95	96	97	98	99	

FIELD TRIP

Write the missing numbers.

35, 36, 37, 38, 39, 40, 41, 42, 43, 44, 45

61, 62, 63, 64, 65, 66, 67, 68, 69, 70

2, 4, 6, 8, 10, 12, 14, 16, 18, 20, 22

10, 20, 30, 40, 50, 60, 70, 80, 90

5, 10, 15, 20, 25, 30, 35, 40, 45, 50, 55

186 (one hundred eighty-six)   Reviewing number sequences to 99

Correcting Common Errors

Some students may need more practice with counting and understanding tens and ones. Have students work in pairs with 50 counting sticks. Have them take turns. One partner says a number greater than 10 and less than 50. The other partner uses the counting sticks and rubber bands to model the number. Both partners must agree that the model is correct before they continue the activity.

Enrichment

1. Write a number from 10 through 99 on each of 20 cards. Give a friend 10 of the cards face down and keep 10 face down. Each draws a card and the player with number having the most tens keeps both. Player with the most cards wins. Play again to compare the ones.
2. Write a number from 1 through 99 on papers and hold one in your hand. Have classmates ask questions such as, "Does your number have 9 tens?" or "Is it greater than 52?" Give only yes or no answers until class guesses your number.
3. Begin with 1 and count by 2's through 17.

Teaching page 186

Tell students they are to write the missing numbers through 99. Have students complete the table independently.

Field Trip

Tell students they are to write the missing numbers in each line. Ask students how they will count in the first line. (by 1's) Ask how they will count in the next 2 lines. (by 1's) Tell students to read the numbers in the next line. (2, 4, 6,) Ask students to tell the pattern in this line. (skip a number, say a number, skip, etc.) Tell students this is called **counting by 2's.** Have students look at the number chart at the top of the page, if needed, to count by 2's through 22 and then on to 30 for more practice. Ask students how they will count in

the next two lines. (by 10's then by 5's) Tell students to refer to the number chart, if needed, to fill in the missing numbers in all the rows.

Extra Credit *Measurement*

Students can learn measurement vocabulary by making **pictograms.** Make a list of words such as: long, short, wide, high, heavy, light and others on a chalkboard or bulletin board. Individually, or in groups, students can choose one describer and cut pictures from magazines to depict that concept. The pictures can be pasted on paper to make a collage to be displayed in the classroom. If done on standard size sheets of paper, they can be three-hole punched and kept in a binder to use as the start of a classroom math dictionary.

Adding by Counting On

pages 187-188

Objective

To count on to add 2- and 1-digit numbers

Materials

99 counting sticks
9 rubber bands
*Chart with numbers 1 through 99

Mental Math

Name the number that is:
1. 7 tens and 9 ones (79)
2. 6 tens and 3 ones (63)
3. 2 tens and 6 ones (26)
4. 0 tens and 3 ones (3)
5. 3 tens and 0 ones (30)
6. 5 tens and 4 ones (54)
7. 8 tens and 2 ones (82)
8. 6 tens and 8 ones (68)

Skill Review

Use the demonstration chart to have students practice counting by 10's, 5's, 1's and 2's.

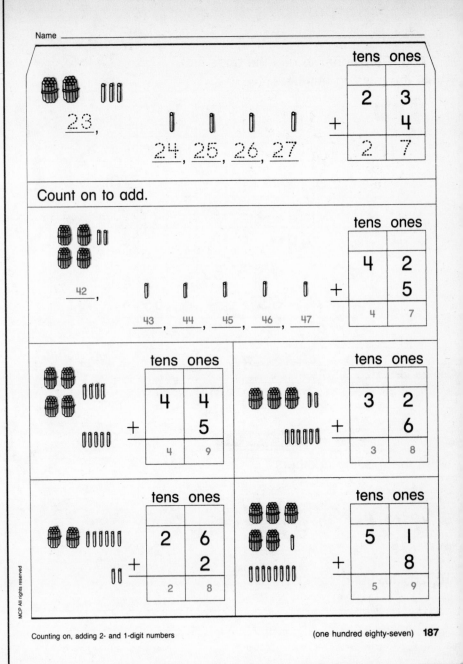

Name _____

		tens	ones
		2	3
23, 24, 25, 26, 27	+		4
		2	7

Count on to add.

		tens	ones
		4	2
42, 43, 44, 45, 46, 47	+		5
		4	7

	tens	ones
	4	4
+		5
	4	9

	tens	ones
	3	2
+		6
	3	8

	tens	ones
	2	6
+		2
	2	8

	tens	ones
	5	1
+		8
	5	9

Counting on, adding 2- and 1-digit numbers   (one hundred eighty-seven) **187**

Teaching page 187

Tell students to show 24 with bundles and ones. Ask how many tens and ones. (2,4) Have students lay out 5 more sticks. Tell students we want to see how many we have in all if we start with 24 and add 5 more. Write **24 + 5 = ___** on the board. Tell students to count with you from 24 to add the 5 more. (24, 25, 26, 27, 28, 29) Ask how many in all. (29) Write **24 + 5** on the board vertically in boxed notation as illustrated:

tens	ones
2	4
	5
(2)	(9)

Note the boxes under tens and ones are for recording trades later. Tell students **we always add the ones first.** Ask how many tens in all and record the 2. Repeat the procedure for 42 + 6, 31 + 7, 16 + 3 and 74 + 3.

Work through the example at the top of the page with the students. Help students with the next problem. Then have them work the 4 problems independently.

187

Add. Remember to add the ones first.

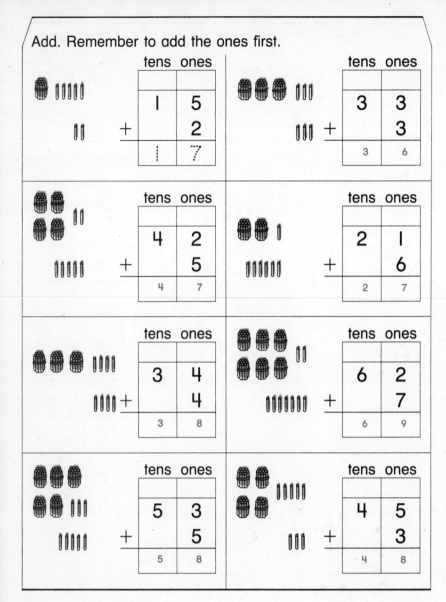

	tens	ones
	1	5
+		2
	1	7

	tens	ones
	3	3
+		3
	3	6

	tens	ones
	4	2
+		5
	4	7

	tens	ones
	2	1
+		6
	2	7

	tens	ones
	3	4
+		4
	3	8

	tens	ones
	6	2
+		7
	6	9

	tens	ones
	5	3
+		5
	5	8

	tens	ones
	4	5
+		3
	4	8

Adding 2- and 1-digit numbers

Correcting Common Errors

If some students have difficulty adding, have them work in pairs with counting sticks and rubber bands. Have them model the first addend, then add the number of counting sticks indicated by the second addend. When they find the total number of counting sticks, they have found the sum.

Enrichment

1. Act out adding 12 + 6. Hold a card that says ten or one to tell what you are.
2. Work with a friend to lay out counters for 2-digit numbers through 99. Tell how many tens and ones. Now count on from the tens to add the ones.

Teaching page 188

Remind students to always add the ones column first and record that number and then record the tens. Work the first problem with the students and tell them to trace the 7 and 1. Tell students to complete the page independently.

Extra Credit *Applications*

Using a thermometer which measures either Fahrenheit or Celsius, ask your students to check the temperature of the classroom every day at 10:00 AM and 2:00 PM. Have them record the temperatures. Continue to collect this information for one week. At the end of this time, have the class compare the results of the morning and afternoon temperature readings. Which is usually the higher reading? Which is the lower? Ask the students to subtract the low temperature from the high temperature for each day. What causes can they identify for the changes in the temperature? Extend the activity by having students make a bar graph for morning and afternoon temperatures.

Facts through 18, Counting On

pages 189-190

Objectives

To review addition facts for sums 10 through 18
To count on to add across decades

Materials

99 counting sticks
9 rubber bands

Mental Math

Name the double plus one for:
1. 4 + 4 (4 + 5)
2. 6 + 6 (6 + 7)
3. 3 + 3 (3 + 4)
4. 5 + 5 (5 + 6)
5. 7 + 7 (7 + 8)
6. 9 + 9 (9 + 10)
7. 2 + 2 (2 + 3)
8. 8 + 8 (8 + 9)

Skill Review

Write **20 + 2 =** ___ on the board. Tell students to start at 20 and count on for 2 more. (20,21,22) Repeat for 63 + 6, 47 + 2, 51 + 8, 14 + 5, 32 + 3 and 84 + 3.

Name _____

Add.

9 +1 10	6 +6 12	7 +7 14	8 +8 16	9 +9 18	5 +6 11	6 +7 13
7 +8 15	4 +7 11	8 +9 17	9 +2 11	2 +8 10	6 +5 11	4 +9 13
9 +4 13	7 +5 12	8 +3 11	1 +9 10	9 +3 12	9 +8 17	5 +7 12
3 +8 11	9 +7 16	8 +5 13	4 +6 10	9 +5 14	8 +3 11	6 +8 14
2 +9 11	8 +7 15	7 +4 11	8 +2 10	9 +6 15	3 +9 12	5 +8 13
4 +7 11	8 +6 14	7 +9 16	5 +9 14	4 +8 12	6 +9 15	7 +6 13

Reviewing addition facts, sums 10 through 18   (one hundred eighty-nine) **189**

Teaching page 189

Tell students to complete the page independently.
Mistakes on this page can indicate need for further drill.

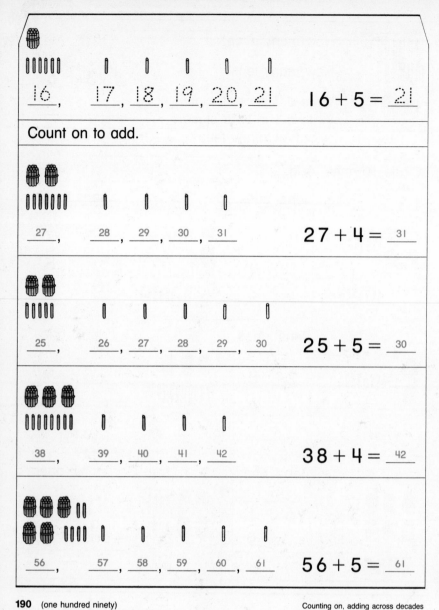

16, 17, 18, 19, 20, 21   16 + 5 = 21

Count on to add.

27, 28, 29, 30, 31   27 + 4 = 31

25, 26, 27, 28, 29, 30   25 + 5 = 30

38, 39, 40, 41, 42   38 + 4 = 42

56, 57, 58, 59, 60, 61   56 + 5 = 61

190 (one hundred ninety)   Counting on, adding across decades

Correcting Common Errors

Some students may need additional practice adding across decades to understand the concept. Have them work in pairs. Tell them to lay down 12 sticks as 1 ten and 2 ones. Have them lay down 9 more sticks and count on from the original 12 to add the 9 sticks. Ask, "Can you bundle another 10 sticks to show the sum?" (yes) Have them do so and then ask, "How many tens and ones do you have now?" (2 tens 1 one) Have them give the number for 2 tens 1 one. (21) Repeat with other addends.

Enrichment

1. Act out 23 + 9. Hold hands to form a circle of 10. Hold a one card if you are a one.
2. Make cards numbered 2, 3, 5, 8 and 9 and place face down in a stack. Make another stack for numbers 26, 33, 46, 75 and 87. Draw a card from each pile and have a friend count on from the larger number to add the smaller number.

Teaching page 190

Write **17 + 3 = __** on the board. Tell students to start at 17 and count on to add 3. (17,18,19,20) Ask a student to write 17, 18, 19 and 20 on the board. Repeat for 43 + 8, 66 + 5, 19 + 3, 38 + 7 and 26 + 9.

Tell students they are to start with the bundles and ones and count on to add more ones. Tell students to trace the 16 to show they start with 16. Then they trace the 17, through 21 to show the numbers they say as they count on 6 more. Have students trace the 21 to show that 16 + 5 = 21. Tell students to complete the page.

Extra Credit *Sets*

Cut heavy plastic or vinyl into rectangles that will fit on desk tops. With permanent marking pens, draw 4 large circles on each placemat. Label each circle with a set attribute such as square, shiny, large, long, etc. Each mat should have a different group of attributes. Have children bring small "junk treasures" from home, in a small bag labeled with their names. Have each child then sort his junk into the appropriate places on the mat. Was there any item that didn't fit into a set? Would it belong to someone else's set? Children may exchange mats several times to sort their junk into other sets. Was any student able to sort all of his junk into sets on any one mat?

Adding, One Trade

pages 191-192

Objective

To add with 1 trade for sums through 99

Materials

99 counting sticks
9 rubber bands
*18 cards with "one" on them

Mental Math

Count on by 1's from:
1. 41 through 50 (41,42,...50)
2. 36 through 44
3. 72 through 81
4. 43 through 52
5. 77 through 84
6. 86 through 94
7. 24 through 32
8. 55 through 61

Skill Review

Write **29 + 3 = __** on the board. Ask students to count on 3 more from 29 to find the sum. Have a student write the numbers 29, 30, 31 and 32 on the board. Repeat the procedure for 26 + 9, 83 + 8, 74 + 7, 46 + 6, and 53 + 9.

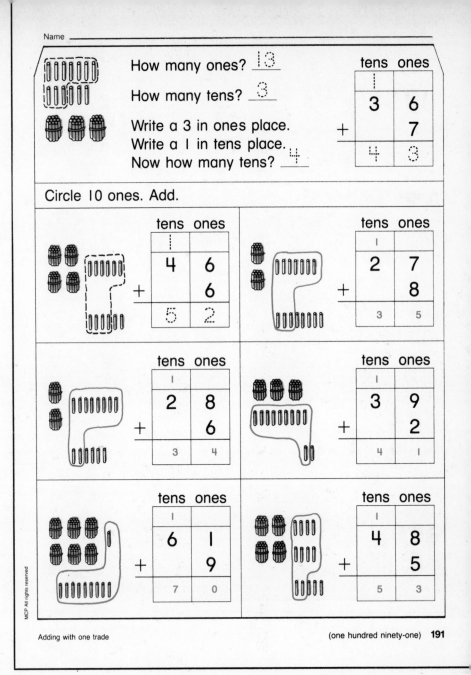

Adding with one trade

(one hundred ninety-one) **191**

Teaching page 191

Write **27 + 6 = __** on the board. Have a student count on 6 more from 27 as you write the numbers on the board. Tell students to lay out 27 sticks and bundle the tens. Ask how many tens and ones. (2,7) Tell students to lay out 6 more sticks. Tell students to add the ones first and tell how many single sticks. (13) Ask how many tens and ones in 13. (1,3) Tell students to bundle the ten sticks and tell how many ones are left. (3) Ask how many tens all together. (3) Draw on the board:

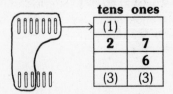

Review how the 10 sticks were bundled so the 1 is recorded in the box under the word tens to show 1 more ten. Count the ones left and record the 3 in the answer box. Have students add the 2 and 1 to record a 3 in the tens answer box.

Go through the first example with the students and have them trace the numbers. Stress adding the ones column first. Go through the next problem with the students and then have them complete the page.

191

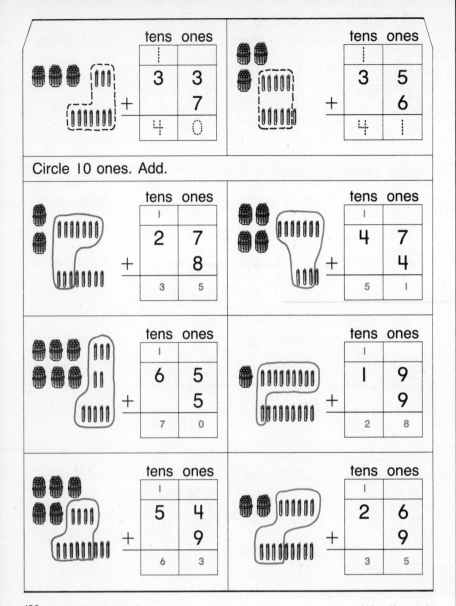

	tens	ones
	3	3
+		7
	4	0

	tens	ones
	3	5
+		6
	4	1

Circle 10 ones. Add.

	tens	ones
	2	7
+		8
	3	5

	tens	ones
	4	7
+		4
	5	1

	tens	ones
	6	5
+		5
	7	0

	tens	ones
	1	9
+		9
	2	8

	tens	ones
	5	4
+		9
	6	3

	tens	ones
	2	6
+		9
	3	5

192 (one hundred ninety-two)

Adding with one trade

Correcting Common Errors

Some students may need additional practice writing more than 10 ones as tens and ones. Have them work in pairs with counting sticks. Give them a list of ones, such as is shown below. Have them use rubber bands to group the sticks in bundles of ten and then rewrite the amount as tens and ones.

14 ones	(1 ten 4 ones)
26 ones	(2 tens 6 ones)
19 ones	(1 ten 9 ones)
22 ones	(2 tens 2 ones)
33 ones	(3 tens 3 ones)
40 ones	(4 tens 0 ones)

Enrichment

1. Draw 24 objects and add 9 more. Circle the groups of ten. Write the problem vertically and show your answer.
2. Write a 5, 6, 7, 8 or 9 on cards in one stack. Write 26, 37, 45, 68 or 79 on each card in a second stack. Draw a card from each and tell how many ones would be left when you add.

Teaching page 192

Go over the 2 examples with students and have them trace the numbers and the lines around the groups of 10 sticks. Remind students to count the ones first and record the ones and then record the newly-circled ten. Have students complete the page independently.

Extra Credit *Probability*

Demonstrate that some events are not as probable as they seem. As a class, discuss the chances of a thumbtack landing point up, when tossed onto a desk from a cup. Divide the class into groups, and give each group a paper cup and a thumbtack. Assign a recorder. Let the students take turns shaking the tack in the cup and spilling it out. Try it at least 25 times.

The recorder keeps track of point-up and point-down events. As a class, discuss the results of the experiment. Now predict the results of an experiment where the paper cup is tossed into the air. Predict how many times it will land upright, up-side-down, or sideways. Test your predictions.

Adding, Some Trading

pages 193-194

Objective

To add with and without 1 trade for sums through 99

Materials

99 counting sticks
9 rubber bands
*Addition fact cards for sums through 18

Mental Math

Name the number that is:
1. 2 more than 9 (11)
2. 6 more than 8 (14)
3. 9 more than 9 (18)
4. 7 more than 9 (16)
5. 9 more than 6 (15)
6. 6 more than 7 (13)
7. 8 more than 8 (16)

Skill Review

Use addition fact cards for review drill to increase speed of recall. Now show the doubles and ask students to give the double plus 1 and its sum.

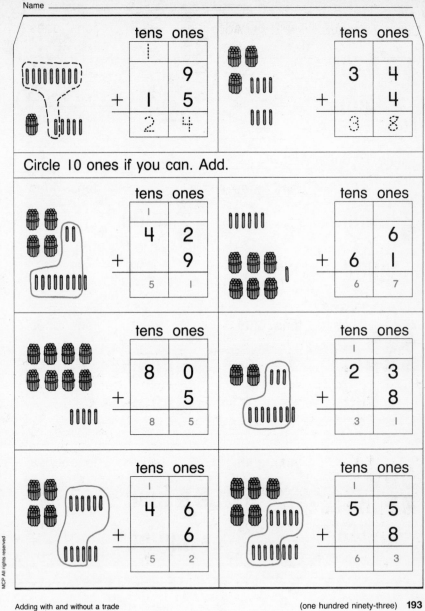

Name _____

Circle 10 ones if you can. Add.

Adding with and without a trade

(one hundred ninety-three) **193**

Teaching page 193

Write **9 + 74** and **67 + 2** vertically on the board in boxed notation as shown on pages 191 and 192. Work through the first problem with the students. Have them use their counting sticks to bundle another ten from 13 ones. Now work through 67 + 2 and ask students how many ones they have when they add 7 and 2. (9) Ask if they have a ten to bundle in 9 ones. (no) Tell students to add the ones and then add the tens and give the sum. (69) Ask students if they will always need to bundle another ten when they add the ones. (no) Ask students when they will need to bundle a ten. (when the ones are 10 or more) Give more addition examples of no trade and 1 trade.

Go through the 2 example problems with the students and have them trace the numbers and lines around the group of 10. Remind students that they will sometimes have more than 10 ones and sometimes less than 10 ones in the problems on this page. Have students complete the page independently.

193

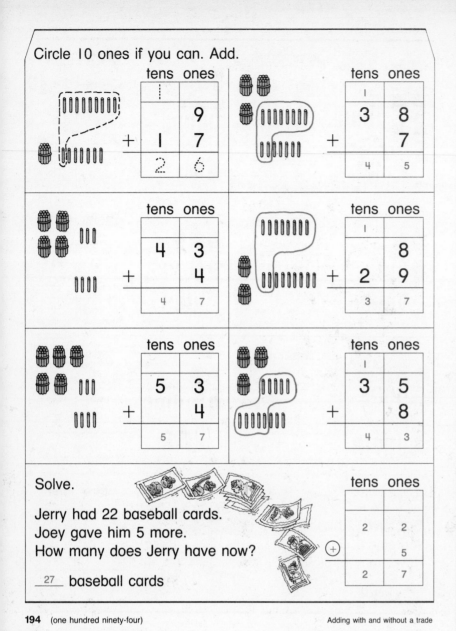

Circle 10 ones if you can. Add.

	tens	ones
		9
+	1	7
	2	6

	tens	ones
	3	8
+		7
	4	5

	tens	ones
	4	3
+		4
	4	7

	tens	ones
		8
+	2	9
	3	7

	tens	ones
	5	3
+		4
	5	7

	tens	ones
	3	5
+		8
	4	3

Solve.

Jerry had 22 baseball cards.
Joey gave him 5 more.
How many does Jerry have now?

___27___ baseball cards

	tens	ones
	2	2
+		5
	2	7

194 (one hundred ninety-four)

Adding with and without a trade

Correcting Common Errors

Watch for students who add each column separately, failing to regroup.

    INCORRECT   CORRECT
                        1
       25   25
     + 8   + 8
     ─────   ─────
      213   33

Correct by having them work with partners using place-value materials to model the problem.

Enrichment

1. Write 5 addition facts whose sums are less than 10 and 5 facts whose sums are 10 or more.
2. Write the problem that tells how many students would be in your class if 9 new students came. Find the total.

Teaching page 194

Remind students that some of these problems will have more than 10 ones. Tell students to complete the first 6 problems independently. Read the story problem with the students and have them write the + sign and find the sum. Remind students to write their answers on the line.

Extra Credit *Applications*

Show students a box of cereal marked 25¢ and another marked 20¢. Ask which costs more. Write **25¢** and **20¢** on the board, and circle the 25. Ask volunteers to gather groceries from the classroom store. Make sure their prices are clearly marked. Then have students arrange ten pairs of items on a table. Number each pair. Ask students to compare the prices of the items. Put a chart of the prices on the board, for example:

1. 15¢   10¢
2.   5¢   30¢
3. 50¢   55¢

Ask students to examine each pair. Finally, have them circle the larger number.

Adding, Some Trading

pages 195-196

Objective

To practice adding with and without 1 trade for sums through 99

Materials

*18 "one" cards

Mental Math

Name the number that is:
1. 6 dimes and 1 penny (61¢)
2. 4 nickels and 1 dime (30¢)
3. 10 pennies and 1 dime (20¢)
4. 1 quarter and 1 dime (35¢)
5. 2 dimes and 9 nickels (65¢)
6. 1 nickel and 1 quarter (30¢)
7. 8 dimes and 14 pennies (94¢)

Skill Review

Have a student begin an addition column for facts having 7 as one addend. (7 + 0 = 7) Have other students complete the column. (7 + 1 = 8, 7 + 2 = 9, . . . 7 + 9 = 16) Develop an 8 column where 8 is one of the addends. Continue for 9, 5, 6, 4 and 3.

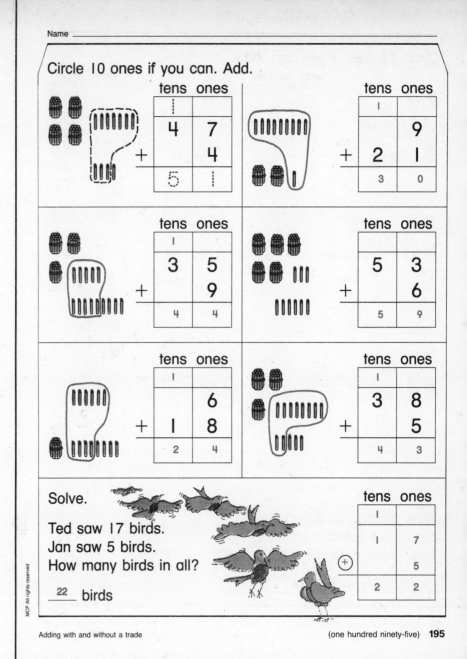

Adding with and without a trade

(one hundred ninety-five) **195**

Teaching page 195

Go through the example with the students and have them trace the numbers and lines around the groups of 10. Remind students they will not always have a group of 10 ones. Have students work the 5 problems independently. Read the story problem as students work it. Be sure students write the + sign and record the answer on the line. Ask students to then read the problems with you and read the answer.

195

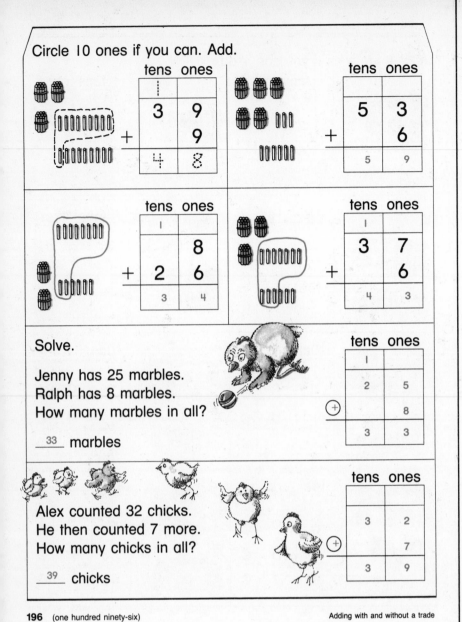

Circle 10 ones if you can. Add.

tens	ones
1 3	9
	9
4	8

tens	ones
5	3
+	6
5	9

tens	ones
1	8
2	6
3	4

tens	ones
1 3	7
+	6
4	3

Solve.

Jenny has 25 marbles.
Ralph has 8 marbles.
How many marbles in all?

tens	ones
1	
2	5
+	8
3	3

__33__ marbles

Alex counted 32 chicks.
He then counted 7 more.
How many chicks in all?

tens	ones
3	2
+	7
3	9

__39__ chicks

196 (one hundred ninety-six)   Adding with and without a trade

Correcting Common Errors

Watch for students who have difficulty deciding whether it is necessary to trade when adding a 1-digit number to a 2-digit number. Some will always add an extra ten when not necessary.

INCORRECT	CORRECT
1	
46	46
+ 3	+ 3
59	49

Correct by having them work with partners and use place-value materials to model the problem.

Enrichment

1. Write and answer 5 addition problems for sums through 99 where the sum of the ones is more than 10. Write 5 problems with a one's sum less than 10.

2. Draw 2 book shelves. Draw 19 books on one shelf and 7 books on the other shelf. Write and answer a problem that tells how many books in all.

Teaching page 196

Go through the example and have students trace the numbers and the line around the group of 10. Tell students to complete the next 3 problems. Now have students read the story problems, tell what is to be done and find the answers.

Extra Credit *Statistics*

Bring a bathroom scale to school to weigh different objects in the classroom such as: books, book bags, phonographs, pairs of boots, etc. Give each student, or group of students, a paper cut-out in the shape of the scale, and hang a string across the front board. Weigh each item. Choose a volunteer for each, to write the name of the item and its weight, on their paper scale. Then have the students clothespin their paper to the string in order from the lightest item to the heaviest item. You could also have a volunteer monitor the line, to help keep items in the correct order. Finally, ask one student to name the item that falls in the middle of your weight line. Explain that those items in the center represent an average weight of all the items weighed.

196

Adding Money, Some Trading

pages 197-198

Objective

To add money with and without 1 trade through 99¢

Materials

9 dimes
18 pennies

Mental Math

How many pennies in:
1. 1 quarter (25)
2. 2 dimes (20)
3. 5 nickels (25)
4. 1 quarter and 1 dime (35)
5. 2 dimes and 1 nickel (25)
6. 25 cents (25)
7. 2 dimes and 5 pennies (25)

Skill Review

Write the following chart on the board and help students fill in missing amounts:

Amount	Words	Dimes	Pennies
25¢	twenty-five cents	2	5
37¢	(thirty-seven) cents	(3)	(7)
(48¢)	forty-eight cents	(4)	(8)
(79¢)	(seventy-nine) cents	7	9

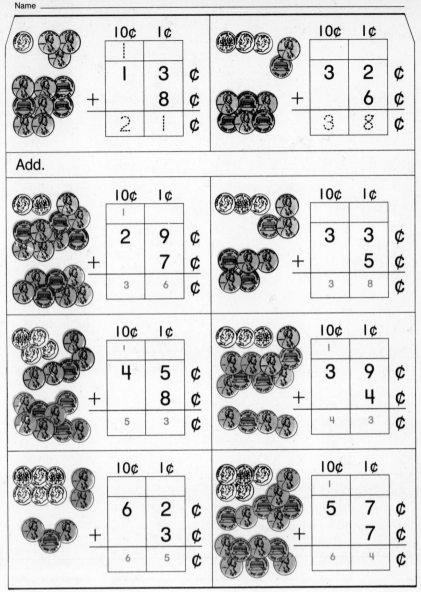

Add.

Adding money with and without a trade

(one hundred ninety-seven) **197**

Teaching page 197

Ask students to name the amounts at the top of the boxes. (10¢ and 1¢) Ask students what was in these spaces on the previous pages they've worked. (tens and ones) Ask students why 10¢ is in the tens place. (means 10 cents) Ask why 1¢ is in ones place. (means 1 cent) Tell students to count the dime and pennies in the first row and tell the amount. (13¢) Ask how many dimes and pennies in 13¢. (1, 3) Ask how many pennies in the bottom row. (8) Ask how many pennies are in 3 pennies and 8 more. (11) Ask how many dimes and pennies are in 11¢. (1, 1) Ask students to trace the 1 under the dime. Tell students to trace the 1 dime. Tell students to trace the 1 recorded in the ones answer column. Tell students to add the dimes column and trace the 2 to show 2 dimes. Ask how much

money in all. (21¢) Work through the next problem with the students and remind them that some of these problems will have trading and some will not. Have students complete the page independently.

197

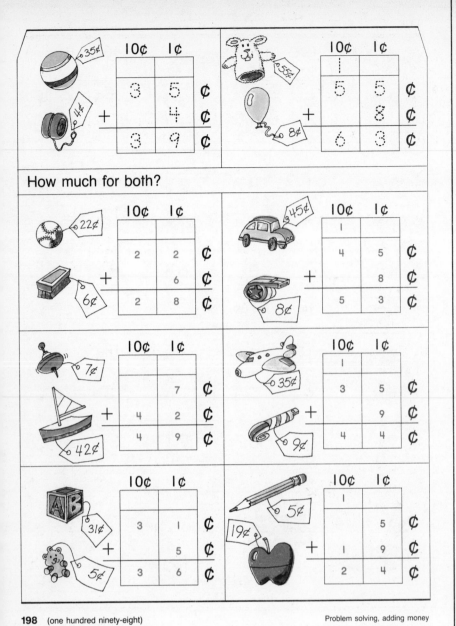

How much for both?

Problem 1 (ball 35¢, yo-yo 4¢):

10¢	1¢	
3	5	¢
	4	¢
3	9	¢

Problem 2 (mouse 55¢, balloon 8¢):

10¢	1¢	
5	5	¢
	8	¢
6	3	¢

Problem 3 (baseball 22¢, eraser 6¢):

10¢	1¢	
2	2	¢
	6	¢
2	8	¢

Problem 4 (car 45¢, whistle 8¢):

10¢	1¢	
4	5	¢
	8	¢
5	3	¢

Problem 5 (top 7¢, boat 42¢):

10¢	1¢	
	7	¢
4	2	¢
4	9	¢

Problem 6 (plane 35¢, candy 9¢):

10¢	1¢	
3	5	¢
	9	¢
4	4	¢

Problem 7 (block 31¢, bear 5¢):

10¢	1¢	
3	1	¢
	5	¢
3	6	¢

Problem 8 (pencil 5¢, apple 19¢):

10¢	1¢	
	5	¢
1	9	¢
2	4	¢

Problem solving, adding money

Correcting Common Errors

Watch for students who add incorrectly because they trade when it is not necessary. Have them work with partners. Before they do any of the problems, have the partners discuss whether trading will be necessary, and write above the problem YES if trading is necessary or NO if it is not. Then have them work independently to find the sums and compare answers when they finish to make sure they agree. Where they do not, partners should discuss and, if necessary, use place-value materials to find a sum on which they can agree.

Enrichment

1. Purchase 2 items from a classroom store with dimes and pennies. Give the clerk the least number of pennies possible for the 2 items.
2. Show 62¢ + 9¢ using 6 dimes. Show the sum with 7 dimes. Tell which way uses fewer coins.

Teaching page 198

Tell students they are to find the cost of the 2 items in each problem. Remind students that they will not always have 10 pennies to trade for a dime in these problems. Work through the 2 examples with the students and then have them complete the page independently.

Extra Credit *Sets*

Divide a bulletin board into 4 sections. Cut the following shapes from construction paper: one large circle, square, triangle and rectangle from red paper; one medium-sized circle, square, triangle and rectangle from blue paper; one small circle, square, triangle and rectangle from yellow paper. Display the shapes in random order and ask volunteers to arrange the shapes into sets on the bulletin board. Ask how many sets can be formed using the shapes, the color, and the size. Which of these groups cannot be divided into 4 sets? (size). Why not? As a follow-up activity, group the shapes into sets on the bulletin board. When the children are not present, place one shape in the wrong set. See if your class is observant enough to notice the error!

Adding, Some Trading

pages 199-200

Objectives

To practice adding with and without 1 trade for sums through 99

To solve addition problems of 2- and 1-digit numbers

Materials

None

Mental Math

Is the sum greater or less than 10?
1. 9 + 8 (greater)
2. 6 + 2 (less)
3. 3 + 9 (greater)
4. 6 + 8 (greater)
5. 4 + 5 (less)
6. 3 + 8 (greater)
7. 5 + 2 (less)
8. 1 + 7 (less)

Skill Review

Tell students a story of Dante running 14 blocks with his mom and then walking 9 more blocks. Ask students how many blocks they went in all. Ask a student to write the problem on the board in the boxed notation you've provided. Ask students to tell the steps to work the problem.

Add.

23 + 6 29	15 + 8 23	27 + 5 32	33 + 4 37	55 + 9 64	42 + 7 49
86 + 7 93	91 + 6 97	47 + 8 55	75 + 5 80	12 + 3 15	29 + 2 31
48 + 1 49	73 + 3 76	38 + 5 43	64 + 9 73	89 + 3 92	17 + 7 24
37 + 2 39	81 + 8 89	55 + 6 61	78 + 2 80	44 + 4 48	63 + 8 71
91 + 4 95	28 + 9 37	67 + 4 71	95 + 4 99	38 + 6 44	58 + 7 65

Adding with and without a trade

(one hundred ninety-nine) **199**

Teaching page 199

Write the first sample problem on the board in boxed notation to show students that the boxes are missing, but the type of problem is the same. Work through the problem on the board with the students. Write the second example on the board without the boxed notation and work through it with the students. Remind students that some problems require them to trade 10 ones for 1 ten and some do not. Tell students to complete the page independently. While students are working, check to see that they are adding and recording the ones first and recording a trade correctly.

199

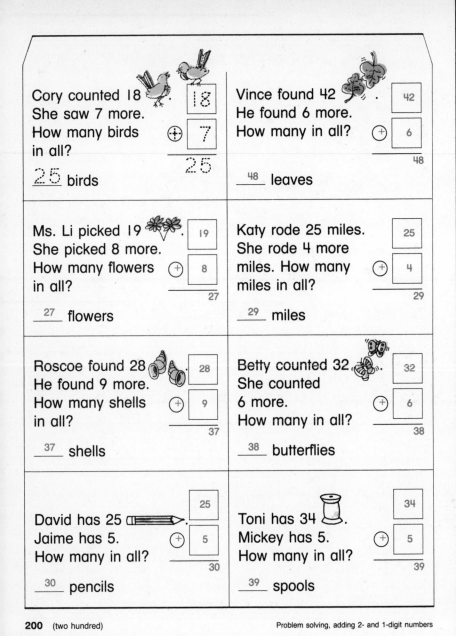

Cory counted 18 🐦. 18 ⊕ 7 ――― 25
She saw 7 more.
How many birds
in all?

25 birds

Vince found 42 🦋. 42 ⊕ 6 ――― 48
He found 6 more.
How many in all?

48 leaves

Ms. Li picked 19 🌸. 19 ⊕ 8 ――― 27
She picked 8 more.
How many flowers
in all?

27 flowers

Katy rode 25 miles. 25 ⊕ 4 ――― 29
She rode 4 more
miles. How many
miles in all?

29 miles

Roscoe found 28 🐚. 28 ⊕ 9 ――― 37
He found 9 more.
How many shells
in all?

37 shells

Betty counted 32 🦋. 32 ⊕ 6 ――― 38
She counted
6 more.
How many in all?

38 butterflies

David has 25 ✏. 25 ⊕ 5 ――― 30
Jaime has 5.
How many in all?

30 pencils

Toni has 34 🧵. 34 ⊕ 5 ――― 39
Mickey has 5.
How many in all?

39 spools

Problem solving, adding 2- and 1-digit numbers

Correcting Common Errors

Some students may have difficulty solving word problems. Have them work with partners. One partner should read the problem. The other partner can retell the problem in his or her own words. Then both partners should discuss how the problem can be solved. They should reverse roles for the next problem.

Enrichment

1. Write all the addition facts with sums greater than 10.
2. Write all the addition facts with sums less than 10.
3. Tell a story using 76 and a number from 0 through 9, so that their sum requires trading 10 ones for a ten.

Teaching page 200

Read through each problem with the students as they write the + sign in the circles and record the answers. Have students also record their answers in the blanks.

Extra Credit *Applications*

Use this activity to introduce the concept of measuring volume before you use cups, teaspoons, and tablespoons in cooking. Set aside one area of the room for messy activity. Cover the floor with plastic if it is carpeted, and use a table with a protected surface. Put a large dishpan filled with water in the middle of the table. Assemble as many different containers as you can including: cup measures, empty cottage cheese and yogurt containers, plastic cups, spoons, and so on. Allow students to go to the table, a few at a time, to experiment with the materials. In this activity, let them fill the containers and empty them into the tub. Some will experiment to see how many cups will fill a larger container, and others will not. Allow them to use the materials in an unstructured way in this introductory activity.

200

Chapter Review

pages 201-202

Objectives

To review addition for sums through 99
To maintain skills learned previously this year

Materials

1 quarter, 9 dimes, 19 nickels, 18 pennies for each pair of students

Mental Math

Will you trade for a ten?
1. 8 ones plus 5 ones (yes)
2. 7 ones plus 0 ones (no)
3. 9 ones plus 8 ones (yes)
4. 4 ones plus 5 ones (no)
5. 1 one plus 9 ones (yes)

Skill Review

Write **12¢** on the board. Ask students to work in pairs to lay out coins to make 12¢. Write out all correct answers in a column on the board as **1 dime, 2 pennies; 2 nickels, 2 pennies; 1 nickel, 7 pennies; 12 pennies.** Ask students which answer has the least number of coins. (1 dime, 2 pennies) Ask students why we might want to use this coin combination to buy something. (quicker and not as heavy) Repeat for 27¢, 42¢ and 36¢.

Teaching page 201

Go through each box of problems and ask students what they are to do. Then have students complete the page independently.

CHAPTER CHECKUP

How many?

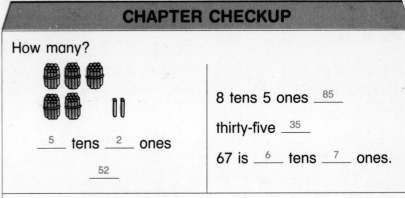

_5_ tens _2_ ones

52

8 tens 5 ones _85_

thirty-five _35_

67 is _6_ tens _7_ ones.

Write the missing numbers.

36, 37, _38_, _39_, _40_, _41_, _42_, _43_, _44_, 45

72, 73, _74_, _75_, _76_, _77_, _78_, _79_, _80_, _81_

Add.

$$
\begin{array}{c} 3 \\ +5 \\ \hline 8 \end{array}
\quad
\begin{array}{c} 9 \\ +6 \\ \hline 15 \end{array}
\quad
\begin{array}{c} 6 \\ +7 \\ \hline 13 \end{array}
\quad
\begin{array}{c} 7 \\ +8 \\ \hline 15 \end{array}
\quad
\begin{array}{c} 6 \\ +4 \\ \hline 10 \end{array}
\quad
\begin{array}{c} 9 \\ +7 \\ \hline 16 \end{array}
\quad
\begin{array}{c} 4 \\ +9 \\ \hline 13 \end{array}
$$

Add.

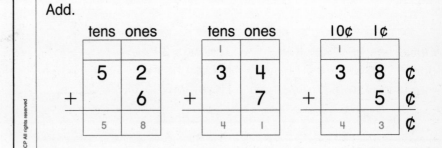

tens	ones
5	2
+	6
5	8

tens	ones
1	
3	4
+	7
4	1

10¢	1¢	
1		¢
3	8	¢
+	5	¢
4	3	

Chapter review   (two hundred one) **201**

ROUNDUP REVIEW

Add or subtract.

$$\begin{array}{r} 14 \\ -\ 8 \\ \hline 6 \end{array} \qquad \begin{array}{r} 17 \\ -\ 9 \\ \hline 8 \end{array} \qquad \begin{array}{r} 5 \\ +9 \\ \hline 14 \end{array} \qquad \begin{array}{r} 14 \\ -\ 6 \\ \hline 8 \end{array} \qquad \begin{array}{r} 7 \\ +5 \\ \hline 12 \end{array} \qquad \begin{array}{r} 9 \\ +7 \\ \hline 16 \end{array} \qquad \begin{array}{r} 8 \\ +5 \\ \hline 13 \end{array}$$

How much for both?

6¢

7¢

$\boxed{6}$ ¢
$(+)$ $\boxed{7}$ ¢
_13_ ¢

__13__ ¢

Solve.
Sharon had 17¢.
She spent 9¢.
How much does
Sharon have left?

$\boxed{17}$ ¢
$(-)$ $\boxed{9}$ ¢
_8_ ¢

__8__ ¢

How many?

__47__

Write the number.

8 tens 8 ones is __88__.

74 is _7_ tens _4_ ones.

sixty-three is __63__.

Add.

$$\begin{array}{r} 42 \\ +\ 6 \\ \hline 48 \end{array} \qquad \begin{array}{r} 54 \\ +\ 8 \\ \hline 62 \end{array}$$

How much for both?

45¢

8¢

$\boxed{45}$ ¢
$(+)$ $\boxed{8}$ ¢
_53_ ¢

__53__ ¢

Cumulative review

Enrichment

1. Draw coins to show 66¢ + 9¢. Draw the sum in coins and use the least number of pennies you can.
2. Write all the numbers from 0 through 99 that have 8 ones.
3. Write all the amounts from 0¢ through 99¢ that will require a trade for a dime, if 1 penny is added.

Teaching page 202

Go through each section of problems and ask students what they are to do. Then have students complete the page independently.

This page reviews addition and subtraction facts, adding money, place value and adding with some trading.

Place Value, Sequencing

pages 203-204

Objective

To review place value and number sequencing through 99

Materials

*Chart with numbers 1 through 99

Mental Math

Name the number that comes before and after:

1. 32 (31, 33)
2. 67 (66, 68)
3. 97 (96, 98)
4. 12 (11, 13)
5. 20 (19, 21)
6. 49 (48, 50)
7. 31 (30, 32)
8. 13 (12, 14)

Skill Review

Have students count by 10's from 10 through 90. Write the numbers in a column on the board. Ask students to count by 5's from 5 through 95. Write the numbers in a column on the board. Have students refer to the demonstration chart if necessary to count by 2's through 98.

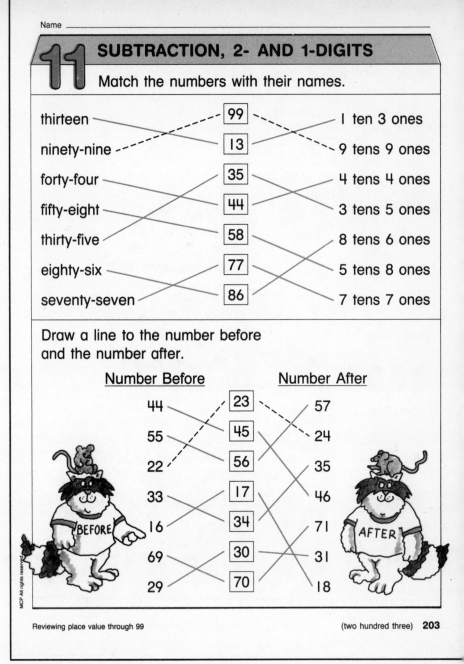

11 SUBTRACTION, 2- AND 1-DIGITS

Match the numbers with their names.

thirteen — 99 — 1 ten 3 ones
ninety-nine — 13 — 9 tens 9 ones
forty-four — 35 — 4 tens 4 ones
fifty-eight — 44 — 3 tens 5 ones
thirty-five — 58 — 8 tens 6 ones
eighty-six — 77 — 5 tens 8 ones
seventy-seven — 86 — 7 tens 7 ones

Draw a line to the number before and the number after.

Number Before | **Number After**

44   23   57
55   45   24
22   56   35
33   17   46
16   34   71
69   30   31
29   70   18

Reviewing place value through 99   (two hundred three) **203**

Teaching page 203

Tell students they are to match the middle row of boxed numbers to their number names and then the numbers to their notations of tens and ones. Have students find the boxed number 99 and trace the line to ninety-nine and the line from 99 to 9 tens 9 ones. Tell students to complete the top half of the page independently. Tell students that the bottom half of this page asks them to tell the number that comes before and after each number in the middle row of boxes. Tell students to find the 23 in the top box and trace the line to the left to show that 22 comes before 23. Tell students to then trace the line from the 23 to the 24 on the right to show that 24 comes after 23. Have students complete the bottom half of the page independently.

203

Count backwards.

99	98	97	96	95	94	93	92	91	
90	89	88	87	86	85	84	83	82	81
80	79	78	77	76	75	74	73	72	71
70	69	68	67	66	65	64	63	62	61
60	59	58	57	56	55	54	53	52	51
50	49	48	47	46	45	44	43	42	41
40	39	38	37	36	35	34	33	32	31
30	29	28	27	26	25	24	23	22	21
20	19	18	17	16	15	14	13	12	11
10	9	8	7	6	5	4	3	2	1

Count backwards.

45, 44, 43, _42_, _41_, _40_, _39_, _38_, _37_, 36

96, 95, 94, _93_, _92_, _91_, _90_, _89_, _88_, 87

71, 70, _69_, _68_, _67_, _66_, _65_, _64_, 63

22, 20, 18, _16_, _14_, _12_, _10_, _8_, _6_, 4

90, 80, _70_, _60_, _50_, _40_, _30_, _20_, 10

55, 50, _45_, _40_, _35_, _30_, _25_, _20_, _15_, 10

Reviewing number sequencing through 99

Correcting Common Errors

Some students may need additional practice with writing numbers from 1 to 99 in order. Draw a number line on the chalkboard showing a section of the numbers from 0 through 99. Point to a number, such as 32, and have students name the number that is

  1 more
  2 more
  1 less
  2 less

Once students can name these numbers using a number line, try the same exercise without a number line.

Enrichment

1. Draw a street with 4 houses on one side. The first house's address is 88 and the last house's address is 91. Write each house's address on its front door.
2. Count backwards from 99 through 1 with a friend. Take turns saying the numbers. Repeat for counting backwards by 2's.

Teaching page 204

Display the chart with numbers 1 through 99. Write the number **5** on the board. Ask students to tell the number that comes before 5. (4) Ask students to name the number that comes before 4. (3) Continue through 0. Tell students that this is called **counting backwards.** Have students count backwards from 5 through 0. Now write 10 on the board and repeat the procedure. Repeat again for 34 through 26, and others. Tell students they are to write the missing numbers to count backwards from 99 through 1. Have students trace the 98 and then complete the table. Tell students they are to fill in the missing numbers to count backwards from 45. Tell students to trace the 42 and continue to write the numbers. Tell students to look at the last three lines of numbers and tell what they are to do. (count backwards by 2's, 10's and 5's) Have students complete all the rows independently.

Extra Credit   *Applications*

Remind students that one place to use mathematics is in the kitchen. Ask if anyone knows what a recipe is. Tell students they will make play dough. Work with small groups to measure these ingredients: 1 cup flour, 1/2 cup salt, 2 teaspoons cream of tartar, 2 tablespoons oil, and one cup water with food coloring added. Carefully heat the oil in a saucepan over a hot plate, at a moderate heat. Help students add the rest of the ingredients, and stir until the mixture forms a clean ball. This happens very quickly so caution is needed. Then remove the pan from the heat and allow the dough to cool before students use it for modeling.

204

Subtraction Facts

pages 205–206

Objective

To review subtraction facts for minuends through 18

Materials

*Subtraction fact cards for minuends through 18
18 counters
sheet of paper

Mental Math

What number comes after:
1. 15 if counting by 5's (20)
2. 11 if counting by 1's (12)
3. 40 if counting by 2's (42)
4. 65 if counting by 5's (70)
5. 79 if counting by 1's (80)
6. 50 if counting by 10's (60)
7. 26 if counting by 2's (28)
8. 25 if counting by 5's (30)

Skill Review

Have students lay out 14 counters. Tell students to take away 5 counters and tell how many are left. (9) Have a student write the problem vertically and horizontally on the board. Repeat for other subtraction facts through minuends of 18.

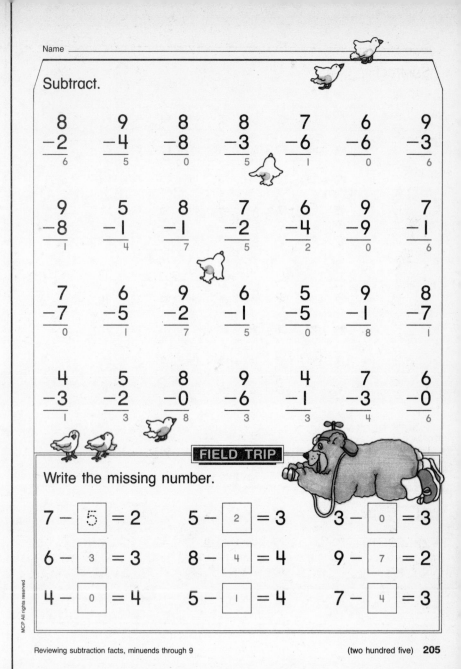

Name _____

Subtract.

8 −2 = 6	9 −4 = 5	8 −8 = 0	8 −3 = 5	7 −6 = 1	6 −6 = 0	9 −3 = 6
9 −8 = 1	5 −1 = 4	8 −1 = 7	7 −2 = 5	6 −4 = 2	9 −9 = 0	7 −1 = 6
7 −7 = 0	6 −5 = 1	9 −2 = 7	6 −1 = 5	5 −5 = 0	9 −1 = 8	8 −7 = 1
4 −3 = 1	5 −2 = 3	8 −0 = 8	9 −6 = 3	4 −1 = 3	7 −3 = 4	6 −0 = 6

FIELD TRIP

Write the missing number.

$7 - \boxed{5} = 2$ $5 - \boxed{2} = 3$ $3 - \boxed{0} = 3$

$6 - \boxed{3} = 3$ $8 - \boxed{4} = 4$ $9 - \boxed{7} = 2$

$4 - \boxed{0} = 4$ $5 - \boxed{1} = 4$ $7 - \boxed{4} = 3$

Reviewing subtraction facts, minuends through 9   (two hundred five) **205**

Teaching page 205

Group subtraction fact cards associated with doubles, cards where the same number is taken away and related fact cards such as 7-2 and 7-5. Use groups of cards for building speed of recall. Have students complete the 4 rows of problems independently.

Field Trip

Tell students they are to fill in the missing number in each subtraction fact. Ask students what number is taken away from 7 to equal 2. (5) Have students trace the 5. Remind students that they know how to write another fact using the same numbers. Ask students to tell another subtraction fact using 7, 5 and 2. (7 − 2 = 5) Help students with the second problem and then have them complete all the problems.

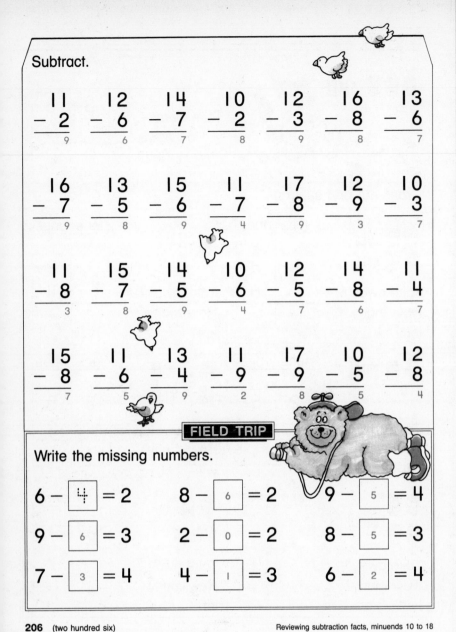

Subtract.

11 − 2 9	12 − 6 6	14 − 7 7	10 − 2 8	12 − 3 9	16 − 8 8	13 − 6 7
16 − 7 9	13 − 5 8	15 − 6 9	11 − 7 4	17 − 8 9	12 − 9 3	10 − 3 7
11 − 8 3	15 − 7 8	14 − 5 9	10 − 6 4	12 − 5 7	14 − 8 6	11 − 4 7
15 − 8 7	11 − 6 5	13 − 4 9	11 − 9 2	17 − 9 8	10 − 5 5	12 − 8 4

FIELD TRIP

Write the missing numbers.

6 − [4] = 2   8 − [6] = 2   9 − [5] = 4

9 − [6] = 3   2 − [0] = 2   8 − [5] = 3

7 − [3] = 4   4 − [1] = 3   6 − [2] = 4

Reviewing subtraction facts, minuends 10 to 18

Correcting Common Errors

Some students may need more review of the subtraction facts. Have them work with partners using subtraction fact cards. Have them work together to pair the cards to show related facts.
EXAMPLE:
$14 − 6 = 8$ $14 − 8 = 6$

Enrichment

1. Write all the subtraction facts through minuends of 18 where 9 is taken away.
2. Write the subtraction facts through minuends of 18 that are the hardest for you to remember. Have a friend quiz you.
3. Complete a subtraction table for minuends through 18.

Teaching page 206

Tell students to complete the 4 rows of subtraction problems. Mistakes in these problems can indicate need for further drill.

Field Trip

Tell students they are to fill in the missing number in each subtraction fact. Ask students what number is taken away from 6 to equal 2. (4) Have students trace the 4. Remind students that to find the missing number in each fact they may want to write another subtraction fact using the two numbers. (6 − 2 = 4)

Extra Credit   *Geometry*

Give each student four pieces of paper and have them label the sheets with a circle, triangle, square, and rectangle. Ask them to look around and find at least two examples of each shape, drawing the examples on the appropriate paper. If class time is limited you may ask students to conduct this exercise at home, bringing their drawings in the next day. Have some examples ready to help those who were unable to find the shapes such as: a paper napkin folded into a triangular shape, a paper plate, a magazine, and a square piece of bread. A good book to read to the class is *Tatum's Favorite Shape* by Dorothy Thole.

Subtracting, No Trading

pages 207-208

Objective

To subtract 1-digit from 2-digit numbers for minuends through 99

Materials

99 counting sticks
9 rubber bands
*Subtraction fact cards for minuends through 9

Mental Math

Count by 2's from:
1. 12 through 24 (12, 14, . . . 24)
2. 1 through 9 (1, 3, 5, 7, 9)
3. 3 through 13
4. 2 through 18
5. 4 through 20
6. 1 through 17
7. 16 through 26

Skill Review

Review subtraction fact cards with the students. Have students work in groups to act out the facts which are more difficult for them.

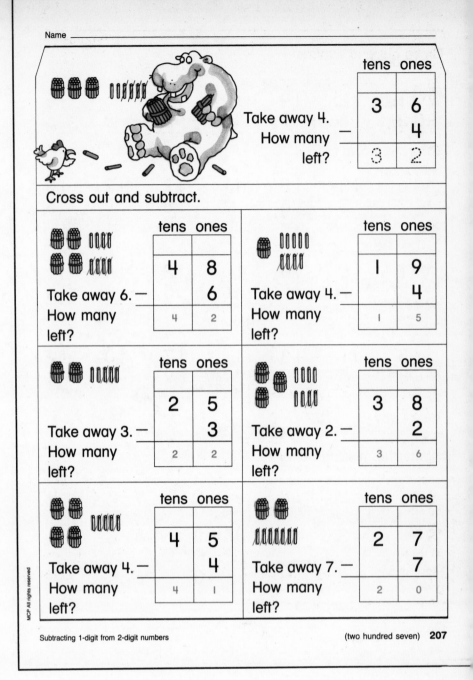

Subtracting 1-digit from 2-digit numbers

(two hundred seven) **207**

Teaching page 207

Tell students to lay out 16 sticks and bundle the ten. Tell students to take away 4 sticks and tell how many are left. (12) Write **16 − 4 = 12** on the board in boxed notation as shown on page 207. Have students tell how many in all, how many were taken away and how many are left. Now tell students to lay out 37 sticks and bundle the tens. Have students take 5 away and tell how many are left. (32) Repeat the above questions as you write **37 − 5 = 32** on the board in boxed notation.

Have students tell how many tens and ones are shown in the example. (3,6) Have students tell the number. (36) Tell students to trace the lines through the 4 sticks to show that 4 ones are taken away. Ask how many ones are left and have students trace the 2. Ask how

many tens are left and have students trace the 3. Go through another example with the students if necessary and have them complete the page independently. Note that this lesson stresses crossing out the sticks taken away. Remind the students to subtract the ones column first.

207

Cross out and subtract.

	tens	ones
Take away 6. −	4	9
		6
How many left?	4	3

	tens	ones
Take away 3. −	3	5
		3
How many left?	3	2

	tens	ones
Take away 2. −	2	7
		2
How many left?	2	5

	tens	ones
Take away 5. −	1	6
		5
How many left?	1	1

	tens	ones
Take away 4. −	4	8
		4
How many left?	4	4

	tens	ones
Take away 4. −	3	4
		4
How many left?	3	0

	tens	ones
Take away 5. −	4	7
		5
How many left?	4	2

	tens	ones
Take away 7. −	3	8
		7
How many left?	3	1

208 (two hundred eight)

Subtracting 1-digit from 2-digit numbers

Teaching page 208

Go through the example problem with the students. Remind students to trace the lines to cross out the sticks in each problem and subtract the ones first. Have students complete the page independently.

Extra Credit *Geometry*

Many objects have similar shapes. Hold up a book and draw the book's rectangular shape on the board. Point to a door in the room and draw its shape on the board. Explain that the book and the door, while very different in size, have similar shapes. Ask students to describe objects in the room that have similar shapes. Some may find identical objects such as: two windows in a row, two identical books, a pair of desks. Others may see similarities not related to size such as: a ball and an orange, or a piece of chalk and a flag pole. Encourage them to find less obvious similarities. For example, point out that a clock and a ball are both round. Have students draw two objects with similar shapes.

Trading

pages 209-210

Objective

To understand trading 1 ten for 10 ones

Materials

99 counting sticks
9 rubber bands

Mental Math

Name the number that is:
1. 7 tens 6 ones (76)
2. 8 tens 1 one (81)
3. 4 tens 8 ones (48)
4. 9 tens 3 ones (93)
5. 3 tens 4 ones (34)
6. 5 tens 2 ones (52)
7. 1 ten 8 ones (18)

Skill Review

Write **7 tens 6 ones = 76** on the board. Ask students to tell what is left if 2 ones are taken away. (7 tens 4 ones or 74) Repeat the activity for 4 tens 4 ones and other problems where no trading is needed.

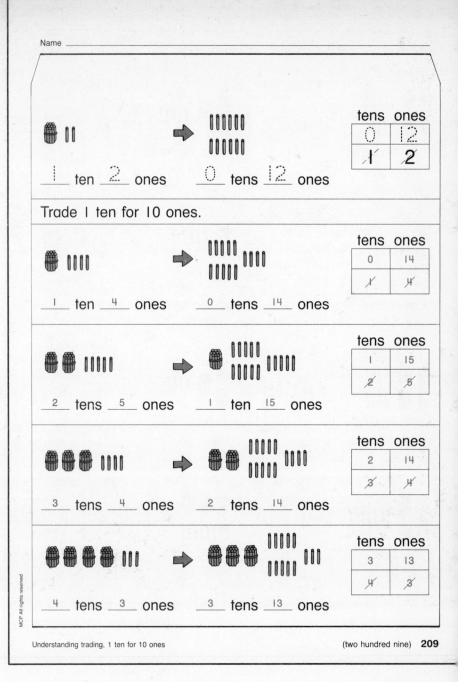

Understanding trading, 1 ten for 10 ones

(two hundred nine) **209**

Teaching page 209

Tell students to lay out 26 sticks and bundle the tens. Ask how many tens and ones. (2,6) Tell students to remove the band from 1 bundle and tell how many tens and ones now. (1,16) Write **2 tens 6 ones = 1 ten 16 ones** on the board. Tell students they traded a ten for 10 ones.

Tell students they will trade 1 ten for 10 ones on this page. Ask students how many bundles of ten are shown. (1) Tell students to trace the 1. Ask how many single sticks or ones. (2) Tell students to trace the 2. Tell students that 1 bundle of ten is traded for 10 ones. Ask how many tens and ones now. (0,12) Tell students to trace the 0 and 12. Tell students the 1 in the tens column is crossed out and a zero is recorded above it to show there are no tens left. Tell students the 2 in

the ones column is crossed out and a 12 is recorded above it to show that there are now 12 ones. Repeat the procedure to talk through each of the four problems.

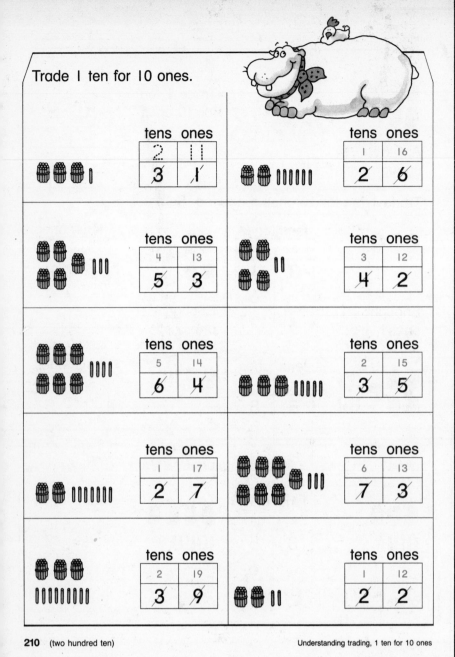

Trade 1 ten for 10 ones.

	tens	ones
	2	11
	3	1

	tens	ones
	1	16
	2	6

	tens	ones
	4	13
	5	3

	tens	ones
	3	12
	4	2

	tens	ones
	5	14
	6	4

	tens	ones
	2	15
	3	5

	tens	ones
	1	17
	2	7

	tens	ones
	6	13
	7	3

	tens	ones
	2	19
	3	9

	tens	ones
	1	12
	2	2

Understanding trading, 1 ten for 10 ones

Correcting Common Errors

Some students may forget to decrease the number of tens by one when they rename. Lead them in a math cheer where they chant, "1 less ten, 10 more ones." Then have them work with partners using counting sticks and rubber bands to show 1 less ten and 10 more ones for each of the following.

5 tens 4 ones   (4 tens 14 ones)
2 tens 6 ones   (1 ten 16 ones)
8 tens 9 ones   (7 tens 19 ones)
3 tens 0 ones   (2 tens 10 ones)

Enrichment

1. Act out trading a ten for 10 ones to subtract 6 crayons from a box of 24 crayons.
2. Draw 2 baskets of 10 balls each and 2 balls beside the baskets. Draw a second picture to show that 4 balls are to be taken away for a game.

Teaching page 210

Have students lay out 31 counters in 3 bundles of tens and 1 one. Tell students to remove the band from 1 bundle and trace the line to cross out the 3 in the example problem. Ask how many bundles of ten are left and have students trace the 2 above the 3. Ask how many ones (11) and have students trace the line to cross out the 1 and trace the 11 above the 1 to show that there are now 11 ones. Go through another problem with the students and then have them complete the page independently.

Extra Credit   *Geometry*

Ask four students to clasp hands so that they form a square. Ask the rest of the class to imagine what they look like viewed from above; how they would appear to a fly on the ceiling. Illustrate their arrangement on the board and ask a student to identify the shape. (square) Now direct the students in opposite corners to change places, but not to let go of each others' hands. Those two who stay fixed may turn, but they must hang on. The comical solution is that all the students will end up facing the outside of the square with their arms stretched behind them. Ask them to return to their original positions, again without letting go of each others' hands. Divide the class into groups of four and let them all try.

210

Subtracting, One Trade

pages 211-212

Objective

To subtract with 1 trade for minuends through 99

Materials

99 counting sticks
9 rubber bands

Mental Math

Name the number that is:
1. 2 tens 6 ones (26)
2. 1 ten 16 ones (26)
3. 4 tens 4 ones (44)
4. 3 tens 14 ones (44)
5. 2 tens 3 ones (23)
6. 1 ten 13 ones (23)
7. 5 tens 7 ones (57)
8. 4 tens 17 ones (57)

Skill Review

Write **2 tens 7 ones** on the board. Ask students if 2 ones can be taken away from 7 ones. (yes) Now ask if 8 ones can be taken away from 7 ones. (no) Continue to ask if 6, 9, 4 and 5 ones can be taken from 7 ones. Write on the board and repeat the exercise for the following: **4 tens 6 ones, 8 tens 2 ones** and **6 tens 5 ones.**

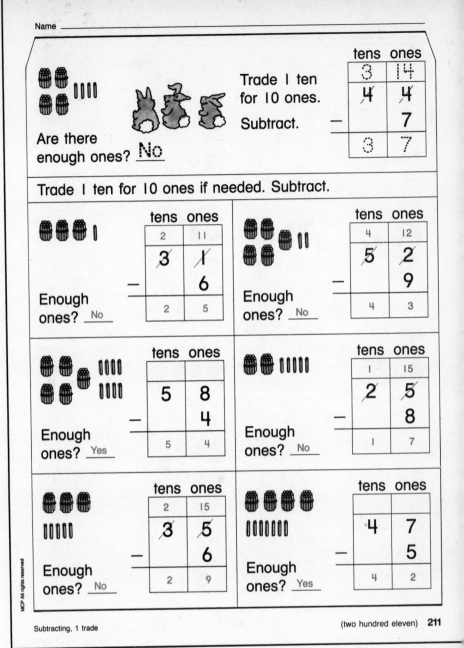

Name _____

Are there enough ones? **No**

Trade 1 ten for 10 ones. Subtract.

tens	ones
3	14
4	4
−	7
3	7

Trade 1 ten for 10 ones if needed. Subtract.

Enough ones? **No**

tens	ones
2	11
3	1
−	6
2	5

Enough ones? **No**

tens	ones
4	12
5	2
−	9
4	3

Enough ones? **Yes**

tens	ones
5	8
−	4
5	4

Enough ones? **No**

tens	ones
1	15
2	5
−	8
1	7

Enough ones? **No**

tens	ones
2	15
3	5
−	6
2	9

Enough ones? **Yes**

tens	ones
4	7
−	5
4	2

Subtracting, 1 trade

(two hundred eleven) **211**

Teaching page 211

Write on the board:

tens	ones
(2)	(14)
3	4
	8
(2)	(6)

Tell students to lay out 34 sticks and bundle the tens. Ask how many tens and ones. (3,4) Tell students we want to take 8 away. Ask students if there are enough ones to take 8 away. (no) Ask students what must be done. (trade 1 ten for 10 ones) Tell students to trade 1 ten for 10 ones and then tell how many tens are left. (2) Cross out the 3 in the tens column on the board and write a **2** above it. Ask students how many ones now. (14) Cross out the 4 and write **14** above it. Tell students we had 4 ones and now have 10 more to make 14 ones in all. Ask students if 8 ones can be taken away from 14 ones. (yes) Ask how many ones are left. (6) Write **6** in the ones column. Ask students how many tens are left. (2) Write **2** in the answer. Repeat the procedure for 40-9, 36-2, 42-5 and 28-4. Note to the students that some problems do not need a trade.

Go through the example using the same procedure as above. Remind students that a trade is not needed in some problems on this page. Have students complete the page.

211

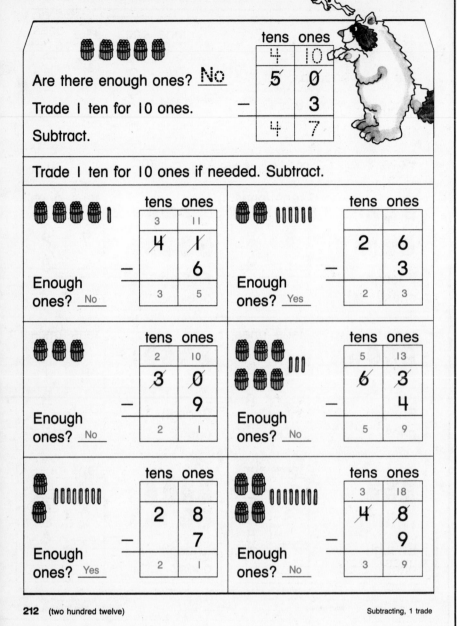

Are there enough ones? No

Trade 1 ten for 10 ones.

Subtract.

tens	ones
4̶	1̶0̶
5̶	0̶
−	3
4	7

Trade 1 ten for 10 ones if needed. Subtract.

tens	ones
3	11
4̶	1̶
−	6
3	5

Enough ones? No

tens	ones
2	6
−	3
2	3

Enough ones? Yes

tens	ones
2	10
3̶	0̶
−	9
2	1

Enough ones? No

tens	ones
5	13
6̶	3̶
−	4
5	9

Enough ones? No

tens	ones
2	8
−	7
2	1

Enough ones? Yes

tens	ones
3	18
4̶	8̶
−	9
3	9

Enough ones? No

Subtracting, 1 trade

Correcting Common Errors

Some students may subtract the top digit from the bottom digit rather than regroup.

INCORRECT

$$
\begin{array}{r}
34 \\
-\ 6 \\
\hline
32
\end{array}
$$

CORRECT

$$
\begin{array}{r}
2\,14 \\
\cancel{3}\cancel{4} \\
-\ \ 6 \\
\hline
28
\end{array}
$$

Have them work with partners using counting sticks and rubber bands to model the problem. Before they begin to subtract, have them ask themselves, "Are there enough ones to subtract?"

Enrichment

1. Write all the 1-digit numbers that can be subtracted from 3 tens 7 ones without a trade.
2. Write and solve 2 problems where 1-digit numbers are subtracted from 2-digit numbers. The first problem should have 1 trade, the other should not.

Teaching page 212

Work through the example with the students. Tell students this page has some problems where a trade of 1 ten for 10 ones is needed but some problems do not need a trade. Remind students to subtract the ones first. Have students complete the page independently.

Extra Credit   *Sets*

Play color and shape bingo. Give each student an 8-inch square of white paper, prefolded into 2-inch squares. Using 4 different colors of paper, cut 16 one and one-half inch squares for each student, and draw various shapes on each side. Include circles, squares, triangles, stars etc. Distribute these 16 squares to students and instruct them to cut out the shapes and paste them in random locations on their white papers. Each child's bingo card will be different. Pass out counters or beans to mark cards. Print a set of word cards, each with a color and shape word, for example: Red Star, Blue Triangle etc. Hold up a card. Students should read the card and cover the appropriate square on their cards. Continue displaying cards and marking the matching set member until one student has 4 in a row. Students can also play this game in pairs or small groups when their work is complete.

Subtracting, Some Trading

pages 213-214

Objective

To practice subtraction with and without 1 trade for minuends through 99

Materials

*Subtraction fact cards for minuends through 9

Mental Math

Name the numbers that can be taken away from:

1. 7 (1 through 7)
2. 9 (0 through 9)
3. 6 (0 through 6)
4. 4 (0 through 4)
5. 2 (0 through 2)
6. 1 (0 and 1)
7. 8 (0 through 8)

Skill Review

Distribute subtraction fact cards equally to all students. Have 1 student collect all cards that are related to doubles. Have the student show each card to the class and give the answer. Have a student collect all facts that have the same minuend. Continue to collect facts that equal the same number, have the same number taken away or have the same numbers in them.

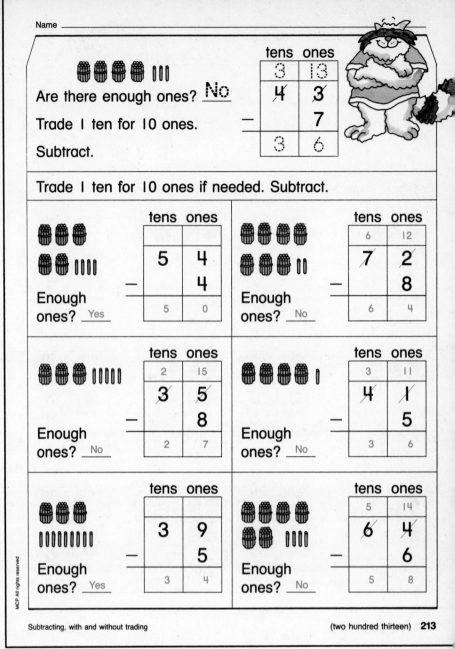

Subtracting, with and without trading

Teaching page 213

Write in boxed notaton on the board: **82-2, 78-9, 25-8, 46-7, 32-5, 53-4** and **21-2.** Ask students to tell if a trade is needed in each problem. Then have students work in pairs. Have the first student work a problem and the second student explain it to the class. Watch students' work to see that the ones column is worked first and a trade is correctly recorded. Repeat for more problems to allow all students to work at the board.

Work through the example with the students. Remind students that if there are not enough ones, they must trade 1 ten for 10 ones and record the trade. Tell students to work the problems on this page independently.

Trade 1 ten for 10 ones if needed. Subtract.

	tens	ones
	4 ~~5~~	10 ~~0~~
−		2
Is a trade needed? **Yes**	4	8

	tens	ones
	3 ~~4~~	11 ~~1~~
−		7
Is a trade needed? Yes	3	4

	tens	ones
	3	9
−		8
Is a trade needed? No	3	1

	tens	ones
	2	7
−		4
Is a trade needed? No	2	3

	tens	ones
	4 ~~5~~	12 ~~2~~
−		3
Is a trade needed? Yes	4	9

	tens	ones
	3 ~~4~~	10 ~~0~~
−		6
Is a trade needed? Yes	3	4

	tens	ones
	3	8
−		2
Is a trade needed? No	3	6

	tens	ones
	1 ~~2~~	13 ~~3~~
−		6
Is a trade needed? Yes	1	7

Subtracting, with and without trading

Correcting Common Errors

Some students may trade when it is not necessary. Remind them that, as they work each problem, they first should ask themselves if there are enough ones from which to subtract. If the answer is no, then they should trade 1 ten for 10 more ones. If the answer is yes, they do not need to trade.

Enrichment

1. Write and solve 4 subtraction problems where 7 or 3 is taken away from 54 or 42.
2. Tell the 1-digit numbers that can be taken away from 55 without a trade.
3. Lay out bundles and single sticks to show a 2-digit number. Tell a partner to take 6 or any other 1-digit number away. Ask your partner to write and solve the problem.

Teaching page 214

Work through the first example, asking if there are enough ones (no) or if a trade is needed. (yes) Tell students to trace the word yes and the line through the 5. Have students trace the 4 above the 5 to show that 1 ten is traded. Tell students to trace the line through the 0 and trace the 10 above to show that 0 ones plus 10 more is 10 ones. Tell students to subtract 2 ones from 10 ones and trace the 8 to show that 8 ones are left. Tell students to trace the 4 to show that 4 tens are left. Work through the next problem with the students to be sure they record the trade correctly. Have students complete the page independently.

Extra Credit *Measurement*

Make a metric bulletin board to demonstrate the use of basic units of metric measure. Discuss the use of metric labels on packaging. Have each student bring labels from home including: two labels for grams, two for centimeters and two for liters. Divide the bulletin board into three sections. Sort the labels by unit and tack them on the corresponding section of the board. Compare the labels in each section. Guide students in discovering that the gram section measures weight, the meter section measures length and the liter measures liquid measure or volume. Save some labels for the students to sort and arrange from smallest measure to largest.

Subtracting, Some Trading

pages 215-216

Objectives

To subtract with and without 1 trade for minuends through 99
To solve subtraction story problems

Materials

99 counting sticks
9 rubber bands
*Subtraction fact cards for minuends through 9

Mental Math

How much money?
1. 2 dimes 5 pennies (25¢)
2. 10 pennies and 6 more (16¢)
3. 1 quarter (25¢)
4. 3 dimes 1 nickel (35¢)
5. 8 dimes (80¢)
6. 1 dime 1 quarter (35¢)
7. 4 nickels 1 dime (30¢)
8. 15 pennies (15¢)

Skill Review

Distribute the subtraction fact cards equally to the students. Ask students to show all fact cards that equal 7, all facts that equal 9, etc.

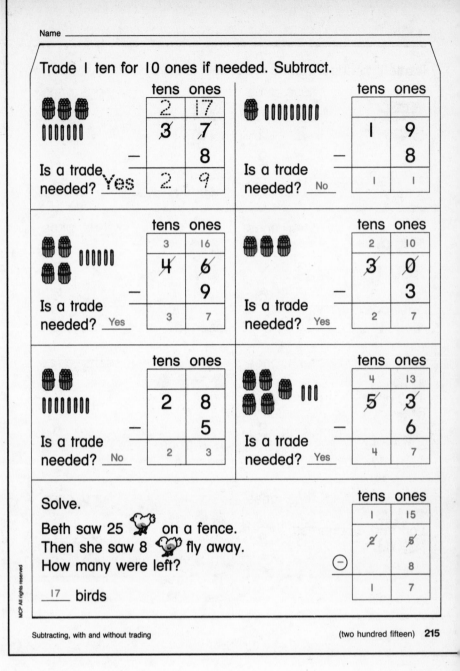

Subtracting, with and without trading

(two hundred fifteen) **215**

Teaching page 215

Ask students if a trade is needed in the example problem. (yes) Tell students to trace the word yes. Work through the problem with the students. Remind students that some problems on this page need a trade. Read the story problem with the students and ask what sign is needed in the circle. (-) Tell students to write the sign in the problem and solve it. Have students complete the page independently.

215

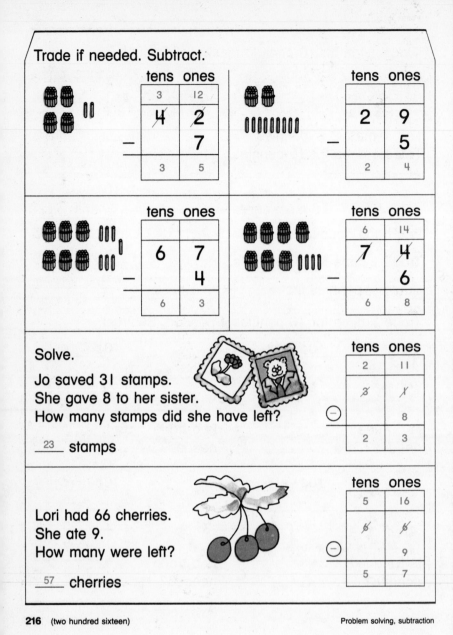

Trade if needed. Subtract.

tens ones

	3	12
	4̸	2̸
−		7
	3	5

tens ones

	2	9
−		5
	2	4

tens ones

	6	7
−		4
	6	3

tens ones

	6	14
	7̸	4̸
−		6
	6	8

Solve.

Jo saved 31 stamps.
She gave 8 to her sister.
How many stamps did she have left?

⊖

tens ones

	2	11
	3̸	1̸
		8
	2	3

__23__ stamps

Lori had 66 cherries.
She ate 9.
How many were left?

⊖

tens ones

	5	16
	6̸	6̸
		9
	5	7

__57__ cherries

Problem solving, subtraction

Correcting Common Errors

Some students may forget to decrease the number of tens when they trade.

INCORRECT	CORRECT
1 7	2 17
3̸7̸	3̸7̸
− 8	− 8
39	29

Have them work with partners using counting sticks and rubber bands to model the problems.

Enrichment

1. Tell a story of having 23 rocks and losing 9. Write the problem and tell how many are left.
2. Draw bundles and singles to show 2 names for 83.

Teaching page 216

Have students tell how many tens and ones are in the first problem. (4,2) Ask students how many ones are to be taken away. (7) Ask students if there are enough ones in 2 to take 7 away. (no) Ask if a trade is needed. (yes) Have students work this problem and the next 3 problems. Now read the first story problem and have students write the minus sign in the circle. Ask students what 2 questions they need to ask in this problem. (Are there enough ones? Is a trade needed?) Have students work both problems independently as you offer reading assistance where needed.

Extra Credit *Geometry*

To expand the concept of measuring shapes, give each student a random length of string. Ask them to find three things in the room that are the same length as the string. Some will see that it is possible to use the string repeatedly to measure long distances; for example, the length of the room is about 8 strings. Others will see that they can measure with part of the string and see that the distance around their wrist is one-half of a string length. Have students make a list of the things they have measured. Have them point them out to the rest of the class. Ask six students to compare the lengths of their strings by asking them to line up before the class in order from shortest to longest piece of string.

216

Subtracting Money

pages 217-218

Objectives

To subtract money for minuends through 99
To solve money story problems

Materials

9 dimes
25 pennies

Mental Math

How much money?
1. 3 dimes 2 pennies (32¢)
2. 2 dimes 12 pennies (32¢)
3. 1 dime 10 pennies (20¢)
4. 4 dimes 3 pennies (43¢)
5. 3 dimes 13 pennies (43¢)
6. 1 dime 14 pennies (24¢)

Skill Review

Tell students to lay out 25 pennies and tell how much money. (25¢) Ask students if there are enough pennies to trade for a dime. (yes) Tell students to trade 10 pennies for a dime. Ask how many dimes and pennies. (1,15) Ask how much money in all. (25¢) Ask students if there are enough pennies to trade for another dime. (yes) Tell students to trade 10 pennies again for a dime and tell how many dimes and pennies and how much money in all. (2, 5, 25¢)

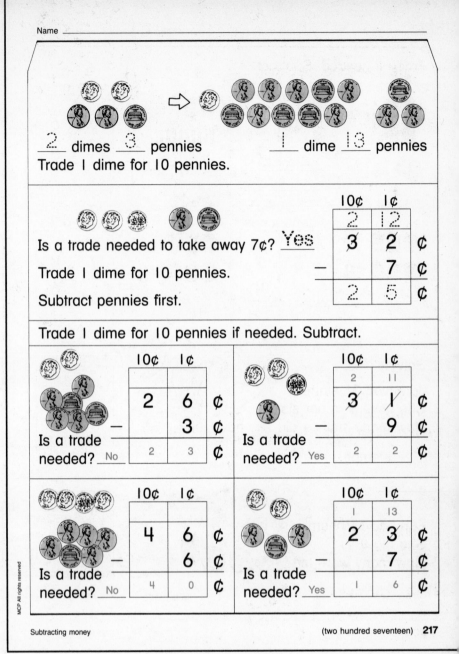

Subtracting money   (two hundred seventeen) **217**

Teaching page 217

Students have 2 dimes and 5 pennies laid out. Tell students a story of having 2 dimes and 5 pennies in your pocket but the parking meter takes only pennies and you need 15 pennies to park. Ask how to get 15 pennies. (trade 1 dime for 10 more pennies) Tell students to trade 1 dime for 10 pennies. Tell students 1 dime can be traded for 10 pennies just like 1 bundle of ten can be traded for 10 ones. Repeat the parking meter story having 2 dimes and 6 pennies and needing 9 pennies. Write the problem **26¢-9¢** on the board in boxed notation. Tell students this problem will tell how much money will be left after 9¢ is put in the parking meter. Ask if a trade is needed. (yes) Work through the trade of 1 dime for 10 pennies again with coins as you show the trade in the problem on the board. Repeat the story for having 3 dimes and 7 pennies and

needing 5 pennies to demonstrate that no trade is needed in some problems.

Have students count the dimes and pennies and trace the 2 and 3. Ask students how many dimes and pennies are shown after 1 dime is traded for 10 pennies. (1,13) Tell students to trace the numbers. Work through the second problem with the students and then remind them that some problems on this page don't need a trade. Have students complete the page independently.

217

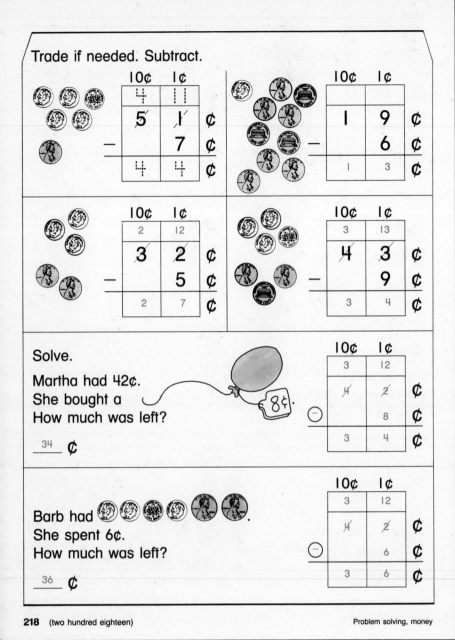

Trade if needed. Subtract.

	10¢	1¢	
	4	11	
	$\cancel{5}$	$\cancel{1}$	¢
−		7	¢
	4	4	¢

	10¢	1¢	
	1	9	¢
−		6	¢
	1	3	¢

	10¢	1¢	
	2	12	
	3	2	¢
−		5	¢
	2	7	¢

	10¢	1¢	
	3	13	
	$\cancel{4}$	3	¢
−		9	¢
	3	4	¢

Solve.

Martha had 42¢.
She bought a 🎈 8¢.
How much was left?

__34__ ¢

	10¢	1¢	
	3	12	
	$\cancel{4}$	$\cancel{2}$	¢
−		8	¢
	3	4	¢

Barb had 🪙🪙🪙🪙🪙.
She spent 6¢.
How much was left?

__36__ ¢

	10¢	1¢	
	3	12	
	$\cancel{4}$	$\cancel{2}$	¢
−		6	¢
	3	6	¢

Problem solving, money

Correcting Common Errors

Watch for students who forget to add the ones to the ten when they regroup. Have students practice trading by working with partners using coins. Have them use dimes and pennies to model the following, then trade 1 dime for 10 pennies and write what they have then.

3 dimes 2 pennies
  (2 dimes 12 pennies)
2 dimes 1 penny
  (1 dime 11 pennies)
1 dime 6 pennies
  (0 dimes 16 pennies)
4 dimes 0 pennies
  (3 dimes 10 pennies)

Enrichment

1. Take 3 dimes and 2 pennies to a classroom store. Purchase an item costing 6 cents. How much money do you have left?
2. Draw 3 dimes and 2 pennies. Draw the same amount of money using only 2 dimes.

Teaching page 218

Talk through the example asking students if there are enough pennies or ones and if a trade is needed. Remind students that each of the next 3 problems may or may not need a trade. Have students work the problems independently. Read each story problem and have students write the sign needed and then complete the problem.

Extra Credit *Numeration*

Using old catalogs, magazines or newspapers, have students cut out various toys, games, prizes, etc. Have them paste each picture on small pieces of cardboard or heavy paper and write a price on the back of each picture. Set up a play store and give students play money. Let them purchase an item by reading the correct price and then counting out the correct amount, using play pennies, nickels, dimes and quarters.

218

Problem Solving, Subtracting

pages 219-220

Objective

To solve problems for minuends through 99

Materials

9 dimes
25 pennies

Mental Math

Name the number that is:
1. 24¢ + 6¢ (30¢)
2. 23 + 1 (24)
3. 3 + 82 (85)
4. 9 + 61 (70)
5. 26¢ + 5¢ (31¢)
6. 72 + 9 (81)
7. 45 + 5 (50)
8. 1¢ + 19¢ (20¢)

Skill Review

Have students work in pairs. Tell the first student to place 4 dimes in one hand and 2 pennies in the other. Ask how much money. (42¢) Have the second student take 1 dime away and place 10 pennies with the 2 pennies. Have students tell the new name for 42¢. (3 dimes 12 pennies) Repeat for 64¢, 98¢, 16¢, 26¢, and 19¢.

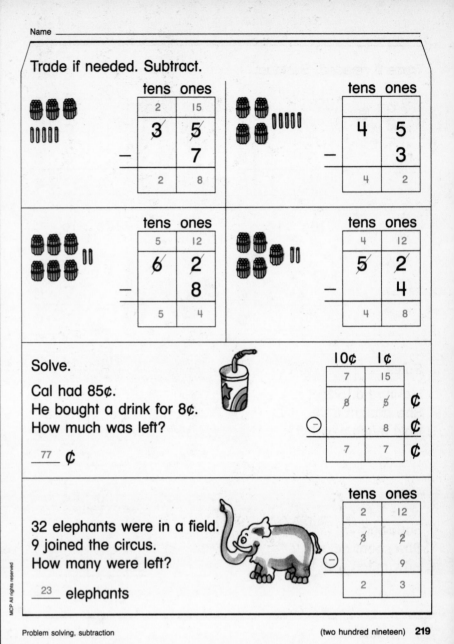

Name _____

Trade if needed. Subtract.

	tens	ones
	2	15
	3̸	5̸
−		7
	2	8

	tens	ones
	4	5
−		3
	4	2

	tens	ones
	5	12
	6̸	2̸
−		8
	5	4

	tens	ones
	4	12
	5̸	2̸
−		4
	4	8

Solve.

Cal had 85¢.
He bought a drink for 8¢.
How much was left?

___77___ ¢

10¢	1¢	
7	15	
8̸	5̸	¢
−	8	¢
7	7	¢

32 elephants were in a field.
9 joined the circus.
How many were left?

___23___ elephants

	tens	ones
	2	12
−	3̸	2̸
		9
	2	3

Problem solving, subtraction

(two hundred nineteen) **219**

Teaching page 219

Remind students that some problems require a trade of 1 ten for 10 ones and some problems do not. Tell students to examine the ones column first, see if a trade is needed and then begin to work the problem. Have students look at the money story problem on this page. Tell students that bundles and single sticks could be used here as dimes and pennies since 1 dime equals 10 pennies just as 1 bundle equals 10 single sticks. Remind students to put the subtraction sign in each story problem. Help students read the story problems as they work independently to complete the page.

Trade if needed. Subtract.

35 − 3 **32**	71 − 6 **65**	29 − 3 26	84 − 9 75	67 − 5 62
87 − 6 81	56 − 4 52	41 − 7 34	73 − 5 68	34 − 8 26
18 − 3 15	45 − 8 37	52 − 9 43	38 − 5 33	95 − 7 88

Solve.

Chuck had 32 🐚.
He gave 6 to Molly.
How many did he
have left?

32
− 6
26

26 shells

Patsy had 28 🃏.
She sold 4 of them.
How many were
left?

28
− 4
24

24 cards

Abby had 82¢.
She spent 8¢.
How much was
left?

82¢
− 8¢
74¢

74 ¢

Larry had 35 🥜.
He ate 9 of them.
How many were
left?

35
− 9
26

26 peanuts

220 (two hundred twenty)   Problem solving, subtraction

Teaching page 220

Write the first problem on the board in boxed notation to help students see that they will work these problems the same way they did in boxed notation. Have students trace the answer. Then talk through the second example as students record the trade and trace the answer. Tell students to complete the 3 rows of subtraction problems independently. Tell students they need to write the sign in each money story problem. Help students read the story problems as they complete the page.

Extra Credit   *Geometry*

Bring examples of patterns with repeated shapes to class, such as: pieces of wallpaper or fabric, graph paper, advertisements or a box of tiles. Show how the same shape can be repeated to form a pattern. Ask students to look around the room to see if they notice a pattern of repeated shapes. Examples in your classroom might include: ceiling or floor tiles, panes of glass in a window, or shelves in a bookcase. For each of the examples you have brought in or that students have found in the room, ask them to identify the basic shape. For example, floor tiles are probably squares; book shelves, rectangles, etc. Ask students to look for a pattern of repeating shapes at home and to bring in a drawing or description of the pattern. When they have done this, ask each to hold up the drawing and explain to the class what the drawing represents, and identify the basic shape being repeated.

Chapter Review

pages 221-222

Objectives

To review subtraction for minuends through 99

To maintain skills learned previously this year

Materials

*Addition fact cards for sums through 18
*Subtraction fact cards for minuends through 18
99 counting sticks
9 rubber bands

Mental Math

Name the number that comes:
1. next after 2, 4, 6, 8 (10)
2. before 90 (89)
3. next after 15, 20, 25 (30)
4. after 12 (13)
5. next after 40, 50, 60 (70)
6. before 8 tens 0 ones (79)
7. after 8 + 2 (11)
8. before 20-1 (18)

Skill Review

Shuffle the addition and subtraction fact cards. Deal the cards equally to all students. Ask students to lay down all cards that equal 7. Repeat for other sums and differences until all cards are laid down. Now ask students to pick up all doubles, all cards related to the sum of 7, etc.

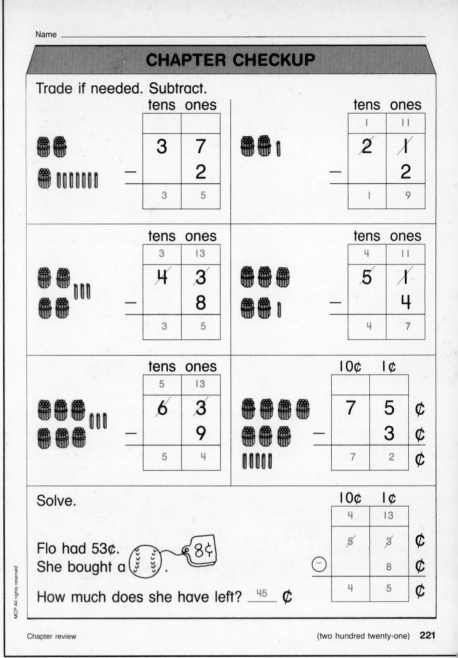

Teaching page 221

Ask students what question they must ask first in a subtraction problem. (Are there enough ones? Is a trade needed?) Remind students to always work the ones column first. Tell students they will need to write the sign in each of the story problems and record the answers in the blanks. Help students read the problems if necessary. Have students complete the page independently.

221

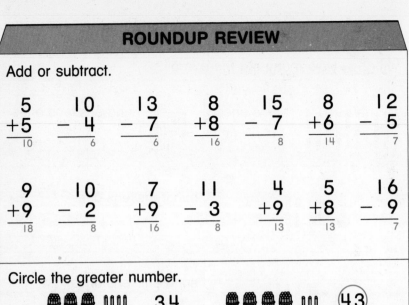

ROUNDUP REVIEW

Add or subtract.

5 +5 **10**	10 − 4 **6**	13 − 7 **6**	8 +8 **16**	15 − 7 **8**	8 +6 **14**	12 − 5 **7**
9 +9 **18**	10 − 2 **8**	7 +9 **16**	11 − 3 **8**	4 +9 **13**	5 +8 **13**	16 − 9 **7**

Circle the greater number.

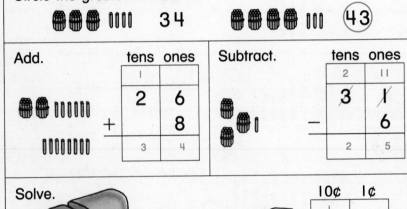

34   **(43)**

Add.

tens	ones
1	
2	6
+	8
3	4

Subtract.

tens	ones
2	11
3̷	1̷
−	6
2	5

Solve.

35¢   9¢

10¢	1¢	
1		
3	5	¢
+	9	¢
4	4	¢

How much for both? __44__ ¢

Cumulative review

222

Enrichment

1. Write the sums through 18 on an addition table. Try to improve your speed of recall.
2. Write the answers for minuends through 18 on a subtraction table. Try to improve your speed of recall.
3. Write an addition and a subtraction problem showing 1 trade. Write one of each with no trade.

Teaching page 222

Ask students what they are to do in each group of problems. Remind students to look at the sign before beginning to work each problem. Tell students they are to write the signs in the last 2 problems. Have students complete the page independently.

This page reviews addition and subtraction facts, comparing numbers, addition and subtracting with trading and adding money.

Multiples of 10

pages 223-224

Objective
To count and write by 10's through 200

Materials
*2 hundred-squares
Crayons
Scissors
10 × 10 grid sheets

Mental Math
Name the number that is:
1. 9 tens (90)
2. 8 dimes (80¢)
3. 4 tens (40)
4. 5 dimes (50¢)
5. 8 tens (80)

Skill Review
Attach a grid sheet to the board. Have students count with you as you count the squares through 90, stressing the multiples of ten. Ask students how many squares in each row. (10) Count by 10's and then by 5's to square number 25. Tell students to count by 10's through 70 and then 6 more to 76. Repeat for other numbers. Have students cut out the strips and singles and show 31, 26, 38, etc. as you name each number, and name its tens and ones.

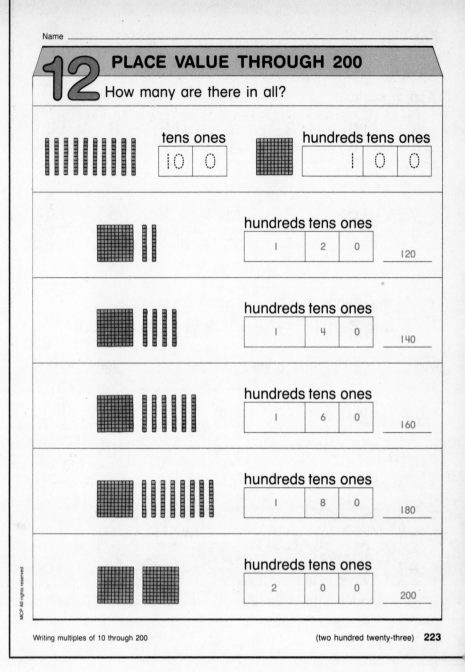

Writing multiples of 10 through 200   (two hundred twenty-three) **223**

Teaching page 223

Have students color all 10 strips on a 10 × 10 grid. Have students count by 10's through 90 and then by 1's through 99. Tell students that 1 more than 99 is 100 or 10 tens. Tell students to cut out the 10 ten-strips and count by 10's again through 100. Show students a hundred-square. Ask a student to place the 10 ten-strips on the hundred-square. Ask how many ten-strips are in 100. (10) Students may need to count the squares by 1's. Write **100 ones = ten, tens = 1 hundred** on the board. Tell students that 1 hundred-square and 1 ten-strip is 110 or 11 tens. Write in a column on the board: **10 tens = 100, 11 tens = 110, 12 tens = 120,** through **20 tens = 200.** Have students count by 10's from 10 through 200. Have students place all their ten-strips and singles in envelopes for later use. Have students tell how many ten-strips are in the first illustration, (10) and trace the 10 and 0. (10) Tell students we write a 1 under hundreds to show there is 1 hundred-square, a zero under tens to show no more tens and a zero to show there are no ones. Have students trace the boxed numbers and 100. Go through the next 2 problems with students and have them complete the page independently.

223

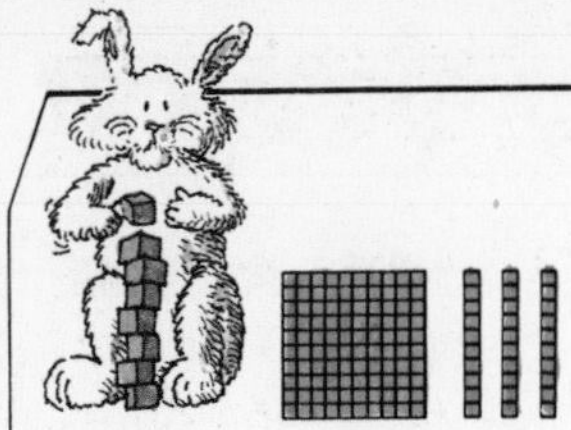

hundreds tens ones

hundreds	tens	ones
1	3	0

130

How many are there in all?

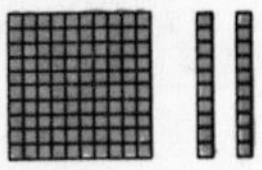

hundreds	tens	ones
1	2	0

120

hundreds	tens	ones
1	7	0

170

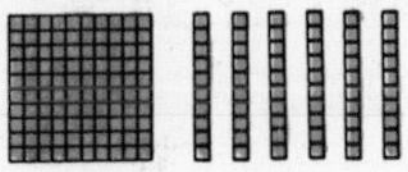

hundreds	tens	ones
1	6	0

160

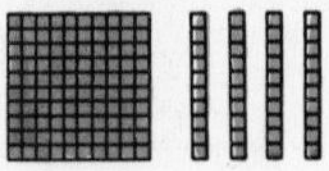

hundreds	tens	ones
1	4	0

140

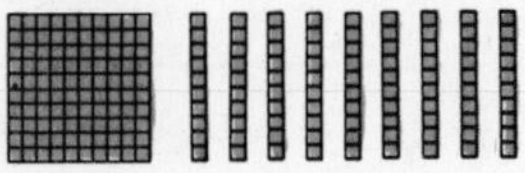

hundreds	tens	ones
1	9	0

190

Writing multiples of 10 through 200

Correcting Common Errors

Some students may have difficulty seeing how a number of tens can be written as hundreds and tens. Have them work with partners using hundred-squares and ten-strips. For each of the following, have them model the problem, then trade 10 ten-strips for 1 hundred-square and rewrite the problem using hundreds and tens.

14 tens	(1 hundred 4 tens)
11 tens	(1 hundred 1 ten)
17 tens	(1 hundred 7 tens)
15 tens	(1 hundred 5 tens)

Enrichment

1. Make a 10's chain. Write the numbers by 10's through 200 and connect them in order.
2. Take turns with a friend to count to 200 by 10's, and tell how many tens are in each number.

Teaching page 224

Have students tell how many hundreds, tens and ones, trace the numbers in the boxes and trace 130. Tell students to complete the page.

Extra Credit   *Measurement*

Ask the class to think of different jobs where measurement is important. Write invitations to people in different types of careers to come to your class. Ask them to discuss and demonstrate the importance of measurement in their jobs. Some careers that might apply include: a baker, carpenter, surveyor, or pharmacist. Student's parents are a good resource for speakers.

224

100 through 200

pages 225-226

Objective

To write numbers from 100 through 200

Materials

*Hundred-squares
Ten-strips
*Single squares
10 × 10 grid
10 × 10 grid numbered 1 through 100

Mental Math

Name the number that comes before and after:
1. 92 (91, 93)
2. 64 (63, 65)
3. 11 (10, 12)
4. 30 (29, 31)
5. 99 (98, 100)

Skill Review

Have students count by 10's through 100. Place a ten-strip on the chalk tray for each decade and ask students how many ten-strips. At 100 ask students what can be traded for 10 tens. (hundred-square) Trade and ask how many hundreds. (1) Place a ten-strip beside the hundred-square and ask how many. (110) Continue placing ten-strips through 200. Discuss the trade for another hundred-square to get 200.

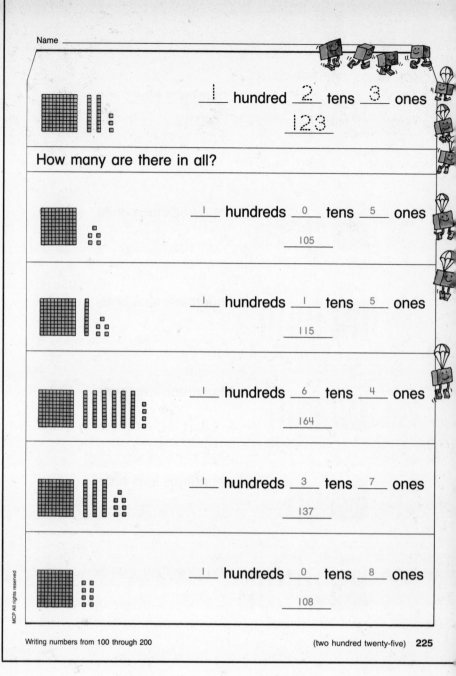

Name _____

___1___ hundred __2__ tens __3__ ones

123

How many are there in all?

___1___ hundreds __0__ tens __5__ ones

105

___1___ hundreds __1__ tens __5__ ones

115

___1___ hundreds __6__ tens __4__ ones

164

___1___ hundreds __3__ tens __7__ ones

137

___1___ hundreds __0__ tens __8__ ones

108

Writing numbers from 100 through 200   (two hundred twenty-five) **225**

Teaching page 225

Write the headings **Hundreds, Tens, Ones** on the board. Show a hundred-square with a single square beside it. Ask how many hundreds, tens and ones. (1, 0, 1) Ask how many in all. (101) Continue adding singles through 109. Record each number as it is developed. At 110, tell students that 10 ones can be traded for a ten. Make the trade and record the number. Continue to develop and record numbers by 1's through 130 for students to see the continuous pattern of trading 10 ones at decade numbers. Now have students demonstrate and record other numbers through 200.

Ask students how many hundreds are shown in the first example. (1) Have students trace the 1. Repeat for tens and ones and have students trace 123 on the line.

Work the next problem together and then have students complete the page independently.

225

How many are there in all?

___1___ hundreds ___6___ tens ___2___ ones

162

___1___ hundreds ___0___ tens ___6___ ones

106

___1___ hundreds ___7___ tens ___4___ ones

174

___1___ hundreds ___9___ tens ___1___ ones

191

___1___ hundreds ___1___ tens ___9___ ones

119

___1___ hundreds ___5___ tens ___7___ ones

157

Writing numbers from 100 through 200

Correcting Common Errors

Some students may write a number such as one hundred forty-five as 10045 with extra zeros in it. Have them use digit cards and a place-value chart to model the problems, placing a 1 in the hundreds place, a 4 in the tens place, and a 5 in the ones place.

Hundreds	Tens	Ones
1	4	5

Enrichment

1. Count the floor tile squares in a room at school or home.
2. Cut 3 numbers from 100 through 200 from a newspaper. Read the numbers to your class and tell how many hundreds, tens and ones in each.

Teaching page 226

Tell students they are to write the number of hundreds, tens and ones, and then write the number for each of the 6 problems. Have students complete the page.

Extra Credit *Measurement*

Clear an area on a table or counter. Have a student label it with a sign that reads MEASURING TOOLS. Have students bring in as many different types of measuring equipment as they can find at home. Include some unusual devices such as: pressure gauges, egg timers, types of clocks and meters. Discuss the use of one or two of the measuring tools each day. Let a student pick one to explain or demonstrate. Also, have students make a list of measuring equipment they see around the school. These could also be demonstrated by the personnel who use them.

91 through 200

pages 227-228

Objectives

To write numbers through 200 in sequence
To count by 2's, 5's, 10's through 200

Materials

*Hundred-squares
*Completed grid for numbers 101 through 200

Mental Math

How many in all?
1. 11 tens (110)
2. 15 tens (150)
3. 1 hundred-square (100)
4. 9 tens 10 ones (100)
5. 20 tens (200)
6. 19 tens 10 ones (200)
7. 17 tens (170)

Skill Review

Show students 1 hundred-square and ask how many 10's. (10) Show a second hundred-square and ask how many 10's in all. (20) Write the number **200** on the board and ask how many hundreds, tens and ones. (2, 0, 0) Write the number **154**. Ask students to tell how many hundreds, tens and ones. (1, 5, 4) Continue for other numbers from 101 through 200.

Name _____

Write the missing numbers.

91	92	93	94	95	96	97	98	99	100
101	102	103	104	105	106	107	108	109	110
111	112	113	114	115	116	117	118	119	120
121	122	123	124	125	126	127	128	129	130
131	132	133	134	135	136	137	138	139	140
141	142	143	144	145	146	147	148	149	150

Write the missing numbers.

94, _95_, _96_, _97_, _98_, _99_, _100_

101, 102, _103_, _104_, _105_, _106_, _107_, _108_

128, 129, _130_, _131_, _132_, _133_, _134_, _135_

FIELD TRIP

Count by tens.

80, 90, _100_, _110_, _120_, _130_, _140_, _150_

Count by fives.

95, 100, _105_, _110_, _115_, _120_, _125_, _130_

Count by twos.

100, 102, 104, _106_, _108_, _110_, _112_, _114_, _116_

Writing numbers through 150 in sequence

(two hundred twenty-seven) **227**

Teaching page 227

Tell students they are to start at 91 and write the numbers in order through 150. Have students find 100 and trace it. Tell students there are other numbers they are to trace and these numbers will help them through the chart. Now have students find the 94 in the first number sequence and trace the next number. Tell students they can use their number chart to help them write the numbers here. Tell students to find the row that reads 80, 90. Ask students if this row is counting by 1's. (no) Ask how they are to count and write the numbers here. (by 10's) Repeat this questioning for the next 3 rows. Show students how to use the chart to help write the numbers by 5's and 10's. Remind students to write every other number when counting by 2's. Direct students to complete the page independently.

227

Write the missing numbers.

151	152	153	154	155	156	157	158	159	160
161	162	163	164	165	166	167	168	169	170
171	172	173	174	175	176	177	178	179	180
181	182	183	184	185	186	187	188	189	190
191	192	193	194	195	196	197	198	199	200

Write the missing numbers.

161, 162, 163, 164, 165, 166, 167, 168

154, 155, 156, 157, 158, 159, 160, 161

177, 178, 179, 180, 181, 182, 183, 184

148, 149, 150, 151, 152, 153, 154, 155

FIELD TRIP

Count by tens.

100, 110, 120, 130, 140, 150, 160, 170, 180

Count by fives.

150, 155, 160, 165, 170, 175, 180, 185, 190

Count by twos.

160, 162, 164, 166, 168, 170, 172, 174, 176, 178

228 (two hundred twenty-eight)   Writing numbers 100 through 200 in sequence

Numbers through 200

pages 229-230

Objective

To read and write numbers through 200 in sequence

Materials

*Number board with 1 through 100
*Number board with 101 through 200
*Blank cards

Mental Math

Name the ordinal number that comes:

1. after 4th (5th)
2. before 3rd (2nd)
3. before 9th (8th)
4. after 9th (10th)
5. between 6th and 8th (7th)
6. between 1st and 3rd (2nd)
7. before 2nd (1st)
8. between 3rd and 5th (4th)

Skill Review

Name a number from 1 through 200 as either the number, or its renaming in hundreds, tens and ones. Ask students to write the number on the board. Repeat for more numbers.

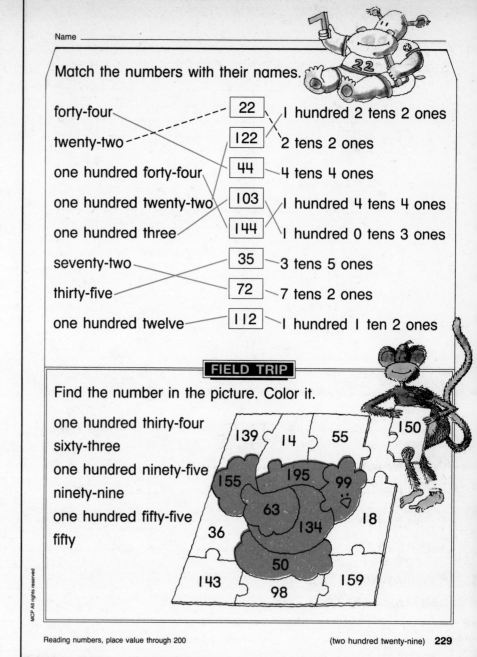

Name _____

Match the numbers with their names.

forty-four — 22 — I hundred 2 tens 2 ones
twenty-two — 122 — 2 tens 2 ones
one hundred forty-four — 44 — 4 tens 4 ones
one hundred twenty-two — 103 — I hundred 4 tens 4 ones
one hundred three — 144 — I hundred 0 tens 3 ones
seventy-two — 35 — 3 tens 5 ones
thirty-five — 72 — 7 tens 2 ones
one hundred twelve — 112 — I hundred I ten 2 ones

FIELD TRIP

Find the number in the picture. Color it.

one hundred thirty-four
sixty-three
one hundred ninety-five
ninety-nine
one hundred fifty-five
fifty

139   14   55   150
155   195   99
63
36   134   18
50
143   159
98

Reading numbers, place value through 200   (two hundred twenty-nine) **229**

Teaching page 229

Display demonstration boards for reference. Write the following numbers on the board in columns; first column: **one hundred fifty-three, one hundred seventy-two, one hundred twenty-five;** second column: **125, 172** and **153;** third column: **1 hundred 7 tens 2 ones, 1 hundred 5 tens 3 ones, 1 hundred 2 tens 5 ones.**

Tell students to read the first number in column one. (one hundred fifty-three) Ask them to match it to the correct number in column two (153) and draw a line to it. Next, ask them to match it to the renaming in column 3 (1 hundred 5 tens and 3 ones) and draw a line to it. Ask a student to come to the board and draw connecting lines for the next two numbers.

Tell students they are to draw a line from the number in the box to its number name in the left column and to its renaming in the right column. Have students trace the lines from 22 to its number name and renaming. Tell students to complete this section independently.

Field Trip

Tell students they are to read each number word, find that number in the picture and color it. Ask students to read each number word with you. Remind students they are to color only the numbers in the picture that match the number words.

229

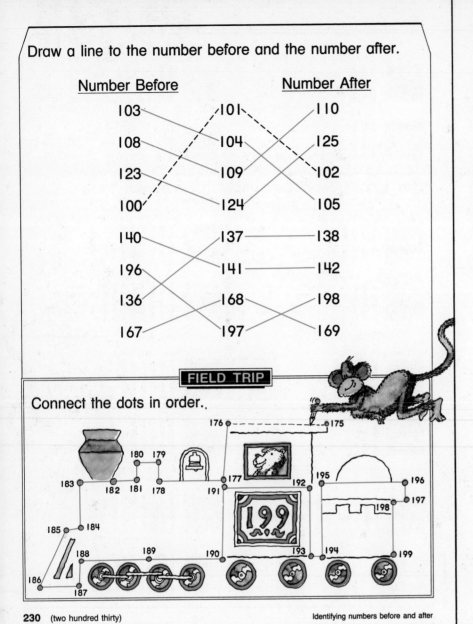

Draw a line to the number before and the number after.

Number Before		Number After
103	101	110
108	104	125
123	109	102
100	124	105
140	137	138
196	141	142
136	168	198
167	197	169

FIELD TRIP

Connect the dots in order.

230 (two hundred thirty)   Identifying numbers before and after

Correcting Common Errors

Some students may have difficulty identifying the numbers that come just before and just after a given number. Draw a number line from 110 to 130 on the chalkboard. Point to different numbers, one at a time, on the number line and have students name the number that comes just before and the number that comes just after. Erase those numbers from the number line and label it from 130 to 150 and repeat the process.

Enrichment

1. Draw doors to 5 doctors' offices one side by 2's from 172 and by 2's from 171 on the other side.
   Number the doors in order on one side by 2's from 172 and by 2's from 171 on the other side.
2. Write the room numbers that would be included if you saw a sign that reads Rooms 116-132.

Teaching page 230

Display the demonstration boards. Write ___**116**___ on the board and ask students to tell the number that comes before 116 and the number that comes after 116. (115, 117) Have a student write the numbers in the blanks. Repeat for 172 and 98. Tell students they are to draw lines from the number in the box to the numbers before and after it. Have students trace the lines from 104 back to 103 and on to 105. Tell students to complete both groups of numbers independently.

Field Trip

Tell students they are to connect the dots in order to create a picture. For practice, have students count by ones from 150 through 200. Ask students to find the smallest and the largest numbers shown in the picture.

Tell students to begin with the smallest number and connect the dots in order to the largest number shown.

Extra Credit *Statistics*

Ask each student to bring in the comics section from a Sunday newspaper. Tell them to choose a comic strip and one character they like. Give each student scissors, paper, and glue. Now ask them to cut out their favorite comic character every time it appears in the strip. Have them glue the figures on the paper and label their picture with the name of the comic strip. Post these picture graphs on a board where students can look at each other's work and compare. Ask the class whose comic strip character appeared most. Which character appeared least? Ask if the character appeared in every frame of the strip.

Comparing Numbers

pages 231-232

Objective

To compare numbers through 200

Materials

*Hundreds boards through 200
*Hundred-squares
*Ten-strips
*Single squares

Mental Math

Tell the time when the long hand is on:

1. 6 and short hand is between 12 and 1 (12:30)
2. 12 and short hand is on 4 (4:00)
3. 6 and short hand is between 6 and 7 (6:30)
4. 12 and short hand is on 5 (5:00)
5. 6 and short hand is between 9 and 10 (9:30)

Skill Review

Have students count by 1's from 45 through 70, 166 through 190, etc. Have students count by 2's from 100 through 140, 68 through 88, etc. Have students count by 5's from 85 through 120, 115 through 160, etc. Have students count by 10's from 60 through 130, 90 through 180, etc.

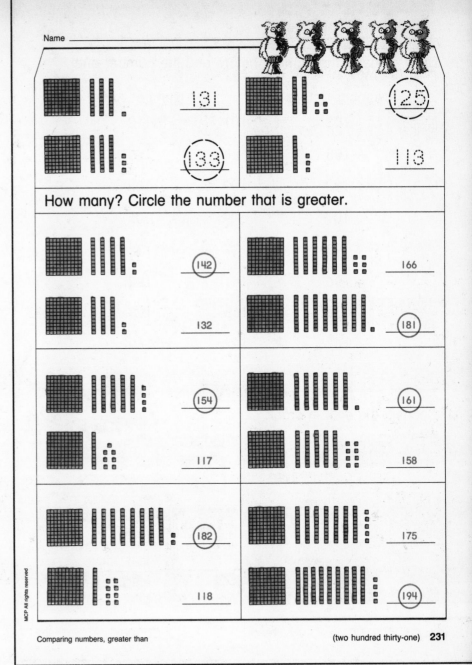

Comparing numbers, greater than

(two hundred thirty-one) **231**

Teaching page 231

Place a hundred-square, 2 ten-strips and 5 single squares in view. Ask students to tell the number. (125) Write **125** on the board. Now show 2 more ten-strips and 1 more single square and ask students the number. (146) Write the number. Ask students how many hundreds, tens and ones in each to compare the numbers. Ask students which is greater, 125 or 146. (146) Have a student circle the greater number. Ask students why 146 is greater. (has more tens, is farther down on the hundreds board)

Tell students they are to write the numbers shown in the 2 illustrations in each box. Ask students how many hundreds, ten and ones are in the first illustration. (1, 3, 1) Have students say the number and then trace 131. Repeat for 133. Now ask students which number

is greater. (133) Tell students they are to circle the greater number. Have students trace around the 133. Go through the second example similarly and then have students complete the page. Students may need the aid of the hundred-squares, tens-strips and single squares.

231

How many? Circle the number that is less.

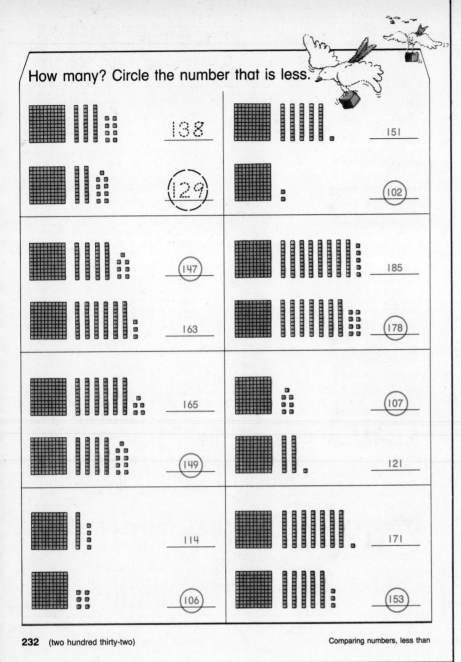

138	151
(129)	(102)
(147)	185
163	(178)
165	(107)
(149)	121
114	171
(106)	(153)

Comparing numbers, less than

Teaching page 232

Tell students they are to write the 2 numbers shown in the illustration in each box, and then circle the number that is less than the other. Go through the sample problem and then have students complete the page independently.

Extra Credit *Logic*

Write these sentences on the board, and have volunteers read each of them aloud:
1. A train weighs more than a tree.
2. A kitten weighs less than a tree.
3. A kitten weighs more than a cookie.

Then ask students to put these items (train, kitten, tree and cookie) in order from the lightest to the heaviest. Then ask them to put the items in order from the heaviest to the lightest.

Repeat the activity using the following sentences. Have them order these items from the shortest to the tallest.
1. A girl is taller than a flower.
2. A flagpole if taller than a door.
3. A girl is shorter than a door.

Make up more puzzles of this sort and encourage each student to make up one.

Counting Money, Dollars

pages 233-234

Objective

To count a dollar, dimes and pennies for amounts to $2.00

Materials

*Hundred-squares, ten-strips and single squares
1 dollar
10 dimes
10 pennies

Mental Math

How much in all?
1. 9 dimes, 4 pennies (94¢)
2. 8 dimes (80¢)
3. 8 dimes, 14 pennies (94¢)
4. 3 ten-strips, 4 singles (34)
5. 1 hundred-square (100)
6. 8 dimes − 1 dime (70¢)
7. 6 dimes − 10 pennies (50¢)

Skill Review

Show 10 single squares and ask students what can be traded for these. (1 ten-strip) Show 10 ten-strips and ask what can be traded for these. (1 hundred-square) Write amounts through 200 and ask students how many hundreds, tens and ones in each number.

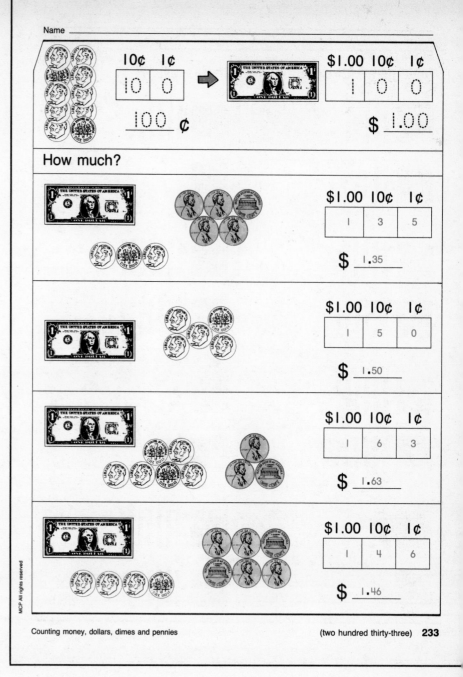

Counting money, dollars, dimes and pennies

(two hundred thirty-three) **233**

Teaching page 233

Tell students to lay out 10 pennies. Ask students if they can trade 10 pennies for another coin. (yes) Ask what coin. (dime) Tell students to lay out 10 dimes. Ask how many pennies in 10 dimes. (100) Tell students 100 pennies can be traded for 10 dimes and 10 dimes can be traded for 1 dollar. Write on the board: **100 pennies = 10 dimes = 1 dollar.** Tell students to lay out 1 dollar, 1 dime and 2 pennies. Tell students this amount is read 1 dollar and 12 cents. Write **$1.12** on the board and point to each part as you read it again. Now have students lay out 1 dollar, 3 dimes and 8 pennies. Write:

Dollars		Dimes	Pennies
(1)	.	(3)	(8)
(1)	.	(6)	(3)

on the board and have students write the 1, 3 and 8 under their headings. Have students read the amount. Repeat for $1.63.

Go through the example with students to stress the value and notation of $1.00. Have students trace the numbers. Repeat the procedure for the first example and then have students complete the page.

233

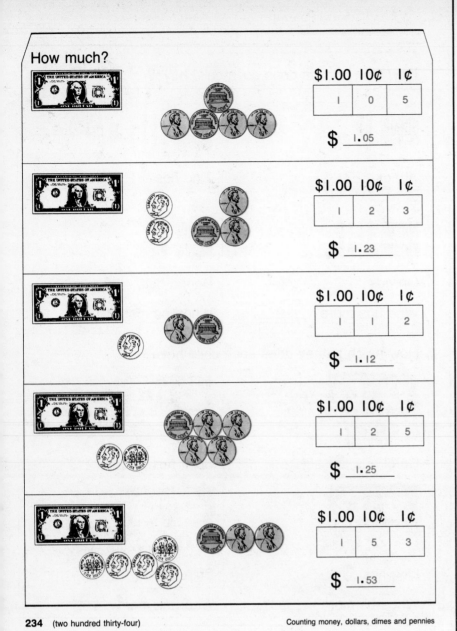

How much?

$1.00	10¢	1¢
1	0	5

$ 1.05

$1.00	10¢	1¢
1	2	3

$ 1.23

$1.00	10¢	1¢
1	1	2

$ 1.12

$1.00	10¢	1¢
1	2	5

$ 1.25

$1.00	10¢	1¢
1	5	3

$ 1.53

234 (two hundred thirty-four)   Counting money, dollars, dimes and pennies

Correcting Common Errors

Some students may need additional practice with writing dollar amounts. Have them work with partners with 1 dollar, 9 dimes, and 9 pennies. One partner should use the dollar, and some of the dimes and pennies to model an amount, and the other partner should write the amount using a dollar sign and cents point. The partners can change roles and repeat the activity with different amounts.

Enrichment

1. Use a dollar, dimes and pennies to draw 3 amounts of money through $1.99. Write the amounts.
2. Write the number 179 in hundreds, tens and ones and as money.

Teaching page 234

Work through the first problem with the students and then have them complete the page independently.

Extra Credit   *Geometry*

Give each student a square sheet of paper. (The size 8 1/2 by 8 1/2 inches is easy to make from standard paper and easy to work with.) Ask students to name the shape of the paper. (square) Now have them fold the sheet in half and name the shape of the folded paper. (rectangle) Now have them fold the sheet in half the other way. Show the class that this results in a square shape again. Demonstrate how they can fold the paper again, this time diagonally. Explain that the folded paper will look like a triangle when they are done. Now have students open the paper and examine the patterns. Give them crayons and tell them to color the page, taking advantage of the fold patterns. Post the colored patterns on a board and let the class compare them. Some will have outlined triangles, others squares, still others, rectangles. Ask individuals to come up and identify as many shapes as they can.

Comparing, Sequences

pages 235-236

Objectives

To find the greater number to solve problems

To write numbers in sequence through 200

Materials

Hundred square

Ten-strips

Single squares

Mental Math

Which is greater?

1. 85 or 115 (115)
2. $1.00 or $1.19 ($1.19)
3. 162 or 102 (162)
4. $1.00 or 99¢ ($1.00)
5. 145 or 146 (146)

Skill Review

Write on the board:

Before		After
(102)	**103**	(104)
(98)	**99**	(100)

Have students fill in the number before and after each number. Then write on the board:

31	(32)	(33)	**34**
108	(109)	(110)	**111**

Have students write the numbers that come between the 2 numbers.

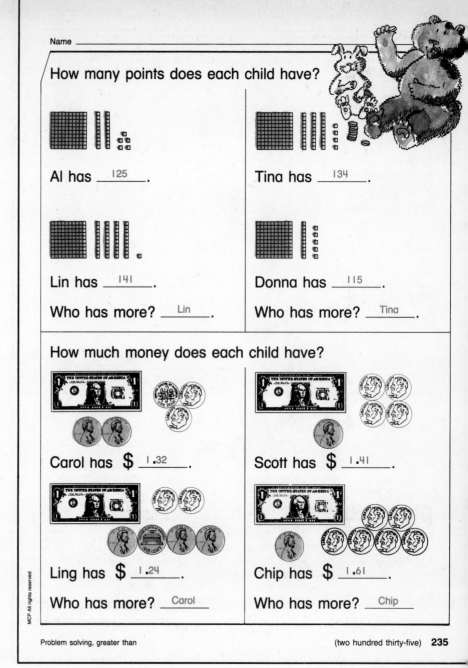

Name _____

How many points does each child have?

Al has ___125___.

Tina has ___134___.

Lin has ___141___.

Donna has ___115___.

Who has more? ___Lin___.

Who has more? ___Tina___.

How much money does each child have?

Carol has $ ___1.32___.

Scott has $ ___1.41___.

Ling has $ ___1.24___.

Chip has $ ___1.61___.

Who has more? ___Carol___

Who has more? ___Chip___

Problem solving, greater than

(two hundred thirty-five) **235**

Teaching page 235

Tell students a story of Damian who has 162 marbles and Donny who has 185 marbles. Ask who has the most marbles. (Donny) Tell more stories for students to compare 2 numbers or 2 money amounts through 200, to find the greater or lesser amounts. Have students write the numbers on the board and circle the number that is greater or less than the other.

Read the first problem to the students. Ask students to tell how many points Al and Lin have and write the numbers. (125, 141) Tell students they are to tell who has more points so they need to compare the hundreds, tens and ones in each number. Ask how many of each in 125 (1, 2, 5) Repeat for 141. (1, 4, 1) Ask which number is more. (141) Ask why 141 is more. (same number of hundreds but 141 has more

tens) Tell students to write the name of the child who has more points. (Lin) Go through each of the next 3 problems similarly with the students.

235

Write the missing numbers before and after.

_28_, 29, _30_

_128_, 129, _130_

_98_, 99, _100_

_198_, 199, _200_

_99_, 100, _101_

_147_, 148, _149_

_168_, 169, _170_

_150_, 151, _152_

_109_, 110, _111_

_118_, 119, _120_

Write the missing numbers.

46, _47_, _48_, 49

146, _147_, _148_, 149

83, _84_, _85_, 86

183, _184_, _185_, 186

129, _130_, _131_, 132

197, _198_, _199_, 200

160, _161_, _162_, 163

103, _104_, _105_, 106

112, _113_, _114_, 115

169, _170_, _171_, 172

FIELD TRIP

Count by tens.

10, 20, _30_, _40_, _50_, _60_, _70_, _80_

_90_, _100_, _110_, _120_, _130_, _140_, _150_

_160_, _170_, _180_, _190_, _200_

236 (two hundred thirty-six)   Writing numbers 100 through 200 in sequence

Teaching page 236

Tell students they are to write the numbers that come before and after the numbers in the center. Have students trace the 28 and 30. Have students work the next problem and then tell students they are to write the missing numbers in the blank. Have students trace the 47 and 48. Have students work another problem and then direct students' attention to the bottom of the page. Tell students they are to write the missing numbers when counting by 10's through 200. Tell students some numbers are given for them to trace as they go along. Tell students to complete the page independently.

Extra Credit *Measurement*

Use a balance scale to teach the concepts of heavier than, lighter than, and weighs the same. Provide a collection of items to be weighed and compared. Number the items. Demonstrate the use of the balance scale. Practice identifying items that are heavier, lighter or weigh the same on the scale. Working individually or in pairs, have students complete this chart for various classroom items:

_____ is heavier than _____

_____ is lighter than _____

_____ weighs the same as _____

236

Chapter Review

pages 237-238

Objectives

To review place value through 200
To maintain skills learned previously
this year

Materials

Hundred-square
Ten-strips
Single squares

Mental Math

Name the next 3 numbers:
1. 101, 102, 103, (104, 105, 106)
2. 94, 96, 98, (100, 102, 104)
3. 100, 110, 120, (130, 140, 150)
4. 85, 90, 95, (100, 105, 110)
5. 176, 177, 178, (179, 180, 181)
6. 90, 100, 110, (120, 130, 140)

Skill Review

Write 2 numbers from 100 through
200 on the board. Ask a student to
tell which number is less and why it
is less. Ask a student to tell which
number is greater and why. Now
have each of 2 students write a
number from 100 through 200 on
the board. Have 1 student tell which
is less and why and the other
student tell which is greater and
why. Repeat so that all students
have turns.

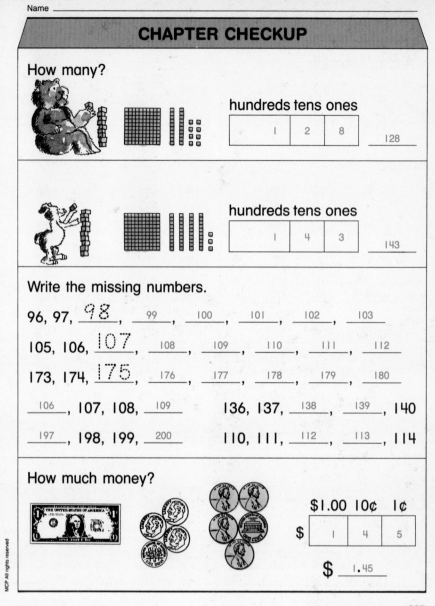

Teaching page 237

Ask students what they are to do in each section of
problems as you read the directions. Have students
complete the page independently.

Add or subtract.

$$\begin{array}{r} 5 \\ +5 \\ \hline 10 \end{array} \qquad \begin{array}{r} 6 \\ +6 \\ \hline 12 \end{array} \qquad \begin{array}{r} 7 \\ +7 \\ \hline 14 \end{array} \qquad \begin{array}{r} 8 \\ +8 \\ \hline 16 \end{array} \qquad \begin{array}{r} 9 \\ +9 \\ \hline 18 \end{array} \qquad \begin{array}{r} 10 \\ -3 \\ \hline 7 \end{array} \qquad \begin{array}{r} 12 \\ -5 \\ \hline 7 \end{array}$$

$$\begin{array}{r} 15 \\ -8 \\ \hline 7 \end{array} \qquad \begin{array}{r} 14 \\ -9 \\ \hline 5 \end{array} \qquad \begin{array}{r} 12 \\ -7 \\ \hline 5 \end{array} \qquad \begin{array}{r} 7 \\ +8 \\ \hline 15 \end{array} \qquad \begin{array}{r} 9 \\ +5 \\ \hline 14 \end{array} \qquad \begin{array}{r} 13 \\ -4 \\ \hline 9 \end{array} \qquad \begin{array}{r} 17 \\ -8 \\ \hline 9 \end{array}$$

Add.

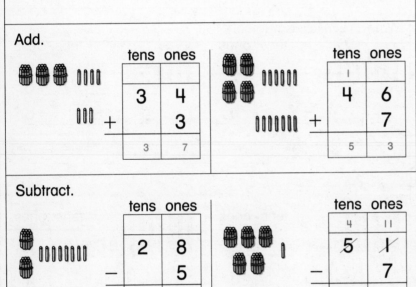

Subtract.

238 (two hundred thirty-eight)   Cumulative review

Enrichment

1. Draw the number 200 in dimes and then in dollars.
2. Draw a street with 4 houses on each side. Number the first house on one side 98 and the last house on that side 104. Number the last 2 houses on the other side 103 and 105. Have a friend fill in the missing house numbers.
3. Write the amounts from $1.16 through $1.21. Draw a dollar bill and coins to show each.

Teaching page 238

Ask students what they are to do in each section of problems. Remind students to look at the sign before working each problem. Tell students to work with the ones column first, in the 4 bottom problems. Tell students a trade may or may not be needed in these problems. Direct students to complete the page independently.

This page reviews addition and subtraction facts and addition and subtraction with some trading.

Adding, Some Trading

pages 239-240

Objective

To review addition of 2- and 1-digit numbers with and without trading for sums through 99

Materials

*Addition fact cards for sums through 18
Ten-sticks
Single squares

Mental Math

Name a fact in the family of:
1. 7 (9 − 2, 3 + 4, 5 + 2, etc.)
2. 9
3. 4
4. 6
5. 8
6. 0
7. 5
8. 3

Skill Review

Show addition facts and have students tell the sum. Have students also tell if the sum is 10 or greater, or if it is less than 10. Have students then tell if a trade for a ten-stick would be needed in an addition problem.

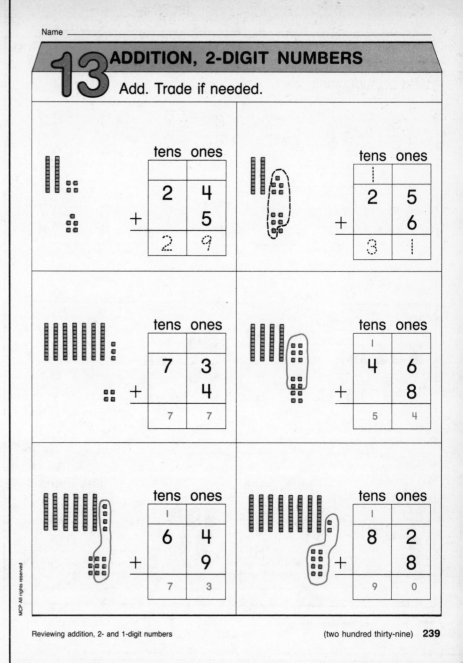

Reviewing addition, 2- and 1-digit numbers

(two hundred thirty-nine) **239**

Teaching page 239

Have students work in pairs to show the numbers 34, 51, 75 and 99, telling how many tens, ones. Have students then show adding 7 to each number. Help students review the trading of 10 single squares for 1 ten-stick. Work each problem on the board to review trading, recording a trade and adding ones first. Also review counting on to find the sums.

Tell students they are to find the sum in each problem. Remind students that some problems do not need a trade. Ask students when they will trade for a ten. (when the sum of the ones is 10 or more) Have 2 students write the first 2 problems on the board and talk through their work. Have students trace the answers and then complete the page independently.

239

Add. Trade if needed.

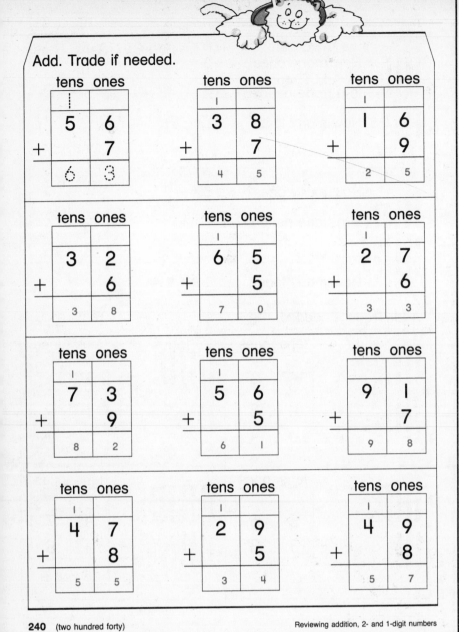

tens	ones
I	
5	6
+	7
6	3

tens	ones
I	
3	8
+	7
4	5

tens	ones
I	
I	6
+	9
2	5

tens	ones
3	2
+	6
3	8

tens	ones
I	
6	5
+	5
7	0

tens	ones
I	
2	7
+	6
3	3

tens	ones
I	
7	3
+	9
8	2

tens	ones
I	
5	6
+	5
6	I

tens	ones
I	
9	I
+	7
9	8

tens	ones
I	
4	7
+	8
5	5

tens	ones
I	
2	9
+	5
3	4

tens	ones
I	
4	9
+	8
5	7

Reviewing addition, 2- and 1-digit numbers

Correcting Common Errors

Watch for students who have difficulty deciding whether or not to trade. Discuss how they trade only when the sum of the ones is 10 or more. Then before they work the problems on page 240, have them look at the ones column and decide whether they will need to trade. If they decide that they will have to trade, have them write YES above the problem; if they decide that they don't, have them write NO. After they have done this for all of the problems, then they can solve them.

Enrichment

1. Work with a friend to sort addition facts into 2 groups, one for sums of 10 or more and one for sums less than 10.
2. Write 2 addition problems through sums of 99 where trading is needed and 2 problems without trading. Trade papers with a friend and work each other's problems.
3. Draw ten-sticks and singles to show the sum of 77 + 7.

Teaching page 240

Tell students that again on this page some problems require a trade and some do not. Note that the visual aids are missing on this page. Allow students to use ten-sticks and single squares if they choose. Have students complete the page independently.

Extra Credit *Geometry*

Remind students that everything has a shape. Have a student stand near the board, on a chair if necessary, and draw a rough silhouette of them with chalk. Ask the student to step away from the drawing and explain that this represents the student's shape. Now have the class break into groups of two or three and supply each of them with a life-size piece of paper. (Newspaper taped together will work, if a long roll of paper is not available.) Ask them to trace each other's shapes on paper. Demonstrate for the class by carefully outlining a student on paper. Remind the class that it will be important for them to lie still while they are being traced. Have the students work together to trace each other. They can fill in the outline, drawing in their faces and clothes.

Two-digit Addition

pages 241-242

Objective

To add 2-digit numbers with and without trading for sums through 99

Materials

Ten-sticks
Single squares

Mental Math

Is a trade for 1 ten needed?
1. 7 ones plus 4 ones (yes)
2. 6 ones plus 0 ones (no)
3. 5 ones plus 5 ones (yes)
4. 15 ones (yes)
5. 5 ones plus 9 ones (yes)
6. 9 ones plus 0 ones (no)
7. 8 ones (no)
8. 17 ones (yes)

Skill Review

Write **34 + 7** vertically on the board and ask students to lay out the numbers with ten-sticks and singles. Go through the problem adding the ones first, questioning if a trade is needed, recording the trade and recording the number of ones and tens in all. Repeat for more problems of 1-digit numbers added to 2-digit numbers. Randomly give problems with and without a trade.

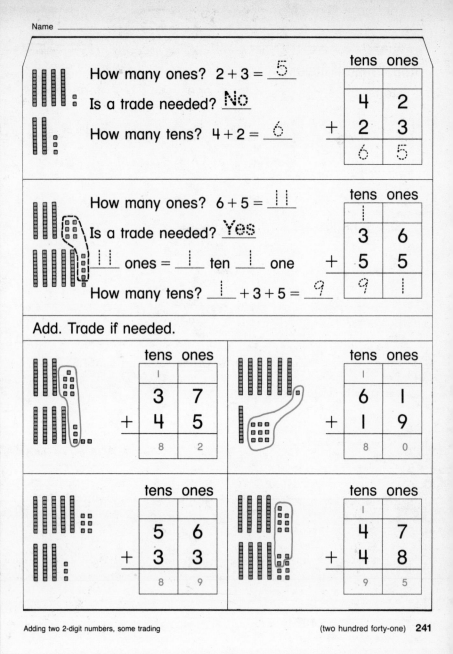

Adding two 2-digit numbers, some trading

Teaching page 241

Have students show 10 with 1 ten-stick. Tell students to lay out 6 more ten-sticks and tell how many tens in all. (7) Ask if there are any ones. (no) Ask students to tell the number. (70) Write the problem vertically on the board and add the ones column and then the tens column, to reach the sum of 70. Repeat for more problems of adding tens with no ones through sums of 90. Now write **23 + 13** vertically on the board and have students lay out ten-sticks and ones for each number. Ask students how many ones. (6) Ask if a trade is needed. (no) Ask students how many tens. (3) Work the problem on the board adding the ones first and then the tens. Repeat for more problems of 2-digit numbers added together for sums through 99. Some problems should require trading and some should not.

Work through the 2 examples with the students to stress adding the ones column first, asking if a trade is needed, recording a trade properly and adding all the tens. Have students trace the answers as you talk through the problems. Have students complete the page independently.

Add. Trade if needed.

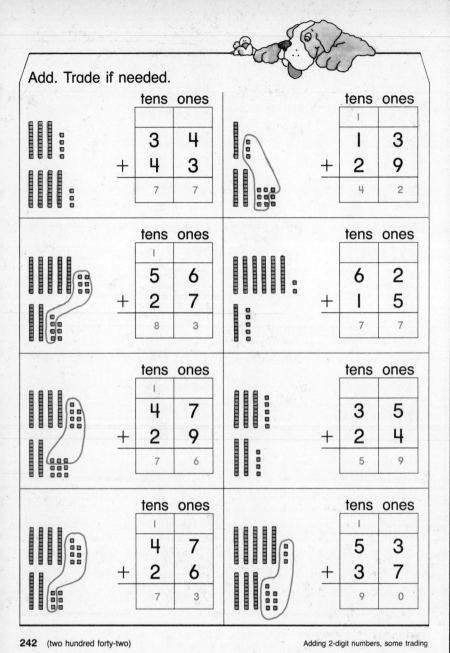

tens	ones
3	4
+ 4	3
7	7

tens	ones
1	
1	3
+ 2	9
4	2

tens	ones
1	
5	6
+ 2	7
8	3

tens	ones
6	2
+ 1	5
7	7

tens	ones
1	
4	7
+ 2	9
7	6

tens	ones
3	5
+ 2	4
5	9

tens	ones
1	
4	7
+ 2	6
7	3

tens	ones
1	
5	3
+ 3	7
9	0

242   (two hundred forty-two)   Adding 2-digit numbers, some trading

Correcting Common Errors

Watch for students who add from left to right. While this will not affect the answer when trading is not required, it will affect it when trading is required and might lead to the following error:

INCORRECT	CORRECT
	1
29	29
+ 13	+ 13
312	42

Have students model the problem with ten-strips and singles. Remind them that they should add toward the plus sign, not away from it.

Enrichment

1. Use the numbers 24, 36, 75 and 48 to write 6 different addition problems. Solve each problem.
2. Write and solve problems where 37 is added to each of the numbers from 50 through 57.

Teaching page 242

Remind students that some problems on this page require trading and some do not. Tell students to add the ones column first, decide if a trade is needed and then proceed to work the problem, being sure to add all the tens. Have students complete the page independently.

Extra Credit   Counting Strategies

Use this activity to help students construct a simple bar graph. Ask several students to name the way they come to school each day. Draw a simple illustration on the board for each type of transportation mentioned, such as school bus, city bus, car or walking. Draw the pictures one below the other in a column. Distribute one, four-inch square of drawing paper to each student. Have students draw a picture of how they most often come to school. As the pictures are completed, attach them to the board in the horizontal row that indicates the kind of transportation used. Study the completed graph with the class. Count the squares in each row. Have students identify the way in which most students come to school and the way in which fewest students come. Point out that each row of squares make a line or bar, and that they have made a bar graph.

Two-digit Addition

pages 243-244

Objectives

To practice adding 2-digit numbers with and without trading for sums through 99
To solve addition problems

Materials

*Clock
Ten-sticks
Single squares

Mental Math

Will you add or subtract?
1. how many in all (add)
2. how many are left (subtract)
3. 4 plus 8 (add)
4. 8 take away 6 (subtract)
5. 10 and 2 more (add)
6. 2 more than 12 (add)
7. 1 less than 9 (subtract)
8. how many altogether (add)

Skill Review

Have students show the following times on the demonstration clock: 12:30, 6:00, 3:30, 4:30, 1:00, 7:30 and 9:00. Have students write the times on the board as they are shown.

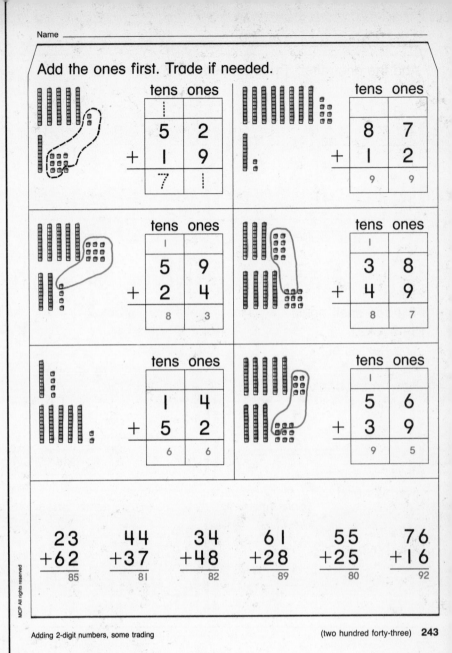

Add the ones first. Trade if needed.

	tens	ones
	5	2
+	1	9
	7	1

	tens	ones
	8	7
+	1	2
	9	9

	tens	ones
	5	9
+	2	4
	8	3

	tens	ones
	3	8
+	4	9
	8	7

	tens	ones
	1	4
+	5	2
	6	6

	tens	ones
	5	6
+	3	9
	9	5

23	44	34	61	55	76
+62	+37	+48	+28	+25	+16
85	81	82	89	80	92

Adding 2-digit numbers, some trading

(two hundred forty-three) **243**

Teaching page 243

Remind students to add the ones column first and determine if a trade is needed. Tell students to complete the page independently.

Tell students that the problems at the bottom of the page are worked in the same way as the problems above.

243

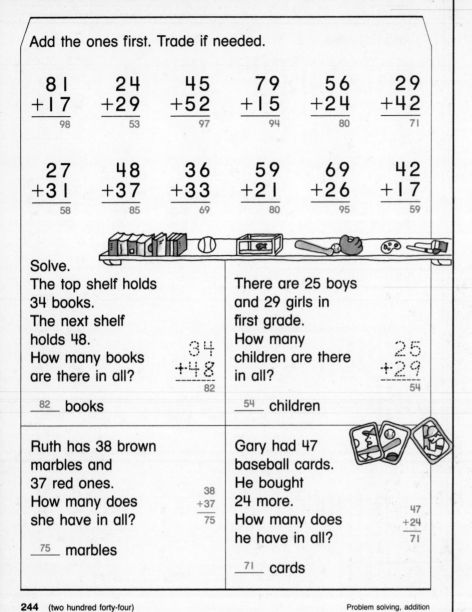

Add the ones first. Trade if needed.

81	24	45	79	56	29
+17	+29	+52	+15	+24	+42
98	53	97	94	80	71

27	48	36	59	69	42
+31	+37	+33	+21	+26	+17
58	85	69	80	95	59

Solve.

The top shelf holds 34 books. The next shelf holds 48. How many books are there in all?

34
+48
‾‾‾‾
82

__82__ books

There are 25 boys and 29 girls in first grade. How many children are there in all?

25
+29
‾‾‾‾
54

__54__ children

Ruth has 38 brown marbles and 37 red ones. How many does she have in all?

38
+37
‾‾‾
75

__75__ marbles

Gary had 47 baseball cards. He bought 24 more. How many does he have in all?

47
+24
‾‾‾
71

__71__ cards

244 (two hundred forty-four)   Problem solving, addition

Correcting Common Errors

Watch for students who regroup but fail to write the renamed ten and thus fail to add it.

INCORRECT	CORRECT
	1
52	52
+29	+29
71	81

Have them work with partners, using place-value materials to model the problems.

Enrichment

1. Tell a story where two 2-digit numbers are to be added together. Have a friend write and solve your problem.
2. Write 4 different addition problems of two 2-digit numbers so that they all have the same sum of 87.
3. Write 4 different addition problems with 44 as one of the addends in each problem. Make all problems have 1 trade. Solve your problems.

Teaching page 244

Tell students a story of Ricky who found 26 rocks and then 14 more. Ask students how to find the total number of rocks in all. (add 26 and 14) Write the problem on the board and have students work through it as you record their answers. Repeat for other stories, with and without trading.

Read each story problem and have students tell how to find the number in all. (add) Tell students to work the problem and record the answer on the line. Now tell students to work the 12 addition problems independently.

Extra Credit   *Measurement*

Collect several containers in different sizes and shapes. Have students use measuring cups to fill each container with rice to determine its volume. Then have a student choose two containers and guess which one has greater volume. The student can then try to prove the answer by filling the containers with rice, and comparing the volumes. Continue by having the student predict the volume of four other containers. Have students record their guesses and measurements on a chart, with three columns titled: container, my guess, measured volume.

Adding Multiples of 10

pages 245-246

Objective

To add multiples of 10 with 1 trade for sums through 180

Materials

Hundred-square
Ten-sticks

Mental Math

Count by 10's from:
1. 80 through 140 (80, 90, . . . 140)
2. 40 through 120
3. 60 through 110
4. 90 through 170
5. 50 through 120
6. 70 through 160
7. 60 through 130

Skill Review

Have students tell a story where the numbers 48 and 23 are to be added together. Have a student write the problem on the board and solve it. Have another student talk through the problem telling the steps to work it. Repeat for other problems of 2 numbers through sums of 99.

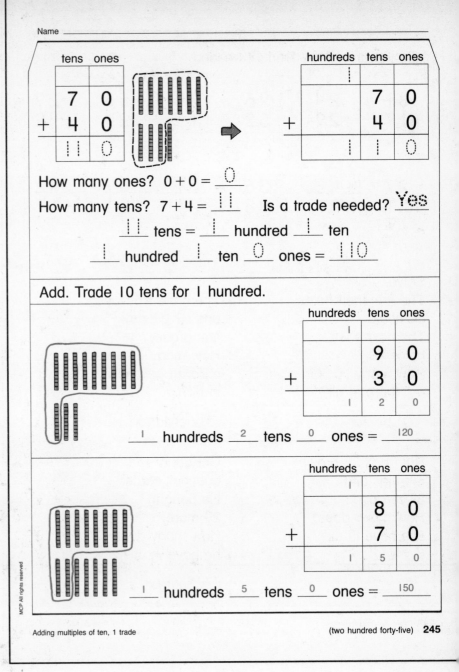

Adding multiples of ten, 1 trade

Teaching page 245

Write **40 + 90** on the board in boxed notation as shown on page 245. Have students show each number with ten sticks. Ask how many ones in all. (0) Ask if a trade is needed. (no) Record the zero in the ones column. Ask how many tens. (13) Ask if there are enough tens to trade for 1 hundred. (yes) Tell students to trade 10 tens for 1 hundred-square. Record the trade on the board. Ask how many tens are left. (3) Record the 3 in the tens column. Ask how many hundreds. (1) Record the 1 in the hundreds column. Ask students to read the number. (130) Ask students to tell how many hundreds, tens and ones are in 130. (1, 3, 0) Repeat for 30 + 80, 70 + 20 and 60 + 90. Note the problem 70 + 20 does not require a trade. Go through the example problem with the students. Remind students there may not always be enough tens

to trade for 1 hundred. Have students complete the page independently.

245

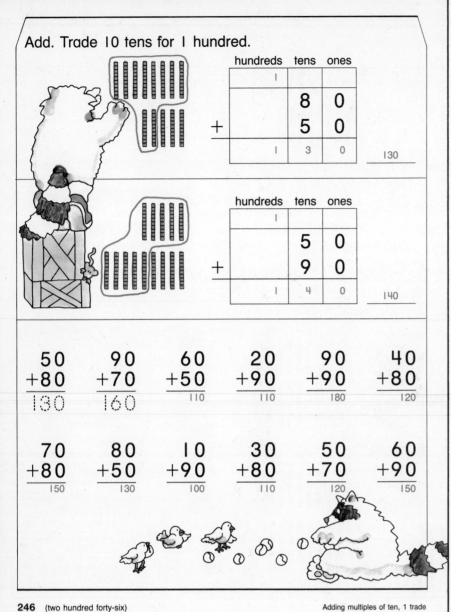

Add. Trade 10 tens for 1 hundred.

hundreds	tens	ones
1		
	8	0
+	5	0
1	3	0

130

hundreds	tens	ones
1		
	5	0
+	9	0
1	4	0

140

50 +80 130	90 +70 160	60 +50 110	20 +90 110	90 +90 180	40 +80 120
70 +80 150	80 +50 130	10 +90 100	30 +80 110	50 +70 120	60 +90 150

246 (two hundred forty-six)   Adding multiples of ten, 1 trade

Correcting Common Errors

Some students may get confused when the sum in the tens column is 10 or more and try to write both digits in the tens column. Have them work with partners and practice writing the following numbers of tens as hundreds and tens.

12 tens (1 hundred 2 tens)
19 tens (1 hundred 9 tens)
15 tens (1 hundred 5 tens)
10 tens (1 hundred 0 tens)

Enrichment

1. Write the numbers by 10's from 10 through 200.
2. Play "Concentration" with cards numbered by 10's from 100 through 200, and cards labeled 10 tens, 11 tens, 12 tens through 20 tens. Place all cards face down and player turns over 2 cards. A match wins another turn.

Teaching page 246

Talk through the first 2 problems to review with students the trading of 10 tens for 1 hundred. Remind students that some problems on this page do not require a trade of 10 tens for 1 hundred. Have students complete the page. Remind them that the last 12 problems are worked the same way as the ones above.

Extra Credit *Applications*

Ask a volunteer to explain why we go to the Post Office. (to mail letters or packages) Equip a table as a classroom post office. Have students design a class stamp, reproduce it and put a supply in your post office. You will also need a simple scale for weighing parcels and letters. Allow students to write letters to each other. Provide shoe boxes and assorted objects that students can wrap as parcels to mail. Appoint two students to work as clerks in the post office, exchanging students' play money for stamps. Show them how to weigh the parcels and explain that students will or every ounce the parcel weighs. Point out that heavy letters may also need more than one stamp. Allow them to paste their stamps on the letters and have them delivered by one of the students designated as mail carrier. This activity would be especially good around Valentine's Day.

246

Adding, Two Trades

pages 247-248

Objective

To add 2-digit numbers with 1 or 2 trades for sums to 200

Materials

Hundred-square
Ten-sticks
Single squares

Mental Math

Is a trade for 1 hundred needed?
1. 7 tens (no)
2. 11 tens (yes)
3. 18 tens (yes)
4. 4 tens (no)
5. 10 tens (yes)
6. 9 tens (no)

Skill Review

Write **9 ones** on the board. Ask students if a trade is needed when the sum of the ones column is 9 ones. (no) Now write **12 tens** and ask students if a trade for 1 hundred is needed. (yes) Write more numbers of tens or ones on the board and ask if a trade is needed for each. When students are comfortable with this exercise, have students tell if a trade is needed and what the 10 ones or 10 tens are to be traded for. (10 ones for 1 ten, 10 tens for 1 hundred)

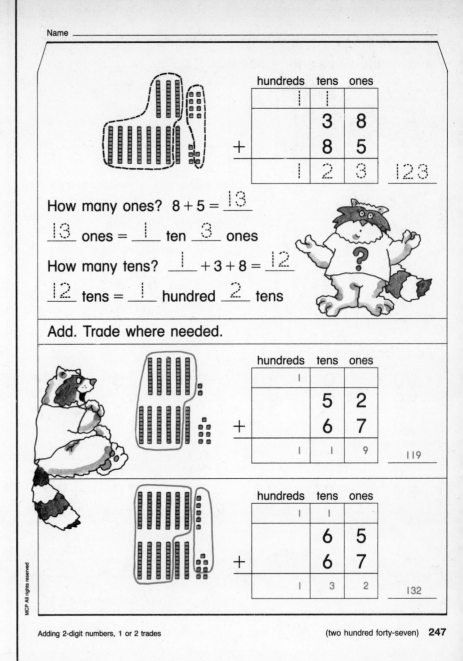

Name _____

hundreds	tens	ones	
1	1		
	3	8	
+	8	5	
1	2	3	123

How many ones? 8 + 5 = 13

13 ones = 1 ten 3 ones

How many tens? 1 + 3 + 8 = 12

12 tens = 1 hundred 2 tens

Add. Trade where needed.

hundreds	tens	ones	
1			
	5	2	
+	6	7	
1	1	9	119

hundreds	tens	ones	
1	1		
	6	5	
+	6	7	
1	3	2	132

Adding 2-digit numbers, 1 or 2 trades

(two hundred forty-seven) **247**

Teaching page 247

Write **46 + 95** in boxed notation on the board. Ask students how many ones. (11) Ask if a trade is needed. (yes) Show the trade on the board and ask how many ones are left. (1) Ask students how many tens in all. (14) Ask if a trade for a hundred is needed. (yes) Show the trade on the board and ask how many tens are left. (4) Ask students how many hundreds. (1) Ask students how many hundreds, tens and ones in the answer. (1,4,1) Have students read the number. Repeat for other addition problems having 1 trade or 2 trades through sums of 200. Work through the sample problem with the students. Have students record the answer to the problem on the line. Have students work the next 2 problems independently.

247

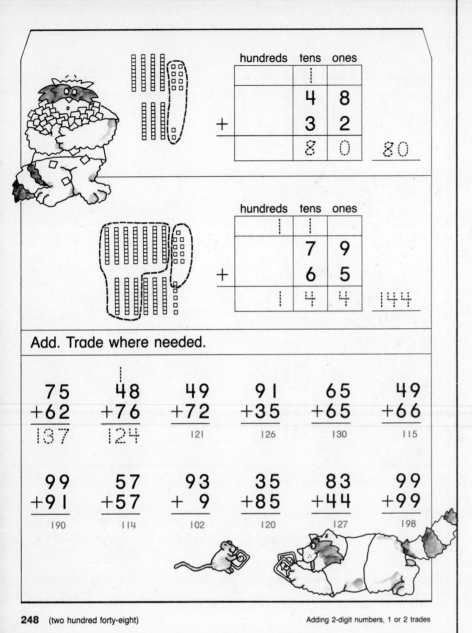

hundreds	tens	ones
	1	
	4	8
+	3	2
	8	0

80

hundreds	tens	ones
1	1	
	7	9
+	6	5
1	4	4

144

Add. Trade where needed.

```
  75      48      49      91      65      49
 +62     +76     +72     +35     +65     +66
 137     124     121     126     130     115

  99      57      93      35      83      99
 +91     +57     + 9     +85     +44     +99
 190     114     102     120     127     198
```

Correcting Common Errors

Some students may trade incorrectly because they reverse the tens and ones or hundreds and tens or both.

INCORRECT   CORRECT
```
   5 2               1 1
   74                 74
  +68                +68
  511                142
```

Have students work with partners and use place-value materials to model the problem.

Enrichment

1. Write 4 different addition problems using the numbers 26, 43, 79, 57 and 88. Trade with a friend to write the sums.
2. Name the addition facts that would, and those that would not, require a trade in the tens column.

Teaching page 248

Go through the two sample problems with students and have them trace the dotted lines and numbers in the problems and on the lines, to record their answers. Remind students that some problems on this page may not have 2 trades. Remind students to add the ones first, then the tens and then the hundreds column. Have students complete the page independently.

Extra Credit *Applications*

To help your students become more aware of their environment, ask them to find and list all the geometric shapes they can find in their classroom or outdoors. Divide a sheet of paper into four sections. Label each section squares, circles, triangles, rectangles. How many squares can they find (books, windows)? How many circles (clocks, manhole covers)? This activity can be carried out over a week to increase student awareness of their surroundings.

Adding, Some Trading

pages 249-250

Objectives

To practice adding 2-digit numbers for sums to 200

To add 2-digit numbers to solve problems

Materials

Hundred-square
Ten-sticks
Single squares

Mental Math

Is a trade needed?
1. 9 ones plus 0 ones (no)
2. 6 tens plus 4 tens (yes)
3. 7 ones plus 9 ones (yes)
4. 6 ones plus 6 ones (yes)
5. 2 tens plus 3 tens (no)
6. 5 ones plus 4 ones (no)
7. 8 tens plus 7 tens (yes)

Skill Review

Write **172** on the board and have students tell how many hundreds, tens and ones. (1,7,2) Repeat for more 2- and 3-digit numbers through 200. Now have a student write a number from 100 through 200 on the board and ask a friend to tell the number of hundreds, tens and ones. Repeat for more students to participate.

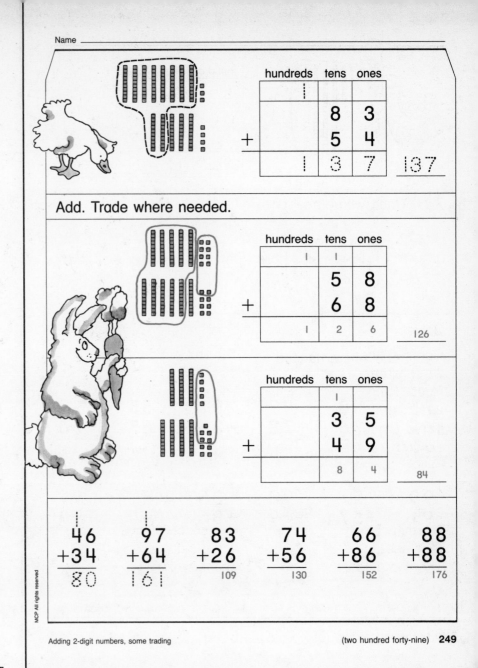

Name _____

Add. Trade where needed.

hundreds	tens	ones
	8	3
+ 5	4	

137

hundreds	tens	ones
1	1	
	5	8
+ 6	8	

126

hundreds	tens	ones
	1	
	3	5
+ 4	9	

84

```
  46      97      83      74      66      88
 +34     +64     +26     +56     +86     +88
 ─────   ─────   ─────   ─────   ─────   ─────
  80     161      109     130     152     176
```

Adding 2-digit numbers, some trading

(two hundred forty-nine) **249**

Teaching page 249

Go through the example with the students to review adding ones first, then the tens column and then recording the hundreds. Continue to ask if a trade is needed after adding each column, and remind students that some of the problems on this page have 1 trade, some have 2 trades and some have no trades. Also remind students to record their answers on the lines. Have students complete the page independently.

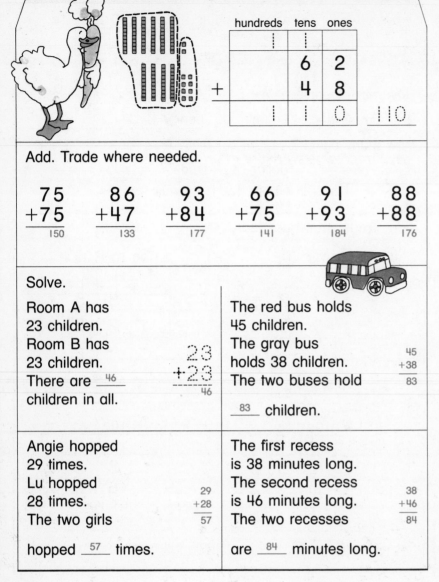

hundreds	tens	ones
	6	2
+	4	8
1	1	0

110

Add. Trade where needed.

75	86	93	66	91	88
+75	+47	+84	+75	+93	+88
150	133	177	141	184	176

Solve.

Room A has
23 children.
Room B has
23 children.
There are __46__
children in all.

23
+23
46

The red bus holds
45 children.
The gray bus
holds 38 children.
The two buses hold

45
+38
83

__83__ children.

Angie hopped
29 times.
Lu hopped
28 times.
The two girls

29
+28
57

hopped __57__ times.

The first recess
is 38 minutes long.
The second recess
is 46 minutes long.
The two recesses

38
+46
84

are __84__ minutes long.

250 (two hundred fifty)   Adding 2-digit numbers, problem solving

Adding Money, Dollars

pages 251-252

Objectives

To add dollars, dimes and pennies for sums to $2.00
To solve money problems

Materials

Hundred-square
Ten-sticks
Single squares
Dollar, dimes, pennies

Mental Math

How many dimes would make:
1. 80¢ (8)
2. 120¢ (12)
3. 180¢ (18)
4. 110¢ (11)
5. 150¢ (15)
6. 50¢ (5)

Skill Review

Write **120¢** on the board. Ask students how many dimes in 120. (12) Ask if there are enough dimes to trade for 1 dollar. (yes) Ask students how many dimes are left. (2) Write **120¢ = $1.20** on the board and tell students 120 cents is the same as 12 dimes and no pennies or 1 dollar and 2 dimes. Repeat for 176¢, 159¢, 119¢, 184¢ and 167¢.

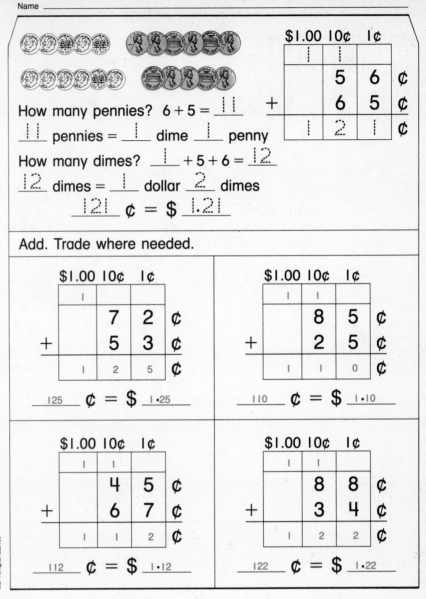

How many pennies? 6 + 5 = 11
11 pennies = 1 dime 1 penny
How many dimes? 1 + 5 + 6 = 12
12 dimes = 1 dollar 2 dimes
121 ¢ = $ 1.21

	$1.00	10¢	1¢	
	1	1		
		5	6	¢
+		6	5	¢
	1	2	1	¢

Add. Trade where needed.

	$1.00	10¢	1¢	
	1			
		7	2	¢
+		5	3	¢
	1	2	5	¢

125 ¢ = $ 1.25

	$1.00	10¢	1¢	
	1	1		
		8	5	¢
+		2	5	¢
	1	1	0	¢

110 ¢ = $ 1.10

	$1.00	10¢	1¢	
	1	1		
		4	5	¢
+		6	7	¢
	1	1	2	¢

112 ¢ = $ 1.12

	$1.00	10¢	1¢	
	1	1		
		8	8	¢
+		3	4	¢
	1	2	2	¢

122 ¢ = $ 1.22

Adding money, dollars, dimes, and pennies

(two hundred fifty-one) **251**

MCP All rights reserved

Teaching page 251

Write **34 + 85** in boxed notation on the board. Ask students how many ones. (9) Record the 9. Ask if a trade is needed. (no) Ask how many tens. (11) Ask if a trade is needed. (yes) Record the trade and ask students how many tens are left. (1) Record the 1 and ask how many hundreds. (1) Record the 1 in hundreds place and ask students to read the answer. (119) Write **34¢ + 85¢** in boxed notation on the board. Write headings of **Dollars, Dimes** and **Pennies.** Ask students to tell how this problem differs from the first problem. (cent signs) Proceed to talk through the problem with the students and record the answers. Write **119¢** on the board and ask students how this would be written in dollars and cents. ($1.19) Review with the students that 11 dimes = 1 dollar and 1 dime.

Work through the sample problem with the students, have them tell the answers and trace the numbers. Have students complete the next 4 problems independently.

251

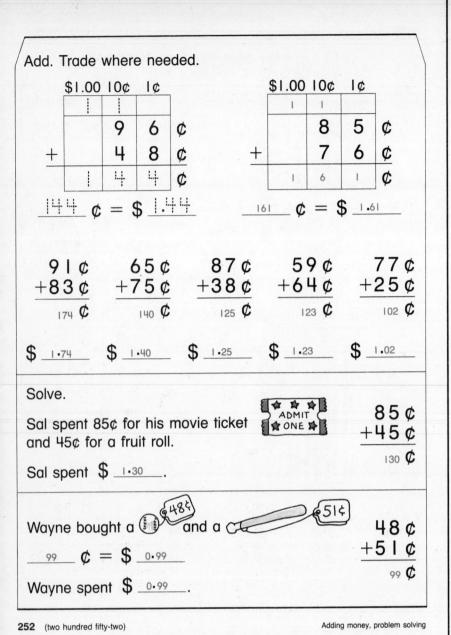

Add. Trade where needed.

	$1.00	10¢	1¢	
	I	I		
		9	6	¢
+		4	8	¢
	I	4	4	¢

144 ¢ = $ 1.44

	$1.00	10¢	1¢	
	I	I		
		8	5	¢
+		7	6	¢
	I	6	I	¢

161 ¢ = $ 1.61

91¢	65¢	87¢	59¢	77¢
+83¢	+75¢	+38¢	+64¢	+25¢
174 ¢	140 ¢	125 ¢	123 ¢	102 ¢

$ 1.74 $ 1.40 $ 1.25 $ 1.23 $ 1.02

Solve.

Sal spent 85¢ for his movie ticket and 45¢ for a fruit roll.

ADMIT ONE

85 ¢
+45 ¢
130 ¢

Sal spent $ 1.30 .

Wayne bought a ⚾ 48¢ and a 🏏 51¢

99 ¢ = $ 0.99

48 ¢
+51 ¢
99 ¢

Wayne spent $ 0.99 .

Adding money, problem solving

Correcting Common Errors

Watch for students who have difficulty adding amounts of money. Discuss with them how the procedure is the same as with adding whole numbers. However, they use a ¢ sign or a $ sign and cents point in the answer. If they continue to have difficulty, have them use dollars, dimes, and pennies to model the problems.

Enrichment

1. Draw a dollar bill and coins to show 4 amounts from $1.50 to $1.99.
2. Draw a dollar bill and coins to show your money if you had 116 pennies and Dad gave you 88 more.

Teaching page 252

Tell students to work the 7 money problems independently. Then read the first story problem and have students discuss and decide how to solve it. (add) Have students work the problem independently. Repeat for the second story problem. Remind the students to write the answers on the answer line.

Extra Credit   *Applications*

Prepare a waterproof table. Put out a dishpan full of water, a cup measure and three other containers. Hold up the cup measure. Tell the students that they are to see how many cups full of water can be emptied into the other containers. Demonstrate with the unit measure and a container other than those to be used in the activity. Show how they can fill the measure repeatedly and empty it into the larger container.

Have students complete a chart that shows how many cups were emptied into each different container. Let students work at the table in small groups throughout the day.

Adding Three Addends

pages 253-254

Objective

To add three 2-digit numbers with or without trading

Materials

Hundred-square
Ten-sticks
Single squares

Mental Math

Name the number that is:
1. 2 more than 91 (93)
2. 7 tens and 14 ones (84)
3. $1.00 plus 2 dimes ($1.20)
4. 80 take away 1 (79)
5. 24 and 6 more (30)
6. 4 dimes and 15 pennies (55¢)
7. before 200 (199)
8. 7 tens and 7 ones (77)

Skill Review

Write **7 + 2 + 8** vertically on the board. Review with the students how to add 7 + 2 to equal 9 and then add 9 + 8 to equal 17. Repeat for more addition problems of three 1-digit numbers.

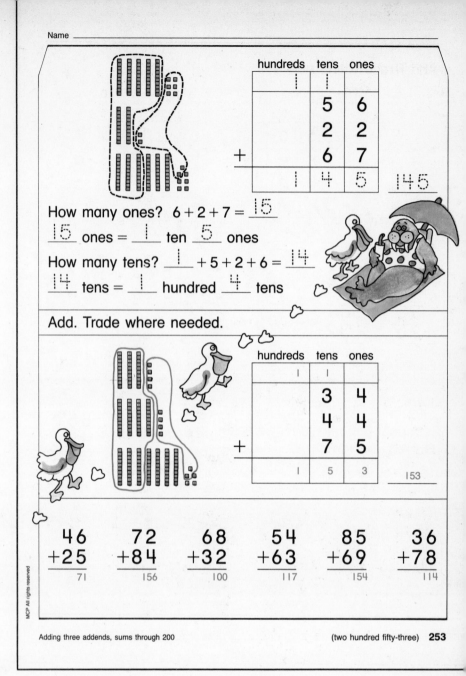

Name _____

	hundreds	tens	ones	
	1	1		
		5	6	
		2	2	
+		6	7	
	1	4	5	145

How many ones? 6 + 2 + 7 = 15
15 ones = 1 ten 5 ones
How many tens? 1 + 5 + 2 + 6 = 14
14 tens = 1 hundred 4 tens

Add. Trade where needed.

	hundreds	tens	ones	
	1	1		
		3	4	
		4	4	
+		7	5	
	1	5	3	153

46	72	68	54	85	36
+25	+84	+32	+63	+69	+78
71	156	100	117	154	114

Adding three addends, sums through 200   (two hundred fifty-three) **253**

Teaching page 253

Write **72 + 69** in boxed notation on the board and have students talk through the problem as you record the numbers. Now write **72 + 69 + 17** in boxed notation. Ask students what is different in this problem from the first. (one more addend) Have students add the ones as you say, "2 plus 9 equals (11) and 11 plus 7 equals (18)." Ask students how many ones in all. (18) Ask if a trade is needed. (yes) Record the trade and ask students how many ones are left. (8) Record the 8 ones and have students add the tens as you say, "1 plus 7 equals (8) and 8 plus 6 equals (14) and 14 plus 1 equals (15)." Ask if a trade is needed. (yes) Record the trade and ask students how many tens are left. (5) Record the 5 tens and ask students how many hundreds. (1) Record the 1 hundred and ask students to read the sum. (158) Repeat the procedure for 44 +

18 + 63 and 29 + 98 + 70.

Go through the example with the students and then help them with the next problem. Have students work the remaining problems independently.

253

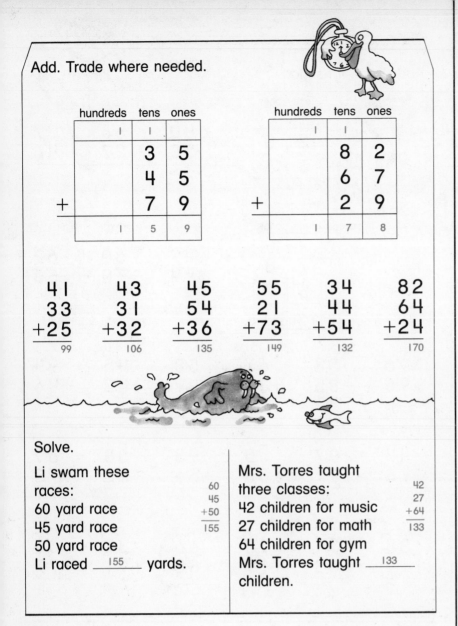

Add. Trade where needed.

hundreds	tens	ones
I	I	
	3	5
	4	5
+	7	9
I	5	9

hundreds	tens	ones
I	I	
	8	2
	6	7
+	2	9
I	7	8

```
  41      43      45      55      34      82
  33      31      54      21      44      64
 +25     +32     +36     +73     +54     +24
 ───     ───     ───     ───     ───     ───
  99      106     135     149     132     170
```

Solve.

Li swam these
races:
60 yard race
45 yard race
50 yard race

```
  60
  45
 +50
 ───
 155
```

Li raced __155__ yards.

Mrs. Torres taught
three classes:
42 children for music
27 children for math
64 children for gym

```
  42
  27
 +64
 ───
 133
```

Mrs. Torres taught __133__
children.

Adding three addends, sums through 200

Correcting Common Errors

Watch for students who have difficulty with column addition because they cannot remember the sum of the first two addends in a column to add to the third addend. Correct by having them write the sum of the first two addends next to these numbers and then use this sum to add to the third addend.

Enrichment

1. Write and solve an addition problem where 44 is added to itself 2 more times.
2. Use the numbers 46, 34, 18 and 12 to write 2 addition problems with 3 addends. Solve your problems.
3. Figure the total number of desks in 3 rooms in your school.

Teaching page 254

Help students with the first two problems at the top of page. Have students work the next 6 problems independently. Then read each of the story problems for students to write the sign and the problem, and work it. Have students record their answer to complete the sentence under each problem.

Extra Credit *Measurement*

Take a fifteen minute field trip to the cafeteria. Have cafeteria workers discuss the importance of using correct weights and measures in their work. Have them show students a sample recipe they use and the proportion of ingredients. Then the students can borrow a collection of measuring equipment to bring back to the classroom. Have them compare the items and arrange them from the smallest unit of measure to the largest.

Sums through 200

pages 255-256

Objectives

To practice addition of 2-digit numbers with and without trading
To solve addition problems

Materials

Hundred-square
Ten-sticks
Single squares

Mental Math

Tell where the clock hands are for:
1. 6:30 (long on 6, short between 6 and 7)
2. 5:00 (long on 12, short on 5)
3. 12:00 (both on 12)
4. 3:00 (long 12, short on 3)
5. 8:30 (long on 6, short between 8 and 9)
6. 2:30 (long on 6, short between 2 and 3)
7. 11:00 (long on 12, short on 11)

Skill Review

Write **79 − 9** on the board. Ask a student to work the problem. Give more subtraction problems of 2-digit numbers minus 1-digit numbers. Give some problems with and without 1 trade for minuends through 99.

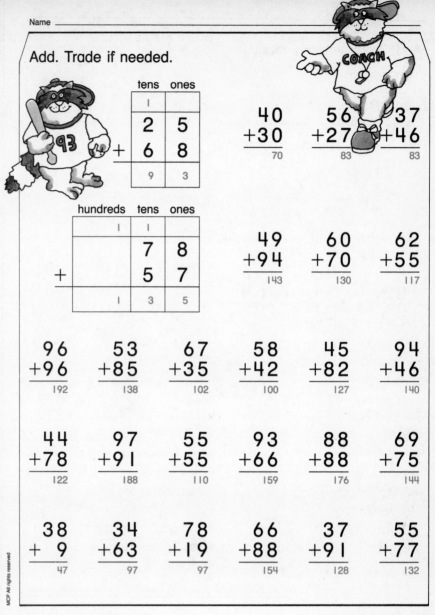

Name _____

Add. Trade if needed.

tens	ones
1	
2	5
6	8
9	3

$$\begin{array}{r} 40 \\ +30 \\ \hline 70 \end{array} \quad \begin{array}{r} 56 \\ +27 \\ \hline 83 \end{array} \quad \begin{array}{r} 37 \\ +46 \\ \hline 83 \end{array}$$

hundreds	tens	ones
1	1	
	7	8
	5	7
1	3	5

$$\begin{array}{r} 49 \\ +94 \\ \hline 143 \end{array} \quad \begin{array}{r} 60 \\ +70 \\ \hline 130 \end{array} \quad \begin{array}{r} 62 \\ +55 \\ \hline 117 \end{array}$$

$$\begin{array}{r} 96 \\ +96 \\ \hline 192 \end{array} \quad \begin{array}{r} 53 \\ +85 \\ \hline 138 \end{array} \quad \begin{array}{r} 67 \\ +35 \\ \hline 102 \end{array} \quad \begin{array}{r} 58 \\ +42 \\ \hline 100 \end{array} \quad \begin{array}{r} 45 \\ +82 \\ \hline 127 \end{array} \quad \begin{array}{r} 94 \\ +46 \\ \hline 140 \end{array}$$

$$\begin{array}{r} 44 \\ +78 \\ \hline 122 \end{array} \quad \begin{array}{r} 97 \\ +91 \\ \hline 188 \end{array} \quad \begin{array}{r} 55 \\ +55 \\ \hline 110 \end{array} \quad \begin{array}{r} 93 \\ +66 \\ \hline 159 \end{array} \quad \begin{array}{r} 88 \\ +88 \\ \hline 176 \end{array} \quad \begin{array}{r} 69 \\ +75 \\ \hline 144 \end{array}$$

$$\begin{array}{r} 38 \\ + 9 \\ \hline 47 \end{array} \quad \begin{array}{r} 34 \\ +63 \\ \hline 97 \end{array} \quad \begin{array}{r} 78 \\ +19 \\ \hline 97 \end{array} \quad \begin{array}{r} 66 \\ +88 \\ \hline 154 \end{array} \quad \begin{array}{r} 37 \\ +91 \\ \hline 128 \end{array} \quad \begin{array}{r} 55 \\ +77 \\ \hline 132 \end{array}$$

Practice, sums through 200   (two hundred fifty-five) **255**

Teaching page 255

Allow students to use manipulatives as they work independently to complete this page.

Solve.

Ellen bought 🪙 *53¢* and ✂ *75¢*.

Ellen spent __128__ ¢ or $ __1.28__.

$$\begin{array}{r} 53¢ \\ +75¢ \\ \hline 128¢ \end{array}$$

Rita has 48 marbles. Wanda has 67 marbles. How many in all?

They have __115__ marbles in all.

$$\begin{array}{r} 48 \\ +67 \\ \hline 115 \end{array}$$

Craig bought a 🚗 *59¢* and a 🚗 *85¢*.
How much did Craig spend?

Craig spent __144__ ¢ or $ __1.44__.

$$\begin{array}{r} 59¢ \\ +85¢ \\ \hline 144¢ \end{array}$$

Lon hopped 37 times on his left foot. He hopped 63 times on his right foot. How many times did Lon hop?

$$\begin{array}{r} 37 \\ +63 \\ \hline 100 \end{array}$$

Lon hopped __100__ times.

Adam jumped a rope 57 times. Then he jumped 65 more times. Adam jumped rope

$$\begin{array}{r} 57 \\ +65 \\ \hline 122 \end{array}$$

__122__ times.

Royce likes to read.
  Monday–43 minutes
  Tuesday–45 minutes
  Wednesday–37 minutes

Royce read for __125__ minutes.

$$\begin{array}{r} 43 \\ 45 \\ +37 \\ \hline 125 \end{array}$$

256 (two hundred fifty-six)   Problem solving, sums through 200

Enrichment

1. Figure the total number of minutes in your lunch periods on Monday, Tuesday and Wednesday.
2. Arrange the numbers 38, 53 and 40 in order from least to greatest and find their sum.
3. Tell a story about your wanting to buy items costing 93¢ and 89¢ but finding you haven't enough money for both. Write and solve the problem to tell how much you would need to buy both items.

Teaching page 256

Tell students a story of buying a dog treat for 79¢ and a can of cat food for 33¢. Encourage students to come up with a plan of how to find the total amount of money spent. Encourage discussion among the students toward reaching a decision to add the 2 amounts. Work through the problem with the students and then have them create story problems for the class to solve. If students want to include 3 addends in their stories, tell them to make their numbers less than 66 so that the sum will be under 200.

Read the first problem with the students and help them decide on a plan for finding the solution. Allow students to then work the remainder of the problem and trace their answers. Now read through each problem with the students to discuss their plan for solution. Have students complete the problems. Offer reading assistance where necessary.

Extra Credit   *Measurement*

Have students make this simple snack by working in groups. Provide each group with the ingredients, a set of measuring cups, spoons and mixing bowls. Let each group make one recipe and share it among themselves.

1¼ c raisins
1½ c mixed nuts
1 c shelled sunflower seeds
1¾ c shredded coconut

Ask students to invent recipes of their own by changing one or two of the ingredients.

Chapter Review

pages 257-258

Objectives

To review addition of 2-digit numbers with and without trading
To maintain skills learned previously this year

Materials

*Clock
Hundred-square
Ten-sticks
Singles

Mental Math

Name the number that is:
1. 38 plus 2 (40)
2. 16 minus 4 (12)
3. 1 more than 99 (100)
4. 1 less than 200 (199)
5. 39 take away 9 (30)
6. 10 plus 40 (50)
7. 100 plus 80 plus 9 (189)

Skill Review

Have students show times on the hour and half-hour and then write those times. Then have students show and write the time that is 30 minutes later than 6:00, 30 minutes later than 4:30, etc.

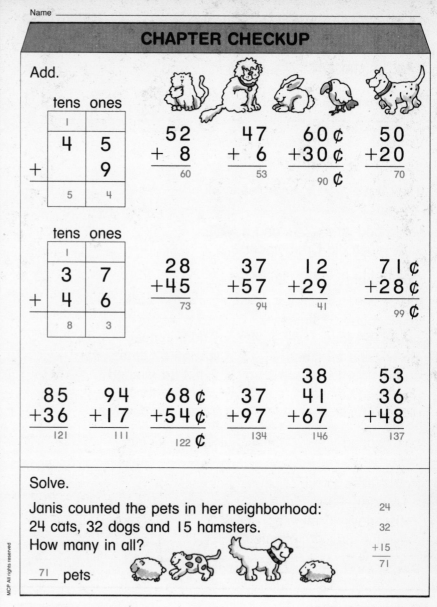

CHAPTER CHECKUP

Add.

tens	ones
1	
4	5
+	9
5	4

$$\begin{array}{r} 52 \\ +\ 8 \\ \hline 60 \end{array}$$

$$\begin{array}{r} 47 \\ +\ 6 \\ \hline 53 \end{array}$$

$$\begin{array}{r} 60¢ \\ +30¢ \\ \hline 90¢ \end{array}$$

$$\begin{array}{r} 50 \\ +20 \\ \hline 70 \end{array}$$

tens	ones
1	
3	7
+ 4	6
8	3

$$\begin{array}{r} 28 \\ +45 \\ \hline 73 \end{array}$$

$$\begin{array}{r} 37 \\ +57 \\ \hline 94 \end{array}$$

$$\begin{array}{r} 12 \\ +29 \\ \hline 41 \end{array}$$

$$\begin{array}{r} 71¢ \\ +28¢ \\ \hline 99¢ \end{array}$$

$$\begin{array}{r} 85 \\ +36 \\ \hline 121 \end{array}$$

$$\begin{array}{r} 94 \\ +17 \\ \hline 111 \end{array}$$

$$\begin{array}{r} 68¢ \\ +54¢ \\ \hline 122¢ \end{array}$$

$$\begin{array}{r} 37 \\ +97 \\ \hline 134 \end{array}$$

$$\begin{array}{r} 38 \\ 41 \\ +67 \\ \hline 146 \end{array}$$

$$\begin{array}{r} 53 \\ 36 \\ +48 \\ \hline 137 \end{array}$$

Solve.

Janis counted the pets in her neighborhood: 24 cats, 32 dogs and 15 hamsters. How many in all?

$$\begin{array}{r} 24 \\ 32 \\ +15 \\ \hline 71 \end{array}$$

_71_ pets

Chapter review   (two hundred fifty-seven) **257**

Teaching page 257

Ask students to look at the sign in each of the first 5 problems and tell what they are to do. (add) Tell students they are to decide how to solve the story problem and to write a + or − sign and solve it. Remind students they are to record the answer to the story problem on the line. Offer reading assistance where needed.

257

ROUNDUP REVIEW

Add or subtract.

| 5
+6
——
11 | 3
+8
——
11 | 9
−4
——
5 | 12
− 5
——
7 | 13
− 7
——
6 | 7
+8
——
15 | 14
− 6
——
8 |

| 15
− 6
——
9 | 8
+8
——
16 | 9
+8
——
17 | 13
− 4
——
9 | 8
−3
——
5 | 7
+7
——
14 | 4
+9
——
13 |

Write the missing number.

105, 106, _107_, _108_, _109_, _110_, _111_, _112_

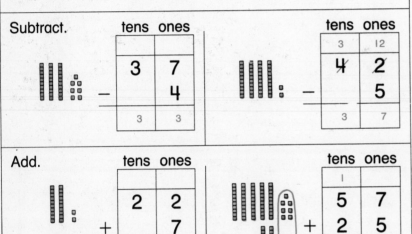

Subtract.

tens	ones
3	7
	4
3	3

3	12
4̶	2̶
	5
3	7

Add.

tens	ones
2	2
	7
2	9

1	
5	7
2	5
8	2

Cumulative review

Enrichment

1. Write all the numbers between 100 and 200 that have a 9 in them.
2. Write and solve the problem that shows the difference between your age and your dad's.
3. Write 2 addition problems with no trading and 2 addition problems with trading.

Teaching page 258

Ask students what they are to do in each section on this page. Remind students to look at the sign in each problem before working it. Have students complete the page independently.

This page reviews addition and subtraction facts, sequencing and addition and subtracting with some trading.

258

Squares and Triangles

pages 259-260

Objective

To recognize squares and triangles

Materials

*Large square and triangle
Triangle and square per pair of students
Crayons

Mental Math

Name the number that:
1. comes after 175 (176)
2. is 4 more than 16 (20)
3. is 1 dollar and 1 dime ($1.10)
4. comes after 10, 20, 30 (40)
5. comes after 6, 8, 10, 12, (14)
6. is 2 less than 10 (8)
7. comes before 130 (129)
8. tells your age

Skill Review

Write **64 + 18** on the board and ask a student to solve the problem. Now write **82 − 8** and have a student solve this problem. Continue for addition problems for sums through 200, and subtraction problems of 2-digit minus 1-digit numbers with minuends through 99.

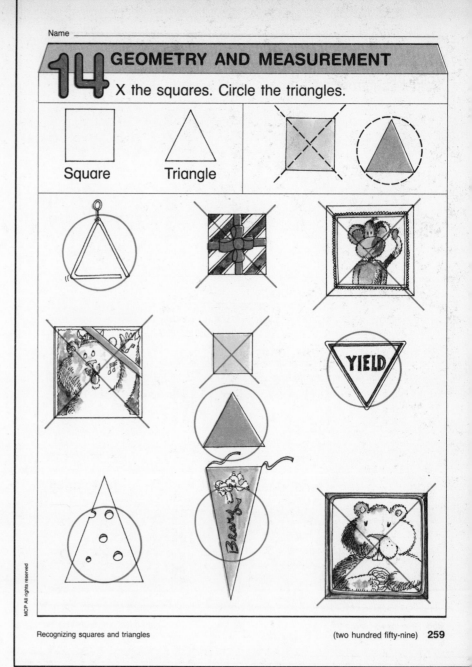

14 GEOMETRY AND MEASUREMENT

X the squares. Circle the triangles.

Square   Triangle

Recognizing squares and triangles   (two hundred fifty-nine) **259**

Teaching page 259

Give squares and triangles of different sizes to each pair of students. Show the demonstration square. Tell students this shape is called a **square** and write the word on the board. Ask students how many sides the square has. (4) Ask how many corners are in a square. (4) Tell students to hold up their squares. Tell students to compare their squares with those held up by other pairs of students. Ask if all the squares are the same shape. (yes) Ask if all the squares have 4 corners and 4 sides. (yes, yes) Tell students all squares have 4 sides that are the same length. Have 16 students stand together to form a square with 4 on each side. Have 12 students form a square and then 8 students do the same. Show the demonstration triangle and ask how many sides and corners. (3, 3) Write **triangle** on the board and tell students a shape with 3 sides and 3

corners is called a triangle. Have students hold up their triangles and compare them to see that all triangles have 3 sides and 3 corners but may be different in shape. Now have students name objects in the classroom that are triangles or squares.

Tell students they are to draw an x on the squares on this page and draw a circle around the triangles. Ask students what shape the first figure is. (square) Ask the shape of the second. (triangle) Tell students to trace the circle around the triangle and the x on the square. Have students complete the page independently.

259

Color the squares red.
Color the triangles blue.

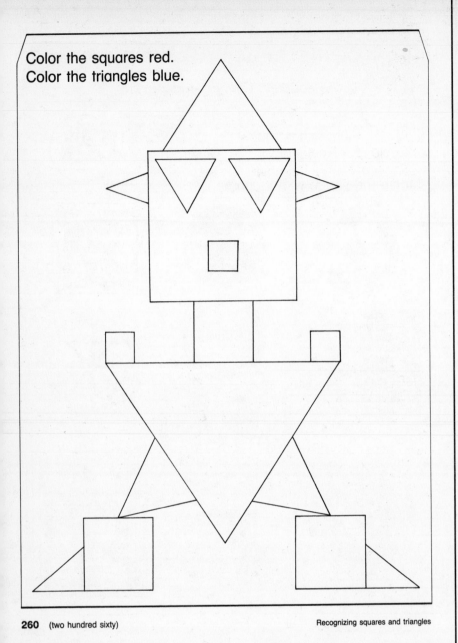

Recognizing squares and triangles

Correcting Common Errors

Some students may have difficulty recognizing squares and triangles since two-dimensional figures are not a part of their everyday world. Have them work with partners with a variety of cutouts of both figures. Have the students arrange the figures to make designs and count to tell how many triangles and how many squares make up their design.

Enrichment

1. Cut from magazines or catalogs pictures that show triangles and squares.
2. Use dotted paper and a ruler to connect 3 dots to draw a triangle and 4 to draw a square.

Teaching page 260

Tell students they are to color the robot's squares red and the robot's triangles blue. Have students complete the page independently.

Extra Credit *Geometry*

Ask the students to find pictures of houses and buildings in magazines. Have them cut the pictures out and glue them on paper. Then have them find geometric shapes (triangles, squares, circles, rectangles) used in the design of the buildings. Ask them to outline, in marker or crayon, the shapes they have found and, label them. Have students exchange papers to check each other on any shapes they missed outlining.

Circles and Rectangles

pages 261-262

Objective

To recognize circles, rectangles, triangles and squares

Materials

*Large square, triangle, circle and rectangle
Square, triangle, rectangle and circle
Crayons

Mental Math

What comes after:
1. 3rd (4th)
2. 8th (9th)
3. 1st (2nd)
4. 6th (7th)
5. 2nd (3rd)
6. 7th (8th)
7. 5th (6th)
8. 4th (5th)

Skill Review

Write the words **square** and **triangle** on the board. Show triangular or square objects in the room, and ask students to name the shape and point to its name on the board. Repeat for more examples.

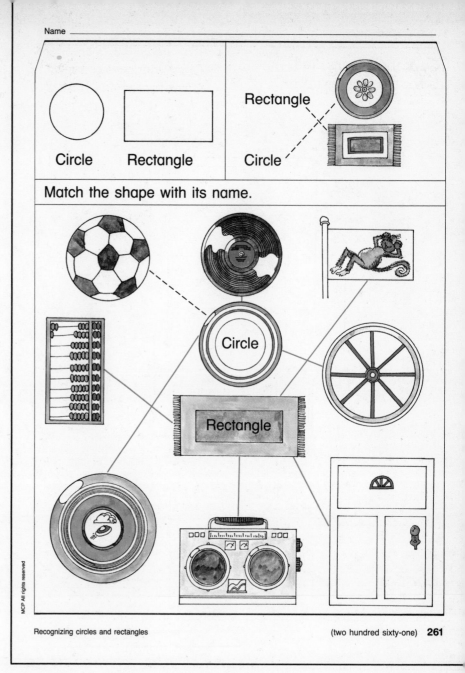

Rectangle

Circle

Circle   Rectangle

Match the shape with its name.

Circle

Rectangle

Recognizing circles and rectangles   (two hundred sixty-one) **261**

Teaching page 261

Have rectangles of different sizes and shapes and varying sizes of circles to give each pair of students a rectangle and circle. Show the demonstration rectangle and tell students the shape is called a **rectangle** as you write the word on the board. Have students hold up their rectangles and compare them. Ask how many corners and sides. (4, 4) Ask if all rectangles are the same shape. (no) Tell students a rectangle has 2 long sides and 2 short sides. (**Note** there is no need to refer to a square as a special rectangle at this time.) Show the demonstration circle. Ask students the name of this shape and write **circle** on the board. Ask students if a circle has corners. (no) Have students hold up their circles and tell if circles are always the same shape. (yes) Tell students a circle will roll. Ask students where circles are found on a bicycle or car.

(wheels) Have students name objects in the classroom that are the shape of a circle or rectangle. As each object is named, have the student come to the board and point to the shape's word.

Tell students they are to match the 2 shapes at the top of the page with their names. Have students point to each word as you read it with them. Have students trace the lines to the circle and rectangle. Have students point to each word in the middle of the page as they say the words. Now tell students to draw a line from each shape on this page to its word name.

261

Color circles red.
Color squares blue.

Color triangles green.
Color rectangles brown.

262 (two hundred sixty-two)

Recognizing geometric figures

Correcting Common Errors

Some students may confuse the various figures. Have them work with partners with a cut-out of each of the four figures. As you verbally describe a figure, they hold it up and name it. EXAMPLES

- A figure with 3 corners (triangle)
- A figure with no corners (circle)
- A figure with 4 sides, 2 long ones and 2 short ones (rectangle)
- A figure with 4 sides, all of them the same length (square)

Note that a square is a special kind of rectangle; that is, it is a rectangle with four equal sides. So, should a student say "rectangle" for the last answer above, he or she is not incorrect.

Enrichment

1. Cut from magazines or catalogs pictures of objects that have the shapes of circles and rectangles.
2. Wear a blindfold and remove a shape from a bag. Tell the shape's name.

Teaching page 262

Tell students they are to color each shape in this picture. Have students read the coloring directions with you. Tell students to color the shape words as follows: circles with a red crayon, squares with a blue crayon, triangles with a green crayon and rectangles with a brown crayon. Now have students color the shapes on the page independently.

Extra Credit   *Applications*

Cut out various sizes of geometric shapes (square, circle, rectangle, triangle) from tagboard or other stiff paper. Have the students use these to trace and cut out the shapes from colored construction paper. They may use each size or shape more than once. Using only these shapes in any combination, have the students create a scene or picture on their desks. When they have arrived at a pleasing combination, allow them to glue their pictures onto a background.

Non-standard Units of Length

pages 263-264

Objective

To measure lengths with non-standard units

Materials

*12-inch strip of adding machine paper
*Large paper clip
12-inch strip of adding machine paper
Small paper clip

Mental Math

What shape is:
1. a wheel (circle)
2. this book (rectangle)
3. a dime (circle)
4. a brick (rectangle)
5. a floor tile (square)
6. a pennant (triangle)
7. a clockface (circle)
8. an exit sign (rectangle)

Skill Review

Write the words **triangle, rectangle, circle** and **square** on the board. Hold up one shape and ask a student to name the shape and point to its name from those on the board. Repeat for each student to have a turn.

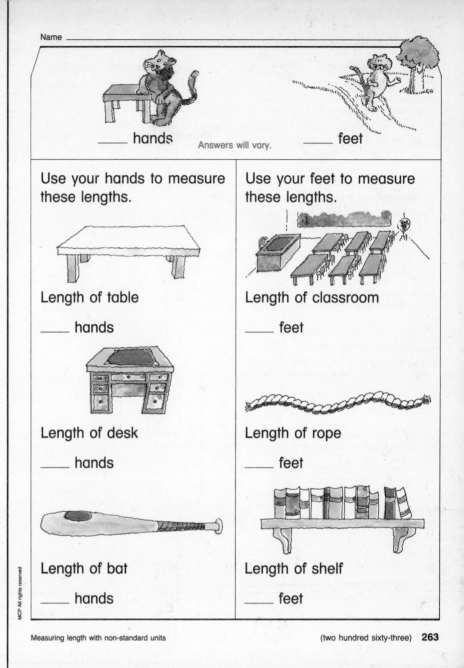

Name _____

_____ hands   Answers will vary.   _____ feet

Use your hands to measure these lengths.

Length of table

_____ hands

Length of desk

_____ hands

Length of bat

_____ hands

Use your feet to measure these lengths.

Length of classroom

_____ feet

Length of rope

_____ feet

Length of shelf

_____ feet

Measuring length with non-standard units

(two hundred sixty-three) **263**

Teaching page 263

Attach a strip of adding machine paper to the chalkboard. Use a large paper clip to demonstrate measuring. Tell students you are going to see how many paper clips long the piece of paper is. Put one end of the clip at the end of the paper and make a mark on the paper at the other end of the clip. Then place the end of the clip at the mark and make another mark on the paper to show the length of 2 clips. Continue to measure to the end of the paper. Note that it will most likely not come out even. Ask students how many clips long the paper is as you count them together. Tell students "the paper is about __ paper clips long." Tell students you have made a paper clip ruler and they will now make one of their own. Have students work in pairs with adding machine paper and a paper clip. Supervise students as they make their rulers. Now ask students if all their papers

and paper clips are the same length. (probably not) Allow students to compare theirs with other students'.

Tell students they are to tell how many hands wide the desk is. (Answers will vary.) Repeat for next example. Tell students they are to measure some objects in the classroom using their hands and feet. Go through each problem to agree on a specific table, desk, etc. in the room to be measured. Then have students proceed to measure the objects. Be sure they use the heel-to-toe method. Results will vary as hands and feet vary in size. Offer reading assistance where needed.

263

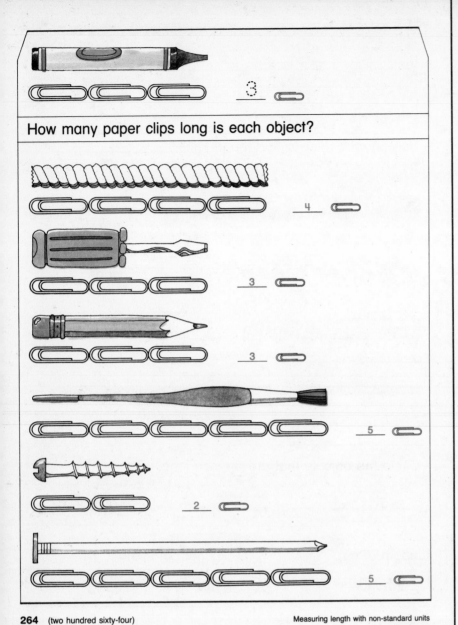

How many paper clips long is each object?

(crayon)	3
(rope/coil)	4
(screwdriver)	3
(pencil)	3
(paint brush)	5
(screw)	2
(nail)	5

Measuring length with non-standard units

Correcting Common Errors

Students may need more experience measuring with non-standard units. Have them work with partners, with one partner using a hand and the other a foot as a measuring unit. Have them use their units to measure objects in the classroom and record the results. Then have them discuss whether it takes more hands or more feet to measure an object. (more hands)

Enrichment

1. Use your paper clip ruler to measure your desktop and this book. Write the measurements and compare with a friend's findings.
2. Measure the length and width of a room in your home with your feet. Tell how wide and long the room is.
3. Use 2 different length pencils to measure your desktop. Compare your findings.

Teaching page 264

Tell students they are to tell how many paper clips long the crayon is. (3) Have students count the clips and trace the 3. Tell students they are to tell the length, in paper clips, for the objects on this page. Have students complete the page.

Extra Credit Sets

"Ping-pong" puzzles are an arrangement of objects with two sets of characteristics. On a table make a cross out of two strings, so that four areas are defined. Gather objects with the characteristics red and green, food, not food; for example: apple and tomato (red, food), red ball and red toy car (red, not food), cucumber and green pepper (green, food), green block and green pen (green, not food). Label each section with a characteristic. Have students take turns placing the objects within the correct section marked off by the string. Extend the activity by changing the pool of objects the students choose from. Be sure to include objects that do not fit into any of the categories.

264

Length in Inches

pages 265-266

Objective

To measure lengths in inches

Materials

6-inch ruler with zero line on the edge
Paper clip

Mental Math

Name the number that tells:

1. corners on a square (4)
2. students in this room
3. the sum of 40 and 10 (50)
4. sides on a triangle (3)
5. long sides on a rectangle (2)
6. corners on a circle (0)
7. numbers on a clock (12)
8. sides on a square (4)

Skill Review

Write **26 + 32 + 78** vertically on the board. Ask a student to work the problem. Then have another student talk through the problem explaining each step. Repeat for more problems with 3 addends that are 1- or 2-digit numbers for sums through 200.

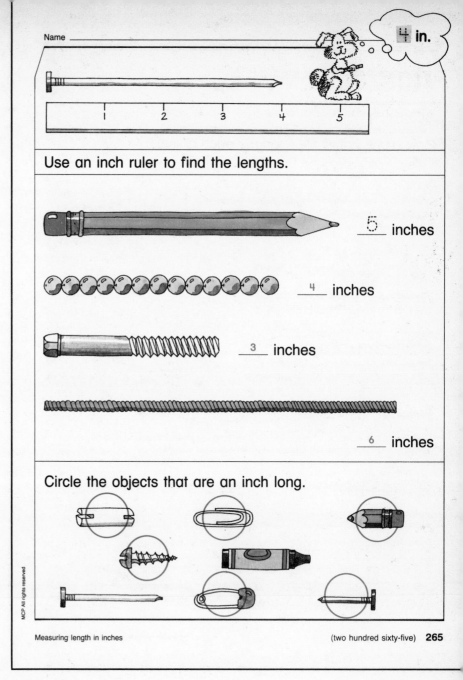

Name _____

4 in.

Use an inch ruler to find the lengths.

5 inches

4 inches

3 inches

6 inches

Circle the objects that are an inch long.

Measuring length in inches

(two hundred sixty-five) **265**

Teaching page 265

Help students make paper clip rulers that are 6 clips long. Making the marks of each clip's length will help students understand the meaning of numbers on a ruler. Tell students to use their paper clip rulers to measure pencils. Ask, "The pencil is how many paper clips long?" Have students measure other objects that are 6 clips or less in length such as crayons, erasers, chalk, strips of paper, etc. Show students an inch ruler. Remind students that paper clips, hands, feet, etc. come in different lengths. Therefore you have to know what length paper clip or hand or foot, etc. someone used, to know how long something really is. Tell students their ruler is marked in **inches.** Tell students to run their fingers from the edge of their rulers to the number 1. Tell students this length is 1 inch and is always the same. Have students compare the 1-inch length on their ruler to friends' rulers. Ask if 1 inch is the same on all the rulers. (yes) Ask students to put their fingers at the end of the ruler and move across to 1 inch, 2 inches, 3 inches, etc. to the end. Ask students how many inches are on their rulers. (6) Ask how long their rulers are in inches. (6 inches) Help students find and measure objects that are 1 inch long. Students may ask about the marks on the ruler between the numbers. Tell students these are used to measure objects to the closest inch. (Parts of an inch are not taught at this time.)

Tell students they are to find the length of the crayon in inches. (4) Have students trace the 4. Tell students to find the length of each of the next 4 objects and write the number. Tell students they are to circle the objects at the bottom of the page that are 1 inch long. Have students complete the page independently.

265

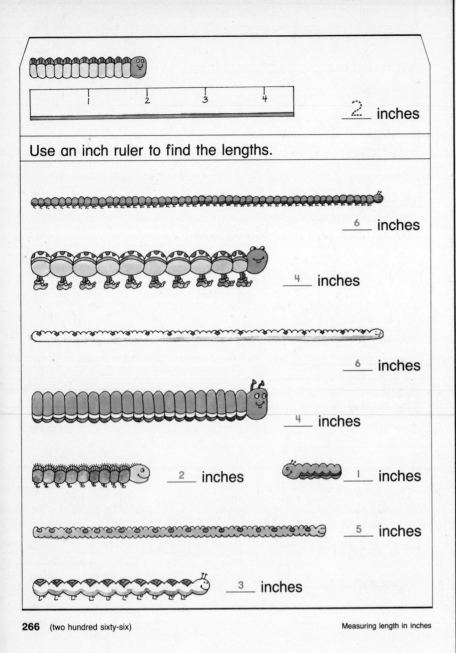

inches

Use an inch ruler to find the lengths.

6 inches

4 inches

6 inches

4 inches

2 inches   1 inches

5 inches

3 inches

266 (two hundred sixty-six)

Measuring length in inches

Correcting Common Errors

Watch for students who measure incorrectly because they do not align the end, or 0 point, of the ruler with the end of the object. Have them work with partners, each checking the other to see that the ruler is properly aligned.

Enrichment

1. Draw lines that are about 1 inch, 2 inches, etc. through 6 inches in length.
2. Measure 4 objects that are 6 inches or less in your house. Draw a picture of each and write its length in inches.

Teaching page 266

Tell students they are to tell the length of the caterpillar in inches. (2) Have students trace the 2. Tell students they are to use their 6-inch rulers to measure each of the caterpillars on this page and write the length. Have students complete the page independently.

Extra Credit *Measurement*

Build a trundle wheel. Cut a circle with a circumference of one meter out of extra heavy cardboard. Also cut a handle similar to that of a wheelbarrow. It should be long enough that the wheel can be pushed along as the student walks. Attach the handle to the center of the circle so that it can roll easily along the floor. Place a heavy mark or dark tape at one point along the

circumference. Start with the tape exactly at the handle. Explain to students that as the wheel rolls, you have measured one meter each time the tape or mark passes the handle. Now measure the hallway or take a hike and measure the distance walked with the trundle wheel. Have students take turns measuring with the wheel.

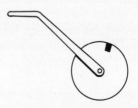

Perimeter in Inches

pages 267-268

Objectives

To measure length in inches
To find perimeter in inches

Materials

6-inch ruler

Mental Math

Name 3 facts that equal:
1. 8 (5 + 3, 2 + 6, etc.)
2. 9
3. 6
4. 5
5. 4
6. 7
7. 3

Skill Review

Write **2 + 4 + 7** vertically on the board and have a student work the problem. Repeat for more 3 addend problems of 1-digit numbers, for sums through 19. Now write the word **inches** beside each of 3 addends and ask students to tell the total inches for each problem.

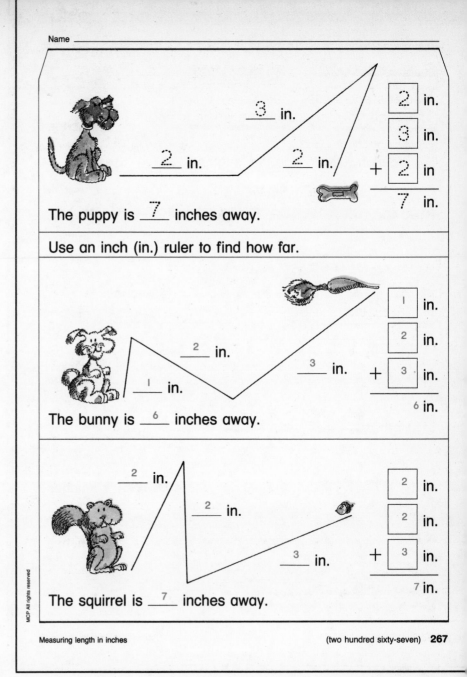

Name _____

The puppy is __7__ inches away.

Use an inch (in.) ruler to find how far.

The bunny is __6__ inches away.

The squirrel is __7__ inches away.

Measuring length in inches

(two hundred sixty-seven) **267**

Teaching page 267

Draw 3 dots across the board and connect them so that the distance between the first two is 3 inches and the distance between the last two is 4 inches. Ask a student to measure the distance between the first 2 dots and write the number above the line connecting the dots. Write the word **inches** beside the number. Repeat for the distance between the last 2 dots. Draw a ball beside the first dot and a box beside the last dot. Ask students how to find the distance in inches from the ball to the box. (add 3 inches and 4 inches) Ask students to tell the total distance. (7 inches) Draw other examples of 2 or 3 addends of 6 inches or less each.

Tell students that **in.** is a short way to write the word inches. Have students find in. in the first problem. Ask students how to find the total distance from the puppy

to the bone. (measure each length and add them) Tell students to verify the 3 lengths with their inch rulers and trace the 2, 3 and 2. Tell students to trace the numbers in the problem 2 in. + 3 in. + 2 in. = 7 in. Read the sentence with the students and have them trace the 7. Help students work through the next problem and then have them complete the page independently.

267

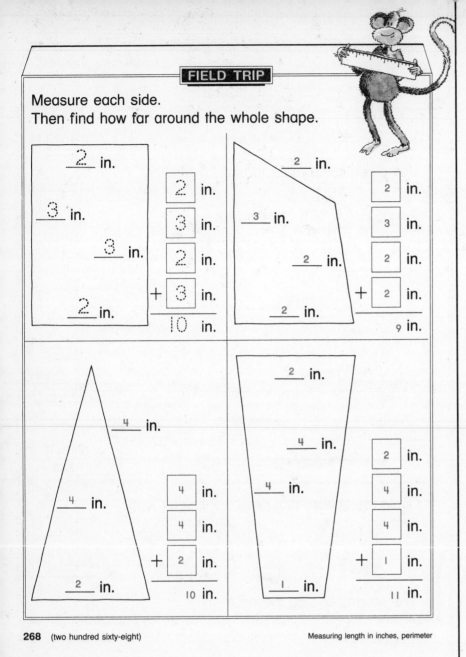

FIELD TRIP

Measure each side.
Then find how far around the whole shape.

Shape 1 (rectangle):
- _2_ in.
- _3_ in.
- _3_ in.
- _2_ in.

Boxes: 2 in. / 3 in. / 2 in. / + 3 in. = 10 in.

Shape 2 (quadrilateral):
- _2_ in.
- _3_ in.
- _2_ in.
- _2_ in.

Boxes: 2 in. / 3 in. / 2 in. / + 2 in. = 9 in.

Shape 3 (triangle):
- _4_ in.
- _4_ in.
- _2_ in.

Boxes: 4 in. / 4 in. / + 2 in. = 10 in.

Shape 4 (trapezoid):
- _2_ in.
- _4_ in.
- _4_ in.
- _1_ in.

Boxes: 2 in. / 4 in. / 4 in. / + 1 in. = 11 in.

268 (two hundred sixty-eight)   Measuring length in inches, perimeter

Correcting Common Errors

Watch for students who do not measure all the lengths when they are finding perimeter. Have them first count how many times they should measure, and then carefully write the measures on the blanks and in the boxes.

Enrichment

1. Construct a triangle using crayons for sides. Find the total distance around it in inches.
2. Measure and cut lengths of string 4 inches, 4 inches, 2 inches and 2 inches. Lay them out to make a shape and find the distance around it.

Field Trip
Teaching page 268

Tell students they are to measure each side, write the numbers and then find the distance around the shape. Have students measure each side of the rectangle to verify the numbers and then trace them. Tell students they will add the 4 numbers together to find the distance in inches around the shape. Tell students to write the numbers in the boxes to make an addition problem. (2 + 3 + 2 + 3) Remind students to add 2 and 3, add that to the 2, and then add 3 to the sum. Have students trace the 10. Ask students how many numbers will be added together to find the distance around each of the shapes. (3 or 4) Write **1 + 1 + 1 + 1** on the board and talk through the process of adding 4 numbers together. Remind students to measure the

length of each side of a shape first, write the numbers in the boxes to make an addition problem, and then add the numbers together to find the total inches in all.

Extra Credit   *Measurement*

To extend the student's understanding of estimation, have them collect some rocks. Have students hold one rock in each hand, and guess which is heavier. Then have them weigh the rocks to check their guesses. Next have them arrange some of the rocks in order from lightest to heaviest using estimation. They can weigh the rocks to see how well they estimated.

268

Length in Centimeters

pages 269-270

Objective

To measure length in centimeters

Materials

*Ruler marked in centimeters
6-centimeter ruler

Mental Math

Give the total length for:
1. 2″ and 8″ (10″)
2. 3″, 5″ and 7″ (15″)
3. 4″, 2″ and 6″ (12″)
4. 1″, 2″ and 3″ (6″)
5. 9″ and 2″ (11″)
6. 4″ and 6″ (10″)
7. 1″, 9″ and 8″ (18″)
8. 3″, 3″, 3″ and 3″ (12″)

Skill Review

Have students work in pairs. Have the first student draw a line that is from 1 inch to 6 inches in length. Have the second student measure the line with a ruler and write its length in inches. Reverse roles for more practice in creating and measuring lines that are 1 inch to 6 inches in length.

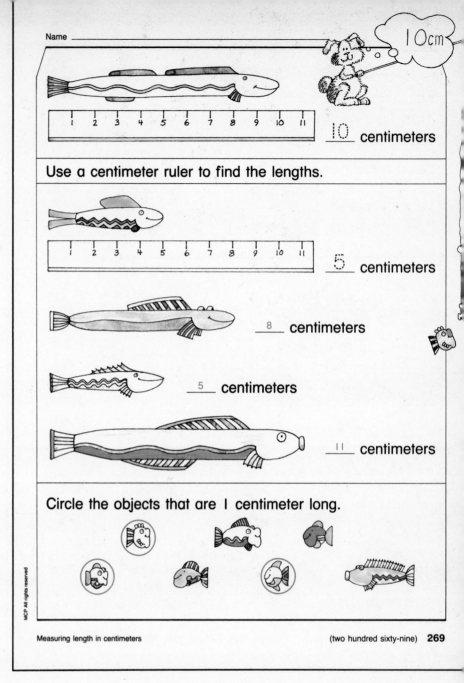

Measuring length in centimeters

(two hundred sixty-nine) **269**

Teaching page 269

Tell students that another way we measure things is in **centimeters**. Tell students a centimeter, like an inch, is always the same length. Tell students to run their fingers from the edge of the centimeter ruler to the number 1. Tell students this is 1 centimeter. Have students find 2 centimeters, etc. to the end of their rulers. Ask how many centimeters long the ruler is. Help students find and measure objects that are 1 centimeter, 2 centimeters, etc.

Tell students they are to tell the length of the fish as measured by the centimeter ruler. (10 cm) Have students trace the 10. Tell students to verify the length of the next fish and trace the 5. Have students find the next three lengths and write the numbers. Now tell students they are to measure each of the fish at the

bottom of the page and circle those that are 1 centimeter long. Have students complete this section independently.

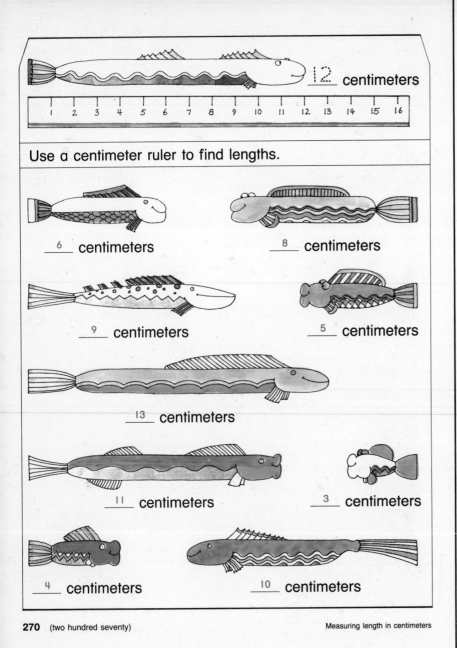

12 centimeters

Use a centimeter ruler to find lengths.

6 centimeters

8 centimeters

9 centimeters

5 centimeters

13 centimeters

11 centimeters

3 centimeters

4 centimeters

10 centimeters

Measuring length in centimeters

Correcting Common Errors

Watch for students who measure incorrectly because they do not align their rulers properly. Have them work with partners, each making sure that the other has placed the end, or 0 point, of the ruler at the end of the object and that the ruler is level with the object; that is, the edge of the ruler does not cross over the object, or one end of the ruler is not farther away from the object than the other end. The best position for the person reading the ruler is squarely in front of it and looking down vertically at the object and the ruler.

Enrichment

1. Measure 4 objects at home that are 12 centimeters or less. Draw a picture of each and write its length in centimeters.
2. Draw a vase with 4 flowers in it. Draw the stems of the flowers 8, 9, 10, and 11 centimeters in length.

Teaching page 270

Tell students they are to find the length of the fish in centimeters. (12) Have students trace the 12. Tell students to use their centimeter ruler to measure each of the fish on this page and write the numbers in the blanks. Have students complete the page.

Extra Credit *Measurement*

Make an inch worm to help demonstrate measurement.

Cut construction paper into 12-inch strips, one for each student. Have students draw lines on the strip at 1-inch intervals using their rulers as guides. Have them fold the strip back and forth on the lines. Then have students draw a 1-inch diameter circle for the face.

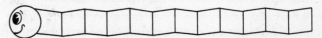

This could also be done with centimeter measurements.

Perimeter in Centimeters

pages 271-272

Objectives

To measure length in centimeters
To find perimeters in centimeters

Materials

*Ruler marked in centimeters
6-inch ruler

Mental Math

Name three 1-digit addends that equal:
1. 10 (2, 3, 5; 1, 8, 1, etc.)
2. 14
3. 16
4. 13
5. 11
6. 15
7. 18

Skill Review

Draw a 4-inch line segment on the board. Have a student measure it in inches and in centimeters. Have another student record the measurements on the board as they are given. Repeat for more line segments of lengths through 6 inches or 11 centimeters.

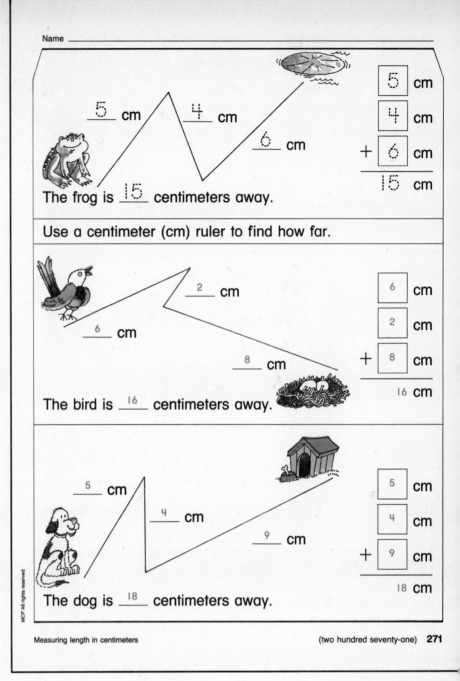

Name _____

_5_ cm   _4_ cm   _6_ cm

5	cm
4	cm
+ 6	cm
15	cm

The frog is _15_ centimeters away.

Use a centimeter (cm) ruler to find how far.

_2_ cm   _6_ cm   _8_ cm

6	cm
2	cm
+ 8	cm
16	cm

The bird is _16_ centimeters away.

_5_ cm   _4_ cm   _9_ cm

5	cm
4	cm
+ 9	cm
18	cm

The dog is _18_ centimeters away.

Measuring length in centimeters

(two hundred seventy-one) **271**

Teaching page 271

Draw 3 dots across the board and connect them so that the distance between the first two is 3 centimeters and the distance between the last two is 4 centimeters. Ask a student to measure the distance between the first 2 dots and write the number above the line connecting the dots. Write the word **centimeters** beside the number written by the student. Repeat for the distance between the last 2 dots. Draw a ball beside the first dot and a box beside the last dot. Ask students how to find the distance in centimeters from the ball to the box. (add 3 centimeters and 4 centimeters) Ask students to tell the total distance. (7 centimeters) Draw other examples of 2 or 3 addends of 6 centimeters or less each.

Tell students that **cm** is a short way to write the word centimeters. Have students find cm in the first problem. Ask students how to find the total distance from the frog to the lily pad. (measure each length and add them) Tell students to verify the 3 lengths with their centimeter rulers and then trace the 5, 4 and 6. Tell students to trace the numbers in the problem 5 cm + 4 cm + 6 cm = 15 cm. Help students work through the next problem and then have them complete the page independently.

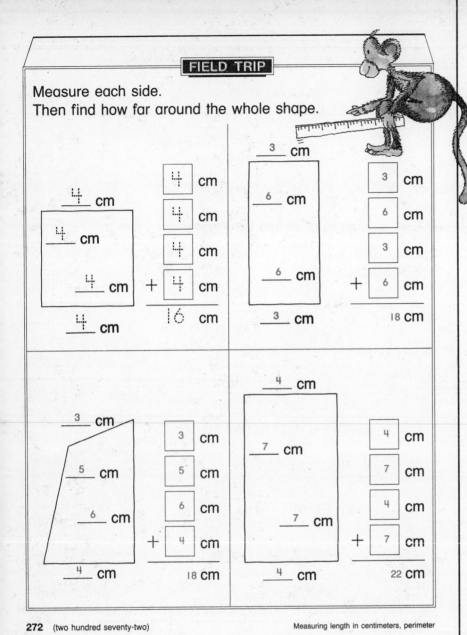

FIELD TRIP

Measure each side.
Then find how far around the whole shape.

4 cm

4 cm
4 cm

4 cm
4 cm
4 cm
+ 4 cm
4 cm
16 cm

3 cm
6 cm
6 cm
3 cm
3 cm
6 cm
+ 6 cm
3 cm
18 cm

3 cm
5 cm
6 cm
4 cm

3 cm
5 cm
6 cm
+ 4 cm
18 cm

4 cm
7 cm
7 cm
4 cm

4 cm
7 cm
4 cm
+ 7 cm
22 cm

272 (two hundred seventy-two)

Measuring length in centimeters, perimeter

Correcting Common Errors

If students need additional practice finding perimeter, have them work with partners with drawings of figures that they make on grid paper. Have students first count the number of sides they must measure, then make sure they measure all that they should and add the measures to find the perimeter.

Enrichment

1. Draw 1-inch and 1-centimeter lines. Draw more lines for 2 in., 2 cm, 3 in., 3 cm, 4 in. and 4 cm.
2. Draw a triangle. Find its perimeter in inches and centimeters.

Teaching page 272

Field Trip

Tell students this page is similar to a page they did earlier, but here they are to find the lengths in centimeters. Tell students they are to measure each side, write the numbers and then find the distance around the shape. Have students measure each side of the first figure to verify the numbers and then trace them. Ask students how to find the total distance in centimeters around the shape. (add the sides) Tell students to write the numbers in the boxes to make an addition problem. (4 + 4 + 4 + 4) Remind students to add 4 and 4 together and then add 4 to that sum and add 4 to that sum. Have students trace the 16. Remind students to measure the length of each side of a shape first, write the numbers in the boxes to make an

addition problem, and then add the numbers together to find the total centimeters in all.

Extra Credit *Statistics*

Draw a line down the center of a large piece of paper. On one side put the heading "Left-handed," and on the other side, "Right-handed." Have students work in pairs to trace each other's hands onto the paper. Explain that if they are right-handed, they should have their partner trace their right hand on the side that says Right-handed. Left-handed students trace hands on the Left-handed side. Have students hold the paper up at the end of the day. Explain that what they have drawn is called a picture graph. Ask if it is easy to tell, even at a distance, whether there are more right or left-handed people in the room. Ask if anyone can explain why this is called a picture graph. (Each person is represented by a picture of their hand.)

272

Chapter Review

pages 273-274

Objectives

To review geometry and measurement
To maintain skills learned previously this year

Materials

*Ruler marked in centimeters
6-inch ruler
Hundred-square
Ten-strips
Single squares

Mental Math

Name the number that:
1. is 1 less than 100 (99)
2. is 9 plus 8 (17)
3. comes before 200 (199)
4. tells sides on a square (4)
5. is 4 more than 17 (21)
6. tells corners on a circle (0)
7. is 10 less than 90 (80)

Skill Review

Draw a triangle on the board. Label its sides 2 cm, 3 cm and 5 cm. Have a student write a problem on the board to find the triangle's perimeter. Have another student solve the problem. Repeat for perimeters in centimeters of other triangles, squares and rectangles.

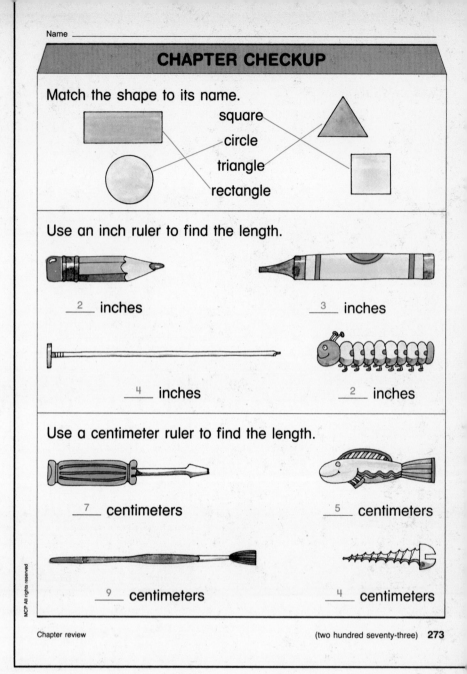

Teaching page 273

Tell students they are to draw a line from the word to its shape. Tell students they are to find the length in inches for each of the 4 items and write the number on the line. Tell students they are to find the length in centimeters of each of the next 5 items and write the number on the line. Have students complete the page independently.

ROUNDUP REVIEW

Add or subtract.

3 +9 — 12	12 − 9 — 3	4 +5 — 9	14 − 9 — 5	4 +9 — 13	8 +7 — 15	11 − 7 — 4
10 − 4 — 6	16 − 7 — 9	6 +5 — 11	7 +9 — 16	11 − 6 — 5	13 − 8 — 5	8 +6 — 14

Write the missing numbers.

102, 103, _104_, _105_, _106_, _107_, _108_, _109_

Add.

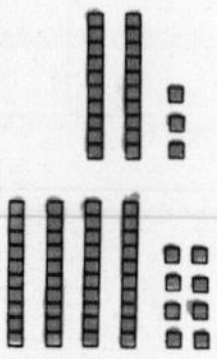

tens	ones
1	
2	3
+ 4	8
7	1

Subtract.

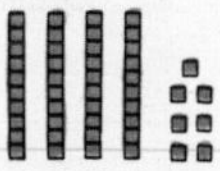

tens	ones
3	17
4̸	7̸
−	8
3	9

Add.

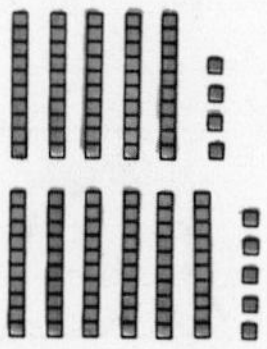

hundreds	tens	ones
1		
	5	4
+	6	5
1	1	9

Cumulative review

Enrichment

1. Draw line segments that are 2, 5, 8 and 9 inches in length. Have a friend measure and write the length of each.
2. Write the ages in numerical order for each person in your family. Fill in the missing numbers to make a number line from 0 through the number that is the age of the oldest member of your family. Circle your family's ages.

Teaching page 274

Read the direction words with the students for each section and ask what they are to do. Remind students to look at the sign in each problem in the first section and in the three problems at the bottom of the page. Have students complete the page independently.

This page reviews addition and subtraction facts, sequencing numbers and addition and subtraction with some trading.

Equal Parts, One Half

pages 275-276

Objectives

To recognize equal parts of a figure
To recognize one half of a figure

Materials

*Sheets of 9 × 12 construction
  paper
Crayons

Mental Math

Name the time:
1. 30 minutes later than 6:00
   (6:30)
2. long hand on 6, short between 2
   and 3 (2:30)
3. both hands on 12 (12:00)
4. short hand on 10, long on 12
   (10:00)
5. 30 minutes later than 6:30
   (7:00)

Skill Review

Draw a rectangle on the board and
label its long sides **6 centimeters**
and its short sides **2 centimeters.**
Have a student write and solve the
problem to find the distance around
the rectangle. Draw another
rectangle measured in inches,
have a student measure the sides
and write the distance around it.
Draw more rectangles, triangles or
squares and repeat the exercise.

15 FRACTIONS AND GRAPHING

Circle the shapes with equal parts.

Which figure has equal parts?

Recognizing equal parts of figures

(two hundred seventy-five) **275**

Teaching page 275

Show students a 9 × 12 sheet of colored paper. Tell
students this is a whole sheet of paper. Fold the paper
so that the 2 parts are not equal in size. Label one **A**
and the other **B**. Ask which is the bigger part and
which is the smaller part. Fold the paper again so there
are 4 parts with 1 obviously-larger part. Label the parts
A, B, C, D. Ask students to tell the biggest part and
the smallest part. Repeat with another sheet of paper
until students can easily identify the biggest and
smallest parts. Now fold a new sheet of paper into 2
equal parts and ask which part is bigger and smaller.
(neither) Tell students the parts are exactly the same
size. Fold the paper again to form 4 equal parts and
ask students if there is a bigger or smaller part. (no)
Tell students the parts are all **equal**.

Tell students the cat wants to know which of the 2
rectangles has 4 equal parts. Ask students to answer
the cat. (the 2nd figure) Tell students to trace the circle
around the answer. Tell students to circle the figure in
each box that has equal parts. Have students complete
the page.

275

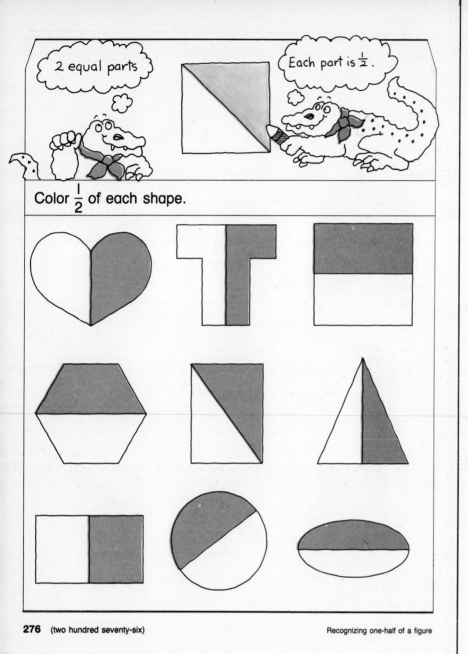

Color $\frac{1}{2}$ of each shape.

Recognizing one-half of a figure

Correcting Common Errors

Some students may need additional practice with the concept of one-half. Have them work with partners with rectangles of different sizes. Have them fold each rectangle in half and choose a color to color one-half. Then have them play "fair shares," where they pretend that a rectangle is a candy bar that they are going to share. One partner draws a line to cut the "candy bar" in half, and the other partner gets to choose the first piece. They trade roles with the next "candy bar."

Enrichment

1. Fold a piece of paper into 2 equal parts. Write each part's name on it.
2. Draw how you will share a cookie equally with a friend. Draw another cookie in 2 parts with a bigger part for yourself.

Teaching page 276

Fold a sheet of paper into 2 equal parts and ask which part is bigger and smaller. (neither) Tell students the 2 parts are exactly the same size and each part is **1 of 2 equal parts** or **one-half** of the whole sheet. Write **one-half** on the board. Point to 1 part and say, "This is 1 part of 2 equal parts." Write ½ on the board and point to each number in the fraction as you repeat that each part is 1 part of 2. Tell students ½ is another way to write one-half. Tell students the first number in the fraction is the part we are talking about and the second number tells us how many parts in all.

Have students point to 1 part of the square and tell its name. (½) Tell students to color ½ of the figure. Now tell students they are to color 1 of the 2 equal parts in each figure on this page. Ask students to tell the name

of the part of each figure they will color. (½) Tell students to complete the page.

Extra Credit *Logic*

Teach students to play "Paper, Scissors, Stone." Explain that the game is played by two people. On the count of three they show a hand to one another. The hand should be either flat to represent a piece of paper, in a fist to represent a stone, or pointing two fingers to represent a pair of scissors. Point out that there is an order of precedence among the objects. Paper covers stone, stone blunts scissors, and scissors cut paper. Explain this means that paper wins over stone, stone over scissors, and scissors over paper. If both players show the same thing, a tie is declared. Have students play the game and keep track of their wins, losses, and ties. Ask each pair to declare a winner at the end of the game.

276

One Third, One Fourth

pages 277-278

Objective

To recognize one third and one-fourth of a figure

Materials

Sheets of 9 × 12 construction paper
*Different sizes and shapes of paper
Crayons

Mental Math

Is a trade needed?
1. 6 + 2 + 1 ones (no)
2. 9 ones from 2 ones (yes)
3. 7 tens + 7 tens (yes)
4. 2 tens from 3 tens (no)
5. 6 + 1 + 4 tens (yes)
6. 4 ones + 9 ones (yes)
7. 2 tens + 7 tens (no)

Skill Review

Give each student a 9 × 12 paper.
Show students how to fold the
paper lengthwise and crosswise to
form two equal halves. Allow
students to choose the way they
want to fold the paper. Have
students write on each part the
fraction that names it. (½) Have
students exchange papers with a
friend and write the names of the
parts on the reverse side. (½)

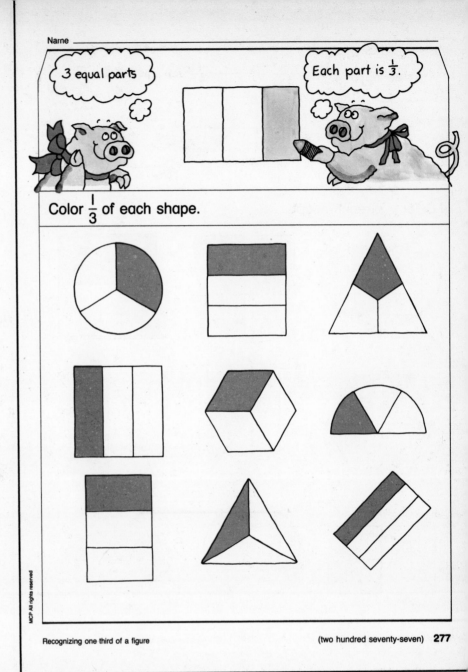

Recognizing one third of a figure

(two hundred seventy-seven) **277**

Teaching page 277

Fold a sheet of colored paper into 3 unequal parts.
Have students tell how many parts. (3) Ask if they are
equal. (no) Repeat for another sheet in 3 unequal
parts. Now fold paper equally into thirds and ask how
many parts. (3) Ask which is the biggest and the
smallest part. (all are equal) Repeat for other sizes and
shapes of paper. Tell students each part is 1 of 3 equal
parts. Write **one third** and ⅓ on the board and read
each to the students. Write ⅓ on each part of the
paper. Ask students to write the fraction on the board
for each part as you point to it.

Tell students they are to find and color 1 of the 3
equal parts of each shape on this page. Ask students to
tell the name for the part colored in the example. (⅓)
Have students complete the page independently.

277

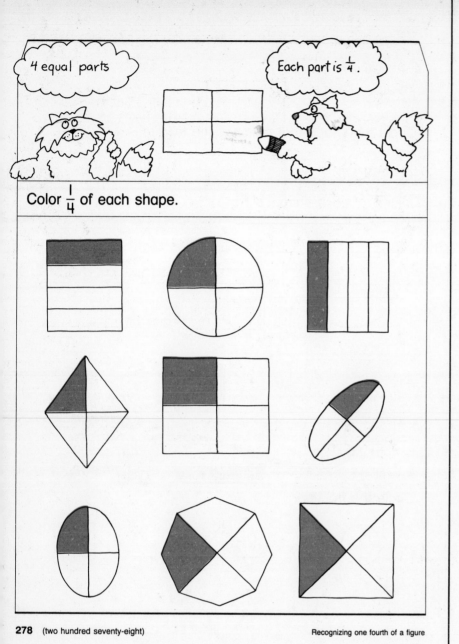

4 equal parts

Each part is $\frac{1}{4}$.

Color $\frac{1}{4}$ of each shape.

       Recognizing one fourth of a figure

Correcting Common Errors

Some students may not completely understand that the parts of the whole must be equal. Have them work with partners and a worksheet showing 3 pairs of figures where one of the pair is divided into a number of equal parts and the other is divided into the same number of parts, but not equal. The 3 pairs should show 2 parts, 3 parts, and 4 parts. Have students circle the figure that is divided into equal parts, or fair shares. Then have them shade one of the parts that shows ½, ⅓, and ¼.

Enrichment

1. Find a recipe in a cookbook at home that has measurements of ⅓ and ¼ in it.
2. Fold a paper into 4 equal parts. Write the name of each part on it.
3. Cut a pre-marked paper into 3 equal parts. Write the name of each part on it.

Teaching page 278

Fold a sheet of colored paper into 4 unequal parts. Have students tell how many parts. (4) Ask if they are equal. (no) Now fold a paper equally into fourths and ask how many parts. (4) Ask which is the biggest and the smallest part. (all are equal) Tell students each part is 1 of 4 equal parts. Write **one fourth** and ¼ on the board and read each to the students. Write ¼ on each part of the paper.

Tell students they are to find and color, 1 of the 4 equal parts of each shape on this page. Ask students to tell the name for the part colored in the example. (¼) Have students complete the page independently.

Extra Credit   *Measurement*

Distribute papers with the following word-search puzzle. Tell students to find these measurements in their unabbreviated form, and circle them.

qt   c   m   ft   cm
in.   l   g   oz   yd

```
O U N C E K C E A M D O A M E T E R
N D P V R A G L D K O P T C R M S T
D N L Q U A R T O W B O N L T Q F I
V K Q Y V L A F X A C Y A R D M D N
J S Z R M D M U G P I I H X L N K C
G F G I S E V P D B J P S L M A S H
Y O A D Z M C H R K T J N I C E U C
A O R U P F C E N T I M E T E R Y E
H T V O E W U M Q B K I M E J Z F N
A I C K B L P R J S X D L R T Y V F
```

278

Recognizing Fractions

pages 279-280

Objective

To recognize halves, thirds and fourths

Materials

*Figures divided into halves, thirds, fourths
Cards divided into halves, thirds, fourths
Crayons

Mental Math

Name the shape that:
1. has no corners (circle)
2. has 4 equal sides (square)
3. has 3 corners (triangle)
4. has 2 long and 2 short sides (rectangle)
5. can roll (circle)
6. has 3 sides (triangle)
7. wheels are (circles)

Skill Review

Attach to the board paper figures which have been divided into halves, thirds or fourths. Have a student go to the board and write the name of a part on one of the sheets. Continue until all parts have been named as ½, ⅓ or ¼. Now point to parts at random and have students say the name as ½, ⅓ or ¼.

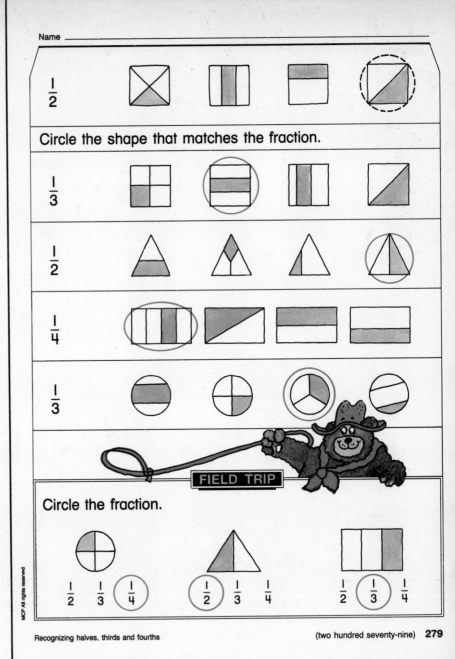

Recognizing halves, thirds and fourths

(two hundred seventy-nine) **279**

Teaching page 279

Tell students they are to circle the shape in each row that matches the fraction on the left. Have students read the first fraction. (½) Ask students if ½ of the first shape is shaded. (no) Continue through the remaining 3 shapes and then have students trace around the last shape to show that ½ of it is shaded. Tell students to find and circle the shape that matches the fraction in each of the next four rows.

Field Trip

Tell students they are to circle the fraction that names the part of each of the 3 shapes that is shaded.

279

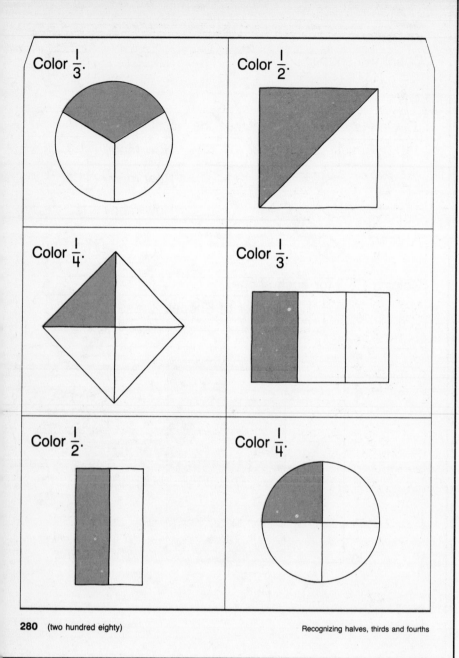

Color $\frac{1}{3}$.

Color $\frac{1}{2}$.

Color $\frac{1}{4}$.

Color $\frac{1}{3}$.

Color $\frac{1}{2}$.

Color $\frac{1}{4}$.

Recognizing halves, thirds and fourths

Correcting Common Errors

Some students may have difficulty interpreting a fraction. Discuss how the bottom number tells how many equal parts are in the whole, and the top tells how many of these equal parts are to be shaded.

Enrichment

1. Fold a paper into 4 equal parts. Write a fraction on each part to tell its name. Repeat for papers in 2 and 3 equal parts.
2. Make up a recipe for Silly Soup using the fractions ½, ⅓ and ¼. Example ½ dog bone, ¼ crayon, ⅓ bucket of water, etc.
3. Draw a picture of you at breakfast. Show that you drank ⅓ of your milk.

Teaching page 280

Tell students they are to color a part of each shape on this page. Have students read the directions in each box. Ask students how many of the 3 equal parts of the circle they will color. (1) Remind students that 1 part is ⅓ of the whole circle. Students will observe that they can color any one part of each shape as they complete the page independently.

Extra Credit *Applications*

Help the students to discover what happens to water when it is left in an open container. Pour water into a large pan. Ask the students to measure the depth of the water. Have them use both an inch ruler and a centimeter ruler to take the measurements. Only approximate measurements are necessary. Record the results on a simple chart. Continue to measure and record the data for one week. Discuss the results with the class. Ask what the students think happened to the water in the pan. Expand the activity by placing one pan of water in the sun and another in the shade.

280

Bar Graphs

pages 281-282

Objective
To construct a bar graph

Materials
*Yardstick
Clock face
Crayons

Mental Math
How much money in all?
1. 1 dollar 2 dimes ($1.20)
2. 5 nickels (25¢)
3. 1 dollar 1 nickel ($1.05)
4. 1 quarter 2 dimes (45¢)
5. 18 dimes ($1.80)
6. 10 dimes 30 pennies ($1.30)
7. 12 nickels (60¢)

Skill Review
Group students in pairs with each having a clock face. Tell each student to show a time on the hour or half-hour. Tell students to then read each other's clock and write the time. Have students continue for more practice in showing, telling and writing times on the hour and half-hour.

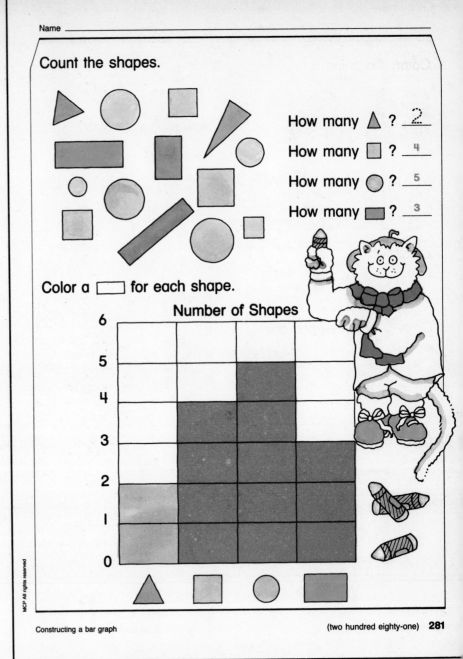

Constructing a bar graph   (two hundred eighty-one) **281**

Teaching page 281

Ask how many students have dogs at home. Write **dogs** ___ on the board and fill in the number as volunteered by the students. Repeat for any other animals students have as pets. Also ask how many students have no live animal pets, to allow all students to respond. Tell students a bar graph is a special way to show how many students have each kind of pet or no pet. Write the animal words needed and the words no pets in a row across the bottom of the board. Use a yardstick to draw vertical lines between the words. Number the lines as illustrated:

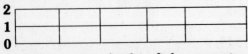

Make your graph as many rectangles high as your greatest number of pets of one kind. Have a student shade the number of rectangles that tells how many

dogs the students have. Continue for all information gained. Be sure students begin shading from the bottom. Now ask students questions such as which pet is the most popular, least popular, etc. Erase the listed information and ask students how many dogs in all, etc. Encourage students to form other questions. Tell students they are to count the number of each shape and write the number. Ask students to verify the number of triangles and trace the 2. Tell students to count the squares, circles and rectangles and write the numbers. (4, 5, 3) Ask students how many triangles. (2) Tell students to color the 2 dotted boxes. Ask students how many squares. (4) Ask how many boxes need to be colored. (4) Tell students to complete the bar graph independently.

281

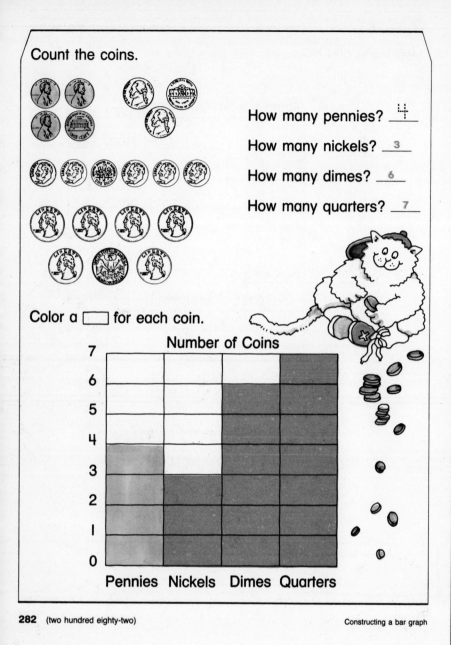

Count the coins.

How many pennies? 4

How many nickels? 3

How many dimes? 6

How many quarters? 7

Color a ☐ for each coin.

Number of Coins

7
6
5
4
3
2
1
0

Pennies Nickels Dimes Quarters

Constructing a bar graph

Some students may have difficulty counting a particular shape because they cannot remember whether or not they counted it already. As they count the number of circles, for example, have them cross out each one as it is counted.

Enrichment

1. Make a bar graph to show how many children are in your family and the families of 3 of your friends. Write your 4 names across the bottom of your graph.
2. Make a bar graph to show how many of your classmates live in a white, red, green or blue house. Which is the most popular color of house?

Teaching page 282

Tell students they are to make a bar graph on this page to show the number of each kind of coin shown. Ask students to verify the number of pennies and trace the 4. Tell students they are to finish the list here by counting the coins and writing the numbers. Tell students they are to then make the bar graph. Have students complete the page independently.

Extra Credit *Logic*

Before class, prepare sets of six cards with each of these words: All, Are, Animals, Birds, Dolls, Toys, Apples, Fruit, People, Mothers, Plates, Dishes, Pencils, and Things You Write With. Then put the following on the board:

ALL CHAIRS ARE FURNITURE.
ALL FURNITURE ARE CHAIRS.

Ask students if both sentences make sense. (no) Have a student explain which makes sense (the first) and why. (Because while chairs are a kind of furniture, there are other kinds of furniture, too. Not everything that is furniture is a chair.) Tell them to use the word cards they have, to make sentences like these. Go over the sentences with the class when they have finished. Read the words aloud and ask volunteers to tell which sentences are correct.

Bar Graphs

pages 283-284

Objective

To interpret a bar graph

Materials

1-inch grid paper
Crayons

Mental Math

How much in all?
1. 10 − 6 + 2 (6)
2. 5 tens 6 ones (56)
3. 2 in. + 3 in. + 1 in. (6 in.)
4. 1 hundred 7 tens 9 ones (179)
5. 99 + 1 (100)
6. 143 + 0 (143)
7. 1 dollar minus 1 penny (99¢)
8. 100 + 60 + 2 (162)

Skill Review

Make a bar graph on the board
showing the number of Mondays
through Fridays in the present
month. Have students count and
record the number of each. Then
have students shade in the boxes to
show the information. Have students
respond to questions about which
day shows up the most, least, how
many of each day, how many in
all, etc.

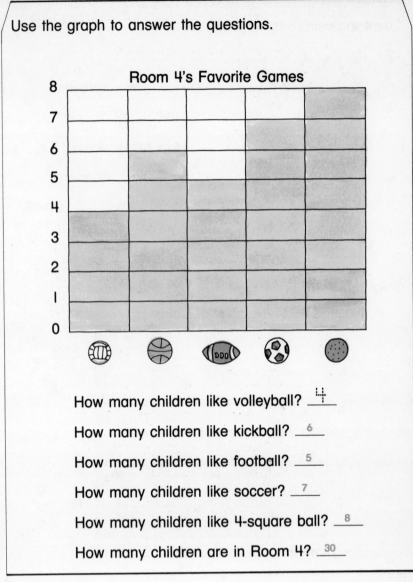

Name _____

Use the graph to answer the questions.

Room 4's Favorite Games

How many children like volleyball? __4__

How many children like kickball? __6__

How many children like football? __5__

How many children like soccer? __7__

How many children like 4-square ball? __8__

How many children are in Room 4? __30__

Interpreting a bar graph

(two hundred eighty-three) **283**

Teaching page 283

Tell students they are to answer questions by referring
to the completed bar graph. Talk through the first
question with the students and have them verify and
then trace the 4. Tell students to complete the
remaining questions independently.

Use the graph to answer the questions.

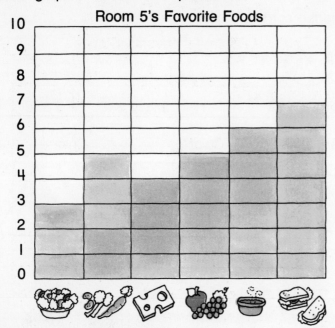

Room 5's Favorite Foods

How many like salads best? __3__

How many like vegetables best? __5__

How many like cheese best? __4__

How many like fruit best? __5__

How many like soup best? __6__

How many like sandwiches best? __7__

How many children are in room 5? __30__

Interpreting a bar graph

Correcting Common Errors

Some students may not make the bar in a bar graph the proper length because they do not count the squares correctly. Have them place their finger on the line at the end of the top bar and slide it over this line to the scale to see if they colored the number of squares that they intended.

Enrichment

1. Make a bar graph to show your classmates' favorite ball games. Have a friend answer questions from your graph.
2. Make a large bar graph on the bulletin board to show how many of your classmates have birthdays in each of the 12 months. Decorate each month with a drawing for a holiday, special occasion or birthday cake.

Teaching page 284

Tell students to use the graph to answer the questions on this page. Read each question with students and have them write its answer on the line.

Extra Credit   *Applications*

Provide each group of students with a class list. Ask one group to take a census of the number of family members each student in class has. Remind them to count themselves. Give them 1/2-inch graph paper and ask them to make a bar graph to represent their count. Another group of students can gather information about the number of pets in each family and make a bar graph of the results. Ask remaining groups to choose a question to use in conducting their survey of each family, and make a bar graph of their findings.

Chapter Review

pages 285-286

Objectives

To review fractions and graphing
To maintain skills learned previously
this year

Materials

Hundred-square
Ten-strips
Singles

Mental Math

Name the number that tells:
1. a fraction for one part of 4 (¼)
2. a fraction for one part of 3 (⅓)
3. 7 tens and 9 ones (79)
4. hundreds in 167 (1)
5. quarters in $1.00 (4)
6. 5¢ plus 85¢ (90¢)
7. 1's on a clock face (5)

Skill Review

Have students help draw a bar
graph on the board to show the
number of students wearing shoes
that are white, brown, black and
other colors. Have students dictate
questions to be answered by the
graph. Write their questions on the
board. Then have students give
answers to the questions.

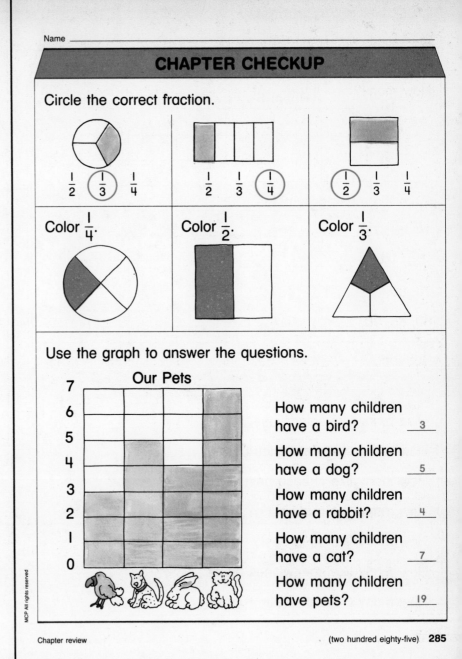

CHAPTER CHECKUP

Circle the correct fraction.

Color ¼.   Color ½.   Color ⅓.

Use the graph to answer the questions.

Our Pets

How many children
have a bird?   3

How many children
have a dog?   5

How many children
have a rabbit?   4

How many children
have a cat?   7

How many children
have pets?   19

Chapter review   (two hundred eighty-five) **285**

Teaching page 285

Read the directions for each of the first 6 boxes and
have students complete each problem. Then read the
directions above the graph and ask students to tell
what the graph shows. Read through the first question
with students and have them complete the page
independently.

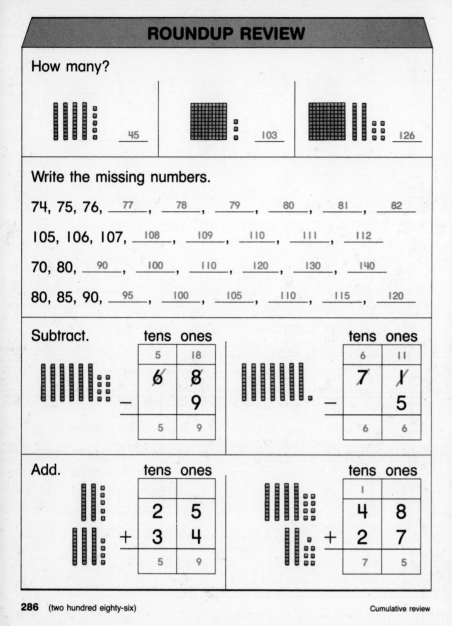

ROUNDUP REVIEW

How many?

45   103   126

Write the missing numbers.

74, 75, 76, _77_, _78_, _79_, _80_, _81_, _82_

105, 106, 107, _108_, _109_, _110_, _111_, _112_

70, 80, _90_, _100_, _110_, _120_, _130_, _140_

80, 85, 90, _95_, _100_, _105_, _110_, _115_, _120_

Subtract.

tens	ones
5	18
6̸	8̸
	9
5	9

tens	ones
6	11
7	1̸
	5
6	6

Add.

tens	ones
2	5
+ 3	4
5	9

tens	ones
1	
4	8
+ 2	7
7	5

286   (two hundred eighty-six)   Cumulative review

Enrichment

1. Cut a piece of paper into 4 equal parts. Write each part's fraction on it.
2. Write and solve a problem to tell how many more students are in your class than there are people in your family.
3. Make a bar graph to show how many sides are in a square, a rectangle and a triangle.

Teaching page 286

Ask students what they are to do in each section. Remind students to look at the sign in each of the last four problems. Have students complete the page independently.

This page reviews place value, sequencing of numbers and addition with some trading.

100 Addition Facts

page 287

Add.

2 +8 10	6 +0 6	1 +2 3	5 +1 6	3 +2 5	1 +9 10	7 +2 9	4 +1 5	7 +3 10	0 +7 7
1 +4 5	3 +3 6	4 +3 7	0 +9 9	3 +5 8	5 +5 10	0 +1 1	9 +1 10	1 +6 7	0 +5 5
6 +4 10	4 +5 9	3 +4 7	1 +3 4	9 +0 9	2 +0 2	6 +2 8	3 +6 9	0 +0 0	5 +0 5
4 +0 4	2 +3 5	0 +2 2	5 +3 8	2 +5 7	0 +4 4	2 +1 3	0 +3 3	6 +1 7	0 +6 6
7 +0 7	4 +2 6	7 +1 8	3 +0 3	3 +7 10	5 +2 7	8 +1 9	2 +6 8	1 +0 1	5 +4 9
1 +8 9	4 +4 8	2 +2 4	2 +7 9	0 +8 8	1 +1 2	8 +0 8	4 +6 10	6 +3 9	1 +7 8
3 +1 4	6 +5 11	2 +4 6	7 +7 14	8 +2 10	1 +5 6	8 +4 12	3 +8 11	8 +6 14	3 +9 12
8 +3 11	9 +4 13	5 +6 11	8 +8 16	9 +5 14	7 +4 11	4 +8 12	7 +6 13	9 +3 12	4 +7 11
9 +7 16	5 +8 13	9 +2 11	7 +5 12	6 +9 15	8 +5 13	2 +9 11	6 +6 12	7 +8 15	4 +9 13
6 +8 14	5 +7 12	9 +8 17	7 +9 16	9 +9 18	8 +7 15	5 +9 14	9 +6 15	8 +9 17	6 +7 13

Reviewing 100 basic addition facts

(two hundred eighty-seven) **287**

Teaching page 287

This page presents the 100 addition facts. It can be used as a written or oral drill, any time during the curriculum. It could also be used as a timed test, to increase students' computation speed.

Subtract.

100 Subtraction Facts
page 288

4 −0 4	9 −3 6	10 − 2 8	4 −1 3	5 −5 0	10 − 1 9	8 −5 3	10 − 6 4	3 −3 0	10 − 7 3
4 −3 1	9 −1 8	6 −5 1	7 −7 0	9 −5 4	9 −4 5	0 −0 0	9 −6 3	7 −0 7	7 −5 2
2 −0 2	5 −4 1	8 −8 0	9 −2 7	5 −3 2	6 −0 6	7 −6 1	3 −1 2	1 −1 0	7 −3 4
10 − 9 1	9 −0 9	10 − 4 6	4 −2 2	5 −1 4	10 − 8 2	3 −0 3	6 −3 3	9 −7 2	10 − 3 7
8 −7 1	5 −0 5	3 −2 1	7 −1 6	8 −4 4	9 −8 1	7 −4 3	8 −1 7	1 −0 1	7 −2 5
6 −1 5	8 −0 8	5 −2 3	6 −4 2	8 −2 6	4 −4 0	8 −6 2	6 −2 4	2 −1 1	6 −6 0
8 −3 5	2 −2 0	10 − 5 5	9 −9 0	15 − 6 9	11 − 5 6	12 − 3 9	13 − 7 6	11 − 2 9	12 − 6 6
11 − 4 7	13 − 5 8	11 − 6 5	14 − 7 7	15 − 9 6	13 − 6 7	12 − 8 4	16 − 9 7	11 − 8 3	12 − 7 5
13 − 9 4	12 − 5 7	13 − 4 9	11 − 9 2	12 − 4 8	14 − 5 9	11 − 7 4	16 − 8 8	15 − 8 7	14 − 8 6
16 − 7 9	17 − 9 8	13 − 8 5	18 − 9 9	14 − 6 8	17 − 8 9	12 − 9 3	11 − 3 8	14 − 9 5	15 − 7 8

Reviewing 100 basic subtraction facts

Teaching page 288

This page presents the 100 subtraction facts. It can be
used in the same manner as the preceding page.

Alternate Chapter 1 Checkup

Objective

To review 0 through 10

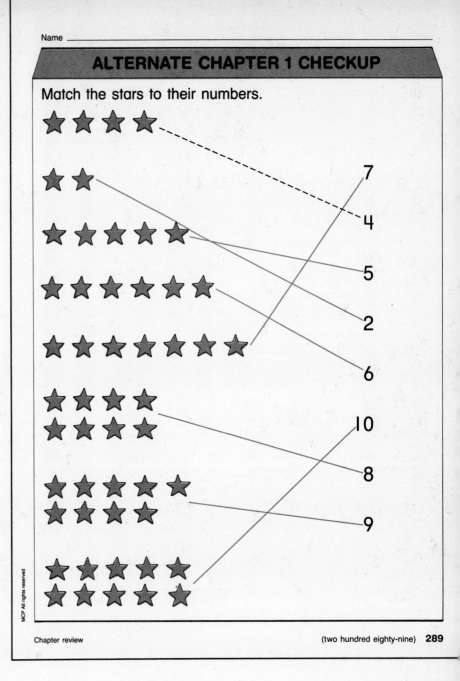

ALTERNATE CHAPTER 1 CHECKUP

Match the stars to their numbers.

7

4

5

2

6

10

8

9

Chapter review   (two hundred eighty-nine) **289**

Name _____

Add.

$5 + 5 =$ _10_ $1 + 3 =$ _4_ $6 + 3 =$ _9_

$2 + 4 =$ _6_ $3 + 3 =$ _6_ $7 + 2 =$ _9_

$1 + 6 =$ _7_ $4 + 4 =$ _8_ $3 + 7 =$ _10_

$\begin{array}{r} 6 \\ +4 \\ \hline \scriptstyle 10 \end{array}$ $\begin{array}{r} 2 \\ +8 \\ \hline \scriptstyle 10 \end{array}$ $\begin{array}{r} 4 \\ +1 \\ \hline \scriptstyle 5 \end{array}$ $\begin{array}{r} 3 \\ +5 \\ \hline \scriptstyle 8 \end{array}$ $\begin{array}{r} 1 \\ +7 \\ \hline \scriptstyle 8 \end{array}$ $\begin{array}{r} 2 \\ +3 \\ \hline \scriptstyle 5 \end{array}$

Solve.

Have 6¢.   Add 2¢ more.

$\begin{array}{r} 5\text{¢} \\ +4\text{¢} \\ \hline \scriptstyle 9\text{ ¢} \end{array}$

$6\text{¢} + 2\text{¢} =$ _8_ ¢

Add.

$\begin{array}{r} 5 \\ 3 \\ +2 \\ \hline \scriptstyle 10 \end{array}$ $\begin{array}{r} 1 \\ 2 \\ +4 \\ \hline \scriptstyle 7 \end{array}$ $\begin{array}{r} 7 \\ 1 \\ +2 \\ \hline \scriptstyle 10 \end{array}$ $\begin{array}{r} 4 \\ 2 \\ +3 \\ \hline \scriptstyle 9 \end{array}$

Chapter review

Alternate Chapter 2 Checkup

Objective

To review addition sums through 10

290

Alternate Chapter 3 Checkup

Objective

To review subtraction facts for minuends through 10

ALTERNATE CHAPTER 3 CHECKUP

Subtract.

6 −4 2	8 −2 6	4 −1 3	5 −3 2	7 −1 6	3 −2 1
8 −5 3	10 − 5 5	9 −3 6	5 −2 3	10 − 9 1	8 −4 4
7 −4 3	9 −8 1	4 −4 0	7 −3 4	10 − 1 9	9 −2 7
9 −5 4	10 − 7 3	7 −5 2	5 −0 5	9 −4 5	8 −6 2

Solve.

7 ¢
−3 ¢
4 ¢

Spent 3¢.

8 ¢
−5 ¢
3 ¢

Spent 5¢.

291

Name _____

Add or subtract.

3 +6 9	8 −2 6	4 +1 5	5 +3 8	7 −1 6	4 +4 8
9 −3 6	6 +2 8	10 − 5 5	10 − 8 2	1 +9 10	8 +1 9
5 +4 9	9 −8 1	3 +7 10	7 −3 4	2 +8 10	9 −2 7

Solve.

How much did both cost?

7¢

_10_ ¢

$+$ 3 ¢

10 ¢

How much money was left?   Bought

9 ¢

_3_ ¢

$-$ 6 ¢

3 ¢

Chapter review

Alternate Chapter 4 Checkup

Objectives

To review addition and subtraction facts related to sums through 10

Alternate Chapter 5 Checkup

Objective

To review place value for 11 through 99

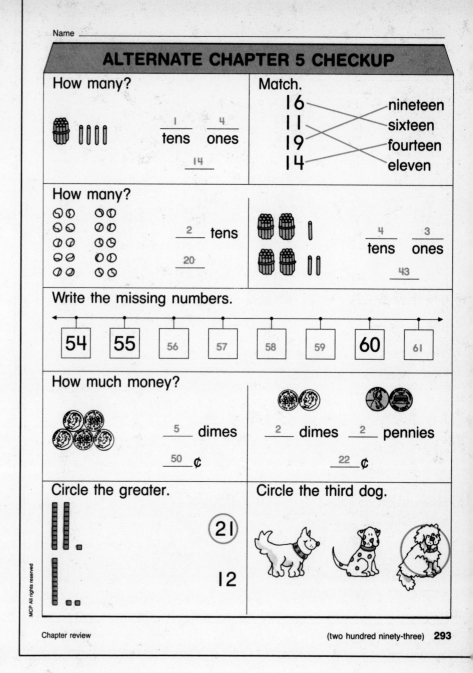

How many?

___1___ ___4___
tens   ones

14

Match.

16   nineteen
11   sixteen
19   fourteen
14   eleven

How many?

___2___ tens

20

___4___ ___3___
tens   ones

43

Write the missing numbers.

| 54 | 55 | 56 | 57 | 58 | 59 | 60 | 61 |

How much money?

___5___ dimes

50 ¢

___2___ dimes   ___2___ pennies

22 ¢

Circle the greater.

(21)

12

Circle the third dog.

293

Name _____

ALTERNATE CHAPTER 6 CHECKUP

Add.

9 +9 18	8 +6 14	6 +7 13	9 +4 13	7 +8 15	6 +6 12	9 +3 12

5 +8 13	9 +6 15	7 +7 14	5 +9 14	8 +4 12	9 +2 11	8 +8 16

$4 + 9 = \underline{13}$ $6 + 8 = \underline{14}$ $9 + 5 = \underline{14}$

$8 + 3 = \underline{11}$ $2 + 9 = \underline{11}$ $7 + 6 = \underline{13}$

$9 + 7 = \underline{16}$ $7 + 5 = \underline{12}$ $8 + 7 = \underline{15}$

$5 + 6 = \underline{11}$ $9 + 8 = \underline{17}$ $5 + 7 = \underline{12}$

$6 + 9 = \underline{15}$ $3 + 9 = \underline{12}$ $4 + 8 = \underline{12}$

$8 + 5 = \underline{13}$ $4 + 7 = \underline{11}$ $6 + 5 = \underline{11}$

How much?

$$\begin{array}{r} 8 \ ¢ \\ + \; 9 \ ¢ \\ \hline 17 \ ¢ \end{array}$$

 9 ¢

 5 ¢

4 ¢

$$\begin{array}{r} 9 \ ¢ \\ 5 \ ¢ \\ + \; 4 \ ¢ \\ \hline 18 \ ¢ \end{array}$$

294 (two hundred ninety-four)

Chapter review

Alternate Chapter 7 Checkup

Objective

To review subtracting from minuends through 18

ALTERNATE CHAPTER 7 CHECKUP

Subtract.

$18 - 9 = \underline{9}$ $13 - 8 = \underline{5}$ $14 - 6 = \underline{8}$

$15 - 3 = \underline{12}$ $18 - 4 = \underline{14}$ $15 - 7 = \underline{8}$

$14 - 5 = \underline{9}$ $17 - 8 = \underline{9}$ $18 - 5 = \underline{13}$

$17 - 6 = \underline{11}$ $12 - 7 = \underline{5}$ $13 - 9 = \underline{4}$

$16 - 7 = \underline{9}$ $16 - 2 = \underline{14}$ $12 - 4 = \underline{8}$

16	14	12	18	13	15
$-\ 9$	$-\ 8$	$-\ 3$	$-\ 7$	$-\ 6$	$-\ 8$
7	6	9	11	7	7

17	13	15	12	14	16
$-\ 5$	$-\ 4$	$-\ 6$	$-\ 8$	$-\ 9$	$-\ 4$
12	9	9	4	5	12

Solve.

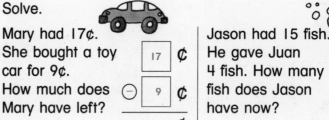

Mary had 17¢. She bought a toy car for 9¢. How much does Mary have left?

$\begin{array}{r} 17 \\ \ominus\ 9 \\ \hline 8 \end{array}$ ¢

_8_ ¢

Jason had 15 fish. He gave Juan 4 fish. How many fish does Jason have now?

$\begin{array}{r} 15 \\ \ominus\ 4 \\ \hline 11 \end{array}$

_11_ fish

Chapter review   (two hundred ninety-five) **295**

295

Name _____

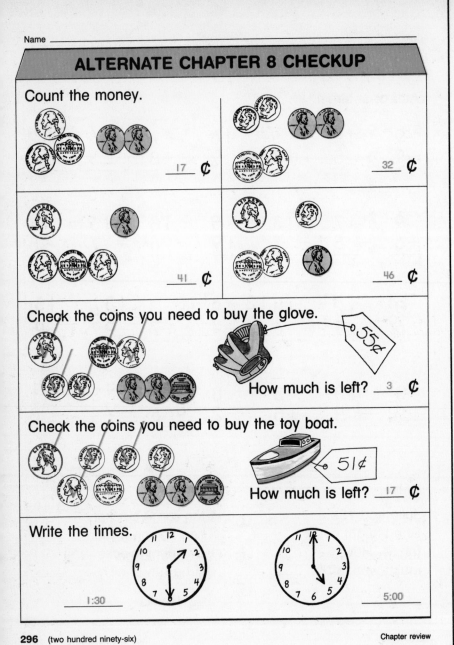

Count the money.

17 ¢

32 ¢

41 ¢

46 ¢

Check the coins you need to buy the glove.

55¢

How much is left? __3__ ¢

Check the coins you need to buy the toy boat.

51¢

How much is left? __17__ ¢

Write the times.

1:30

5:00

Chapter review

Alternate Chapter 8 Checkup

Objective

To review counting money, solving money problems and telling time

Alternate Chapter 9 Checkup

Objective

To review adding and subtracting for sums and minuends through 18

Name _____

ALTERNATE CHAPTER 9 CHECKUP

Add or subtract.

9 +9 ── 18	14 − 5 ── 9	6 +7 ── 13	16 − 9 ── 7	7 +8 ── 15	6 +3 ── 9	12 − 5 ── 7
9 +6 ── 15	17 − 8 ── 9	13 − 7 ── 6	5 +9 ── 14	18 − 6 ── 12	15 − 7 ── 8	8 +8 ── 16
8 +6 ── 14	12 − 9 ── 3	14 − 6 ── 8	9 +4 ── 13	7 +7 ── 14	16 − 7 ── 9	4 +5 ── 9
3 +9 ── 12	13 − 4 ── 9	8 +5 ── 13	8 −2 ── 6	15 − 6 ── 9	8 +4 ── 12	11 − 3 ── 8

Solve.

Julia had 18¢. She bought a 🎀 for 6¢. How much was left?

18 ¢
⊖ 6 ¢
─────
12 ¢

12 ¢

Stan ran 9 blocks. Then he ran 4 more. How many blocks did he run in all?

9
⊕ 4
───
13

13 blocks

Chapter review

(two hundred ninety-seven) 297

297

Name _____

How many?

___4___ tens ___2___ ones

___42___

7 tens 3 ones __73__

forty-four __44__

58 is __5__ tens __8__ ones.

Write the missing numbers.

48, 49, __50__, __51__, __52__, __53__, __54__, __55__, __56__, 57

65, 66, __67__, __68__, __69__, __70__, __71__

Add.

$\begin{array}{r} 7 \\ +9 \\ \hline 16 \end{array}$
$\begin{array}{r} 4 \\ +6 \\ \hline 10 \end{array}$
$\begin{array}{r} 5 \\ +7 \\ \hline 12 \end{array}$
$\begin{array}{r} 9 \\ +4 \\ \hline 13 \end{array}$
$\begin{array}{r} 7 \\ +8 \\ \hline 15 \end{array}$
$\begin{array}{r} 5 \\ +6 \\ \hline 11 \end{array}$
$\begin{array}{r} 3 \\ +9 \\ \hline 12 \end{array}$

Add.

tens	ones
4	5
+	4
4	9

tens	ones
1	
5	7
+	7
6	4

10¢	1¢	
1		
6	2	¢
+	9	¢
7	1	¢

Chapter review

Alternate Chapter 10 Checkup

Objective

To review addition for sums
through 99

Alternate Chapter 11 Checkup

Objective

To review subtraction for minuends through 99

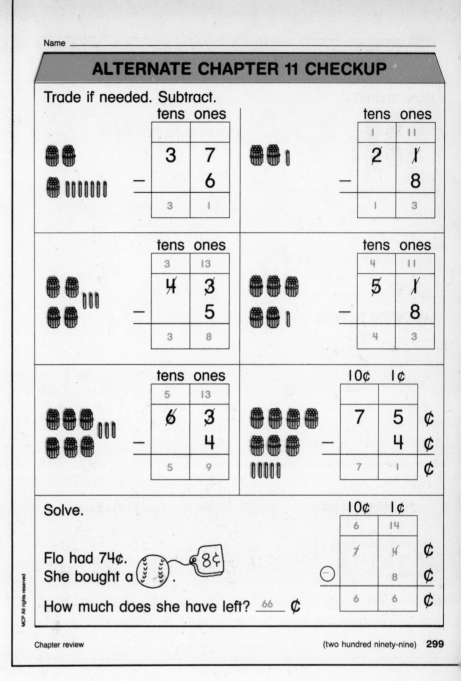

ALTERNATE CHAPTER 11 CHECKUP

Trade if needed. Subtract.

tens	ones
3	7
	− 6
3	1

	tens	ones
	1	11
	2	1̶
	− 8
	1	3

tens	ones
3	13
4̶	3̶
	− 5
3	8

tens	ones
4	11
5̶	1̶
	− 8
4	3

tens	ones
5	13
6̶	3̶
	− 4
5	9

10¢	1¢	
7	5	¢
	− 4	¢
7	1	¢

Solve.

Flo had 74¢.
She bought a ⚾ . 8¢

How much does she have left? _66_ ¢

10¢	1¢	
6	14	
7̶	4̶	¢
−	8	¢
6	6	¢

299

ALTERNATE CHAPTER 12 CHECKUP

How many?

hundreds	tens	ones
1	2	4

___124

hundreds	tens	ones
1	3	3

___133

Write the missing numbers.

77, 78, _79_, _80_, _81_, _82_, _83_, _84_

102, 103, _104_, _105_, _106_, _107_, _108_, _109_

154, 155, _156_, _157_, _158_, _159_, _160_, _161_

_111_, 112, 113, _114_   173, 174, _175_, _176_, 177

_148_, 149, 150, _151_   196, 197, _198_, _199_, 200

How much money?

$1.00	10¢	1¢
1	3	3

$ ___

$ _1.33_

Alternate Chapter 12 Checkup

Objective

To review place value through 200

Alternate Chapter 13 Checkup

Objective

To review addition of 2-digit numbers with and without trading

---

ALTERNATE CHAPTER 13 CHECKUP

Add.

tens	ones
1	
2	2
+	9
3	1

$$\begin{array}{r} 45 \\ +\ 7 \\ \hline 52 \end{array}$$

$$\begin{array}{r} 38 \\ +\ 6 \\ \hline 44 \end{array}$$

$$\begin{array}{r} 30\,¢ \\ +40\,¢ \\ \hline 70\ ¢ \end{array}$$

$$\begin{array}{r} 60 \\ +20 \\ \hline 80 \end{array}$$

tens	ones
1	
4	8
+ 2	9
7	7

$$\begin{array}{r} 31 \\ +39 \\ \hline 70 \end{array}$$

$$\begin{array}{r} 77 \\ +16 \\ \hline 93 \end{array}$$

$$\begin{array}{r} 26 \\ +48 \\ \hline 74 \end{array}$$

$$\begin{array}{r} 54\,¢ \\ +29\,¢ \\ \hline 83\ ¢ \end{array}$$

$$\begin{array}{r} 88 \\ +19 \\ \hline 107 \end{array}$$

$$\begin{array}{r} 92 \\ +16 \\ \hline 108 \end{array}$$

$$\begin{array}{r} 35\,¢ \\ +76\,¢ \\ \hline 111\ ¢ \end{array}$$

$$\begin{array}{r} 47 \\ +46 \\ \hline 93 \end{array}$$

$$\begin{array}{r} 51 \\ 24 \\ +66 \\ \hline 141 \end{array}$$

$$\begin{array}{r} 27 \\ 73 \\ +42 \\ \hline 142 \end{array}$$

Solve.

Justin counted the pets in his neighborhood: 33 cats, 41 dogs and 12 hamsters. How many in all?

$$\begin{array}{r} 33 \\ 41 \\ +12 \\ \hline 86 \end{array}$$

__86__ pets

ALTERNATE CHAPTER 14 CHECKUP

Match the shape to its name.

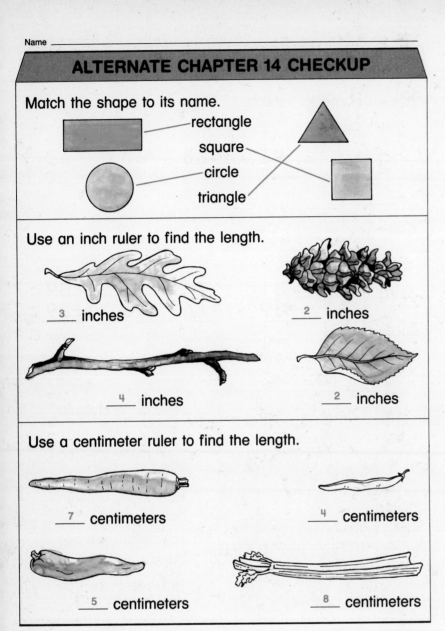

rectangle

square

circle

triangle

Use an inch ruler to find the length.

_3_ inches

_2_ inches

_4_ inches

_2_ inches

Use a centimeter ruler to find the length.

_7_ centimeters

_4_ centimeters

_5_ centimeters

_8_ centimeters

Chapter review

Alternate Chapter 14 Checkup

Objective

To review geometry and measurement

Alternate Chapter 15 Checkup

Objective

To review fractions and graphing

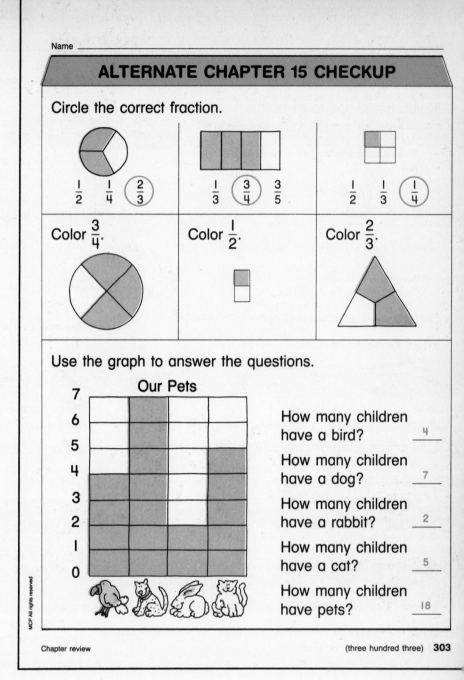

ALTERNATE CHAPTER 15 CHECKUP

Circle the correct fraction.

$\frac{1}{2}$ $\frac{1}{4}$ $\boxed{\frac{2}{3}}$ $\frac{1}{3}$ $\boxed{\frac{3}{4}}$ $\frac{3}{5}$ $\frac{1}{2}$ $\frac{1}{3}$ $\boxed{\frac{1}{4}}$

Color $\frac{3}{4}$.   Color $\frac{1}{2}$.   Color $\frac{2}{3}$.

Use the graph to answer the questions.

Our Pets

How many children have a bird? ___4___

How many children have a dog? ___7___

How many children have a rabbit? ___2___

How many children have a cat? ___5___

How many children have pets? ___18___

Chapter review   (three hundred three) **303**

303

Glossary

Addend A number that is added.
In $7 + 2 = 9$, the addends are 7 and 2.

Basic fact A number sentence that has at least two one-digit numbers.
The sentence below are examples of basic facts.
$4 + 3 = 7$; $12 - 5 = 7$.

Cardinal number A number, such as **three,** used to count or to tell how many.

Circle A plane figure with all of its points the same distance from a given point called the center.

Denominator The number below the line in a fraction.
In ⅗, 5 is the denominator.

Difference The answer to a subtraction problem.

Digit Any of the ten number symbols: 0, 1, 2, 3, 4, 5, 6, 7, 8 and 9.

Equation A mathematical sentence that uses the = symbol.
$16 - 4 = 12$.

Even number A whole number with 0, 2, 4, 6 or 8 in the ones place.

Fact family The related number sentences for addition and subtraction that contain all the same numbers.
$2 + 4 = 6$ $6 - 4 = 2$ $4 + 2 = 6$ $6 - 2 = 4$

Fraction A number that names a part of a whole.
½ is a fraction.

Geometry The branch of mathematics that studies points, lines, plane figures, and figures.

Graph A picture of relationships among numbers and quantities.

Greater than (>) A relationship between two numbers with the greater number given first.
$10 > 7$; ½ > ¼

Less than (<) A relationship between two numbers with the lesser number given first.
$2 < 4$; ¼ < ½

Minuend A number from which another number is subtracted.
In $18 - 5 = 13$, 18 is the minuend.

Multiple The product of a number and a whole number.
Some multiples of 3 are 3, 6 and 9.

Number sentence An equation or an inequality.
$3 + 2 = 5$; $4 < 7$

Numerator The number above the line in a fraction.
In ⅗, 3 is the numerator.

Odd number A whole number with 1, 3, 5, 7 or 9 in the ones place.

Ordinal number A number, such as **fifth,** used to tell order or position.

Perimeter The distance around a shape that is the sum of the lengths of all its sides.

Place value The value of the place where a digit appears in a number. In 137,510, the 7 is in the thousandths place.

Plane figure A shape that appears on a flat surface. For example, circle, square, and triangle.

Product The answer to a multiplication problem.

Rectangle A four-sided plane figure with four right angles.

Right angle An angle that has a measure of 90 degrees.

Sequence Numbers following one another in a pattern.

Square A plane figure with four sides of equal length, and four right angles.

Subtrahend The number that is subtracted from the minuend.
In $18 - 5 = 13$, 5 is the subtrahend.

Sum The answer to an addition problem.

Triangle A plane figure with three sides.

Whole numbers Those numbers used in counting and zero.

Index